The Fugitive Identity of Mediation

Despite much having been written about what mediation is, direct observations of commercial mediations are limited. This book grants an opportunity to observe mediation in action and also provides external commentary about the actions observed.

The book approaches mediation ethnographically as a social process that is informed by structures, rules and norms that colour the environment within which it operates. Through the ethnographic method, a process leading to negotiated order is examined, baring its elements, identifying its influences and studying the movement to order. The result is the reconceptualization of mediation. The mediator is invited into the negotiation as third-party intervener. He creates the process of mediation, defining the process by his actions, which ultimately merges mediator with process. This book provides a window to the lived experience of participants to mediation; it explores their understandings of and interactions within a process they have experienced *together* and demonstrates how mediation is a process inextricably linked to negotiation where the mediator becomes part of the negotiation process, at times separate from the parties, aligned with the parties or in opposition to the parties. *The Fugitive Identity of Mediation* will be of interest to scholars, mediators, parties who participate in the process, and to those active in public policy discourse.

Debbie De Girolamo is a Lecturer in Law at the School of Law, Centre for Commerical Law Studies, Queen Mary, University of London. She is also a Guest Teacher at the London School of Economics and Political Science.

The Fugitive Identity of Mediation

Negotiations, Shift Changes and Allusionary Action

Debbie De Girolamo

LONDON AND NEW YORK

First published 2013
by Routledge
2 Park Square, Milton Park, Abingdon, Oxfordshire OX14 4RN

Simultaneously published in the USA and Canada
by Routledge
711 Third Avenue, New York, NY 10017

First issued in paperback 2014

Routledge is an imprint of the Taylor & Francis Group, an informa business

© 2013 Debbie De Girolamo

The right of Debbie De Girolamo to be identified as author of this work has been asserted by her in accordance with sections 77 and 78 of the Copyright, Designs and Patents Act 1988.

All rights reserved. No part of this book may be reprinted or reproduced or utilised in any form or by any electronic, mechanical, or other means, now known or hereafter invented, including photocopying and recording, or in any information storage or retrieval system, without permission in writing from the publishers.

Trademark notice: Product or corporate names may be trademarks or registered trademarks, and are used only for identification and explanation without intent to infringe.

British Library Cataloguing in Publication Data
A catalogue record for this book is available from the British Library

Library of Congress Cataloging in Publication Data
A catalog record of this book has been requested

ISBN 978-0-415-51720-1 (hbk)
ISBN 978-1-138-88479-3 (pbk)
ISBN 978-0-203-52170-0 (ebk)

Typeset in Garamond
by Cenveo Publisher Services

For Ben

Contents

Acknowledgments   x

1   **Unmasking the mediation process: An ethnographic approach to the study of mediation**   1

    The Mediator's Story 1
    Mediation as a dispute resolution process 4
    Overview of study 9
    Disputing through an ethnographic lens 11
    The ethnographic process 16
       The ethnographic approach 16
       The ethnographic method 22
       An ethnographic application to this study 27
    Summary 31

2   **My village**   33

    The fieldwork site 34
    The mediators 39
    The parties 41
    The mediations 42
    Summary 44

3   **Mediation: Exploring the prism**   45

    Mediation defined 47
    Models of mediator intervention 52
       Neutrality: a discussion 52
       Mediator vision 55
    Mediator behaviour 58
    Mediation as assisted negotiation 63

viii   *Contents*

A mediation model 68
Summary 71

4   Negotiated order: The processual framework of negotiation   72

Strategy and patterns: approaches to process 74
Phases of negotiation revealed 81
The six phases 84
  Unilateral articulation of positions 84
    Case Study 1: Personal injury negotiation – the falling crane 84
    Case analysis 87
  Information exchange 89
    Case Study 2: Nuisance claim – the showering softballs 89
    Case analysis 91
  Testing of positions 92
    Case Study 3: The services contract – website malfunction 92
    Case analysis 93
  Shift in position 94
    Case Study 4: Management services contract – unpaid invoices 94
    Case analysis 96
  Bargaining proposals 98
    Case Study 5: Corporate liquidation – shareholder conduct 98
    Case analysis 100
  Joint decision-making for final agreement 102
    Case Study 6: Employment dispute – the disabled worker 102
    Case analysis 104
The processual arc 105
Summary 107

5   The native voice   109

Case Study 7: Technology foul-up 113
Case analysis 118
Case Study 8: Partnership gone awry 121
Case analysis 129
Case Study 9: The fishing logo 132
Case analysis 139
Summary 142

6   The mediation quintet: Hidden identities   149

Case Study 7: Technology foul-up 153
Case analysis 164

Case Study 8: Partnership gone awry 167
Case analysis 182
Case Study 9: The fishing logo 186
Case analysis 196
Summary 200

7 Epilogue: The fugitive identity of mediation – negotiations, shift changes and allusionary action   206

Implications 209
Limitations to this study 210
What next? 212
Coda 214

Appendix A: Interview protocol for mediators post-mediation   215
Appendix B: Interview guideline for participants post-mediation   217
Bibliography   218
Index   236

Acknowledgments

I owe a debt of gratitude to many people. First and foremost, to Professor Simon Roberts, who was a selfless, dedicated and supportive doctoral supervisor when this book was a doctoral project. With infinite patience, guidance and encouragement, Professor Roberts introduced me to a different way of approaching the analysis of disputing processes. He opened a whole new world of 'seeing and doing' and for that I am particularly grateful. He has become a great mentor, colleague and dear friend on whose advice I continue to rely and which he so generously gives. It is due to his efforts that I have been enriched by this experience. I am also grateful for the support and advice of Fiona Cownie, Michael Palmer, Marian Roberts, Tony Bradney, Bryan Clark, Penny Brooker, Linda Mulcahy, Loukas Mistelis, Ann Kaegi and Fred Zemans throughout the various stages of the development of this project. A word about the title for this study – after much deliberation about an appropriate title, it was Professor Roberts who suggested a reference to the fugitive nature of mediation. Many thanks to him for his very apropos suggestion.

The scope of this research study could not have been possible without the generosity of the British organization that took a chance to open its doors to a research study even though it was sceptical about the research methodology and was not given any clue as to what exactly would be evaluated! The organization walked the talk: it is a thought-leader in the field and its willingness to be subjected to objective study without restriction illustrates its commitment to the development of the field. Heartfelt thanks go to everyone at the organization who participated in my study. They opened their arms to me and my work, and ensured that I obtained the data I needed and attended on as many mediations as I required for my project.

This project would not have evolved as it did without the inhabitants of my mediation villages. Great thanks go to each and every mediator who welcomed me without qualms into their world and for letting me put them under a microscope. It was a privilege to see them in action. Equally, many thanks must go to the parties and their legal representatives who permitted my involvement with such grace while under the pressure of conflict.

None of this – the doctoral project and this book – would have been possible had it not been for my parents' belief in the value of academic pursuit.

Rosetta and Michael De Girolamo have been selfless in their commitment to my education and enthusiasm for this endeavour. It is their pride in my accomplishments and their unwavering support that encourage me to strive higher than I believe possible.

I am very grateful for the support of other members of my family through the evolution of this project – Daniela, Massimo, Michael, Luca, Frances, Anna, Jim, Ruth and Phineus. Special thanks to my sister, Daniela De Girolamo, who took on what I consider to be the most painful of all jobs: that of proofreader when this project was a doctoral study. She was meticulous in her review, undaunted by the task despite the short time-line I imposed upon her, providing insightful comments with a healthy dose of humour that have become stories of lore. Any errors that remain or created anew in this regeneration are entirely due to my own folly.

I dedicate this book to Ben Babcock, who suffered through its full evolution, yet always took an active interest in its development, pushed boundaries of thought, engaged in spirited debate about my propositions or writing style, read and reread drafts without complaint, provided a supportive ear and infinite encouragement, but above all and most importantly, helped to ensure that this journey was not a lone endeavour.

1 Unmasking the mediation process

An ethnographic approach to the study of mediation

> Look at us and listen to us. Do not interpret, do not reconstruct. You ask for proof? We are no more than what we are. Utterly, irreducibly ourselves. Not by being entirely of real life, but by being entirely outside it. We offer ourselves to you unconditionally.
>
> The Father, *Six Characters in Search of an Author*[1]

The Mediator's Story

It was time to meet the parties. As usual, the Mediator met with each privately before inviting them to the large boardroom for the first joint meeting of the day. He began with the defendants. He entered their sanctum. It was a boardroom, as they often are, and would be the defendants' home for the duration of the mediation. It was a room in which they could speak freely without the burden of being observed by the other party.

Introductions were made. As the defendants were not familiar with the process, the Mediator described it: *"This is trying to give parties an opportunity to reach resolution. It is a powerful day because it is your day, your resolution; to try to resolve it, you will speak to us privately and in public. There is some desire to do a settlement."* The defendants' solicitor inquired how the Mediator saw the process unfolding. The Mediator stated, *"I will invite both to make an opening {statement}. It is an opportunity because {everyone} will be sitting around the table."* In describing the nature of the opening session, the Mediator noted its importance. *"Take the opportunity to say what you think is powerful and I will give each of you the chance to say it ... I want to achieve clarity today and at the end of the day, if there is no settlement, we need an understanding of each case and from understanding comes empowerment. The opening session depends on how it goes.*

---

1 L. Pirandello, *Six Characters in Search of an Author*, a new version by Rupert Goold and Ben Power (London: Nick Hern Books, 2008) at 54. The character, Father, is responding to the film producer's assertion that the Father and the other characters are not real and their stories are not real without their creator.

We are not negotiating at the table; rather, we are exploring the case. I will let it run as long as progress is made regarding what the case is about."

After minor administrative matters were attended to, the meeting ended. The Mediator made his way to the Claimant Team.

On entering the room, where he was greeted by a large corporate team, the Mediator began, *"I've come to personally introduce myself and as a courtesy to introduce the process. You know about the process – you're lawyers. Because the defendants are two lay clients, I spent time with them. Unless you have questions, let's kick off."* The claimants' solicitor said that he is a mediator and knows about *"the opening session, eating biscuits, waiting and settling at 10 p.m."* The Mediator spoke about his approach in response. *"My approach is to run the opening as long as is useful to the parties. I find myself trading issues between the parties otherwise and here it is a long way {between rooms}. I would rather get it all out in the joint session. We need to discuss a few things."* There was some discussion about the party rooms being at a distance from each other and soundproof. The Mediator said, *"It is partly psychological, the distance between the parties."*

The mediation agreement was signed, logistics of the day discussed and the wet weather commented upon. With that, the Mediator moved to the joint meeting room.

Both teams entered the large boardroom after being invited to do so by the Mediator. The Mediator commented on the presence of the square table: *"There is nothing we can do with a square table. It is confrontational."* Everyone seated themselves at the table and the Mediator began the session: *"Thanks for coming here. I would like to say a few words because I spoke privately to you. Everyone knows everyone, or do we need introductions? The objective is to reach a negotiated resolution to the dispute. My role is to help you to reach a negotiated solution. I am not a judge, I am not an arbitrator. I am not here to make decisions. We will talk about the case, but I won't say who is right or wrong.*[2]

"The whole process is confidential as per the mediation agreement. If there is no solution, everything discussed is without prejudice. The private session is confidential to us, except if authorized by you. The objective is to enable you to speak frankly.

"About the opening session, I will bring it to an end if it reaches its maximum benefit, the 10 per cent rule. Then, private {meetings}. How long, depends. This is your day, your process, your opportunity, if nothing else, to be clear and confident regarding what the case is about, what the other side's case is about. This is your opportunity. Anything else?"

Once the claimants had discussed logistics for the day, the Mediator invited the claimants to give their opening statement. Discussion ensued about the issues in the case. After the parties had their say, the Mediator concluded the joint session. *"We know the issues now. I want to avoid the situation*

---

2 This case is examined in detail in D. De Girolamo, "A View from Within: Reconceptualizing Mediator Interactions" (2012) 30(2) *Windsor Y.B. Access Just.* (in press).

where we are trading arguments and points. I will discuss the case with you, but I want you to say that you tried to persuade the other side. This is the opportunity for it and if you did do it, then now is the time to discuss in private. We will start with the claimants. Thank you for your contribution."

The parties retired to their private rooms and waited for the Mediator to attend upon them. This first joint session was the only session at which all parties attended. After its conclusion, the Mediator met with the Claimant Team first as he advised. He then met with the Defendant Team. Thereafter, he met with each team on an alternating basis. The sequence continued until an offer was accepted. Once an offer was accepted, the parties worked together to draft the agreement. The Mediator chatted socially with the parties while the solicitors drafted the agreement. He was available to the parties if needed, but did not actively participate in drafting the agreement. The parties returned to the large boardroom where they first came together that morning and signed the agreement, while admiring the vast views of the London skyline that could be seen through the large windows. Everyone was in good spirits and the day ended amicably.

Mediation as negotiation is the definitive image given of mediation by this Mediator. The Mediator's objective for the mediation is to reach a negotiated resolution. It is his view that it affords the opportunity for the parties to persuade each other and through this persuasion to reach settlement. Communication provides the opportunity for persuasion. It is a powerful tool: the Mediator implores the parties to take full advantage of it. He assures them of the confidentiality of the process and its without prejudice nature in order to encourage them to say what they believe is necessary to say. For the Mediator, it is important that the parties exchange information directly and fully with one another. For him, negotiation cannot progress without such candour between the parties: it provides the 'bedrock' to the negotiations.[3] He sees mediation as affording a considerable opportunity for the parties to seek clarity of position, if not resolution. We see that he achieves this objective when the defendant solicitor comments during the process that *"mediation makes you see the other side's view"*.[4]

The Mediator does not lose sight of the fact that the parties are in a state of conflict. This is emphasized in two comments made about the physical

---

3 This is the Mediator's view. In an interview conducted with the Mediator prior to the mediation, the Mediator explained the necessity for candour between parties: *"I like the parties to provide to each other all of the information they need about the case, what they think their good points are so we achieve a level of knowledge and insight, and the parties share about issues, and their respective position on the issues and what supports those positions. We need that bedrock. There are situations where parties are desperate to do a deal without knowing those things."*

4 This statement was made once an agreement in principle was reached and in response to the Mediator's comment that *"no two mediations are the same because it is about people"*.

environment. First, he notes that the requirement for party meeting rooms to be at a distance from one another feeds a psychological need of parties to be apart from one another. And second, he is unhappy about the existence of a square table in the joint session meeting room because a square table is confrontational. As for the process, the Mediator stresses to the parties that they remain in control of the day, of the process, of their decisions. The focus on party control and party participation in the process suggests an underlying goal of empowerment. Indeed, he speaks of empowerment to the parties. The Mediator appears to be attempting to empower the parties to take charge of their dispute and to become responsible for its resolution.

Mediation as a dispute resolution process

Mediation is a social dispute resolution process.[5] It is a multifaceted social interaction whose goal is to contribute to the resolution of disputes.[6] Parties enter the process in conflict. If successful, they leave the process with the conflict resolved. Social interaction and change occur during the process to affect outcome. The parties of the Mediator's Story (described above) experienced such resolution as a result of interaction and change that occurred during a process called mediation and through a persona called the mediator.

The Mediator's Story has all the ingredients of a generally accepted view of mediation: it speaks to facilitation, recognition, self-determination, empowerment and resolution. It encapsulates a view of mediation as generally understood in the literature. Mediation, however, is not as simple as this story suggests. Beneath the story lies a different story, one challenging mediation orthodoxy. It is to the hidden stories that this book is directed.

From a somewhat one-dimensional viewpoint, the Mediator's Story suggests a diversity of definitions, some of which are reflective of the literature, as we shall see in a subsequent chapter. Definitions of mediation encompass a number of concepts. Mediation has been seen as a process to: reach a compromise agreement; create an optimal agreement; improve communication; engender empowerment; increase awareness of others; enhance moral growth; seek fairness and justice; and promote community through harmony.

---

5 Portions of this chapter have been published in D. De Girolamo, "Seeking Negotiated Order Through Mediation: A Manifestation of Legal Culture?" (2012) 5 *J. Comp. Law* 118, and in D. Nelken, ed., *Using Legal Culture* (London: Wildy, Simmonds & Hill, 2012) 153, in which the author examines a definition of legal culture through the exploration of the place of law in the social process of mediated negotiations.

6 The words 'conflict' and 'dispute' are used interchangeably in this study. Although some writers distinguish between the words to connote different concepts within the mediation and negotiation literature, for purposes of this study, the words are used interchangeably to signify a state of opposition existing between parties regarding views, entitlements or resources, for example.

It is said to be a process that facilitates, guides and reconciles parties in their disputes. Within the diversity, however, lies a kernel of commonality: mediation is a process that facilitates a negotiation. Notwithstanding the view one takes about the elemental nature of mediation and the interventions of the third party, negotiation lies at the heart of mediation. Parties seek mediation when they are unable to resolve a dispute directly with the other party or where the legal system encourages them to mediate to achieve a social policy objective. If they were able to do so directly, they would engage in direct negotiations. A bilateral negotiation becomes a trilateral process as parties seek to negotiate a resolution of their dispute with the assistance of an independent, non-aligned party who has no authority to determine or impose an outcome.

Mediation is multidimensional in nature; it is many things to many people. It is a complex process of interactions that is situated within a framework of structures, rules and norms. When conflicts arise between parties, they have choices regarding the method of resolution. However they choose to address the conflict, they know that, in western society, there is generally the option of adjudicating the conflict through the judicial system. Even if they select a binary negotiation process or one that seeks the assistance of a third party in the form of a mediator, the law in the form of rules and norms may ultimately determine the amount, nature, validity or enforceability of the claims, or it may merely colour them. Either way, rules and norms are present and may be drawn upon to effect resolution. As Mnookin says, parties in dispute bargain in the shadow of the law.[7]

---

[7] R. Mnookin and L. Kornhauser, "Bargaining in the Shadow of the Law: The Case of Divorce" (1979) 88 *Yale L. J.* 950. There is some debate on this point. For example, while Riskin is of the view that mediation has become legalized and therefore places parties in a negotiation within the shadow of the court, Kovach sees the shadow to be illusory given the vanishing trial and Tarpley sees mediation as moving the parties away from law's shadow. Hensler, on the other hand, sees the necessity for the shadow for effective bargaining. Another view, articulated by McEwen and Wissler, and Oberman, is that mediation is not positioned within the shadow of the law since it is squarely *within* the legal system. Nolan-Haley echoes this latter view, stating that law informs the process. See P.J. Gardner, "A Conversation with Leonard L. Riskin" (2005) 46 *N.H.B.J.* 5 at 6; K.K. Kovach, "The Vanishing Trial: Land Mine on the Mediation Landscape or Opportunity for Evolution: Ruminations on the Future of Mediation Practice" (2005) 7 *Cardozo J. Conflict Resol.* 27 at 32; J.R. Tarpley, "ADR, Jurisprudence, and Myth" (2001–02) 17 *Ohio St. J. Disp. Resol.* 113 at 121; D.R. Hensler, "Suppose It's Not True: Challenging Mediation Ideology" (2002) *J. Disp. Resol.* 81 at 96; C.A. McEwen and R.L. Wissler, "Finding Out If It Is True: Comparing Mediation and Negotiation through Research" (2002) *J. Disp. Resol.* 131 at 133; S. Oberman, "Mediation Theory vs. Practice: What Are We Really Doing? Re-solving a Professional Conundrum" (2005) 20 *Ohio St. J. Disp. Resol.* 775 at 801–2; J.M. Nolan-Haley, "Court Mediation and the Search for Justice Through Law" (1996) 74 *Wash. U. L. Q.* 47 at 65–6.

Mediation is positioned in the law through its structures, rules and norms. Its position in the law must be acknowledged, but ultimately it must be extracted from the law. In order to see through the process for a clearer understanding of it, the process itself must be laid bare. This becomes particularly relevant in light of two considerations: first, the definitions of mediation, which suggest a process that works outside of the law (for example, parties reach agreement without regard to the law or seek remedies beyond what the law can offer); and second, the institutionalization of mediation within the civil court system through legislative schemes.

Mediations are often positioned within the litigation process itself. In England and Wales, the rules of court explicitly include settlement as an objective of the judicial system, requiring the court to actively manage cases, which includes encouraging and facilitating parties' efforts to settle a dispute.[8] To assist with this objective, rule 44.3(5) of the Civil Procedure Rules (CPR) gives power to the court to order cost sanctions against parties who act unreasonably in failing to take steps to settle their dispute.[9] These rules, together with various Court of Appeal decisions, make it clear that settlement has become a primary objective within the judicial system of England and Wales.[10] Although not explicitly mandating mediation, England and Wales have institutionalized mediation within their legal system through these rules. Lord Clarke, a senior member of the British judiciary, stated in 2008, "Mediation and ADR form part of the civil procedure process. They are not simply ancillary to court proceedings but form part of them."[11] The court has embraced mediation as part of the judicial system through its interpretation and application of the rules.[12]

---

8 The Civil Procedure Rules, 1998 SI 1998/3132, rules 1.4(1), 1.4(2), and 26.4(1).
9 Ibid. rule 44.3(5).
10 For example, *Halsey* v *Milton Keynes General NHS Trust* [2004] EWCA Civ 576; *Burchell* v *Bullard et al.* [2005] EWCA Civ 358.
11 The Right Hon Lord Clarke of Stone-cum-Ebony, Justice of the Supreme Court, "The Future of Mediation", speech given at the Second Civil Mediation Council National Conference, Birmingham, 8 May 2008 (as then Master of the Rolls). Available at: www.judiciary.gov.uk/Resources/JCO/Documents/Speeches/mr_mediation_conference_may08.pdf (accessed 22 August 2012). A different approach is taken by Lord Neuberger, President of the Supreme Court (then Master of the Rolls) who argues that mediation does not form part of the civil justice system; it is "an important adjunct to … our civil justice system". The Right Hon Lord Neuberger of Abbotsbury MR, "Has Mediation had its Day?", Gordon Slynn Memorial Lecture, 10 November 2010. For a copy of the lecture, see *The Expert and Dispute Resolver* (published by The Academy of Experts), Winter 2010 Vol. 15 No. 3, 8 at 10. Despite the divergence, however, the views support the existence of a relationship between the civil justice system and mediation.
12 For further discussions of the court's embrace of mediation in England and Wales, see generally, P. Brooker and A. Lavers, "Mediation Outcomes: Lawyers' Experience with Commercial and Construction Mediation in the United Kingdom" (2005) 5 *Pepp. Disp. Resol. L. J.* 161; J. Jacob, *Civil Justice in the Age of Human Rights* (Aldershot: Ashgate,

Simon Roberts goes further and suggests that adjudication is no longer the primary function of the law courts – settlement is. Private dispute resolution mechanisms are positioned directly within legal institutions where courts are now sponsors of settlement and act as legitimizers for negotiation.[13] Roberts examines the trajectory of cases filed in the Mayor's and City of London Court and the impact of the CPR on the adjudication and settlement of cases, concluding that "it is time to re-conceptualize the court as an arena for structured bilateral negotiations, one in which the dominant mode of interaction is often protracted conversation between the parties themselves. This is the drama in which both active judicial sponsorship of settlement and the theoretical availability of trial and judgment provide a background structure to the process. But beyond that they play a residual role."[14] Further he states, "So, the 'rule of law', long associated with trial and judgment, may now provide legitimacy for a quite different process as the courts move to sponsorship of settlement."[15] Chase uses a different term than sponsorship to connote the position of mediation in law: he refers to the legalization of ADR as a result of the court annexation of mediation and its regulation by the law and lawyers.[16]

This evolution of mediation into the judicial realm of adjudication is seemingly unnatural. The fundamental nature of adjudication differs from that of mediation. Mediation facilitates negotiation. It offers consensual, collaborative negotiation assisted by a non-aligned third party, the mediator. The mediator does not determine outcome. It is a private process, taking place within boardrooms, thus closed to public scrutiny. In other words, anything goes. Adjudication, in contrast, is rule-based, third-party decision-making where outcomes are imposed by a judge not negotiated between the parties.

2007) at 92–104; D. Gladwell, "Alternative Dispute Resolution and the Courts" (1 May 2004) *Civil Court News* 26; D. Cornes, "Commercial Mediation: The Impact of the Courts" (2007) 73 *Arbitration* 12; D. Spenser Underhill, "The English Courts and ADR – Policy and Practice since April 1999" (2003) 14 *Eur. Bus. L. Rev.* 259; D. Spenser Underhill, "The English Courts and ADR – Policy and Practice since April 1999 (Part II)" (2005) 16 *Eur. Bus. L. Rev.* 183; H. Genn, *Judging Civil Justice* (Cambridge: Cambridge University Press, 2010) at 92–121; H. Genn et al., *Twisting Arms: Court Referred and Court Linked Mediation under Judicial Pressure* (May 2007) Ministry of Justice Res Ser 1/07, Ministry of Justice, London at 2–8, 14; S. Prince, "ADR after the CPR: Have ADR Initiatives Now Assured Mediation an Integral Role in the Civil Justice System in England and Wales?" in D. Dwyer, ed., *The Civil Procedure Rules Ten Years On* (Oxford: Oxford University Press, 2009), 321 at 327–34.

13 S. Roberts, "'Listing Concentrates the Mind': The English Civil Court as an Arena for Structured Negotiation" (2009) 29 *Oxford J. Legal Stud.* 457.
14 Ibid. at 476.
15 Ibid. at 478.
16 O.G. Chase, *Law, Culture, and Ritual: Disputing Systems in Cross-cultural Context* (New York: University Press, 2005) at 95.

Rules may or may not be determinative of outcome in a mediated solution; rules are one of the cornerstones of the adjudicated decision. Mediation is a social process resulting in negotiated order; adjudication is imposed normative order.

The word 'mediation' has become infused with legal meaning. Settlement through mediation has been added to the judicial repertoire. Mediators are often trained in the law: retired judges and lawyers have become mediators and are frequently preferred by disputants to those with no legal training. In addition, parties are often represented by lawyers in mediation and thus have their claims or disputes defined legally. As a result, mediation is a process influenced by the law, its institutions and participants.[17] This is important to consider because the use of legal terminology sets the discourse about mediation within a legal framework. The result is that the nature of mediation may be obscured. In their study of order in a social system not yet infused with 'law', Llewellyn and Hoebel recognize the impact of using western terminology to describe their findings, as the meaning of words such as government, power, property have become tainted by understandings attributed them by western society and therefore their import in a non-western context will colour the universality of their applicability.[18]

Labels impose constructions, which may or may not be reflective of reality. For clarity of purpose, this study is not about mediation as defined in the literature or promoted by the judicial system. It is about a dispute resolution process where people strive to resolve conflict without resorting to an authority for the imposition of a decision.

No one can dispute that much has been written about mediation: about its process and outcome, and about its disputant, lawyer and mediator participants. However, as Conley and O'Barr state, "all is not as it seems".[19] People think that they know what happens in mediation: we have heard from disputants, lawyers and mediators who have been part of the drama, and from those who theorize from afar. We need to examine the drama itself and we must do it from outside the drama, while at the same time connected to the drama. As Mansell, Meteyard and Thomson say, "it is difficult to see *through* rules if one sees through rules".[20] I propose to study the dispute resolution process

---

17 For an in-depth exploration of the relationship between mediation and lawyers within the context of civil justice, and in particular, the primary place of lawyers in mediation and its impact on the process, see B. Clark, *Lawyers and Mediation* (London: Springer, 2012).
18 K.N. Llewellyn and E.A. Hoebel, *The Cheyenne Way: Conflict and Case Law in Primitive Jurisprudence* (Norman: University of Oklahoma Press, 1941) at 19.
19 J.M. Conley and W.M. O'Barr, "Back to the Trobriands: The Enduring Influence of Malinowski's Crime and Custom in Savage Society: Bronislaw Malinowski" (2002) 27 *Law & Soc. Inquiry* 847 at 871.
20 W. Mansell, B. Meteyard and A. Thomson, *A Critical Introduction to Law* (London: Cavendish, 2004) at 30.

called mediation in relation to the structures, rules and norms and social processes within which and by which mediation occurs, while at the same time free from their constraints. Studying mediation in this way is a function of perspective requiring the abandonment of parochial views. Abandoning parochial views and laying bare the interactions and changes that occur during the mediation process will be achieved by using ethnography as the methodological approach to this research.[21]

Overview of study

This research into mediation will take the form of an ethnographic study following in the tradition pioneered by Bronislaw Malinowski and continued by others.[22] These ethnographers strove to uncover the structures of order in the societies they studied and in a number of cases they specifically studied the resolution of disputes. Such ethnographic studies provide a relevant analytical framework to conduct this research and address its challenges. In this research, mediation will form part of the 'village' or 'alien society' studied to provide greater clarity into the mediation process.

The ethnographic methodology is a fundamental aspect of this examination of the mediation process. Its 'thick description' seeks to make clear that which may be obscure. The ethnographic exploration of mediation and its interactions will take place on two levels: the processual structure of mediation and mediator–party interactions will provide the analytical focus for this study. This chapter began with a story about mediation, following with a discussion about its nature and its position within the legal panorama of dispute resolution processes. It discusses the theoretical framework of the research and sets out the methodology used, explaining why it is an appropriate approach for the examination of the mediation process. The theoretical framework and methodology are discussed with reference to relevant ethnographic literature. The essence of the chapter is to introduce the reader to the aims of the study and its methodology: a methodology that is steeped in an anthropological tradition.

Chapter 2 introduces the reader to the mediation village of my ethnographic enterprise. It describes the fieldwork undertaken, the organization which generously agreed to lend itself to the ethnographer's endeavour, the mediators and parties who populated the village, and the structure of the village through its mediation process and framework. The intent is to situate the reader within the village.

---

21 This methodological approach is the subject matter of this chapter and will be explored in detail below.
22 A detailed examination of the contribution made to ethnography by Malinowski and others is undertaken later in this chapter.

Chapter 3 speaks of the gap existing between theory and practice in the mediation field and considers the literature's treatment of mediation, focusing primarily on its diverse definitions, and approaches to mediator interventions and behaviours. The chapter continues with a consideration of mediation's origins as a negotiatory process, and concludes with the introduction of a native view of the process and mediator role.

Chapter 4 explores a processual approach to negotiation theory in light of its relevance to mediation. It is through a negotiatory framework that mediation is posited; therefore, an understanding of the negotiation panorama underpinning its structure is required. The purpose of this approach is to ultimately reveal the processual phases of mediation on the basis that mediation is, at its heart, a negotiation in search of resolution to conflict. The focus of the chapter will be on the ethnographic data revealed during the 12-month period of fieldwork research. Six case studies, each textualized from the ethnographic data of six mediations, are set out and each is analysed through a processual negotiatory framework. Together they constitute the negotiation process. Six processual stages of negotiation and, by definition, mediation are disclosed through the data: unilateral articulation of positions; information exchange; testing of positions; shift in position; bargaining proposals; and joint decision-making for final agreement.

In the two following chapters, a move is made from the exploration of process to an exploration of mediator–party content. Chapter 5 focuses on the native voice as heard from the data; that is, it considers the words of the participants to mediation. In particular, it explores what mediators and parties say about the process and about the mediator's role during the process. Also explored is what is not said. For example, we will see the importance placed on communication by the mediator; inconsistencies in what is said to parties about mediator role and mediation process as compared to what is said to the researcher; the integration of mediator with process where the mediator is in control of a process lacking in transparency; the negotiatory framework within which mediators work as dealmakers while seeing themselves as facilitators and benign interveners; and the self-awareness or lack thereof of mediator strategy. Again, the data will be set out in case study format. Three mediations provide the data. Analysis will follow each case study. A summary of themes emerging from the data will conclude the chapter.

Chapter 6 considers mediator–party interactions. In particular, it considers the figure of the mediator, his position in the mediated negotiation, and the manner in which he interacts with the parties. The three cases of Chapter 5 are revisited in this chapter to highlight relational patterns between native voice and action. The cases are reported in the case study form of Chapter 5; however, the focus in this chapter is on the interactions between participants. Analysis of the data will follow each case study and again, a summary of emerging themes will conclude the chapter. The chapter will disclose shifting and hidden identities emerging from the data where mediators move beyond the labelled constructs of the literature. Within the underlying framework of negotiation – a framework readily accepted and promoted by mediators – mediators take on several identities in the quest for the deal of a mediated resolution. Specifically, the mediator takes on ever-shifting identities of party, party adviser and third-party intervener in their mediations, forming a quintet of identities to describe mediator interaction. These identities forge the fugitive nature of mediation, where process and mediator merge, where definitional labels are illusory and identities are hidden. Participants in the process are not aware of the nature or fluidity of the changes that occur. They do not recognize the high level of mediator intervention that takes place in the mediated negotiation. These and other themes emerging from the data will be explored.

Chapter 7, the final chapter, provides an epilogue summarizing the themes disclosed by the data and its analysis. It speaks to the fugitive identity of mediation, a process wholly integrated with negotiation. In recapping themes of shifting identities, party perceptions, unity of process and mediator, it suggests that mediation becomes a depersonalized negotiation during which the mediator engages in depersonalized advocacy in both a normative and a social context. The chapter also explores the implications of the findings as well as limitations to the work, particularly in relation to the ethnographic methodology. It concludes with the hope that its findings compel further exploration of issues raised by the study and a reaffirmation that the capacity for continued learning in the field remains unabated.

Disputing through an ethnographic lens

Although parties may make use of rules and norms to promote their claims, such rules and norms may not be determinative of outcome in a non-adjudicatory process. This creates the need to look at the process itself to determine the influences that lead to resolution. Elements in the process, outside of the law, which impact the evolution of a dispute must also be examined particularly where rules are not definitive of outcome, as these elements will become more relevant to the dispute.[23]

In order to study a process of dispute resolution, it must be examined free from its legal framework. Consequently, relevant components of the process that may be obscured by the weight of the legal trappings of structures, rules and norms will come to light. Accomplishing this will require reliance on ethnography, a research method developed by anthropologists in their study of society. This method has been used to examine disputes and resolution of disputes in societies free from western concepts of law and legal institutions.

---

23 S. Roberts, *Order and Dispute: An Introduction to Legal Anthropology* (Harmondsworth: Penguin, 1979) at 136, 182.

12 *Unmasking the mediation process*

In particular, social structures, relationships, norms and processes have been examined to determine how order was maintained in acephalous societies.[24]

Malinowski's *Crime and Custom in Savage Society*, although an exploration of the problem of order, sets the stage for inquiry into the manner in which disputes were handled in one society.[25] Evans-Pritchard spoke of the self-help way of the Nuer, but also noted the presence of the leopard-skin chief who would, though rarely, intercede on behalf of the disputants to effect a resolution.[26] Llewellyn and Hoebel, in seeking to learn of the law-jobs of the Cheyenne, spoke of present dispute resolution processes such as negotiation, mediation and conciliation as processes that do the work of law without involving the institutions of law.[27] Turner examined village structure and, through the social drama, illustrated the relationship between conflict and order: it was through conflict that order was created and social forms were produced.[28]

Gulliver's *Social Control in An African Society*[29] and *Neighbours and Networks*[30] further inform the relevance of anthropological methods to the study of disputes and their resolution. In considering the broader question of order and how it is maintained in a society where there is no central authoritarian figure,[31] these studies examine society's response to conflict; more specifically, they examine the systems in place for the resolution of conflict. Gulliver explores how breaches of the norms of social behaviour were dealt with: for

---

24 This chapter will review some of these investigations in the paragraphs below.
25 B. Malinowski, *Crime and Custom in Savage Society* (London: Routledge, 2002 edition). Malinowski was interested in law and order in alien society, and thus began the search for law in society. The following discussion regarding ethnographic studies is an introduction to the study of conflict and its resolution in order to highlight the suitability of the approach to the research in issue. An examination of its methods specifically follows later in the chapter, together with a discussion as to its appropriateness to the study of mediation.
26 E.E. Evans-Pritchard, *The Nuer: A Description of the Modes of Livelihood and Political Institutions of a Nilotic People* (New York: Oxford University Press, 1969) at 151–84.
27 Llewellyn and Hoebel, see note 18 at 307.
28 V.W. Turner, *Schism and Continuity in an African Society: A Study of Ndembu Village Life* (Oxford: Berg, 1996 edition) at 93. The 'social drama' was Turner's term for case studies: in examining the processes of social conflict, Turner followed several instances of dispute in the order in which they arose.
29 P.H. Gulliver, *Social Control in An African Society: A Study of the Arusha: Agricultural Masai of Northern Tanganyika* (London: Routledge, 2000 edition).
30 P.H. Gulliver, *Neighbours and Networks: The Idiom of Kinship in Social Action among the Ndendeuli of Tanzania* (London: University of California Press, 1971).
31 It must be recognized that there was the presence of centralized government with the advent of colonialism. The colonial governments introduced a western-styled judicial system in these societies. These works, though, look at the breach of normative order and resolution of the breach outside these external systems which were imposed on the Arusha and Ndendeuli, the subjects of these studies.

example, were there recognized procedures to deal with such breaches; how was it determined that a breach occurred; how were damages established; how were disputes resolved and obligations enforced?[32] He particularly seeks to understand how disputes are resolved absent centralized authority, coercion or self-help.[33]

The Arusha reduced the complexity of their social interactions thus: "We discuss and discuss the matter (in dispute) and then we agree. When we agree, that is the end. What else is there to do?"[34] However, resolution is not so simple. Gulliver looks at the social relationships constructing social order and the impact of norms on disputing outcomes.[35] He uncovers the importance of the social relationship of kin, age and community in both the formulation of the conflict and its resolution.[36] Binary negotiation is conducted through a support network constituted by each disputant for the purpose of resolving conflict. Promotion and constraint on disputing positions are exerted to move the disputing parties to an outcome that is acceptable not only to the party, but also to the community at large. Within these relations, norms play a role.[37] They are not determinative of the outcome, but are integral to the evolution towards resolution. Norms form the basis of the Arusha claims.[38] The Arusha do not rely on norms to settle their dispute. Rather, they are prepared to get as close as they can to their claim in face of the weaknesses and strengths of each party and in terms of what they can negotiate. For the claimant, the key is to show how the defendant's behaviour breaches a norm; for the defendant, it is to show either that there is no divergence from the norm or there is another more important norm requiring divergence. In the end, they negotiate for what they can get rather than for what they are entitled to obtain.[39]

Settlement for the Arusha is a political not a legal function. They do not look to judicial authority for a determination of their conflict. Instead, they use social process informed, but not determined, by norms.[40] Norms exist in some form in all groups of humans – where there is a group there are norms.[41] One cannot escape them. The issue is the impact of those norms on society and their role in social order.

32 Gulliver, see note 29 at 1.
33 Ibid. at 232.
34 Ibid.
35 Ibid. at 275.
36 Ibid. at 2–3.
37 Ibid. at 240.
38 Ibid. at 241.
39 Ibid. at 242–53.
40 Ibid. at 297–99.
41 Llewellyn and Hoebel, see note 18 at 276.

14 *Unmasking the mediation process*

This issue is also pertinent in Gulliver's *Neighbours and Networks*. In examining the social fabric and function of society through the analytical framework of kinship, the issue of norms once again becomes seminal to the question of how society deals with disputes. The process there too is political, not legal, and there too norms are relevant, but not determinative.[42]

Comaroff and Roberts take the analysis further in their study of the Tswana.[43] They see disputes as falling within an integrated paradigm of norms and processes.[44] The debate between the rule-centred theory of law and the processual approach of Malinowski and others is clearly articulated by the authors.[45] Tswana implement social processes and norms in the resolution of their conflict. A rule-centred paradigm alone is not sufficient to understand how a non-western society deals with disputes when they arise in society, and on the other hand, one cannot deny the existence of some form of rules in such society.[46]

Tswana society is based on *mekgwa le melao*, custom and rules.[47] Rules are understood by all to exist and Tswana behaviour tries to fit within the rules. These rules, however (with the exception of a small number of limited cases), do not determine outcome.[48] Tswana society is individualistic, competitive and motivated by personal interest. Rules may be negotiated for advantage.[49] Social interaction within the customs and laws of society determines outcome. Tswana live within a circular paradigm: rules exist but they inform behaviour rather than control behaviour; and social interaction manipulates the rules but does not change the rules.

The Tswana example illustrates that dispute processes which invoke norms are not to be found only in rule-centred paradigms and, at the same time, that social processes of interaction are not the only factors governing outcome. Rather, society's experience with dispute resolution processes can be reflected in a dual system of norms and social interaction. Rules inform the process and the socio-cultural process manipulates the rules for individual gain.[50] A convergence of rules and processes is the result. This convergence illuminates the possibility that dispute resolution processes may not be wholly dependent on rules, nor wholly free of them.

---

42 Gulliver, see note 30 at 179–80, 184.
43 J.L. Comaroff and S. Roberts, *Rules and Processes: The Cultural Logic of Dispute in an African Context* (Chicago: University of Chicago Press, 1981).
44 Ibid. at 20, 28–9, 216.
45 Ibid. at 4–16.
46 Ibid. at 17.
47 Ibid. at 70–9.
48 Ibid. at 239.
49 Ibid. at 19.
50 Ibid. at 247.

An examination of dispute processes should not be viewed only in the context of determinative rules or only in the context of social processes, but rather in a paradigm that blends both rules and social processes. The Tswana dispute process illustrates this on a micro level: it requires this blended paradigm, for without it we would not be able to understand the Tswana process of resolution. The blended paradigm also provides an appropriate analytical framework for a macro-level analysis of dispute processes in other societies. As such, it is particularly relevant to the study at hand.

Turner's *Schism and Continuity in an African Society* is another work that assists in the understanding of dispute processes of other societies. It is also relevant to this study. Turner examines not only the structures of society but also the processes of human interaction. On one level of his examination, he meticulously outlines the structural principles of village life such as village history, membership, mobility, kinship and ritual.[51] He intersperses this with "processional forms" which "developed out of clashes and alignments of human volitions and purposes, inspired by private and public interests and ideals".[52] Turner further states that an analysis of social life requires an examination of the relationship between process and structure.[53] In order to understand processes, there needs to be an understanding of the structures, and vice versa. Each adds dimension to the other.

These studies assist in positioning mediation within the spectrum of dispute resolution processes. Mediation represents a convergence on two levels: a convergence of rules and processes as articulated by Comaroff and Roberts, and a convergence of structures and processes as suggested by Turner. First, rules breathe life into competing claims that create conflict and then seek to influence outcome. Outcome, however, is also dependent on process; that is, social interaction among all actors in the resolution process and the changes that result from such interaction. Facts are manipulated to fit within the normative order; yet the normative order is not implemented in such a way as to determine outcome. Second, mediation operates within society's structures while it is itself a structure. It is the structure of third-party assisted negotiation situated within the larger structure of a rule-centred institution or model, which reflects an individualistic, adversarial, adjudicative approach to decision-making. Its processes operate within these structures. Processually, it is concerned with interaction and change among disputing parties in the face of conflict. The examination of dispute resolution through mediation cannot ignore these bi-level intersections between rules and processes on one hand, and processes and structures on the other.[54]

---

51 Turner, see note 28 at xxv, 328.
52 Ibid. at xxii.
53 Ibid.
54 For the purpose of clarification, 'rules' here refer to ascriptive norms; 'structures' are the principles upon which 'villages' are built; and 'processes' are those elements that inform social interaction.

16 *Unmasking the mediation process*

Through an examination of the convergences, the relationships between structures, rules and norms, and social processes will be made clearer. It is within these convergences that I am interested in discovering through this study: (i) the interactions that take place among the actors in a process called mediation that is situated in a legally centred world; (ii) the resulting changes occurring from such interactions; and (iii) their influences on the process. Changes from the interactions may relate to the views, attitudes, perceptions, responses and conduct of individuals in the process. At a minimum, resolving a dispute requires a transformation of the facts and circumstances into a form that is conducive to a settlement.[55] Considering the very nature of change, whatever change occurs in mediation would likely involve interaction among all participants involved in the process – the parties, their representatives and the mediator. Mediation recognizes the potential for resolution through the dynamic social interaction of negotiated order. It is through this examination of convergences that we may achieve greater understanding of mediation as a means by which to achieve negotiated order. This is the premise on which I entered the field. It is this theoretical construct that guided the search for meaning, the imponderabilia of life.[56]

The ethnographic process

The ethnographic approach

Any discussion of ethnography must begin with Bronislaw Malinowski and his revolutionary *Argonauts of the Western Pacific*. "Imagine yourself suddenly set down surrounded by all your gear, alone on a tropical beach close to a native village while the launch or dinghy which has brought you sails out of sight."[57] Ethnography grew out of the colonial era where the discovery of societies unlike our own sparked great interest. To learn about these societies, Malinowski was emphatic that one had to live among the natives:

> Living in the village with no other business but to follow native life, one sees the customs, ceremonies and transactions over and over again, one has examples of their beliefs as they are actually lived through, and the full body and blood of actual native life fills out soon the skeleton of abstract constructions. That is the reason why, working under such conditions as previously described, the Ethnographer is enabled to add

---

55 These concepts are seen in the manipulation of facts by the Tswana. For example, Comaroff and Roberts, see note 43 at 214, 244.
56 B. Malinowski, *Argonauts of the Western Pacific* (Long Grove: Waveland, 1984 edition) at 18 for his search for the imponderabilia of life.
57 Ibid. at 4.

something essential to the bare outline of tribal constitution, and to supplement it by all the details of behaviour, setting and small incident. He is able in each case to state whether an act is public or private; how a public assembly behaves, and what it looks like; he can judge whether an event is ordinary or an exciting and singular one; whether natives bring to it a great deal of sincere and earnest spirit, or perform it in fun; whether they do it in a perfunctory manner, or with zeal and deliberation.

In other words, there is a series of phenomena of great importance which cannot possibly be recorded by questioning or computing documents, but have to be observed in their full actuality. Let us call them the imponderabilia of actual life.[58]

The spirit of ethnography has not changed since Malinowski's time. As Conley and O'Barr state: "Today, ethnography is still defined as the qualitative, long term study of a society by a researcher who lives among the people, learns their language, and strives to participate in their culture."[59] In their consideration of the rise of the occult in South Africa, Comaroff and Comaroff speak of the role of the anthropologist in conducting ethnographic research. It is well worth hearing their words for encapsulating its importance:

our skills and sensibilities ought to be put to the effort of detecting emergent social processes and patterns from diverse, discordant acts and facts; that the sacred charter of the discipline is to explain the existence of such partly obscured, barely audible, often nascent phenomena in the world.[60]

Ethnography involves fieldwork. In other words, it is the study of active phenomena. Whether it is the study of a foreign society, an organization, or an event, it requires an in-depth examination of the phenomena through active participation with the phenomena itself. It is not a static endeavour. It is dynamic. Because of its nature, it provides the opportunity for researchers to gather layers and layers of data.

This task is made more difficult by the fact that the data is not easily obtained or understood.[61] Although Malinowski's comments come from

---

58 Ibid. at 18.
59 J.M. Conley and W.M. O'Barr, "Legal Anthropology Comes Home: A Brief History of the Ethnographic Study of Law" (1993–94) 27 *Loy. L.A. L. Rev.* 41 at 45.
60 J. Comaroff and J.L. Comaroff, "Occult Economies and the Violence of Abstraction: Notes for the South African Postcolony" (1999) 26 *American Ethnologist* 279 at 283.
61 Malinowski repeatedly states that the ethnographer must extract data that the native cannot articulate from his own world-view: see note 56 at 454. See also, R.F. Fortune, *Sorcerers of Dobu: The Social Anthropology of the Dobu Islanders of the Western Pacific* (London: Routledge, 1963) at 135. Fortune illustrates this when he speaks about concepts that are

studies of Melanesian societies, the task of the present-day ethnographer has not strayed too far from the fundamental role espoused by him: to create generalizations out of imponderable facts.[62] As Geertz states, the ethnographer "sorts winks from twitches and real winks from mimicked ones".[63] Ethnography permits us to see beyond the act: it provides an opportunity to understand why people behave as they do. For Hammersley, it lets us "see things differently, to see possible parallels and links that we had not noticed".[64]

What comes from this life among the 'natives'? According to Geertz, thick descriptions from the ethnographer's data collected from the observations of, discussions with, and participation in native life. The data is complex, multilayered and replete with hidden understandings, requiring effort to be exerted to make sense of it:

> The point for now is only that ethnography is thick description. What the ethnographer is in fact faced with – except when (as, of course, he must do) he is pursuing the more automatized routines of data collection – is a multiplicity of complex conceptual structures, many of them superimposed upon or knotted into one another, which are at once strange, irregular, and inexplicit, and which he must contrive somehow first to grasp and then to render. And this is true at the most down-to-earth, jungle field work levels of his activity: interviewing informants, observing rituals, eliciting kin terms, tracing property lines, censuring households ... writing his journal. Doing ethnography is like trying to read (in the sense of 'construct a reading of') a manuscript – foreign, faded, full of ellipses, incoherencies, suspicious emendations, and tendentious commentaries, but written not in conventionalized graphs of sound but in transient examples of shaped behaviour.[65]

Malinowski noted that missionaries, traders, travellers and government officials provided information about new societies. Their accounts, although informative, were not ethnographies.[66] The fieldwork must be recorded, and it must be analysed to determine the value of the data in relation to the phenomenon studied. Malinowski says that it is the job of the ethnographer to find meaning from that which he observes. He needs to siphon from the

---

not part of the native world-view such as 'bad' and 'good'. The ethnographer must learn about native concepts so that foreign meaning is not attributed to the data.
62 Fortune, ibid. at xix.
63 C. Geertz, *The Interpretation of Culture* (New York: Basic Books, 1973) at 16.
64 M. Hammersley, *What's Wrong with Ethnography? Methodological Explorations* (London: Routledge, 1992) at 14.
65 Geertz, see note 63 at 9–10.
66 Malinowski, see note 56 at 9, 17–18.

Unmasking the mediation process 19

mass the relevant and important details in order to construct a social world comprehensible to all.[67] Gulliver acknowledges that it can be no more than an 'approximation to reality' that is achieved through the ethnographic effort, but stresses the need to record the observations as accurately as possible.[68]

Malinowski sees the dual nature of ethnography: "the writer is his own chronicler and the historian at the same time".[69] In essence, he sees the ethnographer's role as one of interpreter whose interpretation is grounded in scientific philosophy. Although the ethnographer's work is creative because it makes clear that which is hidden, it remains an investigative exercise of natural science since the work is based on the objective realities of the phenomena observed.[70] For Malinowski, therefore, ethnography is a scientific exercise,[71] born perhaps out of his desire to legitimize ethnography as a research methodology: it is his theoretical charter. Both Malinowski and Gulliver emphasize the importance of interpretation to ascribe meaning, but the interpretation must be grounded in the data the ethnographer has observed.[72]

For Geertz, ethnography *is* interpretation. He recognizes the importance of observation but personalizes the observation through his interpretations. Geertz describes the exercise as interpretive rather than scientific. He bases this view on his belief that the ethnographer cannot be privy to every aspect of the society she observes and therefore it is not possible to reconstruct reality: the best that can be done is to make educated guesses as to the meaning of the acts. It is not science, he says; it is cultural interpretation.[73]

Geertz's ethnographer interprets what he sees by giving it meaning. An example of Geertz's interpretive approach is best illustrated in his study of the Balinese cockfight.[74] Geertz sees the Balinese cock as the Balinese man, with pun intended by Geertz. The cockfight becomes the Balinese society: it is a symbol of man's desires and internal tendencies that are suppressed by societal norms.[75] For Geertz, it reflects the social strata of Balinese society as portrayed by the Balinese:

> What sets the cockfight apart from the ordinary course of life, lifts it from the realm of everyday practical affairs, and surrounds it with an aura

---

67 Ibid. at 84.
68 Gulliver, see note 30 at 358.
69 Malinowski, see note 56 at 3.
70 Ibid. at 397.
71 Ibid. at 3, 6.
72 See generally, ibid. 1–25, 84, 337 and in Fortune, see note 61 at xxvii. Also Gulliver, see note 30 at 358.
73 Geertz, see note 63 at 20.
74 Ibid. at 412–53.
75 Ibid. at 417–20, 443, 446.

of enlarged importance is not, as functionalist sociology would have it, that it reinforces status discriminations (such reinforcement is hardly necessary in a society where every act proclaims them), but that it provides a metasocial commentary upon the whole matter of assorting human beings into fixed hierarchical ranks and then organizing the major part of collective existence around that assortment. Its function, if you want to call it that, is interpretive: it is a Balinese reading of Balinese experience, a story they tell themselves about themselves.[76]

But is this really the way the Balinese see themselves? There is no indication from Geertz's report of any data coming from the Balinese regarding their perspective on the cockfight. Crapanzano makes this point in his critique of Geertz's handling of the Balinese cockfight, and also notes that Geertz does not describe the cockfight in detail but only provides his construction of it. This, Crapanzano says, is not ethnography; it is interpretation of culture.[77] Geertz, however, sees the power of ethnography in its interpretation of culture: the observation is transformed into a constructed reality through interpretative activities.[78]

According to Clifford, ethnography is about interpretation of action for the construction of meaning:

Ethnography is actively situated between powerful systems of meaning. It poses its questions at the boundaries of civilizations, cultures, classes, races, and genders. Ethnography decodes and recodes, telling the grounds of collective order and diversity, inclusion and exclusion. It describes processes of innovation and structuration, and is itself part of these processes.[79]

The ethnographer constructs his text through translation of his experience.[80] Clifford emphasizes the importance of translating observations into the textualization of experience:

Whatever else an ethnography does, it translates experience into text. There are various ways of effecting this translation, ways that have

---

76 Ibid. at 448.
77 V. Crapanzano, "Hermes' Dilemma: The Masking of Subversion in Ethnographic Description" in J. Clifford and G.E. Marcus, eds, *Writing Culture: The Poetics and Politics of Ethnography* (Berkeley: University of California Press, 1986) at 74–5.
78 Geertz, see note 63 at 20.
79 J. Clifford, "Introduction: Partial Truths" in Clifford and Marcus, see note 77 at 2–3.
80 J. Clifford, "On Ethnographic Allegory" in Clifford and Marcus, see note 77 at 115; see also T. Asad, "The Concept of Cultural Translation in British Anthropology" in Clifford and Marcus, see note 77 at 143–4, 159.

significant ethical and political consequences. One can 'write up' the results of an individual experience of research. This may generate a realistic account of the unwritten experience of another group or person. One can present this textualization as the outcome of observation, of interpretation, of dialogue. One can construct an ethnography composed of dialogues. One can feature multiple voices, or a single voice. One can portray the other as a stable, essential whole, or one can show it to be the product of a narrative of discovery, in specific historical circumstances. I have discussed some of these choices elsewhere (1983a). What is irreducible, in all of them, is the assumption that ethnography brings experience and discourse into writing.[81]

For Clifford, ethnography is an allegorical account "at the level both of its content (what it says about cultures and their histories) and of its form (what is implied by its mode of textualization)".[82] It creates a powerful story where the boundary between art and science becomes blurred.[83]

These contrasting descriptions of ethnography have common themes. They recognize the difficulty of extracting data and the need to do it as objectively as one can. They also recognize the creative and interpretative aspect of ethnography while at the same time acknowledging the need for an account that is supported by the data, so that it is not merely supposition. Ultimately, ethnography is a method of: (i) research for the collection of a particular type of data; (ii) textualization of data; and (iii) ascribing meaning to the textualized data. In achieving this textualization, the ethnographer tries to make clear that which is obscure. Whatever label is given to this textualization, be it Malinowski's scientific induction, Geertz's interpretation or Clifford's allegory to name a few, the outcome is the same: reconstruction of observed reality as experienced and deduced by the ethnographer. The data must support the textualization and analysis if it is to add to human knowledge. Ethnography is not just about facts. It is not just about theory. It is about facts and theory. Insufficient analysis or theory unsupported by the data is not ethnography.[84] Ultimately, it is a combination of Malinowski's scientific

---

81 Clifford, ibid.
82 Ibid. at 98.
83 Clifford, ibid. and see note 79 at 3.
84 L. Wacquant, "Scrutinizing the Street: Poverty, Morality, and the Pitfalls of Urban Ethnography" (2002) 107 *Am. J. of Sociology* 1468 at 1489, for example; W.J. Wilson and A. Chaddha, "The Role of Theory in Ethnographic Research" (2009) 10 *Ethnography* 549, in which they review Wacquant's critique of three ethnographies in the aforementioned article. They conclude that ethnography must be more than mere description to be valid; it should provide 'inductive theoretical insights' or a combination of inductive and deductive analysis: see at 562–3.

method and the literary, interpretative approach espoused by Geertz and Clifford.[85]

The ethnographic method

The foregoing discussion considered the elements of ethnography – data collection, textualization and the analysis of the data. This section examines in greater detail the various approaches to the analysis of the data, over which there is significant debate.[86] The same question is asked over and over: what is an appropriate approach to the ethnographic method? Again, it is necessary to begin with Malinowski in order to appreciate the evolution of the methodology that has been applied since he lived with and reported on the Trobrianders. *Argonauts of the Western Pacific* serves two purposes: as an ethnographic account of a particular aspect of Trobriand society and as a text on ethnographic methodology.

In his introductory chapter, Malinowski sets out the rules of the scientific method of ethnography and continues throughout the Trobriand narrative to comment on issues of method. He begins with the call for transparency: the clear line between the observation of native acts, statements and interpretations on the one hand, and the deductions of the researcher on the other.[87] He also speaks of the importance of systematic collecting and recording of data, the approach to questioning native informants, the need for a comprehensive account of native life, and the demand for inductive generalizations from the data obtained.[88] In this regard, Malinowski's theoretical approach was to see how each element of society fitted within the whole. He examined all aspects of society: he considered, for example, kinship, agricultural, religious, political, social, economic and psychological elements of society to understand an important Trobriander ceremony, the *kula*.[89] In so doing, he showed the integral role of each in the maintenance of order within the *kula* exchange. Conley and O'Barr describe this as a functionalist approach where all aspects of social life comprise the whole and from which individual action is determined.[90]

---

85 Malinowski, see note 56 at 25; Geertz, see note 63; Clifford, see notes 79 and 80.
86 For example, see generally, Clifford and Marcus, see note 77.
87 Malinowski, see note 56 at 3.
88 Ibid. at 1–25.
89 Simplistically, the *kula* is a ritual of commodity exchange between the communities of the Trobriand Islands. The commodities are red shell necklaces and white shell bracelets. Members of the communities exhange these items in a highly ritualized, ceremonial, symbolic and ordered manner. The *kula* is a primary social institution, comprising various activities and obligations, which is central to the life of the Trobriander. For greater detail, see Malinowski, note 56 at 81–4.
90 Conley and O'Barr, see note 19 at 853–4.

In his preface to Fortune's *Sorcerers of Dobu*, Malinowski hails the functionalist approach taken by Fortune, and in so doing, describes the approach:

> [The anthropologist] has to investigate the relations between custom, institution and type of behaviour. For we are now more and more interested in the connections between the component parts of an institution in the relations of institution to institution and of aspect to aspect. We are interested, that is, rather in meaning and function than in form and detail. Only an inductive generalization or a functional relation is to the modern anthropologist a real scientific fact.
>
> The functional anthropologist has constantly to make inductive generalization from what he sees, he has to construct theories and draw up the charters of native institutions. In short, he has constantly to theorize in the field, theorize on what he sees, hears and experiences.[91]

Although Malinowski makes his observations in relation to a functionalist approach, his comments are relevant for all ethnographers, whatever theoretical framework is applied. As Malinowski says, the anthropologist has to make sense of what she sees and hears. She needs to put her observations into the context of the social reality of the people she is observing. In doing so, she makes decisions about the relevance and importance of actions taken by her subjects. She must then construe such actions.

A movement away from the functionalist approach came with the study of conflict in *The Cheyenne Way*, which applied the case method in its study of crises.[92] The functionalist approach was not applicable for Llewellyn and Hoebel's purposes; they introduced the new case method approach to ethnography.[93] They examined the 'law' of the Cheyenne by examining a series of cases dealing with breaches of norms and customs of Cheyenne society as recalled by Cheyenne informants. The brilliance of *The Cheyenne Way* was the innovative use of cases to determine how order was maintained in society, rather than a piecemeal examination of society to reveal the whole of society, as was undertaken by the functionalists.

Turner, in *Schism and Continuity in an African Society*, further developed this method through the 'social drama'.[94] Turner used cases to illustrate how the structures of society functioned in practice. For him, it was important to examine the actions of the actors and thus examine the relationship between the processual and structural components of society. Structures were static;

---

91 Fortune, see note 61 at xxix.
92 Llewellyn and Hoebel, see note 18 at 28–9.
93 For an interesting discussion of the context surrounding the making of *The Cheyenne Way*, see A.K. Mehotra, "Law and the 'Other': Karl N. Llewellyn, Cultural Anthropology, and the Legacy of the Cheyenne Way" (2001) 26 *Law & Soc. Inquiry* 741.
94 Turner, see note 28.

processes were not. Processes of human interactions uncovered the irregularities in society.[95] Turner summarizes his approach as follows:

> This book represents an attempt to combine two kinds of anthropological examination. The first is a synchronic analysis of Ndembu village structure. The second is an experiment in diachronic micro-sociology. My spatial unit of study has been the village, my unit of time the social drama. I have tried to marry the general to the particular by analysing a series of social dramas in the history of a single village. That village's membership was organised by the structural principles isolated during the synchronic study of a number of villages. But these principles were there interrelated in a unique way. In the social dramas I have tried to show how in specific situations certain principles came into conflict, and how attempts were made to maintain the unity of the disturbed group despite such conflict.[96]

Gulliver applied this approach and refined it further to examine conflict and its resolution. In *Social Control in An African Society* he studied "the social contexts in which [these] disputes and processes occurred, and the nature of the systems of social relationships in which the disputants were involved".[97] He examined the societal structures of age, kinship and community and the individual interactions within these structures to discover the ways the Arusha dealt with disputes. In *Neighbours and Networks*, he examined the structure of the kinship network among the Ndendeuli and the interaction among individuals within this structure, again in relation to conflict and its resolution. This consideration looked at the impact of the social structure on disputes, and vice versa. In so doing, he acknowledged Turner's contribution to his approach.[98]

Comaroff and Roberts continued to build on the foundation laid by Turner and Gulliver in their examination of the relationship between the Tswana rules and customs, and their manifestation in human action.[99] The methodology applied by Comaroff and Roberts is reflective of the dualism in Tswana society: as stated earlier, rules inform the process and the process manipulates the rules.[100] Their theoretical model, which articulates the convergence between rules and processes, was informed by the data collected from Tswana society. *Rules and Processes* illustrates the need to create an analytical framework that best suits the reality of the observed society:

> everyday life – and the disputes that occur in its course – is at once rule-governed yet characterized by the individualistic pursuit of utility, for

---

95 Ibid. at xxv.
96 Ibid. at 328.
97 Gulliver, see note 29 at x.
98 Gulliver, see note 30 at 63, 355.
99 Comaroff and Roberts, see note 43.
100 Ibid. at 239–40.

which purpose rules may be deployed as resources. It is in this dualism, we argue, that the meaningful construction of the Tswana dispute process is expressed.[101]

As seen from these studies, there is no question that theoretical analysis emerges from the data collected by the ethnographer. But where does the theory fit, if anywhere at all, in the initial fieldwork phase of the ethnographic enterprise? Should an ethnographer go into the field with a fully developed theoretical hypothesis in pursuit of a theory to be proved, disproved, modified or developed; or alternatively, should the ethnographer begin her endeavour free of any theoretical concepts or theoretical encumbrance so as to let the facts uncover the theory? The place of theory in the ethnographic account is a source of debate. Those who advocate an extended case method, for example, would argue that the selection of the fieldsite should be dependent on the theory that the researcher is intent on investigating.[102] This is in contrast to those who say that one should enter the field unencumbered by theoretical objectives.[103]

A balance must be struck between the need for a general theory to guide data collection and the need for a clear lens through which to observe the data. The ethnographer should go into the field with an idea of what she might find and an idea of the nature of the data that she seeks. For Llewellyn and Hoebel, general theory provides a framework for the data collection: it guides the observer's inquiry into the phenomenon and helps the observer to see its relevance.[104] This is suggestive of Malinowski's views that some theory is required to guide the ethnographer in her search for information. Some theory, says Malinowski, is necessary in order to recognize the implications presented by the facts on the development of theory.[105] Fully formed theory, however, will blind the effort because it will render the ethnographer inflexible to the ideas and possibilities suggested by the data.

Although he advocates a different approach to the interpretive function of the ethnographer, Geertz is in agreement with these views on the need for general theory. He echoes the need for general theory to help inform the data and also the development of more specific theory once the data is collected so that the data then informs the theory. He succinctly describes the ethnographer's

---

101 Ibid. at 216.
102 I. Tavory and S. Timmermans, "Two Cases of Ethnography: Grounded Theory and the Extended Case Method" (2009) 10 *Ethnography* 243 at 244, 250, 254.
103 Wacquant, see note 84, in which Wacquant critiques this approach to ethnography at 1481 and 1523. See also R. Behar, "Ethnography and the Book that was Lost" (2003) 4 *Ethnography* 15 at 16, where she states that ethnographers search for stories that they did not know they were looking for.
104 Llewellyn and Hoebel, see note 18 at 19.
105 Malinowski, see note 56 at 9.

experience with respect to the collection of data and the formulation of theories in relation to that data:

> This backward order of things – first you write then you figure out what you are writing about – may seem odd, or even perverse, but it is, I think, at least most of the time, standard procedure in cultural anthropology. Some pretenders to high science and higher technique aside, we do not start out with well-formed ideas we carry off to distant places to check out by means of carefully codified procedures systematically applied. We go off to those places, or, increasingly these days, ones closer by, with some general notions of what we would like to look into and of how we might go about looking into them. We then in fact look into them (or, often enough, look instead into others that turn out to be more interesting), and after doing so we return to sort through our notes and memories, both of them defective, to see what we might have uncovered that clarifies anything or leads on to useful revisions of received ideas, our own or someone else's about something or other.[106]

In the consideration of a general theory that is brought to an ethnographic study, care must be taken not to blur the general theory with the ethnographer's personal conceptions. General theory, as described by Llewellyn and Hoebel, Malinowski and Geertz above, provides helpful and useful guidance to the fieldworker in the collection of data since it helps the fieldworker to see through the minutiae of detail that is present in everyday life. Ultimately, it is the watching and hearing that produces the basis for analytical discourse.[107] General theory assists in exploration of the data. Theory comes from the data, but it does not lie solely in the data; rather, it must spring from the data. The data does not provide the explanation; it generates the theory.[108]

The existence of a personal lens, however, will impede the investigation and interpretation of the data. It will cause the ethnographer to see only recognizable data; that is, data that is known and already understood by the ethnographer. Hammersley believes that the anthropological method of ethnography liberates the ethnographer from her frameworks, which comprise her day-to-day realities.[109] Roberts does not see it quite so simply.

---

106 Geertz, see note 63 at v–vi.
107 J. Comaroff and J.L. Comaroff, "Ethnography on an Awkward Scale: Postcolonial Anthropology and the Violence of Abstraction" (2003) 4 *Ethnography* 147 at 164; H. Englund and J. Leach, "Ethnography and the Meta-narratives of Modernity" (2000) 41 *Current Anthropology* 225 at 226.
108 J. Comaroff and J.L. Comaroff, "Response to Moore: Second Thoughts" (1999) 26 *Am. Ethnologist* 307 at 309.
109 Hammersley, see note 64 at 14.

According to him, the ethnographer "is prone to fit the material under investigation, consciously or unconsciously, into a conceptual and institutional framework of his own, distorting the material as he does so".[110] This is a risk that cannot be avoided. Efforts, however, can be taken to minimize the risk, including: (i) a full awareness of one's preconceptions and the intent to keep them from affecting the ethnographer's understanding of what he sees; (ii) full attention to what is being said and done; and (iii) ensuring that the theoretical framework chosen to ascribe meaning to the data is not shaped "by parochial features drawn from his society or the one that he has investigated".[111]

Once the data is collected, it must be analysed and reported. It must not be mere description, a criticism often made of ethnography.[112] Malinowski sees this step as objective scientific reporting, yet he dances through narrative and description, interpreting what he sees, hears and experiences.[113] Evans-Pritchard's approach was to start and end with a personal narrative and in between provide a pastoral report about a pastoral people with detail sufficient only to support his interpretation of the Nuer social system.[114] Like Malinowski, he sought to create a scientific report. Although lacking the detail of Malinowski's report, Evans-Pritchard's simple and literary report provides the reader with a vivid picture of the Nuer and the structures of their society. The extent of the 'thick description' must be guided by the phenomenon under observation and the ethnographer's general theory of investigation. The resulting analysis and report will be informed by that data.

An ethnographic application to this study

My approach in this ethnographic endeavour is to textualize interpretations of the observations from the immersion in the active phenomena of the study. Ethnography is about recording what one sees and to strive to do it objectively; that is, not from the native's perspective nor from the ethnographer's personal perspective, but rather from the data's perspective. The ethnographer, like the Cree hunter, "can only tell what [she] knows".[115] That is the first step. The second is the analysis of the data from which meaning is ascribed to the data. Generalizations are made about the data: this is the interpretative exercise that forms part of the ethnographic exercise. It involves interpretation of the data, supported by the data. Crapanzano states

---

110 Roberts, see note 23 at 17.
111 Ibid. at 18.
112 For example, G.E. Marcus, "Contemporary Problems of Ethnography in the Modern World System" in Clifford and Marcus, see note 77 at 167.
113 M.L. Pratt, "Fieldwork in Common Places" in Clifford and Marcus, see note 77 at 38–9.
114 R. Rosaldo, "From the Door of his Tent: The Fieldworker and the Inquisitor" in Clifford and Marcus, see note 77 at 96.
115 Clifford, see note 79 at 8.

that the ethnographer does not record the truth of the data; he records the interpretation of the data.[116] Clifford refers to these recordings as 'true fictions'.[117] People label ethnography as all sorts of different things. In the end, its identity is dictated by its function: the function in this study is deductive interpretation of the data collected and informed by a theory of investigation.

My ethnography uses a classic approach in the sense that it is guided by a general theoretical framework, but was not started for the purpose of investigating a specific theory. My purpose was to learn about mediation from a particular methodological perspective, recognizing its structural, processual and normative elements and being curious about the interactions that occur through these elements. Armed with this conceptual and theoretical framework, I entered the field free from the constraints of embedded theory, enabling me to explore what the data exposed in relation to those ideas, leading to the 'aha' moment of ethnography.[118] Analytical constructs flow from the revelations.[119]

It is also classic in the sense that it is guided by Malinowski's belief that the observation and the recording of the observation must be full and meticulous. Although not a structural functionalist approach in the tradition of Malinowski, this study strives for Malinowski's scientific approach in the sense of recognizing, and hopefully satisfying, the need for sufficient details to support the ethnographer's analysis. With data in hand, the interpretative approach of Geertz, Clifford and Marcus is applied as I search for meaning in the data, considering what it conveys about the process, its actors and the place of mediation in a socio-legal world. This approach interprets the data and reconstructs it as it does so into an analysis of a process existing within a particular theoretical paradigm.

I am not seeking to create new theories for the ethnographic enterprise. This book is not an exploration about the ethnographic method. I invoke

---

116 Crapanzano, see note 77.
117 Clifford, see note 79 at 6–7.
118 Willis and Trondman speak of the 'aha' effect of ethnography as moments when new understandings are gleaned from the discourse and the shape of social order is reworked: P. Willis and M. Trondman, "Manifesto for Ethnography" (2000) 1 *Ethnography* 5 at 11–12. I experienced this moment after the conclusion of the fieldwork and as I was going through a review of my notes. It was not unlike the process described by Geertz where the ethnographer realizes the implication of what she has observed and experienced when faced with the data once outside of the field: Geertz, see note 64 at v–vi.
119 See discussion above at notes 107 and 108 regarding the place of general theory in the ethnographic enterprise. See also J. Katz, "From How to Why: On Luminous Description and Causal Inference in Ethnography (Part 2)" (2002) 3 *Ethnography* 63 at 66, where Katz sees a benefit of ethnography residing in its revelations that bring forth hiding practices as well as hidden practices.

ethnography for its purpose in exposition rather than for the creation of new methodological approaches for the field. There exists sufficient criticism about the method and use of the method in the literature and it is not my intention here to give voice to it.[120] My approach is simply this: ethnographic data offers the opportunity to stimulate theoretical creativity – to generate new theories, to move them in alternative directions, or at minimum to cause us to question our assumptions that theories as currently articulated are the only valid ones available to us. It is to that end that I am using ethnography – to show what rarely is seen in public and to invite a new approach to the characterization of mediation.

In carrying out this research method, however, one must be cognizant of the weaknesses of the methodology and be vigilant to lessen or remove their impact. One obvious criticism of the method is, as Roberts noted above,[121] the fact that the observer writes from her own perspective and therefore must strive to set aside her preconceived ideas. Roberts is referring to the personal lens of the researcher. At the very least, the ethnographer should be aware that values may inform description, and as a result they need to be uncovered. Evans-Pritchard provides an example of this where he cannot see the possible reasons why the Nuer were reticent to speak to him: he suggested that it was due to their nature; yet it may have been due to his identification with the colonial government.[122] Clammer and Mansell speak of the effect of the observer's culture as impeding the seeing. Mansell speaks of it in the sense that ethnography involves the translation of culture through the eyes of one who is most familiar with western traditions and therefore has been trained to see only particular things.[123] Clammer is concerned with the ethnographer

---

120 Some voice, however, is necessary for illustrative purposes: as mentioned earlier, Wacquant (see note 84) critiques three ethnographic studies, citing problems of lack of theoretical framework, insufficient data to support analytical conclusions, bias, restricted analytical constructs, and general disagreement over the theories proposed by the ethnographers of their data. The ethnographers each respond to these critiques in their own articles: E. Anderson, "The Ideologically Driven Critique" (2002) 107 *Am. J. of Sociology* 1533; M. Duneier, "What Kind of Combat Sport is Sociology?" (2002) 107 *Am. J. of Sociology* 1551; K. Newman, "No Shame: The View from the Left Bank" (2002) 107 *Am. J. of Sociology* 1577. In addition, there is further review of the Wacquant article and the responses to it in Wilson and Chaddha, see note 84. This series of articles is offered as an example of the extent to which controversy is generated by the ethnographic method. This appears to be a typical scenario where disagreements over methodology or analytical conclusions abound. One could say that these articles represent a fine tradition in the field. For another example, see also Comaroff and Comaroff, see note 60; S. Falk Moore, "Debate: Reflections on the Comaroff Lecture" (1999) 26 *Am. Ethnologist* 304; Comaroff and Comaroff, see note 108.
121 Roberts, see note 23 at 17.
122 Evans-Pritchard, see note 26 at 12–13; Rosaldo, see note 114 at 91.
123 Mansell, Meteyard and Thomson, see note 20 at 15, 29.

who observes his own culture and may not see that which is significant.[124] Hammersley speaks of this in a slightly different manner: he sees ethnographic descriptions as being determined by the purpose, values and assumptions of the observer, and therefore they are not realistic portrayals.[125]

These criticisms are significant for this particular research project, especially in light of my training both in the law and in the practice of mediation. In Bohannan's opinion, lawyers "proceed within the view permitted by the blinkers of their own society".[126] There is a need, according to Bohannan, to systematically define "the cultural blinkers of one's own society, upbringing and prejudices so that one can see the ideas and prejudices of other people when one looks for them".[127] In response, I say that the ethnographic approach and analytical framework of this study assisted me to work without blinkers. To the extent that prejudices remain, they will be recognized and acknowledged. More beneficially, however, my training in the law and in mediation practice informed the collection of my 'thick description'. I knew what I was looking at, and this, says Malinowski, is crucial to the fieldworker who may miss the significance of an observation otherwise: knowledge of the ceremony permits acute observation.[128]

As a lawyer and as a mediator, I have familiarity with the structures, I understand the language, and I know the rules of the game. As such, I was better able to 'see' the interactions of the actors. Twining describes the benefit of such knowledge:

> At one level, there should not be a sharp divide between insider and outsider perspectives. Interpretive sociology teaches that in order to understand a social practice one has to grasp the perspective of the actors. In order to describe chess one must understand the rules, moves, strategy and tactics as the players see them. In order to understand Tiv or Barotse legal processes one must grasp the concepts of the actors (the emics) as well as the language of the external observer (the etics). Conversely, it often helps participants to have some understanding of the context in which they are operating, the role expectations, the factors that constrain and allow leeways of discretion, the economic realities of their situation, the likely consequences of their actions, among other things. Such awareness may not always be a necessary condition for effective action, but it is often a useful part of the equipment of the reflective practitioner. A degree of empathy with actors is a necessary part of interpretive sociology but the

---

124 J. Clammer, "Approaches to Ethnographic Research" in R.F. Ellen, ed., *Ethnographic Research: A Guide to General Conduct* (London: Academic, 1984) 63 at 82.
125 Hammersley, see note 64 at 24–5, 28.
126 P. Bohannan, *Justice and Judgment Among the Tiv* (London: Oxford University Press, 1957) at v.
127 Ibid.
128 Malinowski, see note 56 at 386–7.

standpoint and role of the sociologist are different from those of the participant. The sociologist of food does not become a skilled cook or vice versa.[129]

Another obvious criticism is the effect of the observer on the observed. The ethnographer is not invisible: he takes a seat at the table of discourse.[130] The concern is that the mere presence of the ethnographer alters the behaviour of the observed.[131] This is less likely to occur in mediation because the participants are present to promote their self-interest. They have nothing to gain by altering their behaviour for the researcher. They are interested in dealing with the conflict, not whether a researcher is in the room. The concern, however, may arise during the questioning of the actors: there, they may respond in ways intended to self-aggrandize, self-promote or to cast themselves in a favourable light. This can be minimized by specific questioning, but most relevantly by the direct observation of their actions in the process. The observation serves as a 'check and balance'.

Other criticisms of the methodology include bias on the part of the ethnographer towards her subjects,[132] lack of systematic selection of locale for the fieldwork,[133] and inability to observe the phenomenon since some aspects may remain hidden from the ethnographer.[134] The ethnographer needs to be aware of such concerns in order to recognize their impact on the study and be in a position to take steps to allay any such impact.

Despite such criticisms, the ethnographic method enriches our understandings of observed phenomena.

Summary

This is a study of negotiated order: its focus is on the social interactions and changes that occur during a dispute resolution process that is at once both law-centred and processually defined. The intent is to illuminate, through the moves of the actors, the nature of a process that creates negotiated order.

---

129 W. Twining, "The Idea of Juristic Method: A Tribute to Karl Llewellyn" (1992–94) 48 *U. Miami L. Rev.* 119 at 154.
130 Crapanzano, see note 77 at 53.
131 See for example, Mansell, Meteyard and Thomson, see note 123 at 30; Bowling and Hoffman speak of the impact of the observer on the observed as the Hawthorne Effect from the perspective of mediator presence impacting the parties' conduct. See D. Bowling and D. Hoffman, "Bringing Peace into the Room: The Personal Qualities of the Mediator and Their Impact on the Mediation" (2000) *Negotiation J.* 5 at 10.
132 D.R. Papke, "How the Cheyenne Indians Wrote Article 2 of the Uniform Commercial Code" (1999) 47 *Buffalo L. Rev.* 1457 at 1464.
133 Clammer, see note 124 at 67.
134 Ibid. at 68.

An ethnographic approach to this study of mediation provides a theoretical and practical convergence through 'thick description' and its translation into meaning. More importantly, it provides the opportunity to unmask a process through which negotiated order is achieved. This ability through ethnographic methods to see beyond one's own reality and thereby aim for clarity of understanding of what is being observed is one reason why ethnography is well suited to the study of law in society and, more particularly, to the study of conflict and its resolution. Arguably, Malinowski generated the interest in examining the law in society with *Crime and Custom in Savage Society*. Llewellyn was intrigued by Malinowski's work, which stimulated his interest for the search for 'laws' among the Cheyenne.[135] The method is not only suitable for the broader context of the law, its nature and role in the order of society, but also for the study of disputing processes. Llewellyn and Hoebel, Gulliver, and Comaroff and Roberts all uncovered a form of third-party intervention that was present in the dispute resolution processes of the societies they examined.[136]

As stated earlier, Marcus sees anthropology as providing a "distinctive mode of understanding reality".[137] Malinowski says that it penetrates life.[138] Riles talks about its role in adding a practical real-world dimension to lawyer theorizing.[139] For Conley and O'Barr, anthropology broadens the capacity for knowledge through an unencumbered world-view:

> Anthropology is especially helpful in discovering and describing the possibilities. It can show how things are done in a variety of specific instances. Legal anthropology can tell us, for example, that Hopewellians do not go to court and that the working-class Bostonians do, or that many small claims litigants are at least as concerned with how they are treated in court as whether they win or lose. In short, anthropology can tell us what to consider.
>
> The difficulty of this task should not be underestimated, particularly when novel issues are involved. We have often observed lawyers listening to anthropologists then commenting "of course ... that's obvious!" Our response, usually given *sotto voce*, is always the same: "Then why didn't *you* think of it?"[140]

---

135 Mehotra, see note 93 at 752–3.
136 For example, Llewellyn and Hoebel, see note 18 at 192; Gulliver, see note 30 at 136; Comaroff and Roberts, see note 43 at 109.
137 Marcus, see note 112 at 168.
138 Malinowski, see note 56 at 517–18.
139 A. Riles, "Representing In-between: Law, Anthropology, and the Rhetoric of Interdisciplinarity" (1994) *U. Ill. L. Rev.* 597 at 634–5.
140 Conley and O'Barr, see note 59 at 63.

2 My village

> I've had an extraordinary day, Mr Byron. I went to a village fair. I had a pint of beer. Then the next thing I remember is waking alone, in this wood, on a bed of bracken. All around me were outstretched green hands, supporting me, surrounding me, swaying in time with the sunlight. A million tiny green fingers, the tips scorched by the sun. And amid the bracken, an army of spiders were building a webbed citadel, with many bridges and rooms and grand windows and staircases. All I could hear was birdsong.
>
> The Professor, *Jerusalem*[1]

As explored in Chapter 1, mediation is particularly suited to the anthropological approach of ethnography. It concerns conflict resolution theory, it is situated in a rule-centred paradigm and it is about social processes. The methodology provides an opportunity to examine negotiated order: to bare its elements, to identify its influences and to study the movement to the attainment of that order. Mediation, currently in England and Wales, as in many western societies, lives within a legal world. It has been invoked by the judicial system as another step in a judicial process. It is managed, used and abused by lawyers. It is converted for their own purposes. Mediation must be unlocked from this world if we are to seek clarity of its process. The hope of accomplishing this goal lies with the ethnographic method of research.

In this ethnographic study, mediation becomes my 'village'. During my period of fieldwork, I was a participant-observer at a British mediation agency through which mediations are conducted at the request of the parties in conflict.[2] During this time, I gathered data about the structures within which the interactions occur, such as the court system, the legal representation of the disputants, the legal formulations of their disputes, the mediation

---

1 J. Butterworth, *Jerusalem* (London: Nick Hern, 2009), a play about an England with a folkloric past and gritty present. The Professor recounts a dream in which the bucolic village of yesteryear faces the onslaught of modernity.
2 A description of the fieldwork experience follows later in the chapter.

agency, and the mediation session. Information about the rules and norms applicable to the dispute and the disputing parties was received. Data was also obtained from: (i) observations of the various interactions that occur during mediations; (ii) questioning 'informants' (for example the agency's personnel); (iii) questioning participants to a mediation to the extent possible both before and after each mediation session; and (iv) documentary data relevant to the 'village and its inhabitants'. My approach to fieldwork reflected Geertz's 'thick description'.[3] My data will be presented through the case study method created by Turner's 'social drama'.[4]

The collection of this data was informed by my 'theory of investigation'.[5] This theory has been articulated in Chapter 1. To summarize, within the convergences of structures, rules and norms, and social processes that make up mediation today, I seek to discover the interactions that take place among its actors, changes that occur from such interactions, and their influences on the process.[6] In so doing, I hope to uncover the reality of mediation – what mediation is for the parties, for the mediators, for the lawyers – in other words, how it is actually experienced.

The fieldwork site

My fieldwork site was at a pre-eminent British organization which specialized in the delivery of conflict resolution and conflict management services (hereinafter referred to as the 'Organization').[7] The Organization was founded by a group of commercial professionals who became familiar with mediation and who believed that mediation could offer great benefit in the resolution of business disputes. The Organization was created before judicial support was institutionalized by the civil justice system of England and Wales through the Civil Procedure Rules. It actively promoted mediation as an alternative means by which commercial disputes could be resolved. It encouraged the judiciary, legislators, commercial organizations and law firms to consider

---

3 C. Geertz, *The Interpretation of Culture* (New York: Basic Books, 1973) and discussion in Chapter 1 on method.
4 V.W. Turner, *Schism and Continuity in an African Society: A Study of Ndembu Village Life* (Oxford: Berg, 1996 edition) at 91–4. The case study method will be more fully explored in Chapter 5.
5 In K.N. Llewellyn and E.A. Hoebel, *The Cheyenne Way: Conflict and Case Law in Primitive Jurisprudence* (Norman: University of Oklahoma Press, 1941), 'theory of investigation' is the title to their second chapter in which they describe their analytical framework to their ethnographic study of the Cheyenne.
6 For a more detailed discussion of the aim of this study, its analytical framework and context within which it explores the mediated negotiation, please see Chapter 1.
7 To preserve anonymity for the members of my village, the organization will not be named and will hereinafter be referred to as the Organization.

the impact of mediation on the resolution of disputes and promoted its role in the litigation process.

The Organization focuses on commercial mediations.[8] Among other things, it is a mediation service provider which advises, guides and administers the mediation process, providing access to its panel of accredited mediators for the mediations it organizes; it is a trainer and educator of dispute resolution services; it is a thought-leader in the field, researching issues impacting conflict and the management of that conflict. It is domestic and international in scope.

The physical locale for my ethnographic study was in London. I attended mediations held at the Organization's premises, and I also travelled to mediations held in various other locations in London and in other cities in England and Wales.

During my year of fieldwork, I lived at the Organization during its business life.[9] I attended its offices during regular business hours – waiting for a bus to take me to the tube station, reviewing the services board to see if I would be late due to tube delays, standing at the spot where I knew the carriage doors would open and I would be able to squeeze into any available space, pushing my way into the tube carriage when the train finally arrived and standing in a crowded, hot and stuffy car hoping that there would be no delays before my exit. Once at my destination, I picked up my builder's tea at the local deli and made my way to the office. Once there, the receptionist would let me into the building and I would make my way up to the offices, wishing staff members good morning as I made my way to my desk. Staff tended to arrive between 9:00 and 9:30 a.m. The workday concluded for most between 5:00 and 5:30 p.m. Once at my desk, I would switch on my computer, check my voicemail message status, and read my emails. This began my workday.

The office was set up in an open configuration. 'Pods' of desks were clustered together in diamond configurations denoting the various departments of the Organization. Staff sat either beside or facing their colleagues within their unit, suggesting a camaraderie of spirit. It was surprising to find that staff worked as though there were invisible walls between them, communicating only when necessary and ignoring the din of their colleagues' work efforts around them. The floor was in an L-shape. The business of the day was exposed for anyone to observe and yet everyone acted as though no one could see them. For me, used to the privacy of lawyers' offices, the openness of my

---

8 Within this general category, subcategories of disputes included employment, property, intellectual property, personal injury, construction, engineering, finance, insurance, IT, medical negligence, partnership, professional negligence and shipping disputes.
9 This includes attendance at mediations, and at interviews with mediators. I took annual leave as did staff during the year (during which I would indicate on my email and voicemail greetings that I was away from the office and indicating the date of my return).

surroundings was uncomfortable and seemingly unnatural. I was envious of the others who conducted their work as though no one could see them. I felt as though I was in a fishbowl with no coral reef to hide within. As the days passed, this dissipated and I acclimatized to my surroundings.

While at the Organization, I was part of its mediation team.[10] For me, the team was the hub of the Organization. It was through this team that mediations were organized. Inquiries about mediation services were handled through the team. Members of the team had law degrees or other postgraduate degrees, as did most other members of the Organization. The team members believed in the need for alternative processes with which to deal with conflict. They had a certain zeal in promoting mediation to the world. They believed in the good of their work.

Team members would answer inquiries received about the process. The inquiries came from lawyers, individuals and corporations or other organizations. If a mediator was requested, information about the dispute would be obtained, such as the nature of the dispute, the quantum involved, the identities of the parties and legal representatives, the nature of the relationship between the parties, the status of the proceedings, the timeframe for the mediation, and any particular qualities required of the mediator. Once this information was received, the team would consider suitable mediators during meetings at which all team members, including managers, attended for the purpose of creating a list of recommended mediators for consideration by the inquiring party. The proposed mediators were members of the Organization's panel of mediators. The inquiring party would advise the team members of the selection and a mediation would then be organized. Once a mediation was confirmed as scheduled, the day-to-day administration of the file would be conducted by another member of the team allocated for that purpose.

My role at the Organization during the year was multi-fold. For the first two months, I learned about it and its processes. For example, I reviewed its documents system, I interviewed team members to learn about their responsibilities, I attended team meetings, and I participated in information exchange. For approximately three months, I acted as a member of the mediation team, handling case inquiries and case files. Some of these responsibilities carried on after this time, despite formally leaving the position. I attended the Organization's seminal mediation accreditation course and faculty training course. I prepared reports on my observations of these training courses. I worked on a research project and completed a report outlining my recommendations with respect to that research project. I continued to

---

10 I should indicate at this time that I was not paid for any services provided by me to the Organization nor did the Organization provide any funds in support of my research activities. It provided me with full access to its facilities, documents, staff and mediations. I am grateful for the opportunity to conduct my fieldwork there. It was a privilege.

participate in team meetings and general staff meetings. I gave advice to team members about various inquiries they received.

Most importantly, I attended 38 mediations within a ten-month period. To the extent I was provided with them, I reviewed party documents in preparation for each mediation. I reviewed case and file histories. I spoke with the mediators prior to the mediation and I formally interviewed them after the session was concluded.[11] I contacted the legal representatives and individuals who attended on those mediations to seek participant feedback about the process. The latter inquiries were also part of the Organization's procedure in which it seeks feedback on the process once a mediation is concluded.[12]

I lived and breathed this world for one year. As the Trobriand Islands were Malinowski's village, this Organization and its mediations were mine. I engaged in its rituals: bringing sweets back from travels and placing them on the 'bird' table for the office to share; speaking about the weekend on a

---

11 Regarding discussions with mediators, when speaking with them before a mediation occurred, there was no set routine: it depended on the time of the call from the mediator and the willingness of the mediator to discuss the case at that time. When the opportunity arose, I would ask questions: for example, 'how do you intend to deal with the mediation', 'have you thought whether it can settle'. I did not ask the mediator for his background, although I would give the mediator my background and role at the mediation – as assistant mediator and as researcher. I would give my professional experience as well. For my assistant role, I would ask the mediator what he would like me to do, offering examples, taking notes, keeping track of time – whatever was needed. As for the post-mediation interview, I interviewed each mediator. These interviews were conducted in person, if at all possible. If the mediator lived outside of London, they were conducted by telephone with the mediator on a speaker-phone so that I was free to take notes. The interviews were not taped, but detailed notes were taken. The mediators were not advised prior to the meeting what I would ask. All I said to them was that I would like to ask a few questions about the mediation or that I would like to talk about the mediation. Only a few (two or three) insisted on knowing what I was going to ask, but I did not provide all the specific questions on those occasions: I provided some examples. The interviews lasted typically one hour to an hour and a half, and they were almost always followed by a debrief by me of their performance at the mediation. Only one mediator did not ask for such a debrief. The mediators were asked set questions: I developed an interview protocol (see K. Kressel, "The Strategic Style in Mediation" (2007) 24 *Conflict Resol. Q.* 251 at 254), which was amended slightly after the sixth mediation at which time additional questions were added. The interview protocol was used rather than informal, open-ended questions so that mediators' perspectives about similar issues could be canvassed. A list of the interview questions can be found at Appendix A.
12 The discussions with the legal representatives occurred well after the mediation and also formed part of the Organization's procedure for follow-up. All were conducted by telephone and were unscheduled. Not all lawyers were willing to speak to me. Some did not return my telephone calls; others placed time limits on the calls. An interview guideline was established, but depending on the affability and willingness of the lawyers to speak to me, reliance on the guideline varied. Appendix B contains a copy of the interview guideline.

Monday morning while making a cup of tea at the Tea Point; scrounging for a private room to conduct private conversations; sneaking into the Organization's reception area for chocolate biscuits for afternoon tea; bringing in the odd treat to place on the mediation team's meeting table to enjoy while considering recommendations; changing the number of confirmed mediations on the team's white board when mediations were scheduled; taking part in the Secret Santa for the Christmas party; and when my fieldwork came to an end, receiving the ritual send-off as given to other staff members who left during the year, with speeches, gift, snacks, drinks and general chatter. A memorable year.

I recorded my observations. My notebooks and I became infamous in the office – what was I writing about all the time, I would be asked. The fact of the matter is that I did not know what would become relevant, what would be needed, what related to what. I was at times merely building puzzle pieces, not putting together the puzzle – that came later. I was intrigued about the Organization and its role in disputing processes. I was interested to learn how parties approached mediation. I wanted to explore all aspects of the process as I immersed myself in the life of the Organization. At moments, I thought the ethnography would become one of the Organization, not of a process it was advocating. Ultimately, it begat my mediation villages: it provided me with the citizens and their conflicts. It spawned an urban ethnography of different locales: the mediation village and the institution through which the data was collected.

As for the 38 mediations I attended, the first three I treated as test cases and hence are not included in the reporting results, unless otherwise noted. The remaining 35 mediations were attended within the period from December 2006 to September 2007. They were randomly selected. As mediations were confirmed as scheduled, a member of the team would let me know that a mediation had been scheduled.[13] As long as the date was available to me, it was a commercial mediation, and it was within a two-hour train ride radius from London, I accepted. Each mediation led to an increased desire to observe more. It was with great fortune that I was able to attend so many mediations. When first embarking on the fieldwork, my hope had been to access five to ten mediations, given the difficulty of obtaining access to such a private process. Indeed, the Organization was not encouraging at first about the ability to access such a number of mediations.

---

13 For those mediations I administered as initial team contact, a similar process occurred. I would indicate to the team member responsible for administration of the file once the mediator was selected that the mediation fitted within the parameters of my research selection criteria and that I was available to attend on the mediation. I was generally appointed to the case in that situation.

I attended these mediations as an assistant mediator.[14] All parties were aware that I was attending also in my capacity as an external researcher. They were aware that I was examining the mediation process and they all consented to my presence.[15] All the mediators were supportive of my attendance, speaking openly with me about the process, their views and their experience throughout the session. The parties also generally commented on my study – for example, making reference to my note-taking ability ("you must have enough for a dissertation just from what you have written today") and wishing me good luck with my studies. At no time during any of the mediations was I asked to leave the room because a party did not wish to speak in my presence. I had the same access to the parties as did the mediator: I was generally in attendance with the parties whenever the mediator was present with them. I took copious notes during each mediation session. I typically filled a 7½ by 9½ inch notebook for each mediation session. I wrote, as best I could, verbatim comments of the dialogue, and noted observations regarding conduct and interactions as they occurred. I was present when the mediation began with the mediator's introduction. I was present when the mediation concluded and parties wished each other goodbye, or left without acknowledgment to the other.

The mediators

The mediators of my village were trained and accredited through the Organization's training programme. At the time of the research, the training programme consisted of 40 hours of lecture and role-play exercises, including an assessment for accreditation purposes. The mediators were trained according to the Organization's mediation model.[16] At some point after accreditation, these

---

14 The Organization had a policy of assigning newly trained mediators to mediations. The assistant mediators attend the mediation with the appointed lead mediator, who has full control and responsibility for the mediation. The assistant mediator's primary goal is to observe the 'live' mediation, to learn about the process, and to help the lead mediator in any way that the lead mediator requires. Usually, in my experience, this involved minor administrative tasks, taking notes and acting as a sounding board to the mediator during private times. An assistant does not have conduct of the process, and the assistant's only substantive participation that may arise during a mediation could involve some questioning of the parties or chairing a meeting between parties during a multi-party dispute.
15 Parties were advised before the mediation that I would be attending as assistant mediator and external researcher. In addition, the mediation agreement signed by the parties prior to the commencement of the mediation contained a paragraph regarding consent to my attendance and use of data. Copies of the mediation agreements are on file with the author.
16 The model has been modified over time, but the basic foundation has not changed. See discussion of the model in Chapter 3.

mediators had been invited to join the Organization's panel of mediators.[17] Not all the mediators were exclusive to the Organization. The majority had their own private practices or were members of other mediation service providers or firms. Those exclusive to the Organization were employees of the Organization and were few in number, comparatively speaking.

Their selection to mediate a dispute would generally occur in one of two ways: either they would be specifically requested by the parties or their names would be provided to the parties along with the names of two other potential mediators. The parties would be given the mediator's curriculum vitae with a brief description of the mediator's expertise and experience. Generally, the parties, through direct negotiation, would make a choice and advise of their choice. The Organization then administered the process. This included scheduling the mediation, providing a form of mediation agreement for all to review and sign, making arrangements for the delivery of the relevant documents to the mediator and booking the rooms for the day.

The mediator, once selected, would be advised of the selection. At this point, the mediator took control of the substance of the mediation that was about to take place. The mediator usually, but not always, contacted the legal representatives of the parties to introduce herself, to talk about the process, to find out about the dispute and possibly to learn about settlement attempts that had been made by the parties.

My mediators were of varied backgrounds. Many were practising lawyers. Of these, some were solicitors at law firms or corporations while others were barristers. Some were non-practising lawyers, having retired from such practice, or having qualified but not engaging in active practice (or having done so early in their careers, but since ceasing), or having left the practice of law to mediate full time. One was a retired judge and two others acted as part-time judge while practising law. Others were not lawyers; instead, they had special expertise in business, banking, property, or employment issues, for example. All had several years of experience since receiving their mediation accreditation. They were senior players in the field. Most were men. Three were women. All were white, middle-aged British professionals. For the purposes of my study, all were selected randomly and hence without regard for their gender, professional qualifications or mediator experience.[18]

Admirably, they were all willing to be subjected to intense scrutiny through my participation in their mediations. They did not limit the scope

---

17 This was true for all but one who, although not a panel mediator, was accredited through the Organization.
18 Of particular note regarding the mediators who are the subject of analysis in this book (in The Mediator's Story of Chapter 1, and in the three case studies of Chapters 5 and 6), one was a solicitor who had retired from active practice, one was a non-lawyer, and two were in active legal practice, one of whom was also a part-time judge.

of the remit despite the fact that they were not informed of the possible outcome of the project. They were not informed of what I was looking for, what I was hoping to find or what I might find – I did not know myself. They were confident in their skills and they were generous with their comments, views and willingness to be observed, analysed and critiqued. For them, it is a solitary pursuit and they were keen to share their experiences and to learn from them.

The parties

These mediations were attended by a team of players. It was not uncommon for a room to house two or three representatives of a company or organization in dispute, a senior solicitor, a junior solicitor or a barrister and a solicitor, or just a solicitor or just a barrister. The permutations and combinations seemed endless. The battle lines were indelibly drawn when entourages filled a boardroom with supporting members of their party. Partisans supporting and encouraging the dispute faced off against one another, similar to Gulliver's Arusha who relied on networks of partisan support to promote claims, protect defences, and sometimes to push for settlement.[19]

The place of law in the discussion was prominent given the presence of the legal representatives.[20] Their presence ensured that their clients would not be able to forget the existence of the normative order of rules or of the structure of the legal system within which their dispute lay. Their voice was strong. Party voice, however, was heard through the involvement of the mediator. The mediators exerted effort to hear the voice of the party in dispute above the legal machinations of the solicitors and barristers who attended with them.

Generally, the parties were sophisticated business persons who needed little or no hand-holding. They were often senior executives, shareholders, managers, senior employees or entrepreneurs. On occasion, family members were at odds over property issues or business shareholdings. Sometimes, one party was an individual, but almost always with a sophisticated knowledge of the dispute, and almost always protected by legal representation.[21]

---

19 See discussion in Chapter 1 about the Arusha by Gulliver: P.H. Gulliver, *Social Control in An African Society: A Study of the Arusha: Agricultural Masai of Northern Tanganyika* (London: Routledge, 2000 edition).
20 For an examination of the place of law in mediation, see D. De Girolamo, "Seeking Negotiated Order Through Mediation: A Manifestation of Legal Culture?" (2012) 5 *J. of Comp. Law* 118, and in D. Nelken, ed., *Using Legal Culture* (London: Wildy, Simmonds & Hill, 2012) 153.
21 Only one of the 38 mediations was attended by parties without legal counsel.

The mediations

Many of the mediations of this study were held at the Organization's offices. On occasion, the parties were willing to attend mediation at the premises of one of the parties in order to save venue costs. Wherever the mediation occurs, each party is given a private room and there is, for almost all mediations, a large boardroom available for meetings between parties. The mediator spends time alone in the large boardroom or other private room when not meeting with either party.[22]

Prior to a mediation, the mediator receives documents from the parties. Generally, the parties forward what they believe are relevant documents in support of their positions. These tended to be court documents if the parties were in litigation. Almost always, they also provide a mediation position statement setting out their positions. Generally, the documents are delivered at the 'eleventh hour' and often constitute the parties' entire document file about the dispute. Many mediators read the documents in preparation for the mediation. Some do not. Most contact the parties' legal representatives prior to the mediation day to discuss the process and the dispute, and generally to obtain information about the party. A minority speaks to the parties for the first time on the mediation day.

On arrival at the mediation venue on the day of the mediation, the mediator, in most cases, meets privately with each party to introduce himself, to describe the process, and to perhaps talk about the case and the parties' desires for the day. As to which party the mediator meets first is generally a function of which party has arrived at the mediation premises and is ready to speak to the mediator. A joint meeting follows these private meetings, at which all parties, together with their business and legal representatives, attend for a joint session chaired by the mediator. The mediator invites the parties to the joint session, often telling them where to sit (having carefully considered the seating plan before the start of the joint session). Introductions are often made around the table. The mediator informs the parties of his role and describes the process. He then invites one party to begin, usually the claimant. The parties, usually through their legal representatives, make a statement about their case and their position. An exchange among all participants may ensue. At the conclusion of the joint session, as determined by the mediator, the parties retreat to their individual private meeting rooms. The mediator announces, prior to the retreat, which party he will first visit, and advises the other that he may be some time before attending to them.

---

22 'Alone' needs to be qualified here. The researcher in her role as both researcher and assistant mediator was present with the mediator. Out of 38 mediations observed, this process was followed for 37 of them. In one instance, the mediator retreated to his office when parties were conferring, leaving the researcher alone.

The mediator then begins a series of private meetings with each of the parties, moving between party meeting rooms. This is when the mediator 'shuttle' begins between parties. The mediator works with the parties individually and privately throughout the day; it is rare that all parties meet again for a joint meeting after the first joint session is concluded. Occasional joint meetings between legal representatives or party representatives may occur at the behest of the mediator. For the most part, however, the work of the mediator is conducted in private with each party, away from the eyes and ears of the other party.[23]

This process is carried out until either the parties reach an agreement in principle or the mediator terminates the mediation, if he believes that agreement cannot be achieved. If an agreement in principle is achieved, it is reduced to writing and it is at this point that the structure becomes less defined. In drafting the settlement agreement, parties may work separately, revising and reviewing drafts in private; the legal representatives may work together; one party's legal representative may work with the other party's team; the mediator may or may not actively assist with the drafting; or it may be a combination of all scenarios. Once a written agreement is completed, it is signed by all parties and the mediation concludes. The execution of the agreement may take place in private or in a final joint meeting where all parties witness its signing.

Coffee, tea and biscuits are the order of the day. Lunch is served to each party in their private rooms. Mediations do not stop for lunch. Supper, if the gods are smiling, is provided for the late-night forays – however, often a biscuit or a stolen apple constitutes dinner. As stated above, the day does not end until a written settlement agreement is signed or it becomes clear to the mediator that settlement cannot be reached between the parties, at which time the mediation is terminated. Personal goodbyes between the parties at the end of a mediation, whether settled or not, are not natural occurrences and cannot be anticipated. The mediator, however, is always accorded this civility.

Although said to be an informal process, the parties attend mediation with legal representatives who are formally attired, as are the parties themselves. Briefcases, computers, mobile telephones, and document briefs fill the rooms. Parties often come with their solicitors and barristers, and sometimes with senior and junior lawyers in tow.[24] The day begins inevitably with the

---

23 See Chapter 3 for a discussion of the relevant mediation framework and the recognition that the private meeting is not atypical of mediation frameworks. Private meetings are prevalent in many models of mediation; in particular, see discussion at note 113 in Chapter 3.

24 For purposes of this study, the term 'solicitor' is used to refer to a party's legal representative, regardless of whether the representative is a solicitor or a barrister, and if a solicitor regardless whether it was the junior or senior solicitor on the case. No distinction is made in the references to the legal team.

signing of the mediation agreement, a condition precedent to the conduct of the mediation, and ends with the signing of the settlement agreement, if reached, a condition precedent to resolution. Although first names are used, jokes made, small talk occurs about football, rugby and cricket, and jackets come off, there hangs in the air the breaches, the damages, the injuries that are sought to be remedied through the formal figure of a mediator who takes the parties through the day.

Summary

My mediation village was welcoming and supportive. It was difficult to halt the observations and conclude the period of fieldwork, as the desire for continued access to this private world was strong. The more I observed, the more I wanted to observe. Ultimately, it was necessary to lay down the pen and begin the analytical journey. My 'aha' moment came in reviewing my notes after leaving the mediation village, when I reflected on what I had seen and heard and on what I had participated in.[25] It was then that I was able to see how the process unfolds as well as the nature of the interventions in this negotiatory process we call mediation.

---

25 Recall Geertz's reference to the backward order of things in Chapter 1: Geertz, see note 3 at v–vi.

3 Mediation
Exploring the prism

> Our characters are children, and their playground is time. One advantage of theatre, over say telecomms, is that one is not bound by reality.
>
> Phillippa, *England People Very Nice*[1]

Despite the many views of what mediation is and what it should be, there remains a need for empirical research that provides greater visibility into the interactions and changes that occur during the mediation process.[2] This will

---

1 R. Bean, *England People Very Nice* (London: Oberon Books, 2009) at 71. In this play within a play, the character of Phillippa is responding to a criticism of her play that is being rehearsed: it was pointed out to her that one of the characters is said to be 16 years of age during the Blitz, yet in 2001 is giving birth to twins at the age of 80.

2 Recent empirical research on mediation has considered mediator roles, disputant views, lawyer experiences and generally the outcomes of various mediation programmes. A call for further work continues to be heard particularly with respect to mediator interactions. K. Kressel, in "The Strategic Style in Mediation" (2007) *24 Conflict Resol. Q.* 251, speaks of the need for 'nuanced and detailed' research on mediator stylistic behaviour at 281. J.M. Conley and W.M. O'Barr, in *Just Words: Law, Language and Power* (Chicago: University of Chicago Press, 1998) at 57, point out the difficulty of attaining access to mediation and the labour-intensity of observations and data preparation. D.J. Della Noce, in "Communicating Quality Assurance: A Case Study of Mediator Profiles on a Court Roster" (2008) 84 *N. Dak. L. Rev.* 769 at 819, suggests that there is a need for empirical research regarding mediator claims that they blend various styles in their approach to mediation. In recent research undertaken of civil court mediations including observational research, J.A. Wall Jr and S. Chan-Serafin refer to the lack of information known about the process itself or interactions between mediator and disputants of 'real-world mediations'; see Wall and Chan-Serafin, "Processes in Civil Case Mediations" (2009) 26 *Conflict Resol. Q.* 261 at 263. The need for specific observational research of mediator interactions is raised by J.A. Wall and T.C. Dunne, "Mediation Research: A Current Review" (2012) *Negotiation J.* 217 at 239, D.J. Della Noce, "Evaluative Mediation: In Search of Practice Competencies" (2009) 27 *Conflict Resol. Q.* 193 at 211, and P. Field, "The Unreliable Narrator?" (Review Essay) (2011) *Negotiation J.* 387 at 391. This makes for further compelling reasons for the need that this research be undertaken. For examples of empirical work in mediation see generally,

assist in linking theory and practice, two elements that sometimes fail to meet. References can be found in the literature to a gap existing between theorists and practitioners in the mediation field.[3] For example, one succinct description of the state of relations between the groups is offered by Lawrence Susskind and Noah Susskind:

> Some academics look down their noses at what they regard as the limited and anecdotal knowledge of practitioners, while some practitioners think ivory-tower intellectuals quibble about abstractions or conduct toy experiments instead of grappling with the complex challenges of the real world.[4]

They call on the need for continued dialogue between the two groups because good theory comes from good practice and good practice from good theory.[5] Another relevant issue is the extent to which mediators do not know the theory behind their practice; that they act without a theoretical framework, and thus work within one that is personal to them.[6]

The need to reduce the chasm between theory and practice is also explored on a meta-level in a series remarking on Nader and Grande's views against importing alternative dispute resolution (ADR) processes into African countries. Commentators speak specifically about this need to bridge the gap between practitioner and scholarly knowledge – between practice and theory.[7] Milner speaks of the necessity for practitioners to gain a better understanding of the process they promote because they tend to idealize the process.[8] Merry, too, raises the cry for a better understanding of ADR processes: "it is essential to distinguish between [ADR's] ideology and its practice: between its promises and what takes place on the ground".[9] Milner and Merry are critical of the contradiction between the theory of what ADR

D.W. Golann, "Is Legal Mediation a Process of Repair or Separation? An Empirical Study and Its Implications" (2002) 7 *Harv. Negot. L. Rev.* 301; J Macfarlane, "Why Do People Settle" (2001) 46 *McGill L. J.* 663; J. Macfarlane, "Cultural Change? A Tale of Two Cities and Mandatory Court Connected Mediation" (2002) *J. Disp. Resol.* 241; H. Genn *et al.*, *Twisting Arms: Court Referred and Court Linked Mediation Under Judicial Pressure* (May 2007) Ministry of Justice Res Ser 1/07, Ministry of Justice, London.

3 N. Susskind and L. Susskind, "Connecting Theory and Practice" (2008) *Negotiation J.* 201.
4 Ibid. at 201.
5 Ibid. at 208.
6 S. Oberman, "Style vs. Model: Why Quibble" (2008) 9 *Pepp. Disp. Resol. L. J.* at 53 illustrates the discourse.
7 The Series, "From the Trenches and Towers" is found in (2002) 27 *Law & Soc. Inquiry* 567.
8 N. Milner, "From the Trenches and Towers: Commentary: Illusions and Delusions about Conflict Management – In Africa and Elsewhere" (2002) 27 *Law & Soc. Inquiry* 621 at 627.
9 S.E. Merry, "From the Trenches and Towers: Commentary: Moving Beyond Ideology Critique to the Analysis of Practice" (2002) 27 *Law & Soc. Inquiry* 609.

offers and that which it delivers. These commentaries epitomize the need for clarity about dispute resolution processes including a convergence of theory and practice.

This study seeks to construct such a convergence. Mediation as a process of dispute resolution was very briefly introduced in Chapter 1. This chapter does not aspire to provide an exhaustive survey of ways the process and the interventions undertaken by mediators have been defined and characterized by scholars and practitioners. Such surveys are plentiful in the literature.[10] It does, however, attempt to illustrate the breadth of the disparate views about mediation and its interventions as developed over time, with particular emphasis on the views of the mediation agency which provided the forum for this research. The review aims to provide a springboard to the live experience of mediation's participants as illuminated by ethnography. We learn about the diverse approaches taken to the mediation process and mediator interactions in order to contextualize the data in the search for that which lives behind the mask of imposed labels. Following the overview discussed in this chapter, the remaining chapters will seek to expose the process and the actors within the process, integrating theory and practice. Theory precedes practice as disclosed by ethnographic data, which in turn precedes the convergence embodied in the ethnographer's analysis of the data.

Mediation defined

Before embarking on a review of some of these definitions to highlight the diversity of views regarding the nature and purpose of mediation, a brief word about prescriptive and descriptive approaches. Moffitt, in his consideration of the definition of mediation, queries whether the definition should be

---

10 See, for example, C. Menkel-Meadow, "Mothers and Fathers of Invention: The Intellectual Founders of ADR" (2000) 16 *Ohio St. J. Disp. Resol.* 1; J.R. Coben, "Gollum, Meet Smeagol: A Schizophrenic Rumination of Mediator Values Beyond Self-Determination and Neutrality" (2004) 5 *Cardozo J. Conflict Resol.* 65; D.T. Weckstein, "In Praise of Party Empowerment – and of Mediator Activism" (1997) 33 *Willamette L. Rev.* 501; J.H. Goldfien and J.K. Robbennholt, "What if the Lawyers Have Their Way? An Empirical Assessment of Conflict Strategies and Attitudes Toward Mediation Styles" (2006–07) 22 *Ohio St. J. Disp. Resol.* 277; J.A. Wall, J.B. Stark and R.L. Standifer, "Mediation: A Current Review and Theory Development" (2001) 45 *J. of Conflict Resol.* 370; R.A. Baruch Bush, "'What Do We Need a Mediator For?': Mediation's 'Value-Added' for Negotiators" (1996–97) 12 *Ohio St. J. Disp. Resol.* 1; S.N. Exon, "The Effects that Mediator Styles Impose on Neutrality and Impartiality Requirements of Mediation" (2007–08) 42 *U.S.F. L. Rev.* 577; D.E. Noll, "A Theory of Mediation" (2001) 56 *Disp. Resol. J.* 78; S. Oberman, "Mediation Theory vs. Practice: What Are We Really Doing? Re-Solving a Professional Conundrum" (2005) 20 *Ohio St. J. Disp. Resol.* 775; L.L. Riskin, "Mediation Quandaries" (1996–97) 24 *Fla. St. U. L. Rev.* 1007.

descriptive or prescriptive in nature.[11] He questions whether mediation should be defined as what it is or what it ought to be. He likens the debate to one between legal positivists and adherents of a 'natural law' view: the former describe the law as it is and the latter describe the law as it ought to be.[12] Moffitt recognizes the various practices that are labelled 'mediation'. He believes that definitional boundaries do not serve to illustrate the nature of mediation because mediation is a human activity that is complex and fluid. He goes further, to suggest that a prescriptive definition would hinder a true understanding of the process as it would hide its nature.[13]

Rather than fixating on either a descriptive or prescriptive definition of mediation *per se*, it is more important to understand the extent of the diversity that exists about the nature of mediation and to recognize that such diversity is based mainly on reflexive ruminations. As stated above, while there has been considerable research based on information received from mediators and participants in mediations, direct observations of private, commercial, non-court mandated mediations are limited, and ethnographic accounts rare.[14]

---

11 M.L. Moffitt, "Schemediation and the Dimensions of Definition" (2005) 10 *Harv. Negot. L. Rev.* 69.
12 Ibid. at 81.
13 Ibid. at 72.
14 As part of the fieldwork research for this study, I attended commercial mediations as a participant-observer, as described in Chapter 1. These occurred in England and Wales where there is no legislative provision directly mandating mediation as can be found in various jurisdictions in Canada and the United States. In referring to non-court mandated mediations, I am referring to mediations that have taken place without the requirement of legislation directly dictating that parties are to mediate their dispute (see Chapter 1 for a discussion of the legislative provisions relevant to mediation in England and Wales). For an example of the type of legislation I refer to, see rule 24.1 of the Rules of Civil Procedure, R.R.O. 1990 Reg. 194 (as am.). Observational studies include those conducted of: community and court programme mediations (see, for example, L. Charkoudian *et al.*, "Mediation by Any Other Name Would Smell as Sweet – or Would It? The Struggle to Define Mediation and Its Various Approaches" (2009) 26 *Conflict Resol. Q.* 293, and L. Mulcahy, "The Possibilities and Desirability of Mediator Neutrality – Towards an Ethic of Partiality?" (2001) 10 *Soc. & Leg. Stud.* 505); civil case mediations (for example, Wall Jr and Chan-Serafin, see note 2, J.A.Wall Jr and S. Chan-Serafin, "Do Mediators Walk Their Talk in Civil Cases?" (2010) 28 *Conflict Resol. Q.* 3, J.A. Wall, T.C. Dunne and S. Chan-Serafin, "The Effects of Neutral, Evaluative, and Pressing Mediator Strategies" (2011) 29 *Conflict Resol. Q.* 127, S. Roberts, "'Listing Concentrates the Mind': The English Civil Court as an Arena for Structured Negotiation" (2009) 29 *Oxford J. Legal Stud.* 457); labour mediation (see, for example, A. Douglas, "What Can Research Tell us About Mediation?" (1955) 6 *Labor Law J.* 545, D.M. Kolb, "Roles Mediators Play: State and Federal Practice" (1981) 20 *Industrial Relations* 1, D.M. Kolb, "Strategy and the Tactics of Mediation" (1983) 36 *Human Relations* 247, D.M. Kolb, *The Mediators* (Cambridge, MA: MIT Press, 1983), D.M. Kolb, "To Be a Mediator: Expressive Tactics in Mediation" (1985) 41 *J. of Social Issues* 11); divorce mediation (see, for example, D. Greatbatch and

It is difficult to obtain access to such mediations due to issues of confidentiality and litigation privilege. This has, in large part, restricted direct empirical research. This ethnography of the mediation experience has provided me with a direct view into actual mediations. The breadth of the ethnographic experience gives me a unique and privileged vantage point to describe, comment on, and analyse the unfolding drama of a conflict in the process of resolution. More particularly, it provides the opportunity to critically assess theories of mediated negotiation against real-life experience. Ultimately, a descriptive analysis will be the outcome, but the stimulus underpinning the analysis is the quest for freedom from the restrictiveness of imposed labels referenced above, labels imposed by those both extraneous to and within the process itself.[15] Mediation is what its actors create through their interactions within a socio-normative context.

R. Dingwall, "Selective Facilitation: Some Preliminary Observations on a Strategy Used by Divorce Mediators" (1989) 23 *Law & Society Rev.* 613); well-known mediators from diverse fields (see, for example, D.M. Kolb and Associates, eds, *When Talk Works: Profiles of Mediators* (San Francisco: Jossey-Bass, 1994)); and mediations conducted in Israel (see, for example, H.S. Desivilya and M.R. Elbaz, "Do Mediators Walk the Talk? A Study of Israeli Mediators" (2008) 63 *Disp. Resol. J.* 63). In addition, there is an ethnographic study by S.L. Burns, *Making Settlement Work: An Examination of the Work of Judicial Mediators* (Aldershot: Ashgate Dartmouth, 2000). In her study, Burns examines how judicial mediators conduct their mediations. She observed retired judges in private mediations, and compared their approaches to those of judges conducting settlement conferences within the judicial process. Burns' study, in terms of both purpose and outcome, is limited to the examination of how judicial mediators conduct their mediations. See also S.L. Burns, "'Think Your Blackest Thoughts and Darken Them': Judicial Mediation of Large Money Damage Disputes" (2001) 24 *Human Studies* 227, and "Pursuing 'Deep Pockets': Insurance-Related Issues in Judicial Settlement Work" (2004) 33 *J. of Contemporary Ethnography* 111. For an ethnographic study of decision-making among the Quakers, see A. Bradney and F. Cownie, *Living Without Law: An Ethnography of Quaker Decision-Making, Dispute Avoidance and Dispute Resolution* (Aldershot: Dartmouth, 2000).

15 Labels can mask the nature of actions. These labels support mediator mythology. For discussions about the mythology of mediation, see S.S. Silbey, "The Emperor's New Clothes: Mediation Mythology and Markets" (2002) *J. Disp. Resol.* 171, and D.J. Della Noce, R.A. Baruch Bush and J.P. Folger, "Clarifying the Theoretical Underpinnings of Mediation: Implications for Practice and Policy" (2002–03) 3 *Pepp. Disp. Resol. L. J.* 39, for example. The effect of labelling is also discussed in S. Oberman, see note 6. For a discussion about labels used by mediators to hide the nature of their actions as engaging in the practice of law, see J.M. Nolan-Haley, "Lawyers, Non-Lawyers and Mediation: Rethinking the Professional Monopoly from a Problem-Solving Perspective" (2002) 7 *Harv. Negot. L. Rev.* 235. C. Picard explores the use of language by mediators to describe their interactions and finds that although they may use the same words, these words often do not reflect similar meanings: "Common Language, Different Meaning: What Mediators Mean When They Talk About Their Work" (2002) *Negotiation J.* 251 at 261. Della Noce examines the use of labels in court roster mediator descriptions of mediator activity, concluding that labels

There are those in the field who see mediation primarily as a means of achieving the settlement of a dispute where a third party is brought in by parties to help resolve their dispute; that it is 'just about settlement', as Hazel Genn states.[16] This definition seems over-simplistic in the sense that it appears to reduce mediation to a settlement meeting chaired by a third party. Others, however, see mediation as more layered, more dynamic, and ultimately, more complex.

Merry and Silbey see mediation as a social process of decision-making leading to agreement without reference to the law.[17] Menkel-Meadow refers to agreement, communication and empowerment in which the mediator facilitates communication and problem-solving leading to Pareto-optimal solutions.[18] Like Merry and Silbey, Menkel-Meadow speaks of mediation as a facilitated process leading to a negotiated agreement between the parties, by the parties – not one imposed upon them. For Menkel-Meadow, the negotiated agreement occurs through improved communication and is an empowering process. Folberg and Taylor also refer to mediation as an empowering process. However, for them, it is a task-oriented process: its primary goal is to effect an agreement between the parties with a neutral person assisting them to reach resolution.[19] Self-empowerment for them is a collateral benefit to resolution.[20]

Boskey, Matz, Kolb and Kressel, and Bush and Folger all expand upon the concept of empowerment. Boskey and Matz consider voluntarism and autonomy to be the very essence of mediation. In particular, they identify the importance of respect for the sanctity of the human free will in voluntarily

---

of mediator actions such as evaluative, facilitative or transformative do not disclose what it is that mediators actually do: Della Noce, "Communicating Quality Assurance", see note 2 at 808, 819–22, for example. See also J. Kidner, "The Limits of Mediator 'Labels': False Debate between 'Facilitative' versus 'Evaluative' Mediator Styles" (2011) 30 *Windsor R. of Legal & Soc. Issues* 167 in which she focuses on the evaluative and facilitative dichotomy and the impact that labelling has on party choice and party participation in the process.

16 H. Genn, *Judging Civil Justice* (Cambridge: Cambridge University Press, 2010) at 117. See also R.P. Burns, "Some Ethical Issues Surrounding Mediation" (2001–02) 70 *Fordham L. Rev.* 691 at 701; D. Bowling and D. Hoffman, "Bringing Peace into the Room: The Personal Qualities of the Mediator and Their Impact on Mediation" (2000) *Negotiation J.* 5 at 9.
17 S.S. Silbey and S.E. Merry, "Mediator Settlement Strategies" (1986) 8 *Law & Policy* 7 at 8.
18 C. Menkel-Meadow, "Lawyer Negotiations: Theories and Realities – What We Learn from Mediation" (1993) 56 *Mod. L. Rev.* 361 at 372.
19 J. Folberg and A. Taylor, *Mediation: A Comprehensive Guide to Resolving Conflicts Without Litigation* (San Francisco: Jossey-Bass, 1984) at 9. The concept of the neutral third party is discussed later in the chapter.
20 Ibid. at 7–8.

coming to agreement with full autonomy throughout the process.[21] Kolb and Kressel note that some mediators see mediation as a way to empower members of a community, encourage citizen participation and establish standards for dealing with cultural disputes.[22] Bush and Folger believe that mediation is about empowerment and recognition. Empowerment gives parties a greater sense of self-worth, self-determination and control, and a better ability to deal with conflict in future. Recognition enables them to understand, consider and acknowledge the other party's view and positions.[23] These authors state that the promise of mediation lies in more than just agreement; it is the potential for human moral growth through strength of self and compassion towards others.[24]

Mediation is also seen more pragmatically as an informal, cooperative and accessible process that is faster and more efficient than the adjudicative process.[25] Still others see it as a quest for fairness and justice.[26]

Mediation has been described as a process suited to community, and in particular to relationships where rights are not the primary concern in the aim of or basis for settling disputes.[27] Mediation as reconciliation is echoed by Moore when he states, "Mediation is one of the processes of interaction that has been invented to allow people to live together."[28] He believes that

---

21 J.B. Boskey, "The Proper Role of the Mediator: Rational Assessment, Not Pressure" (1994) 10 *Negotiation J.* 367; see also D.E. Matz, "Mediator Pressure and Party Autonomy: Are they Consistent with Each Other?" (1994) 10 *Negotiation J.* 359 at 362.
22 D.M. Kolb and K. Kressel, "The Realities of Making Talk Work" in Kolb and Associates, eds, see note 14 at 466.
23 R.A. Baruch Bush and J.P. Folger, *The Promise of Mediation* (San Francisco: Jossey-Bass, 1994) at 87–8, 89–91.
24 Ibid. at 230–2, 242–3, 246.
25 This pragmatic view has been a primary motivator behind the proliferation of court-sponsored processes. See, for example, J. Macfarlane, *Court-Based Mediation of Civil Cases: An Evaluation of the Ontario Court (General Division) ADR Centre* (Toronto: Queen's Printer, 1995); R.G. Hann *et al.*, *Evaluation of the Mandatory Mediation Program, submitted to the Civil Rules Committee: Evaluation Committee for the Mandatory Mediation Pilot Project* (Queen's Printer, 2001); Lord Woolf, *Access to Justice Interim Report*, Department for Constitutional Affairs, June 1995.
26 See, for example, D.E. Peachy, "What People Want From Mediation" in K. Kressel, D.G. Pruitt and Associates, eds, *Mediation Research: The Process and Effectiveness of Third Party Intervention* (San Francisco: Jossey-Bass, 1989) 300; T. Tyler, "Procedure or Result: What do Disputants Want from Legal Authorities?" in K.J. Mackie, ed., *A Handbook of Dispute Resolution: ADR in Action* (London: Sweet & Maxwell, 1991) 19.
27 S.E. Merry, "Varieties of Mediation Performance: Replicating Differences in Access to Justice" in A.C. Hutchinson, ed., *Access to Civil Justice* (Toronto: Carswell, 1990) 257 at 273.
28 C.M. Moore, "Why Do We Mediate?" in J.P. Folger and T.S. Jones, eds, *New Directions in Mediation Communication Research and Perspectives* (Thousand Oaks: Sage, 1994) 195 at 202. This echoes Lon Fuller's well-known edict about the nature of mediation: "the central

mediation is community: it gives people "a sense of belonging, recognition, or acceptance as being part of the community".[29] This concept of community, the need to preserve relationships and the ability for reconciliation is reflective of traditions of dispute resolution found in various cultures. Many communities have a mediation-enriched tradition whereby a third party is asked to intervene in a dispute with a view to assisting parties to resolve their conflict. This tradition is found in Japanese culture, in the customs of many African and Pan-Asian groups and in various Christian religious groups such as the Amish, Mennonites and Quakers.[30]

We see that mediation can be narrowly construed solely as a means to effect settlement or broadly as a way to protect a community of members at odds with each other. Mediation appears to serve a multitude of masters; however, whether it seeks to implement its transformative properties, procedural fairness, substantive justice or administrative efficiency, or whether it seeks to enhance communication and self-awareness, at its core, mediation ultimately remains a process invoked to attain negotiated order.

Models of mediator intervention

Neutrality: a discussion

Evident in many definitions of the mediation process is the description of the third-party intervener as being neutral or impartial, having no interest in the dispute or its outcome.[31] It is said that he is there to assist the parties in their

---

quality of mediation [is], namely, its capacity to reorient the parties toward each other, not by imposing rules on them, but by helping them to achieve a new and shared perception of their relationship, a perception that will redirect their attitudes and dispositions toward one another". L. Fuller, "Mediation – Its Forms and Functions" (1970–71) *S. Cal. L. Rev.* 305 at 325.

29 Moore, ibid.
30 See discussion generally in Chapter 1 about ethnographic studies of disputing processes in Africa, for example; L. Nader, "When is Popular Justice Popular?" in S.E. Merry and N. Milner, eds, *The Possibility of Popular Justice: A Case Study of Community Mediation in the United States* (Ann Arbor: University of Michigan Press, 1993) 435 at 444–5; S.E. Merry, "Sorting out Popular Justice" in Merry and Milner, ibid. at 38–49; Bradney and Cownie, see note 14.
31 See, for example, C.W. Moore, *The Mediation Process: Practical Strategies for Resolving Conflict* (San Francisco: Jossey-Bass, 1996) at 51–3, 197–8; M.D. Lang and A. Taylor, *The Making of a Mediator: Developing Artistry in Practice* (San Francisco: Jossey-Bass, 2000) at 161–2, 179–81; K.K. Kovach, "Mediation" in M.L. Moffitt and R.C. Bordone, eds, *The Handbook of Dispute Resolution* (San Francisco: Jossey-Bass, 2005) 304; S. Roberts and M. Palmer, *Dispute Processes: ADR and the Primary Forms of Decision-Making* (Cambridge: Cambridge University Press, 2005) at 197; S. Blake, J. Browne and S. Sime, *A Practical Approach to Alternative Dispute Resolution* (Oxford: Oxford University Press, 2012)

negotiation in a neutral fashion. This is a standard view of mediation intervention within the western model of mediation. Definitions of this concept of neutrality vary widely. For example, it has been seen as encompassing notions of impartiality or as a concept differentiated from impartiality; it has been referred to as representing an equidistance between the parties or as an exercise of lack of bias; it has been related to consensuality of party decision-making or aspects of the process dealing with procedural or outcome neutrality.[32] While recognizing such distinctions, for purposes of analytical discussion the terms 'neutrality' and 'impartiality' herein refer to the non-aligned status of the third-party intervener, standing equidistant between parties and treating parties as such, whether that is because of lack of personal interest in the dispute and its outcome or lack of bias towards the participants or the subject matter of the dispute, for example.[33] Whether the term is neutrality, impartiality or non-alignment, it is expected that, at a minimum, a distance be maintained between the parties and the mediator.

It must also be noted that there is some debate as to whether neutrality or the like has any place in mediation; in particular, whether neutrality should be practised or whether it can be achieved.[34] Mulcahy sees neutrality as an

---

at 200; C. Izumi, "Implicit Bias and the Illusion of Mediator Neutrality" (2010) 34 *Wash. U. J. L. & Pol'y* 71 at 74–7, in which Izumi makes clear through a review of the literature that mediator neutrality is "universally understood to be a vital attribute of the mediation process" (at 74).

32 For examples of these approaches to the definition of neutrality, see S. Cobb and J. Rifkin, "Practice and Paradox: Deconstructing Neutrality in Mediation" (1991) 16 *Law & Soc. Inquiry* 35 (neutrality as impartiality and equidistance); C. Harper, "Comment – Mediator as Peacemaker: The Case for Activist Transformative-Narrative Mediation" (2006) *J. Disp. Resol.* 595 (neutrality as impartiality and lack of bias); P.M. Young, "Teaching the Ethical Values Governing Mediator Impartiality Using Short Lectures, Buzz Group Discussions, Video Clips, a Defining Features Matrix, Games, and an Exercise Based on Grievances Filed Against Florida Mediators" (2011) 11 *Pepp. Disp. Resol. L. J.* 309 (for a view that neutrality and impartiality are interchangeable terms); H. Astor, "Mediator Neutrality: Making Sense of Theory and Practice" (2007) 16 *Soc. & Legal Studies* 221 (neutrality as composed of four elements: treating parties equally; impartiality; consensuality of the process; and freedom from influence); Izumi, ibid. (four elements of neutrality include having no interest; procedural and outcome neutrality and avoidance of bias); J.A. Wall, T.C. Dunne and S. Chan-Serafin, "The Effects of Neutral, Evaluative, and Pressing Mediator Strategies" (2011) 29 *Conflict Resol. Q.* 127 (reflecting on a neutral strategy as being one where the mediator shows no bias, does not evaluate and does not influence parties' positions).

33 In this study, the terms are used interchangeably; Izumi, see note 31 at 78, points to the treatment of the words as synonymous; and Kovach, see note 31 at 311, uses the words interchangeably to denote a mediator who is free from bias. See also, generally, Roberts and Palmer, see note 31 at 153–72.

34 See, for example, L.E. Susskind, J.B. Stulberg, B.S. Mayer and J. Lande (Panel Discussion) "Core Values of Dispute Resolution: Is Neutrality Necessary?" (2012) 95 *Marquette L. R.* 805.

aspiration that is not realized; Garcia speaks of mediator interactions as impacting neutrality even with the most facilitative of moves; Harper and Astor say that mediators cannot be neutral; Mayer argues that neutrality is a concept difficult to describe and one that limits mediator actions; and Kydd and Honeyman suggest that the neutral mediator is weak while a biased mediator can be successful.[35] On the flip side of this debate, we have those who advocate the necessity for neutrality in the process for various reasons: for example, Goldberg and Shaw see failure to reach resolution where mediators are not neutral; Alfini and Stulberg see it as a core value of the process; Exon explores the extent to which the requirement finds a place in various codes of conduct and legislative enactments; and others suggest its relevance as a tool of legitimacy.[36]

This brief overview gives a flavour of the discord regarding the place of neutrality (and all its variations) in the mediation process. It is not within

35 For Mulcahy, see note 14 at 508, 521–3. For Garcia, see A.C. Garcia, "Negotiating Negotiation: The Collaborative Production of Resolution in Small Claims Mediation Hearings" (2000) 11 *Discourse & Society* 315 at 335–7. For Harper and Astor on the inability of mediators to be neutral: Harper, see note 32 at 602, and Astor, see note 32 at 222. Mayer does not see neutrality to be a defining concept of mediation: mediator identity is about more than just neutrality. See B.S. Mayer, "What We Talk About When We Talk About Neutrality: A Commentary on the Susskind-Stulberg Debate" (2012) 95 *Marquette L. R.* 859. For Kydd and Honeyman, who see success and failure as dependent on notions of neutrality and bias, see A. Kydd, "Which Side Are You On? Bias, Credibility and Mediation" (2003) 47 *Am. J. Pol't Science* 597 at 607–8, and C. Honeyman, "Bias and Mediators' Ethics" (1986) *Negotiation J.* 175.

36 These examples are in addition to the discussion about neutrality as being an element in the definition of mediation in note 31 above. See also S.B. Goldberg and M.L. Shaw, "The Secrets of Successful (and Unsuccessful) Mediators Continued: Studies Two and Three" (2007) *Negotiation J.* 393, who find that neutrality is essential to the establishment of trust and confidence between party and mediator, both of which are necessary for mediation to be successful; J.J. Alfini, "Mediation as a Calling: Addressing the Disconnect Between Mediation Ethics and the Practices of Lawyer Mediators" (2007–08) 49 *S. Tex. L. Rev.* 829 at 831, where he says that mediator impartiality and party self-determination are core values fundamental to good mediation practice; J.B. Stulberg, "Must a Mediator be Neutral? You'd Better Believe It!" (2012) 95 *Marquette L. R.* 829, examines the importance of neutrality as a core element of the mediation process as justice demands that mediators be neutral; Exon examines the requirement of impartiality for ethical practice in various state codes of conduct in America, see note 10 at 582–9, and also in "How Can a Mediator Be Both Impartial and Fair? Why Ethical Standards of Conduct Create Chaos for Mediators" (2006) *J. Disp. Resol.* 387; and for the suggestion that neutrality brings legitimacy to the process, see A. Taylor, "Concepts of Neutrality in Family Mediation: Contexts, Ethics, Influence, and Transformative Process" (1997) 14 *Mediation Q.* 215: R. Zamir, "The Disempowering Relationship Between Mediator Neutrality and Judicial Impartiality: Toward a New Mediation Ethic" (2011) 11 *Pepp. Disp. Resol. L. J.* 467 at 514, Mulcahy, see note 14 at 509.

the purview of this chapter to examine the mythology related to the role of neutrality in mediation or to examine the definitions of neutrality or its sister terms 'impartiality' or 'equidistance' in any more detail than that which has been presented.[37] For now, it is important to note that it plays a role in contextually situating mediation within an understanding that the third-party intervener is generally accepted as a neutral intervener among the parties. More particularly, the process is approached as a consensual, collaborative negotiation facilitated by a non-aligned third party who does not determine outcome. As Marian Roberts succinctly states:

> The mediator is distinguished as a disinterested, non-aligned third person, facilitating communication exchanges between the parties that lead towards their own consensual joint decision-making. The mediator has neither a stake in nor any authority to impose an outcome on those parties. The non-determinative nature of the mediator's authority and a non-partisan alignment within the parties' negotiations are recognized to be the two core characteristics of a mediator's role and function.[38]

This statement articulates the premise from which this ethnographic journey begins.

Mediator vision

The nature of a mediator's interventions depends on the mediator's vision of what mediation should be.[39] Kolb and Kressel say that it depends on whether the mediator views the dispute through a transformative or a pragmatic lens.[40] They distinguish between problem-solving and communication objectives by referring to 'frames' that are "interpretative schemes that mediators use to make sense of and organize their activities while at work on a

---

37 Many scholars have, in their writing about neutrality in mediation, canvassed various aspects of the literature on this particular issue as noted in the references above. See generally Mulcahy, see note 14 at 508–14; Zamir, ibid. at 479–87; Young, see note 32 at 318–26.
38 M. Roberts, *Developing the Craft of Mediation: Reflections on Theory and Practice* (London: Jessica Kingsley Publishers, 2007) at 69.
39 This is not a new concept. For example, see K.K. Kovach, "The Vanishing Trial: Land Mine on the Mediation Landscape or Opportunity for Evolution: Ruminations on the Future of Mediation Practice" (2005) 7 *Cardozo J. Conflict Resol.* 27 at 66, and Della Noce, Bush and Folger, see note 15 at 42; J.P. Folger, "'Mediation Goes Mainstream' – Taking the Conference Theme Challenge" (2002–03) 3 *Pepp. Disp. Resol. L. J.* 1; B. Jarrett, "The Future of Mediation: A Sociological Perspective" (2009) *J. Disp. Resol.* 49; C.A. Picard and K.R. Melchin, "Insight Mediation: A Learning-Centered Mediation Model" (2007) *Negotiation J.* 35 at 40.
40 Kolb and Kressel, see note 22 at 468.

dispute".[41] The authors conclude that "there is a tendency for practitioners to define their roles and structure their activities according to whether it is settlement they seek or a change in the ways the parties communicate with each other".[42]

Although different labels are attached to the various activities conducted by mediators, there appears to be support for Kolb and Kressel's conclusion regarding the existence of two basic visions. Briefly, the models suggested by the literature include as follows:

Satisfaction and transformation stories: Bush and Folger's satisfaction story is one where the dispute is reframed into a mutual problem to lead to a win-win solution, whereas the transformation story attains empowerment and recognition through communication controlled by the mediator.[43]

Bargaining and therapeutic strategies: Merry and Silbey describe bargaining strategy as taking "a pragmatic view that the parties should settle because they must live together, while therapeutic mediation emphasizes the value of handling conflict through rational discourses".[44]

Task-oriented and socio-emotional approaches: Kressel and Pruitt define the task-oriented approach as attacking issues, suggesting proposals and achieving agreement. The social-emotional approach emphasizes improved relationships through the parties' efforts to work through the conflict to their own solutions.[45]

'Trashing, bashing and hashing it out': Alfini refers to three approaches. Trashing deals with evaluating the dispute and rebuilding the issues to achieve agreement; bashing refers to making offers more realistic; and hashing it out focuses on communication as the means through which the parties are led to resolution.[46]

Evaluative v. facilitative/directive v. elicitive orientations: Riskin originally proposed a continuum between two approaches. The evaluative approach moves from predicting outcomes and developing position-based proposals to probing interests and developing interest-based proposals. The facilitative approach moves from assisting the parties to articulate and assess their needs, positions and proposals to helping the parties understand issues and interests

---

41 Ibid. at 469.
42 Ibid.
43 Bush and Folger, see note 23 at 16–17, 84–5.
44 Merry and Silbey, see note 17 at 22.
45 K. Kressel and D.G. Pruitt, "Conclusion: A Research Perspective on the Mediation of Social Conflict" in Kressel, Pruitt and Associates, see note 26 at 423–4.
46 J.J. Alfini, "Trashing, Bashing, and Hashing It Out: Is This the End of 'Good Mediation'?" (1991) 19 *Fla. St. U. L. Rev.* 47 at 66–73.

and developing broadly based proposals.[47] Nearly a decade later, Riskin replaced the labels 'evaluative' with 'directive', and 'facilitative' with 'elicitive', to indicate a broader range of mediator orientations because a better understanding of mediator orientations is achieved, he says, "by focusing on the extent to which *almost any conduct* by the mediator *directs* the mediation process, or the participants, toward a particular procedure or perspective or outcome, on the one hand or, on the other, *elicits* the parties' perspectives and preferences – and then tries to honor or accommodate them".[48]

Norm-generating, norm-educating and norm-advocating models: Waldman spurns the above models and suggests a three-fold model focusing on normative values within each mediation and the extent to which norms are used in resolution. The norm-generating model shies away from social or legal norms with parties creating new norms on which to base settlement; the norm-educating model ensures that the parties are conversant with relevant norms affecting their dispute; and the norm-advocating model presses for the incorporation of a particular norm in the decision-making process and resolution.[49]

Narrative approach: The focus is on discourse in this approach. Winslade characterizes mediation as stories, with disputants embedded within a social constructionist view of conflict and impacted by cultural influences. Parties must change their stories of conflict in order to resolve the conflict, and in so doing create new discursive realities that do not include the original conflict.[50]

Strategic style: The goal to solving a problem is to examine and deal with the root causes of conflict, according to Kressel. Mediators attack the underlying or latent causes of conflict, and in so doing assist the parties to address it.[51]

Insight framework: Picard and others blend transformative, narrative and problem-solving approaches to achieve insight into conflict by dealing with threats to the values held by disputants as perceived by them. Once insight is gained, resolution is more amenable.[52]

---

47 L.L. Riskin, "Understanding Mediators' Orientations, Strategies, and Techniques: A Grid for the Perplexed" (1996) 1 *Harv. Negot. L. Rev.* 7 at 17, 24–34.
48 L.L. Riskin, "Decisionmaking in Mediation: The New Old Grid and the New New Grid System" (2003–04) 79 *Notre Dame L. Rev.* 1 at 30–1.
49 E.A. Waldman, "Identifying the Role of Social Norms in Mediation: A Multiple Model Approach" (1996–97) 48 *Hastings L. J.* 703.
50 J. Winslade, "Mediation with a Focus on Discursive Positioning" (2006) 23 *Conflict Resol. Q.* 501. See also J. Winslade and G. Monk, *Narrative Mediation: A New Approach to Conflict Resolution* (San Francisco: Jossey-Bass, 2000).
51 Kressel, see note 2 at 252, 255–6.
52 Picard and Melchin, see note 39 at 40. See also N. Sargent, C. Picard and M. Jull, "Rethinking Conflict: Perspectives from the Insight Approach" (2011) *Negotiation J.* 343, and C. Picard and

Whatever the approach taken, mediation is guided by the goal underlying the approach. It is necessary to understand the goal fuelling the mediator's interventions in order to understand the influence being invoked by the mediator.

Mediator behaviour

During the process, mediators will employ whatever techniques are necessary to further their vision of mediation. As with the prior sections above, a brief canvass of various techniques and strategies described in the literature will be conducted to help contextualize the ethnographic data of the later chapters.

Carnevale examines mediator behaviour and concludes that mediation is a strategic game in which mediators make use of four strategies:

- *integration*, which involves joint problem-solving and, more particularly, a resolution reflecting the common interests and positions of the parties;
- *pressing*, whereby the mediator places limits on the alternatives available to the parties by discrediting the alternatives, attaching costs to them or reducing their benefit;
- *compensation*, which gives something desirable to one or both parties; and
- *inaction*, whereby the mediator lets the parties handle the dispute on their own.[53]

The tactics used in these strategies include caucusing, controlling the agenda, guiding communication, using time constraints and humour, and balancing power.[54] Carnevale concludes by stating that mediator strategy is dependent on mediator perception of common ground and the value placed on the parties' aspirations and beliefs.[55] For example, if a mediator believes that there is much common ground between the parties and believes in the parties' aspirations, an integrative strategy will be used. If there is little perceived common ground and a low regard for the parties' aspirations, pressing will be the dominant strategy.[56]

Another approach to mediator intervention taken by Kressel and Pruitt involves three categorizations:

M. Jull, "Learning Through Deepening Conversations: A Key Strategy of Insight Mediation" (2011) *Conflict Resol. Q.* 151.
53 P.J.D. Carnevale, "Strategic Choice in Mediation" (1986) 2 *Negotiation J.* 41 at 41–7.
54 Ibid. at 47–8.
55 Ibid. at 53.
56 Ibid. at 54. See also P.J.D. Carnevale, D.E. Conlon and K.A. Hanisch, "Experimental Research on the Strategic-Choice Model of Mediation" in Kressel, Pruitt and Associates, see note 26, 344.

- *reflexive intervention*: efforts used by mediators to orient themselves to the dispute, such as developing rapport, gaining entry into the dispute and diagnosing the prognosis of the dispute;
- *contextual intervention*: efforts to alter the climate between the parties so as to foster resolution; and
- *substantive intervention*: efforts to deal directly with the issues, explore areas of interest and compromise.[57]

These interventions appear to be dependent on the mediator's intended purpose as opposed to the mediator's perception of the parties' values in the dispute, as suggested by Carnevale. Kressel, more recently, developed what he sees to be a strategic style to mediating whereby mediators take a pragmatic, efficient, diagnostic and directive approach to resolution. A goal is formulated and strategy implemented for the achievement of the goal. The strategy includes the search for the underlying latent cause of the conflict. Once that is revealed, the mediator takes a pragmatic view of the conflict: he does what is needed to achieve what he sees to be the desired result.[58]

Jones sees strategy to be a combination of process and content intervention.[59] She also refers to three categories of behaviour and tactics:

- *communication-facilitation*, which involves searching for information (i.e. requests for and clarification of information), supportive communication (i.e. empathy, humour, impartiality), and instruction (i.e. mediator's role, process used, ground rules);
- *substantive-directive*, which involves tactics such as discussing solutions (i.e. proposing or evaluating), pressuring (i.e. invoking social norms or costs of disagreement, and stopping the process), power-balancing (i.e. equalizing resources, preventing dominance), and formalizing the agreement (i.e. final agreement, implementation, discussion of future disputes); and
- *procedural*, which involves the establishment of the environment (i.e. private, safe, informal, neutral), agenda-setting (i.e. selection of the order of issues), caucusing (i.e. when, why).[60]

---

57 K. Kressel and D.G. Pruitt, "Themes in the Mediation of Social Conflict" (1985) 41 *J. of Social Issues* 179 at 188–92; see also K. Kressel, "Mediation" in M. Deutsch and P.T. Coleman, eds, *The Handbook of Conflict Resolution: Theory and Practice* (San Francisco: Jossey-Bass, 2000) 522.
58 Kressel, see note 2.
59 T.S. Jones, "A Taxonomy of Effective Mediator Strategies and Tactics for Non Labour Management Mediation" in M.A. Rahim, ed., *Managing Conflict: An Interdisciplinary Approach* (New York: Praeger, 1989) 201 at 221; W.H. Ross Jr, "Beliefs of Mediators and Arbitrators Regarding the Effects of Motivational and Content Control Techniques in Disputes" in Rahim, *Managing Conflict*, at 209.
60 Jones, ibid. at 225–9.

Others look at mediator behaviour in the context of a mediation framework. Pruitt speaks of a five-stage mediation process whereby mediators (i) gather information, (ii) determine the issues, (iii) facilitate or undertake an evaluation of the alternatives, (iv) promote decision-making, and (v) assist with implementation.[61] Oberman sees mediators enacting the following common strategies: (a) setting the process; (b) exploring issues through storytelling; (c) using empathy and information as a basis for intervention; (d) moving away from self-interests by focusing on the present and future; and (e) using social and legal norms in reality testing.[62]

Riskin tackles mediator strategies and techniques from the perspective of mediator participation. Given the debate spurred by his evaluative/facilitative grid (which continues today despite Riskin's subsequent amendment to the grid), it is useful to canvass the elements of his original grid (hereinafter referred to as the 'Old Grid') to understand the dichotomy created in the field between evaluation and facilitation as appropriate approaches. According to the Old Grid, mediator orientation is either facilitative or evaluative, and within these two classifications, broad or narrow.[63] The broad category focuses on interests while the narrow category focuses on positions. Evaluation and facilitation refer to the actions of the mediator in pursuing the goals of the mediation. Riskin describes the techniques of the evaluator as urging and pushing parties to accept settlement, developing and proposing agreement, predicting outcomes as well as the impact of not settling, educating as to interests and assessing strengths and weaknesses of the disputants' cases. The words used to describe the facilitative mediator reflect a much more gentle and distant intervention: the facilitator helps parties to develop and evaluate proposals, asks about the likely outcomes and consequences of not settling, helps the parties understand interests and develop options to respond to those interests, and asks about the strengths and weaknesses of each case.[64] The narrow-evaluative strategy ensures that parties understand strengths and weaknesses of their case, whereas the broad-evaluative strategy emphasizes interests through evaluative techniques. Conversely, the narrow-facilitative approach lets the parties formulate their own assessment of their positions and the broad-facilitative approach helps parties explore interests and options.[65]

As mentioned above, the Old Grid became the New New Grid, in which the evaluative mediator became the directive mediator and the facilitator

---

61 D.G. Pruitt et al., "Process of Mediation in Dispute Settlement Centers" in Kressel, Pruitt and Associates, see note 26, 368 at 376–89.
62 Oberman, see note 10 at 808.
63 Riskin, see note 47 at 17, 26–34.
64 For a chart form of the evaluative/facilitative/broad/narrow categorizations as described herein, see ibid. at 35.
65 Ibid. at 26, 30, 28, 32.

became the elicitor. In what appears to be an attempt to silence those who see the Old Grid as evoking an either–or proposition, Riskin goes to great pains to stress that mediators are both directive and elicitive in their interactions. He says:

> For example, almost every mediator will direct on some issues and elicit on others. And nearly any move by a mediator can have both directive and elicitive aspects or intents or effects. Thus, a mediator might direct the parties toward a particular understanding of their situation in order to elicit options from them. Similarly, when a mediator asks whether one party would consider a future business relationship with the other, this obviously has an elicitive thrust. But merely asking the question can be directive, too, in the sense that it directs the party's attention toward a particular issue and, at least for the moment, away from other issues.[66]

It is interesting to note that the New New Grid has not received the attention accorded the Old Grid, and reference continues to be made to the nomenclature of the Old Grid.[67]

The Old Grid appeared to suggest a rigid dichotomy of behaviours which in turn led to ferocious debate about the categorization of mediators as either facilitative or evaluative.[68] The use of the facilitative and evaluative

---

[66] Riskin, see note 48 at 32–3. As part of his New New Grid, Riskin includes a series of grids illustrating participant influences in three areas of decision-making: substantive, procedural and meta-procedural decision-making. For the purposes of this study, it is sufficient to note the development of the directive and elicitive mediator in what amounts to Riskin's apologia for the Old Grid.

[67] For example, Kressel, see note 2 at 251–2. Kressel refers to three approaches in mediation – facilitative, evaluative and transformative – and then discusses a fourth, his strategic approach. It is interesting to note that he references Riskin's 2003 article, yet uses the language of Riskin's 1996 article. Also Della Noce, "Evaluative Mediation", see note 2 at 194, where she too references the 'big three' as being facilitative, evaluative and transformative mediation styles and proceeds to use the nomenclature in her examination of evaluative practices.

[68] To illustrate the responses generated by Riskin's Old Grid, see K.K. Kovach and L.P. Love, "Mapping Mediation: The Risks of Riskin's Grid" (1998) 3 *Harv. Negot. L. Rev.* 71, in which the authors are critical of evaluation and its role in mediation; J. B. Stulberg, "Facilitative versus Evaluative Mediator Orientations: Piercing the 'Grid' Lock" (1996–97) 24 *Fla. St. U. L. Rev.* 985, in which the author criticizes the descriptions applied to evaluation and facilitation activities; J.J. Alfini moderates a discussion by a panel of academics and practitioners about the efficacy of evaluation in specific case scenarios in "Evaluative versus Facilitative Mediation: A Discussion" (1996–97) 24 *Fla. St. U. L. Rev.* 919. Even Riskin developed his New New Grid to deal with the reaction created by the Old Grid, see note 48. See E. Patrick McDermott and R. Obar, "'What's Going On' in Mediation: An Empirical Analysis of the Influence of a Mediator's Style on Party Satisfaction and

62 *Mediation*

nomenclature became typical in the exploration of mediator styles and approaches. With these two forming an anchor, together with the Bush and Folger transformative approach to mediation, the field soon developed a tripartite categorization based on these approaches.[69] Along with these primary approaches, others soon developed including narrative, insight, activist transformative-narrative mediation, just to name a few.[70] Wall and Dunne, in their review of the literature of the past decade, refer to the numerous categories of strategic behaviours that have developed and reduce them to six, all but one of which reflect the primary three categories. They are: pressing, neutral, relational, analytic, clarification and multifunctional. The latter, multifunctional, seems to point to a more flexible approach.[71]

Many see mediator interactions as being flexible, responsive and adaptable.[72] Some still speak in terms of evaluation and facilitation, suggesting that mediators move between these categories throughout a mediation while others suggest a need to move away from rigid categories to a more eclectic approach that uses a combination of strategies.[73] A panoply of tactics is

---

Monetary Benefit" (2004) 9 *Harv. Neg. L. Rev.* 75 for an overview of the literature on the facilitative/evaluative dichotomy.

69 Riskin, see notes 47 and 48; Baruch Bush and Folger, see note 23. For examples of the categorizations of these approaches as primary approaches: Exon, see note 10; B. Jarrett, "The Future of Mediation: A Sociological Perspective" (2009) *J. Disp. Resol.* 49. See also discussion in note 67.

70 For a discussion about narrative mediation, see Winslade, and Winslade and Monk, see note 50. With regard to the evaluative/facilitative dichotomy, it is referred to as a blended problem-solving or pragmatic approach alongside transformative and narrative mediation: for example, Picard and Melchin, see note 39 at 40; M. Alberstein, "The Jurisprudence of Mediation: Between Formalism, Feminism and Identity Conversations" (2009–10) 11 *Cardozo J. Conflict Resol.* 1, and "Forms of Mediation and Law: Cultures of Dispute Resolution" (2007) 22 *Ohio St. J. Disp. Resol.* 321; Harper, see note 32.

71 Wall and Dunne, see note 2 at 236–7.

72 See, for example, D. Golann, "Variations in Mediation: How – and Why – Legal Mediators Change Styles in the Course of a Case" (2000) *J. Disp. Resol.* 41; J.W. Stempel, "The Inevitability of the Eclectic: Liberating ADR from Ideology" (2000) *J. Disp. Resol.* 247; F.E.A. Sander, "Achieving Meaningful Threshold Consent to Mediator Style(s)" (2007–08) 14 *Dispute Resolution Magazine* 8 at 10; Exon, see note 10 at 589; Kressel, see note 2 at 275; Riskin, see note 48, too sees the flexibility of mediator actions which is reflected in his New New Grid.

73 For a discussion of mediation as both evaluative and facilitative, see R. Birke, "Evaluation and Facilitation: Moving Past Either/Or" (2000) *J. Disp. Resol.* 309, and K.M. Roberts, "Mediating the Evaluative-Facilitative Debate: Why Both Parties are Wrong and a Proposal for Settlement" (2007–08) 39 *Loy. U. Chi. L. J.* 187. Golann sees mediators moving along the facilitative/evaluative grid: see Golann, ibid., and D. Golann and M.C. Aaron, "Using Evaluations in Mediation" (book chapter) in *Mediating Legal Disputes: Effective Strategies for Lawyers and Mediators* (American Bar Association, 2009) at 327–41. Stempel, in two articles, sees the benefit of the eclectic approach: see Stempel, ibid., and

available to mediators in the pursuit of a mediated solution. These approaches and strategies are suggestive of the ever-changing roles that mediators invoke. Mediators may be seen to be passive, facilitative, evaluative, questioning, directive, procedural, reflexive, or contextual interveners, for example. Gulliver points to a continuum of strategies that a mediator follows, alternating between strategies as the circumstances require, moving "from virtual passivity, to 'chairman,' to 'enunciator,' to 'prompter,' to 'leader,' to virtual arbitrator".[74] These categories reflect levels of mediator intervention in the process and can all occur in one mediation. Mackie and others list what they see to be the various roles of a mediator during the course of a mediation, including: process manager, facilitator, problem-solver, information-gatherer, reality tester, scapegoat/lightning conductor/sponge, observer and witness, messenger, negotiation coach, advocate, dealmaker and post-breakdown resource.[75] These roles suggest an intervention in which the mediator is a catalyst for change. Bowling and Hoffman refer to the 'integrative mediator' who "has an extraordinary opportunity to shape the direction of the parties' interactions and discussions".[76] This is because, they say, the process is fluid and the relationship between the mediator and the parties is in flux.[77]

Mediation as assisted negotiation

Recall the words of the Mediator of my ethnographic village that begin this study: *"The objective is to reach a negotiated resolution to the dispute. My role is to help you to reach a negotiated solution. I am not a judge, I am not an arbitrator. I am not here to make decisions. We will talk about the case, but I won't say who is right or wrong ... This is your day, your process, your opportunity, if nothing else, to be clear and confident regarding what the case is about, what the other side's case is about. This is your opportunity."*[78] Such an introduction is suggestive of a normative understanding of mediation among mediators. *"The objective is to reach a negotiated resolution to the dispute. My role is to help you to reach a negotiated solution."* This is a typical and frequent assertion made by the mediators of my village.[79] Notwithstanding the view one takes about the elemental nature of mediation and the interventions of the third party, negotiation lies at the heart of

---

"Identifying Real Dichotomies Underlying the False Dichotomy: Twenty-first Century Mediation in an Eclectic Regime" (2000) *J. Disp. Resol.* 371.
74 P.H. Gulliver, *Disputes and Negotiations: A Cross-Cultural Perspective* (New York: Academic Press, 1979) at 220.
75 K. Mackie *et al.*, *The ADR Practice Guide: Commercial Dispute Resolution* (Haywards Heath: Tottel, 2007) at 286–8.
76 Bowling and Hoffman, see note 16 at 21.
77 Ibid.
78 See Chapter 1 for fuller introductory words by the mediator.
79 For a detailed examination of this assertion, see later discussion in Chapter 5.

mediation. Parties seek mediation when they are unable to resolve a dispute directly with the other party. If they were able to do so directly, they would engage in direct negotiations. De Bono refers to third-party intervention as converting "a two-dimensional fight into a three-dimensional exploration" in search of an outcome.[80]

Mediation is heavily characterized as assisted or facilitated negotiation. Bush refers to a generally accepted description of mediation as assisted negotiation whereby the third party facilitates the parties' negotiation.[81] Roberts and Palmer see the need to examine mediation in the context of the processual shape of negotiations as a process auxiliary to negotiation.[82] Gulliver adds a further dimension: he sees mediation as an integrated part of negotiation that cannot be separated as a distinct stand-alone process.[83] As Gulliver believes, one cannot possibly begin to understand the process of mediation without understanding the process of negotiation. For Gulliver, the negotiation map comprises eight processual phases: (i) search for a negotiation arena; (ii) setting the agenda; (iii) exploration of the range of the dispute; (iv) narrowing the differences; (v) preliminaries to final bargaining; (vi) final bargaining; (vii) ritual confirmation or, in other words, tending to formalization of the settlement agreement; and (viii) implementation of the agreement.[84] Arguably for Gulliver, this is the shape of a mediated negotiation as well.

Others, although seeing mediation as a negotiation process (whether it is called facilitated or assisted negotiation), describe mediation as having stages distinct from negotiation phases such as those described by Gulliver.[85] We have seen a description of a five-stage process offered by Pruitt and Oberman above.[86] Another example outlines four basic phases during which the business of mediation is conducted: (i) preparation; (ii) opening joint session; (iii) private meetings; and (iv) conclusion.[87] Negotiation may have been the original structure in which disputing parties were engaged, it is

80 E. de Bono, *Conflicts: A Better Way to Resolve Them* (London: Harrap, 1985) at 124.
81 Bush, see note 10 at 3. Bush goes on to say, however, that this is *one* possible approach to mediation practice; see at 4.
82 Roberts and Palmer, see note 31 at 173.
83 See generally, Gulliver, see note 74, and particularly at 213. Examples of others who view mediation as negotiation include Roberts, see note 38 at 133; Mackie *et al.*, see note 75 at 11 and 43; C.A. McEwen and R.L. Wissler, "Finding Out if it is True: Comparing Mediation and Negotiation through Research" (2002) *J. Disp. Resol.* 131, in which the authors look at the ways mediators assist negotiators; Bush, see note 10, in which the author considers the ways in which a mediator adds value to the assisted negotiation through a transformative framework.
84 Gulliver, see note 74 at 122–70. Gulliver's negotiation phases will be explored in further depth in Chapter 4.
85 For example, Bush, see note 10; and Mackie *et al.*, see note 75 at 40.
86 See discussion regarding Pruitt and Oberman's phases at notes 61 and 62 herein.
87 Mackie *et al.*, see note 75 at 43–4.

argued, but it becomes altered as a result of the introduction of a third party and its impact on the process and the parties; therefore, the processes are said to be distinguishable.[88]

Whatever the relationship between negotiation and mediation espoused in the literature, it is clear that the third-party intervention in a negotiation adds a contextual layer to party negotiations. The result appears to be a definition reflective of this added dimension: mediation is consensual negotiation assisted by an independent third party who does not have authority to impose a resolution.

If one follows the theory that mediation is assisted negotiation, one must look at the interventions of the mediator in the negotiation framework.[89] It is within such a framework that a mediator sets out to achieve an intended goal of the mediation, whether that is to settle the dispute, repair relationships, educate disputants about their rights and obligations, enhance communication, or transform views of self and others. Studies in this area speak of the influence that the mediator has on the negotiation; how he shapes the interaction, changes perspectives and clears the path for agreement.

During this consensual and assisted negotiation, a mediator may invoke a number of the strategies canvassed above during the course of the process. Some commentators speak specifically of the mediator's role in the negotiation itself: overcoming negotiation barriers through her control of the information exchange; reconceptualizing the dispute; giving voice to the parties; diffusing tension; challenging positions; and expanding the proverbial pie.[90] As does Gulliver, Marian Roberts, in her conversations with 16 mediators about their craft, firmly puts negotiation at the centre of the mediation process and speaks of the mediator's role within that process as an orchestrator of negotiations and manager of information exchange between the parties.[91]

The key, Roberts says, is the need to know how and when to transition between phases of the negotiation.[92] Recall that Gulliver supports this view

---

88 Ibid. at 162–3.
89 Roberts and Palmer, see note 31, and Gulliver, see note 74. For a different approach to the negotiatory framework, see Della Noce, Bush and Folger, see note 15 at 44. These authors suggest that the negotiatory framework is imported from other fields by mediators for application in their practice as a result of an absence of knowledge of or reliance on articulated mediation theory.
90 For example, Burns, see note 16 at 703; P.Y. Wolfe, "How a Mediator Enhances the Negotiation Process" (2005) 46 *N.H.B.J.* 38 at 47; Bowling and Hoffman, see note 16 at 9. See also generally, K. Mackie, "Breakthrough: Overcoming Deadlocked Negotiations", and T. Willis, "Creative Solutions When Only Money is at Stake" in C. Newmark and A. Monaghan, eds, *Butterworths Mediators on Mediation: Mediator Perspectives on the Practice of Commercial Mediation* (London: Tottel, 2005) at 106 and 124 respectively.
91 Roberts, see note 38 at 133.
92 Ibid. at 133.

in referring to a continuum of strategies that a mediator may follow during the course of a mediation.[93] Gulliver also sees the mediator as integral to the information exchange between the parties, playing an influential role in the way information is delivered and received.[94] He positions this role squarely within a negotiation framework. He speaks of the negotiation dyad becoming a negotiation triad and refers to the presence of the mediator in a two-party negotiation. He describes the impact of that mediator on the process in the following way:

> The intervention of a mediator turns the initial dyad of a dispute into a triadic interaction of some kind. The disputing parties retain their ability to decide whether or not to agree to and accept proposals for an outcome, irrespective of the source of the proposals. Yet clearly the mediator exercises influence in some degree, whether he remains largely passive or virtually controls the exchange of information and the learning process. He himself interacts with each party and with both together, and they may communicate to and through him. He becomes a party in the negotiations. He becomes a negotiator and as such, he inevitably brings with him, deliberately or not, certain ideas, knowledge, and assumptions as well as certain interests and concerns of his own and those of other people whom he represents. Therefore he is not, and cannot be, neutral and merely a catalyst. He not only affects the interaction but, at least in part, seeks and encourages an outcome that is tolerable to him in terms of his own ideas and interests. He may even come into conflict with one or both of the parties.[95]

Marian Roberts picks up on this idea that a mediator becomes a party in the negotiations in those mediations where parties are separated from each other during the process. She refers here to the private meetings: meetings where the mediator meets with each party privately and works with each separately to come to resolution. In discussing the role of the mediator in what she terms 'shuttle mediation' (that is, shuttling between parties), she says, "the mediator may act as a simple conduit, passing messages back and forth, or may negotiate actively on behalf of those disputants who obviously cannot negotiate directly".[96] Others concur with the vision of the mediator as active negotiator suggested by Roberts.[97] In a different vein, Mulcahy and Burns

---

[93] Gulliver, see note 74 at 220.
[94] Ibid. at 219.
[95] Ibid. at 213–14.
[96] Roberts, see note 38 at 154.
[97] Robert Dampf, a practitioner mediator, advises lawyers about the mediator's role in the process: "Select a mediator who has a good track record as a negotiator and a lawyer. Remember, the mediator's job is to negotiate effectively with both sides. It is very

refer to mediators as go-betweens during mediation, becoming a party advocate against non-parties or aligning themselves against a party to play 'devil's advocate' against that party.[98] Exon, when examining the ability of mediators to maintain impartiality, says that they become advocates for the benefit of one party when they evaluate the dispute, thus impacting their impartiality negatively.[99] Bowling and Hoffman see the mediator as someone who is not external to the conflict but is "personally involved – being influenced by the process as much as influencing it".[100] Mayer approaches advocacy in yet a different context: he raises it as a way to expand beyond what he sees to be a limited role of third-party neutral. He explores an expanded role for mediators as conflict specialists which would include the traditional third party role together with other roles such as advocate for the parties. Although not speaking of roles to be conducted within one mediation, Mayer raises interesting points on the extent to which the roles played by advocates and mediators can complement one another.[101]

When scholars and practitioners state that the mediator becomes a party to the negotiation, it appears to be in the context of a third party becoming involved in the parties' negotiation, and in the context of that third party

---

helpful if he is an experienced lawyer who can 'separate the wheat from the chaff'. While the mediator must be impartial, it is important for him to be able to challenge a red herring legal argument that has no real merit. The mediator must know the difference between an argument that will fly, one that has a slight chance for take-off, and one that will never get off the ground at all. A mediator who is *only* a message carrier is not truly helping the process." See R.S. Dampf, "The Two Sides of Mediation: Tips from the Mediator: Of Sticks and Stones" (1997) 45 *L.A. Bar J.* 138 at 138. For another example of a practitioner's view of the mediator as negotiator, see J.C. Freund, *The Neutral Negotiator: Why and How Mediation Can Work to Resolve Dollar Disputes* (New Jersey: Prentice-Hall Law & Business, 1994) at 12–16. N.H. Katz sees the role of the mediator through a political frame: that is, as political leader who acts as advocate or negotiator, assisting parties with bargaining which allows them to 'save face and survive'; see N.H. Katz, "Enhancing Mediator Artistry: Multiple Frames, Spirit, and Reflection in Action" in M.S. Herrman, ed., *The Blackwell Handbook of Mediation: Bridging Theory, Research, and Practice* (Oxford: Blackwell, 2006) 374 at 376–8. The reference to mediator as advocate also occurs in Charkoudian *et al.*, see note 14 at 307, when charting mediator behaviours, and in D. Dyck, "The Mediator as Nonviolent Advocate: Revisiting the Question of Mediator Neutrality" (2000) 18 *Mediation Q.* 129, where the author refers to the need for mediator activism to ensure balance in parties' narratives, referring to the activism as advocacy.

98 Mulcahy, see note 14 at 519–21; Burns, "Think Your Blackest Thoughts", see note 14 at 241, and "Pursuing 'Deep Pockets'", see note 14 at 120, 150. Burns' latter point about the alignment by the mediator against parties is seen in Greatbatch and Dingwall's work, see note 14 at 638.
99 Exon, see note 10 at 605.
100 Bowling and Hoffman, see note 16 at 11–12.
101 B. Mayer, *Beyond Neutrality: Confronting the Crisis in Conflict Resolution* (San Francisco: Jossey-Bass, 2004).

actively positioning himself within the negotiation to impact it in the various manners described above. For example, Tarpley refers to the mediator as a negotiator, using negotiation skills to assist the parties with their negotiations:

> 'Good' mediators are 'good' negotiators ... Mediators utilize all of the skills of a good negotiator and facilitate the most difficult task of all – seeing the situation through the lens of the other party. The task of the mediator is to get the parties beyond their 'partisan perceptions' of how their position fits a bargaining marker or standard and into the realm of perception of the other party.[102]

As Gulliver states, mediator presence and participation in a two-party dispute turns the 'initial dyad' into 'a triadic interaction of some kind'.[103] Two parties become three, with the third interacting with the others in different ways.

A mediation model

To this point, diverse views of not only what mediation is but also what mediators do have been considered. Specifically, a suggestion is made that the various approaches reflect two fundamental philosophies in mediation theory: either the importance of settlement or the need for improved and expanded communication. At this point, we need to focus on the mediation model that is the subject of this ethnographic study. It is a model that follows the pragmatic lens of settlement – the goal of mediation is to achieve settlement for the parties. The Organization of my fieldwork site sees mediation as a confidential, flexible, self-determinative process where a 'neutral person actively assists parties' with the negotiation of their dispute.[104]

The elements that were canvassed earlier in this chapter are evident: the 'neutral' third party; the process as a negotiation; parties in control of the decision; and flexibility of the process. The training manual which is provided to all of the Organization's trainees,[105] and which articulates the

---

102 J.R. Tarpley, "ADR, Jurisprudence, and Myth" (2001–02) 17 *Ohio St. J. Disp. Resol.* 113 at 121–2.
103 Gulliver, see note 74 at 213.
104 The Organization sets out its philosophy in its training manual (the 'Manual'). To protect the anonymity of the participants of this study, the full citation of the Manual is not provided; however, a copy is on file with the author. This definition is taken from the Manual.
105 The Manual, ibid., is provided to attendees on the Organization's mediation training course at which participants are assessed for accreditation purposes. The training is based on the principles set out in this Manual. The attendees are provided with a copy of the

Mediation 69

basic philosophy under which its panel mediators are accredited, speaks about the influence that the mediator brings to the process:

> The very presence of a mediator changes the dynamics of the negotiating process. The mediator brings negotiating, problem solving and communication skills, and deploys them from a position of independence and neutrality, making progress possible where direct negotiations have stalled.[106]

Gulliver's view that mediation is a negotiation process is echoed here, as well as his view that mediator presence alters the dynamics of the negotiation. Mediation is a negotiation process and the Organization often refers to the mediator as a negotiator in this process, a negotiator who acts in the capacity of third-party neutral who guides the parties in their negotiation. Neutrality is emphasized in its mediation philosophy: for the Organization, the mediator is a neutral third party who has no interest in the dispute or its outcome.[107] The mediator's function is to assist the parties with their negotiation. More particularly, the mediator works with the parties to rethink their views about their disputes, to coach parties to use effective negotiating strategies to move to settlement, and to overcome barriers to resolution.[108] In summary, the mediator as negotiator will use her negotiation skills for the equal benefit of the parties; act as negotiation coach; assist the parties to overcome

---

Manual prior to attendance at the course and are expected to have read the book in preparation for the course.

106 Ibid.

107 Such requirements of neutrality are not unusual. Many codes of conduct and training manuals of training organizations describe mediator interventions to be neutral or other aspects of neutrality. See, for example, Directive 2008/52/EC of the European Parliament and of the Council of 21 May 2008 on certain aspects of mediation in civil and commercial matters, Article 3(b), which defines a mediator as "any third person who is asked to conduct mediation in an effective, impartial and competent way". See also European Code of Conduct for Mediators, Article 2, which sets out obligations of independence and impartiality: http://ec.europa.eu/civiljustice/adr/adr_ec_code_conduct_en.pdf (accessed 29 July 2012). In the United States, the Model Standards of Conduct for Mediators sets out impartiality requirements for mediators in Standard II: http://www.americanbar.org/content/dam/aba/migrated/dispute/documents/model_standards_conduct_april2007.authcheckdam.pdf (accessed 29 July 2012). A discussion of the neutrality requirements of the Model Standards of Conduct for Mediators as well as other state requirements is found in Exon, see note 10 at 582–9. For an example of a mediation organization having neutrality and impartiality in its concept of mediation see JAMS at: http://www.jamsadr.com/adr-mediation/ and <http://www.jamsadr.com/mediators-ethics/> (accessed 29 July 2012).

108 This is an encapsulation of the discussion regarding the negotiation role as perceived by the Organization, see note 104.

problems; be aware of the relationships among and between the parties; tactically manage the exchange of information; understand the concepts surrounding the formulation of offers; and be a neutral diplomat, focusing on settlement.[109] While carrying out these activities, the mediator must act within the confines of a defined role – that is, as neutral and as facilitator. He must not intrude into party interests and must be vigilant that it remains the parties' negotiation and not his.[110]

The mediated negotiation takes place within a framework that provides a basic structure to help guide mediators in their work. Briefly, the framework includes (i) the preparation phase, involving the initial contact to mediate and preliminary communication with the parties, dealing with documentary exchange, and obtaining the history of the dispute; (ii) the opening phase, dealing with the arrival of parties at the mediation, private pre-mediation meetings with the parties, and the opening joint sessions at which the parties make opening statements; (iii) the exploration phase, involving private meetings and/or joint sessions, the aims of which are to build relationships and trust, information exchange, clarification of issues and interests and 'preparing the way for settlement negotiations'; (iv) the bargaining phase, during which the mediator facilitates movement by working creatively, negotiating, overcoming barriers, coaching the parties, and 'shaping' the settlement; and (v) the concluding phase, dealing with the finalization of the settlement agreement.[111]

It should also be noted that the Organization's model with its various elements is not exclusive to the field of commercial mediations: many of its elements are evident in mediations carried out in other fields.[112] The main distinctive feature of this model is the use of private meetings with parties, rather than one joint session as would occur in family or community mediation, for example. It needs to be noted, however, that the observed mediations are not the only mediations to make extensive use of private meetings and

---

109 Ibid.
110 Ibid.
111 Ibid.
112 For example, those elements include the mediator's statements to the parties regarding the mediator's role to assist the parties to reach resolution, their lack of authority to impose decisions, their neutrality/impartiality and the purpose of the session. Many of the elements of the phases, including clarification of issues, interests and needs, working creatively, overcoming barriers, identifying possible solutions, are also generally evident in mediations of a multitude of disputes, notwithstanding the nature of the dispute or the institutional or organizational context within which it occurs. These elements are stock elements described in the literature, bits and pieces of which can be found in many of the articles cited herein. However, a general treatise about the mediation process which has relevance to many areas of mediation practice and which speaks to these same similar elements and phases can be found in Moore, see note 31 at xiv, 66–7.

where extended joint sessions are rare. It is a typical framework used by other organizations for commercial mediations as well as for court-connected mediations.[113] It must also be noted that the existence of this framework did not necessarily mean its strict adherence by the mediators. During the observed mediations, the use of the framework was at the discretion of each mediator – some phases were followed, others ignored. Indeed, the framework was not in express use as a procedural guide during the mediation sessions; it formed the basis for the mediators' training. The framework does, however, form the basic foundation for the mediations I observed, and as such, must be acknowledged.

Summary

This study does not intend to cover familiar ground. Mediation will continue to be many things to different people. It will continue to be a pliable concept, bending to the desire of those who invoke it. Rather than argue for one definition of mediation against another or debate interventionist strategies, the purpose of this chapter is to ground the research data within the mediation literature and expose its internal structure as a negotiation in preparation for the exploration of the nature of mediator interactions and the process itself. Ultimately, its aim is to provide an overview of a multifaceted process so as to better understand that which is emitted from it. Thus grounded, the fugitive identity of mediation may be unmasked and the relationship between theory and practice may be explored and, hopefully, established.

---

113 See, for example, mediations conducted by JAMS in the United States: www.jamsadr.com/mediation/defined.asp (accessed 27 August 2012); and in England, see ADR Chambers UK: www.adrchambers.co.uk/mediation (accessed 27 August 2012); In Place of Strife, The Mediation Chambers: www.mediate.co.uk/what_is_mediation/index.html (accessed 27 August 2012); and for mediations under the Ontario Mandatory Mediation rule, see C.M. Hanycz, "Through the Looking Glass: Mediator Conceptions of Philosophy, Process and Power" (2004–05) 42 *Alta. L. Rev.* 819, which provides a discussion on the practice in court-connected mediations.

4 Negotiated order

The processual framework of negotiation

> Look – let me see what I can get. We will always have three hundred grand and Mike Wallace on the table from CBS. But if I can get Frost to pay a whole lot more, and secure better terms – it'd be a shame to pass ... You need to know your opponent's breaking point. And to assess that you might call late at night. Or at the weekend. If they take the call, it means they're desperate, and from that moment on, you know you've got the upper hand ... There's give and take. They give you the money, you take it and get the next train out of town.
>
> Swifty, *Frost/Nixon*[1]

Before an analysis of mediation can begin, one must understand the context within which it operates. Recall the discussion of the nature of mediation as assisted negotiation in Chapter 3. Simply, a third party assists parties in dispute with their negotiation of a resolution to their conflict. It is further suggested that mediators participate in the negotiation.

Following the discourse of Chapter 3, it is treated here as axiomatic that negotiation provides the framework for mediated solutions.[2] Mediation does not exist without negotiation; negotiation exists without mediation.[3] An understanding of the elements of mediation can only be gleaned through an understanding of negotiation.[4] It provides the analytical charter for the

---

1 P. Morgan, *Frost/Nixon* (London: Faber & Faber, 2006). The play's character, Swifty Lazar, Richard Nixon's agent, is telling Nixon about negotiating a deal with David Frost for a series of interviews Frost wants to conduct with Nixon on Frost's television show at 13–15.
2 Portions of this chapter have been published in D. De Girolamo, "The Negotiation Process: Exploring Negotiator Moves Through a Processual Framework" (2013) 28(2) *Ohio St. J. Disp. Resol.* (in press).
3 This description of the relationship between mediation and negotiation was articulated by one of my village mediators during the course of mediation. The mediation is reported in Case Study 8.
4 Pruitt and Carnevale speak of the need for an integrated theory of negotiation and mediation. They see an integrated model as a communication network where the mediator straddles the communication line between the parties, creating two communication lines with

study of mediation as assisted negotiation, a framework critical to the development of theory.[5] The first step to a theoretical and practical understanding of mediation as it exists in the real world is to gain an insight into the structure of negotiation. Its structure is mediation's processual shape, since it is the process by which negotiated order is achieved. To understand the negotiation process is to understand the process of the mediation, as mediation takes place within a negotiatory framework. It is within this conceptual framework of negotiation that mediation will be analysed in subsequent chapters. The intent is to highlight the nature of the interactions of parties at the mediation table – it will contextualize the interactions to illustrate the reality of the mediation process experienced by its participants.

The study of negotiation offers the researcher a number of analytical frames through which to conduct an exploration. Theorists have approached negotiation as a series of strategic moves defined by the nature of the moves, as irrational human behaviour due to cognitive realities affecting decision-making or as a process of interactions.[6] Arguably, negotiation is an amalgam of all three. Negotiation involves decision-making, interaction through communication between the decision-makers, norms and psychological factors impacting on the decision-makers, the resource desired or protected by the decision-makers and a little-known opponent faced by each of the decision-makers. In essence, negotiation is about joint decision-making involving parties in conflict who strive to communicate with an opponent within a normative and psychological context about a resource they want or do not wish to give up. The process involves social interaction. Cognitive influences

---

each line linking the mediator with one of the parties. Although this is not specifically what this chapter seeks to do, the Pruitt and Carnevale reference is noted as an example of another attempt to combine mediation and negotiation analytical theory. See generally, D.G. Pruitt and P.J. Carnevale, *Negotiation in Social Conflict* (Buckingham: Open University Press, 1993) at 196.

5 L.G. Stenelo, *Mediation in International Negotiations* (Malmo, Sweden: Nordens boktryckeri (Studentlitteratur), 1972), translated by E.C. Coble. As Stenelo states, a "conceptual framework can be seen as an embryo to a theory" providing a 'classification instrument'; see at 14.

6 Sebenius offers a summary of four such frameworks: "To take but a few examples, these range from the popular Getting to Yes (Fisher, Ury and Paton 1991) world of interests and best alternative to a negotiated agreement, to more formal game-theoretic accounts of strategic interaction and asymmetric information (see Schelling 1960; Raiffa, Richardson and Metcalfe 2002), to the behavioral lenses of cognitive and social psychologists (see Bazerman and Neale 1991; Thompson 2001), and to the '3-D' world of setup, deal design, and tactics intended to create and claim value on a sustainable basis (see Lax and Sebenius 2006)." J.K. Sebenius, "Review Essay: What Can We Learn from Great Negotiations?" (2011) *Negotiation J.* 251 at 253. See also, for example, C. Menkel-Meadow, "Why Hasn't the World Gotten to Yes? An Appreciation and Some Reflections" (2006) *Negotiation J.* 485, and R. Hollander-Blumoff, "Just Negotiation" (2010–11) 88 *Wash. U. L. Rev.* 381 for summaries of the legal negotiation literature.

inform the social interaction. Strategic moves occur within the process. Neither cognitive influences nor strategic moves alone, however, constitute negotiation. They are elements of a process that *is* negotiation. Decisions need to be made within a process of continual social interaction. This process furnishes the foundation of negotiation. It is this view of negotiation that will inform the analysis.

Strategy and patterns: approaches to process

For the purpose of this study, focus will be on the process of negotiation; that is, the moves of the parties from the beginning to the end of a negotiation. This is pitted against a strategic approach which sees negotiation as strategic decision-making and action, defining negotiation through tactics used by negotiators to achieve their strategic goals. Strategies are plans invoked to attain negotiation goals, while tactics are the tools used to implement the strategies. The negotiation becomes a competitive, cooperative or integrative strategic exercise in the furtherance of particular goals.

The processual theorists do not generally use strategy as an analytic tool to examine negotiation. They reduce negotiation to stages or categories of patterns. They seek to uncover what occurs during the process itself. Process is not about either strategy or tactics. It is about the way in which the negotiation unfolds and the patterns, if any, that are discernible. Strategies and tactics are used throughout the process for certain purposes, but they are not what ultimately define the negotiation process for these theorists.

It can be difficult to discern the divide between the two concepts of process and strategy. Some use strategic moves to define the patterns of action; others delineate stages without applying a strategic focus. As an example of the former where strategic moves are relevant, Stevens argues that the phases of negotiation are clearly demarcated by the strategies undertaken by parties in the phases.[7] Stenelo too agrees that there is strategic identification of phases, but is of the view that strategy alone will not identify the particular phase of the negotiation.[8] For him, the identification of strategic goals and the strategies used to achieve these goals will demarcate the particular stages of a negotiation. Stenelo and Stevens, arguably, see an integrated model of process and strategy: strategy and strategic goals define the process.

Beginning with Stevens, competitive and cooperative strategies define the particular stages of negotiation. For him, there are two stages of negotiation, being the early and later (pre-deadline) stages. Negotiators are competitive in the early stages of the negotiation and become cooperative in the later stages.[9]

---

7 C.M. Stevens, *Strategy and Collective Bargaining Negotiation* (New York: McGraw-Hill, 1963) at 10, for example.
8 Stenelo, see note 5 at 86–7.
9 Stevens, see note 7 at 10–11.

The competitive tactics include not only coercion and deception, as noted by Stevens, but also 'vigorous speeches in support of firm positions', surprise and consternation in response and large initial offers delivered as part of a functional ritualistic exchange of information.[10] The tactics of cooperation and coordination are not as easily discernible: the issue in the later stage is how to convey one's changed position without undermining one's bargaining power.[11]

Although for Stevens the strategies demarcate the point at which the negotiation is proceeding, he concedes that the strategies are not rigid. For example, there can be strategic movement between the stages in that cooperative moves may occur in the early stage. Despite this, Stevens continues to be of the view that the two-stage negotiation cycle, as he terms it, is supportable.[12] He states further that a divide exists between the stages and is crossed during the process. It is the crossing of the divide that shifts the strategic action from competitive to cooperative action. The divide is the manifestation of a contract zone, defined as "a range of outcomes each of which is preferred by both parties to no contract" that is critical to the negotiation; without one, there cannot be agreement.[13]

Strategies, however, are an insufficient determinative of the stages of negotiation, according to Stenelo. He does not believe that one can ascertain how far a negotiation has progressed by looking only to the tactics used by the parties. In his view, one needs to look at the substantive goals sought to be achieved as well as the strategies used to achieve the goals.[14] He divides the negotiation process into three stages using strategic goals as the 'primary classification criterion'.[15] In the initial stage, parties seek to determine the negotiation range, defined as the parties' estimate of all the possible outcomes for resolution. In so doing, during this stage, the parties deal with the agenda and other procedural issues. It is imperative, says Stenelo, that the parties jointly define the strategic goal to be reached before the negotiation can proceed any further. The strategies used in this initial stage include information exchange to help establish the bargaining range, persuasive strategies to alter the other party's view of the bargaining range and the use of commitments through initial demands.[16]

The intermediate stage finds the parties dealing with the establishment of the contract zone, defined by Stenelo as "the total number of acceptable negotiation outcomes which remain after all the parties, on the basis of the current

---

10 Ibid. at 59–64.
11 Ibid. at 98–9, 104.
12 Ibid. at 11.
13 Ibid. at 10, 97.
14 Stenelo, see note 5 at 89.
15 Ibid. at 91.
16 For a discussion of the initial stage, ibid. at 91–101.

negotiation range, have rejected certain alternatives as unacceptable".[17] This differs from the negotiation range of the first phase in that the negotiation range estimates all possible outcomes, while the contract zone estimates acceptable outcomes. The action required in this stage is compromise, yet the parties seek to minimize commitment and desire to retain as much bargaining freedom as possible while trying to influence the other to yield. The resulting strategies used include testing of positions, concessions, bluffs, threats and promises.[18]

The final stage involves joint action. The parties work together to reach agreement within the parameters set by the contract zone. Their actions are limited by the reduction in the number of alternatives available to them. The strategies used in this final stage may include those used in the earlier stages: influencing the evaluations of the alternatives through use of principles and information exchange (to a lesser degree than occurred in the initial stage).[19]

The reliance on strategies as indicators of the process of negotiation is not particularly helpful. The Stevens and Stenelo characterizations are broad, and ultimately do not serve to distinguish the processual components of negotiation. The discussion is about strategies. Strategies denote the early and late stages of the process, yet strategies may jump the processual boundaries of their stages. As for Stenelo's added requirement of strategic goal in defining process, goals are like the strategies that are used to attain them: they also may change throughout the course of the negotiation and may not be restricted to processual demarcation. In the end, what we are discussing in the Stenelo and Stevens models are strategies, not process.

Ann Douglas, in her consideration of the negotiation process of the labour industry, begins to move away from a strategic approach in considering process, yet does not forsake strategy completely.[20] She too reduces the process to three phases and she too examines the actions taken by the parties in each phase. One might argue that she also defines the process by actions taken. On closer look, however, one sees that she separates the stages according to what occurs as a result of the parties' actions during the negotiation rather than by strategic moves taken by the parties. She is not concerned with the strategic approaches and decisions made by the parties to progress the negotiation; she is concerned with actions taken and results achieved during the negotiation. Their actions define three stages of the process: (i) *establishing the bargaining range*; (ii) *reconnoitring the range*; and (iii) *precipitating the decision-making crisis*.

---

17 Ibid. at 101.
18 For a discussion of the intermediate stage, ibid. at 101–6.
19 For a discussion of the final stage, ibid. at 106–11.
20 A. Douglas, "The Peaceful Settlement of Industrial and Intergroup Disputes" (1957) 1 *Conflict Resolution* 69.

In the first phase, 'establishing the bargaining range', the parties set out their positions. There appears to be a great divide between the parties: they ferociously state positions that appear to be irreconcilable. This is a necessary stage because it permits parties to assess how firm the other will be in the process. Critical in this stage, says Douglas, is the awareness by all that the chasm existing between the parties as illustrated in this first phase must be reduced and movement towards one another's position must occur if there is to be agreement.[21]

In the second stage, 'reconnoitring the range', the parties seek to determine the bargaining range, referred to as "a stretch of territory within which the parties propose to move around until they can reach consensus on a single settlement point".[22] Parties assess the extent to which there will be movement from the opponent's original stated position. This is the phase during which the parties attempt to discern the potential areas of agreement, whereas in phase one the parties seek to determine areas of disagreement. According to Douglas, however, it is difficult to distinguish between these two phases of the process, except to the acute observer. The movement is subtle. It is in the second phase that assessments of the opponent are made and judgments based on the assessment taken: parties are assessing how firm to be and what concessions the other will make.[23]

The third phase, 'precipitating the decision-making crisis', is when the parties must decide whether the final offer is on the table, and whether to accept that offer.[24]

Gerald Williams' phases of negotiation differ from the Stevens, Stenelo and Douglas models in that he does not apply the concept of the bargaining ranges, extensively used by the other three.[25] Williams seems to use a more generalized approach to define negotiation stages, relying on the nature of negotiator actions. Williams describes the phases as follows: (i) *orientation and positioning*, which refers to the first involvement of lawyers in the dispute, the exchange of communication, and the formulation and articulation of opening positions, with particular strategies framing the positions;[26] (ii) *argumentation*, which works to reduce the distance between the parties that exists in the first stage through information exchange and concessions;[27] (iii) *emergence and crisis*, which involves uncovering and lowering expectations through the use

---

21 For a discussion of phase one, ibid. at 72–5.
22 Ibid. at 73.
23 For a discussion of phase two, ibid. at 75–80.
24 For discussion of phase three, ibid. at 80–1.
25 G.R. Williams, *Legal Negotiation and Settlement* (St Paul, MN: West Publishing Co., 1983) at 72–84.
26 Ibid. at 72–9.
27 Ibid. at 79–81.

of deadlines and the inter-relational dynamics of the parties;[28] and (iv) *agreement*, where the details are worked out or final breakdown occurs and the parties cease to negotiate.[29] Zartman too moves away from bargaining ranges as an anchor to the process, and instead looks more generally to the phases of a negotiation.[30] His model is similar to Williams' in that they both focus on preparation, communication and bargaining action (although not termed as such). Zartman describes his three phases as *diagnosis, formulation* and *specification*, where the first involves preparatory work, the second deals with the search for a shared understanding of the nature of the problem, the terms of trade and a sense of justice, and the last phase focuses on the details of the agreement emerging from the previous phase, 'formulation'.[31]

The most comprehensive treatise on the negotiation process is provided by Gulliver in *Disputes and Negotiation*.[32] Although having regard to a western labour dispute, he primarily relies upon ethnographic data obtained from his study of the Ndendeuli and Arusha of Tanzania to deconstruct the process.[33] For Gulliver, there is a hybrid processual model of negotiation. One aspect of the model is a cyclical network of information exchange and learning, and the other is a developmental model of eight stages of the negotiation process. The cyclical network informs each of the eight stages of the process.[34] As information is exchanged, learning is enhanced and assessments are made. Strategies and tactical decisions are dependent on the flow of, and the assessments made from, the information disclosed. Strategies about the extent of information to

---

28 Ibid. at 81–3.
29 Ibid. at 84–5.
30 W. Zartman, "Processes and Stages" in A.K. Schneider and C. Honeyman, eds, *The Negotiator's Fieldbook: The Desk Reference for the Experienced Negotiator* (Washington, DC: American Bar Association, Section of Dispute Resolution, 2006) 95. Negotiation as a *capoeira*, a Brazilian dance, is explored in M. Young and E. Schlie, "The Rhythm of the Deal: Negotiation as a Dance" (2011) *Negotiation J.* 191, which sees negotiation going through three phases: dance of position, dance of empathy, dance of concessions.
31 Zartman, ibid. at 96–7.
32 P.H. Gulliver, *Disputes and Negotiations: A Cross-cultural Perspective* (New York: Academic Press, 1979). Green and Wheeler would disagree, seeing Gulliver's processual framework as merely descriptive without offering guidance on how to move through the phases: G.M. Green and M. Wheeler, "Awareness and Action in Critical Moments" (2004) *Negotiation J.* 349 at 353. Holmes, on the other hand, finds Gulliver's framework applicable in wider circumstances including the analysis of hostage negotiation: M.E. Holmes, "Optimal Matching Analysis of Negotiation Phase Sequences in Simulated and Authentic Hostage Negotiations" (1997) 10 *Communication Reports* 1.
33 P.H. Gulliver, *Neighbours and Networks: The Idiom of Kinship in Social Action among the Ndendeuli of Tanzania* (London: University of California Press, 1971); P.H. Gulliver, *Social Control in An African Society: A Study of the Arusha: Agricultural Masai of Northern Tanganyika* (London: Routledge, 2000 edition). See Chapter 1 herein for discussion.
34 Gulliver, see note 32 at 82.

Negotiated order 79

be exchanged are invoked, as are strategies about how to maintain and attain preferred goals. Parties readjust their preferences and action plans as information is exchanged. They make decisions about their views, expectations and desired outcomes based on the information they disclose and receive during the process. As information and learning continue, issues become clearer and potential outcomes are revealed.[35]

Inextricably linked to the cyclical processual model of information exchange and learning is the 'developmental model', comprising successive phases through which negotiators progress as they get closer to resolution. It is not a linear model, as the one suggested by Menkel-Meadow;[36] rather, it is one in which the phases could overlap, two or more could occur simultaneously, or there is a return to a prior phase.[37] Gulliver believes, however, that the phases must be completed by the parties for an agreement to be reached. His eight phases constitute the whole of the negotiation process; negotiators must pass through all for agreement to be achievable because they must experience for themselves the learning and adjustment that occur with each phase.[38] Douglas is also of the view that the phases must be played out before the parties reach the point where they are ready to accept the other's 'best and final offer'.[39] If they are not, agreement will not be reached.

Gulliver's eight phases, which must be traversed by the parties, are as follows:

1 *Search for an arena* – Once the dispute is acknowledged, a decision must be made as to where the negotiation will take place.
2 *Composition of agenda and definition of issues* – The issues to be dealt with and the frame within which the issues will be examined are explored.
3 *Establishing maximal limits to issues in dispute* – The parties begin to discuss their positions, advising of their preferences and seeking to learn of the other's 'real' preferences. The phase is marked by "shows of strength and suggestions or forthright assertions of resoluteness and threat. Comments are made on the alleged moral and practical weakness of the opponent

---

35 For the discussion about the cyclical model of information exchange and learning, ibid. at xvii, 83–120.
36 C. Menkel-Meadow, "Toward Another View of Legal Negotiation: The Structure of Problem-solving" (1983–84) 31 *U.C.L.A. L. Rev.* 754 at 759–60. Menkel-Meadow sees a linear model of negotiation comprising orientation (the competitive strategy that colours the approach, whether it is adversarial or problem-solving) that leads to a mindset about attainable outcomes (through meeting needs or maximizing gains), which affects the behaviour (strategic behaviour is referred to here), which affects the solution (whether it is a compromise or a creative one).
37 Gulliver, see note 32 at 121.
38 Ibid. at 174–9.
39 Douglas, see note 20 at 79–80.

and the errors or mendacity in his statements. Personal and group animosities are often brought into the open: animadversions to social, moral, and personal faults in ad hominem attacks on members of the other party, in contrast to the high motives and meritorious qualities of one's own party. Ideological banners are waved (e.g., workers' rights, the moral unity of the group, ideal norms of neighborliness) and supporting references are made to cultural rules, ethical standards, and evocative symbols."[40] The aim, during this phase, is to determine where to set initial demands despite the fact that there appears to be a deep divide between the parties, with little hope for agreement.

4   *Narrowing the differences* – There is movement from disagreement to coordination with an offer that reflects a possible outcome rather than a preferred outcome. A number of strategies may be used during this phase, including dealing with issues in the order as they are placed on the agenda, dealing with the most important issues first, reducing the issues to a common objective, dealing with less difficult issues first, and trading on issues. Concessions and compromise occur, and alternatives considered.

5   *Preliminaries to final bargaining* – The parties clarify facts and set the stage for final bargaining by finding a viable range, narrowing viable alternatives, agreeing on trading between issues or alternatives, and creating a bargaining formula.

6   *Final bargaining* – A stage consisting of the exchange of proposals of a specific and substantive nature on the terms necessary for agreement. The main strategy used here includes concession-making.

7   *Ritual affirmation by the parties of the agreement* – Some act of blessing, recording, confirming, or announcing the achievement of the agreement is carried out once the parties have reached agreement.

8   *Execution of the agreement*.[41]

The phases reflect the ever-moving social interaction between individuals. The models are not intended to reflect the definitive model of the negotiation process, says Gulliver. They are to provide insight into real-life negotiation and as such, are not precise. In fact, the model "reflects the untidiness of actual social behaviour".[42] Despite the 'untidiness', however, there is a pattern that is exposed that "reflects the reality of a general, overall trend from relative ignorance, uncertainty, and antagonism toward increased understanding,

---

40   Gulliver, see note 32 at 137.
41   For discussion about phase one, ibid. at 122–6; for phase two, ibid. at 126–35; for phase three, ibid. at 135–41; for phase four, ibid. at 141–53; for phase five, ibid. at 153–60; for phase six, ibid. at 160–8; for phase seven, ibid. at 169; for phase eight, ibid. at 170.
42   Ibid. at 173.

greater certainty, and coordination".[43] Where this pattern is missing, according to Gulliver, the negotiation fails.[44] This accords with his insistence, as previously mentioned, that each of the phases must be experienced if the parties are to reach agreement. The phases form part of an integrated whole without which agreement will not be reached.

Roberts and Palmer adopt the Gulliver model, with some tweaks.[45] They would separate Gulliver's second phase of 'composition of agenda and definition of issues' into distinct sequential phases. They see the need to do so because the identification of issues is a difficult phase requiring party engagement and transformations of views. As such, it should stand alone to signify its substantive value. The other change deals with the lack of an intermediate step between Gulliver's 'final bargaining' and 'ritual affirmation'. Roberts and Palmer view Gulliver's 'ritual affirmation' as assuming that agreement is easily reached from 'final bargaining'. The authors see a need to recognize when agreement is reached in the process. As they explain, 'final bargaining' may be the moment when the parties are aware of agreement being within reach, but there is still work to do to get to agreement. Once agreement is reached, 'ritual confirmation' occurs.[46]

It is the processual framework, as espoused by all these scholars, through which the investigation of negotiation occurs in this chapter. There is no doubt that strategy plays an important role in negotiation. Decisions need to be made throughout a negotiation about how to progress it further. These decisions can be described as strategic decisions in the sense that they are aimed at a plan, even if the plan is, at its most simplistic, to achieve some sort of outcome. However, the decisions need to be made within a process of continual social interaction. It is the frame of social interaction that denotes the process; it is human behaviour that creates and carries out the strategic move.

Phases of negotiation revealed[47]

As a participant-observer at mediations, I was an observer of the negotiation process. As Menkel-Meadow states, observing mediations can illuminate the negotiation process: it discloses what negotiators do during the process; it discloses the process itself.[48] Gulliver speaks of the need to understand the

---

43 Ibid.
44 Ibid.
45 S. Roberts and M. Palmer, *Dispute Processes: ADR and the Primary Forms of Decision-making*, (Cambridge: Cambridge University Press, 2005) at 129–30.
46 Ibid. at 130.
47 The following discussion of the phases, including case summaries and analysis, have been published in De Girolamo, see note 2.
48 C. Menkel-Meadow, "Lawyer Negotiations: Theories and Realities – What We Learn from Mediation" (1993) 56 *Mod. L. Rev.* 361 at 371–5. With respect to negotiations themselves, Menkel-Meadow notes the need for "a good empirical picture of what negotiators

real-life patterns of negotiation. His examination of negotiation is based on real-life data.[49] Similarly, this study of negotiation relies on real-life data to deconstruct the negotiation process through an analysis of what occurs during the process. It intends to build on existing theoretical knowledge of the process through real-life data analysis. The perspective follows Gulliver's approach in many ways – it provides a descriptive analysis of the negotiation process through ethnographic data of negotiations obtained during observations of mediations.[50] In so doing, it is influenced by Gulliver's methodology and revisits his processual model as well as those espoused by other processual theorists such as Stevens, Stenelo and Douglas.[51] An attempt will be made to articulate a processual framework for negotiation through case-study analysis of mediations observed during my period of fieldwork research.[52] These phases are described and analysed through six case studies, each reflecting a stage in the process. Together, they offer a processual framework for negotiation.

For the purposes of this study, the negotiation begins upon arrival at the arena established by the parties in advance of the negotiation session. It is recognized that the establishment of the arena may well involve negotiation and bargaining; however, this stage is not the subject of this analysis. Although some theorists describe the pre-negotiation activities as a phase to negotiation, the intent of this chapter is to understand the mechanics of the interactions that occur during the actual negotiation session at which these interactions take place.[53] In addition, the ethnographic data regarding this preliminary phase is to a large extent unknown, with the exception of the known fact that the parties have agreed to have the Organization administer

---

    actually do outside of laboratory settings in a wide variety of real-world settings": see C. Menkel-Meadow, "Chronicling the Complexification of Negotiation Theory and Practice" (2009) *Negotiation J.* 415 at 423–4.

49 Gulliver, see note 32 generally and specifically at 65.
50 Ibid. at 60–7.
51 See earlier discussion herein regarding their views.
52 The methodology of case study analysis was discussed in Chapter 1 and will be explored further in Chapter 5. For the purposes of this chapter, portions of six mediated negotiations are textualized. The textualization differs from the case studies of Chapters 5 and 6 in that the focus in those chapters is on mediator and party interaction, whereas the focus in this chapter is on processual action. See further discussion of the case study method in Chapter 5 and of the ethnographic approach in Chapter 1.
53 Most notably of the theorists, Gulliver describes phase one as establishing the arena for the negotiation: Gulliver, see note 32 at 122–6. See, for other examples, Williams, see note 25 at 72–9, Zartman, see note 30 at 96–7 and C.M. Hancyz, "Strategic Negotiation: Moving Through the Stages" in C.M. Hanycz, T.C.W. Farrow and F.H. Zemans, *The Theory and Practice of Representative Negotiation* (Toronto: Emond Montgomery, 2008) 67 at 69–81.

the process, including scheduling the dates and arena for the mediation, as discussed earlier.[54]

My observation of mediations suggests six distinct phases during which parties attempt to resolve their dispute. It must be remembered that these phases are examined in the context of the negotiation process, not the mediation process, despite the fact that they occur during mediations that form part of my ethnographic data.[55] As a result, the case description and subsequent analysis do not focus on the presence of the third-party intervener; instead, they focus on the negotiation process through which the parties move to reach agreement.

On the basis of the ethnographic data emerging from my fieldwork experience, I propose a six-phase process of negotiation: (i) *unilateral articulation of positions*; (ii) *information exchange*; (iii) *testing of positions*; (iv) *shift in position*; (v) *bargaining proposals*; and (vi) *joint decision-making for final agreement*. Obviously, this last phase, 'joint decision-making for final agreement', is not reached where impasse remains and the parties do not reach consensus. Similar to the pre-negotiation activities, this analysis does not examine post-negotiation activities of the parties.[56] For the purposes of this analysis, the negotiation ends when the parties leave the arena. Each of these phases is discussed below and the chapter concludes with an analysis of these phases within a processual arc forming the structure of the negotiation process.

---

54 In this preliminary phase involving the Organization, negotiation of the dates, arena and mediator selection is often required. This negotiation occurs either directly between the parties and/or their representatives, or through the Organization's personnel. If the former, the ethnographic data is scarce as I was not present for those negotiations. If the latter, then the team members (sometimes, the author) were the intermediaries who communicated with the parties individually to determine preferences and organize the requirements for the mediation to take place, and therefore in those circumstances some information is known.

55 See Chapter 2 for discussion of the mediation village and the context within which the negotiations occurred. Also, recall the discussion about the normative order within which mediation occurs, in Chapter 1. The existence and impact of the normative order on the mediation process will be seen in this and subsequent chapters. For the purposes of this chapter, it is necessary to be aware of the position of negotiation within a normative order. Negotiation is not isolated from the influences of such an order: Menkel-Meadow, see note 36 at 766; Gulliver, see note 32 at 193; Roberts and Palmer, see note 45 at 114. See also D. De Girolamo, "Seeking Negotiated Order Through Mediation: A Manifestation of Legal Culture?" (2012) 5 *J. of Comp. Law* 118, and in D. Nelken, ed., *Using Legal Culture* (London: Wildy, Simmonds & Hill, 2012) 153, which examines the relationship of rules, norms and social process in the context of a legal culture analysis.

56 Also, as is the case with the pre-negotiation activities, the ethnographic data is not sufficient to present a cogent articulation of events occurring post-negotiation.

The six phases[57]

Unilateral articulation of positions

Invariably the mediators invite the parties to make a preliminary presentation of their positions. This is the first phase of the negotiation process. It begins the negotiation. The parties are insular – they think only of their own positions.

Case Study 1: Personal injury negotiation – the falling crane

The Claimant, Henry Smith, was injured while performing his job. He was a photographer's assistant for a building supply magazine. He was on a construction site, holding large lights attached to the photographer's camera, when he and the photographer, Joe Austen, walked beneath the path of a building crane to photograph the crane for the magazine. While being lowered, a piece of the crane broke off and fell on Smith, breaking his back. Smith sued his employer, the owner of the land on which the crane was situated, the owner of the crane, the photographer Austen, and a crane repair expert who supplied the crane and who was on site at the time of the injury, all for negligence. All parties were in attendance, as were their legal representatives.

The parties entered an enormous boardroom for their first meeting. The room was awash in a sea of blue from all the lawyers' suits. Smith sat at the head of the room, clothed in grey and sitting in his wheelchair, flanked by his wife and his legal team.

The first articulation of position was by Smith's counsel. He began by referring to the fact that if the matter were not resolved, then Smith would take the case to trial. He spoke of Smith's age and pointed to the fact that Smith had no choice but to follow Austen while Austen was photographing the crane. He referred to Austen's evidence. He said Smith was taken by surprise. Smith was forced to run with Austen; he was not told to stay back. He referred to the evidence regarding the moments before the crane collapsed: no one told Smith to stay back. The barrister then spoke of the legal responsibility of the various defendants: of the employer for failing to ensure a safe workplace and for being vicariously liable for the actions of Austen, one of its employees; of the owner of the land for failing to cordon off the area around the crane and for failure to warn of the danger; of the crane expert who failed to warn and exclude persons from the site; and of Austen who led Smith to danger as the person in charge of the shoot. He spoke of foreseeable risk, the danger associated with the site, and the failures of the defendants to prevent injury. In support of the position, some evidence was referred to. The barrister concluded by anticipating the positions of the defendants and categorically denying contributory negligence on the part of Smith.

---

57 For the sake of anonymity, the names of the participants and selective details of the disputes in the case studies have been altered.

The employer-defendant, Construction Enterprises, began through its barrister by offering statements of sympathy to Smith and a recognition that it was prepared to contribute to a settlement – however, only on the basis of a fair proportion of responsibility to be divided among the defendants and also Smith. Construction Enterprises made clear from the outset that contributory negligence was to be included in the determination of an appropriate outcome. The barrister then promptly denied that Construction Enterprises was in fact the employer of Smith or Austen, as alleged by Smith; however, the barrister acknowledged a potential contractual obligation owed to them by Construction Enterprises. This was immediately followed by an articulation of the causes of the injury, laying blame on others including Smith: the area should have been cordoned off by the owner of the property to create a barrier to the crane, as he invited the crane to be photographed and therefore should have made the area safe for guests; the crane expert should have ensured the safety of the area and provided warnings of the danger as he ought to have known that the crane would break as it was being lowered; Austen should have seen the danger and should not have wandered beneath the crane; and due to the sheer folly of Smith walking beneath the crane when it was being lowered, Smith was contributorily negligent. For this argument, the barrister used the analogy of a tree being felled: no one would walk under a tree as it was being felled. As for Construction Enterprises' responsibility, it was so obvious that someone should not walk beneath the crane that there was no need to issue a warning. He concluded by apportioning the responsibility as 15 per cent to Smith, with the remaining 85 per cent of the liability to be attributed to the owner of the land at 30 per cent, Construction Enterprises at 10 per cent, Austen at 20 per cent and the crane expert at 40 per cent.

The owner of the land was next in the progression of the articulation of the positions. Through his barrister, he also expressed his sympathies and acknowledged the horrific consequences that resulted from the accident before embarking on the reasons why he was not responsible for the injury. Three parties were responsible: Smith, Austen and Construction Enterprises. Construction Enterprises had been given warnings and instructions that it should have passed to its employees; Smith and Austen had heard these instructions; and it was self-evident that Smith and Austen should not have walked beneath the path of the crane, using the tree-felling analogy introduced by Construction Enterprises. He said that Smith was plainly foolish for walking under the crane and bore considerable responsibility. The owner of the land was responsible for taking reasonable steps to make the area reasonably safe, which it did by advising parties where to stand and by advising where the crane would be lowered. The barrister ended by stating that he had not heard anything suggesting his client was liable.

The crane expert followed. He began also by expressing his sympathies for Smith and advised that he would not repeat the allegations concerning Smith's liability. He described himself as having expertise with the crane and being a business associate of the landowner. He supplied the crane but had no further involvement with the crane, nor had any responsibility. The landowner who owned the crane retained an experienced engineer who looked after the crane. The crane expert had no authority over visitors to the site. He was merely on the site to provide a piece of equipment at the request of the landowner. He was not in control of the operation. His view of liability, in descending order of apportionment, was as follows: (1) Construction Enterprises was primarily responsible as Smith was its employee and it was in charge of the shoot. It failed to conduct a risk assessment to ensure the safety of its workers. (2) The next party bearing responsibility was Austen, who was responsible for Smith. (3) Smith was contributorily negligent, but the crane expert declined to develop reasons for this view. (4) Finally, the remaining share of responsibility was on the landowner. However, if the crane expert were to be found liable, he would turn to his insurers who were made a party to the action and who were denying insurance coverage under the terms of an insurance policy.

Austen began in the same way as the others: he expressed his sympathy for Smith. He referred to the fact that Smith and he were cousins and that Smith had received an expression of regret from Austen directly, but it would be inappropriate not to echo the expressions of sympathy stated by the others. He began differently from the others, not referring immediately to his view of the liabilities, but rather to a need that the issue between the crane expert and his insurer be determined so that there was certainty for each of the parties about the crane expert's liquidity and insurance status, as it may impact Smith's willingness to accept an apportionment offered by the defendants. For Austen the landowner was the principal villain, as he had invited Construction Enterprises to photograph the crane and so it was incumbent on him to ensure that everything was safe because he knew when the crane would be lowered and what was involved. There was plenty of time for warnings to be given. The landowner and crane expert should have warned them and there was no evidence that such warning was given. The barrister for Austen then went through the evidence in detail supporting Austen's position. He went on to stress the crane expert's responsibility for the crane: he should have ensured that the crane worked safely; he knew what dangers were involved and he should have taken precautions. Construction Enterprises was also responsible. It was responsible for the health and safety of all involved. As for Smith's case against Austen, Smith relied on the special relationship between them and on Austen for his safety. Austen pointed out that he was added as a party after the action commenced against the others. Until that point, Austen was going to testify in support of Smith. He pointed to the fact that they do not owe each other a duty of care beyond Donoghue v. Stevenson – that of reasonable care to be exercised to those who could be foreseeably affected by his conduct. The analogy of the tree-felling did not apply; rather, it was one of two adults holding hands crossing the street. Smith was responsible for his own safety.

The final defendant to speak was the crane expert's insurer. He too began by expressing sympathy for Smith. The barrister said that he would not discuss insurance law. He said he did not know how anyone could say that the crane expert had been in charge. It was the landowner who was in charge. Although having expressed sympathy for Smith, he then began to discuss Smith's conduct. He said the key point in the case on liability was the fact that Smith and Austen chose to walk under a crane being lowered. It was an insult to a man's intelligence to advise him not to walk under the crane in such circumstances, not because it was foreseeable that something would fall off the crane – it was foreseeable that the crane itself could fall. It was complete folly to walk under the crane. The barrister denied that the dispute between the insurer and the crane expert needed to be resolved in order to resolve the claim. The insurer would not roll over. It was in an extremely strong position and was getting stronger as each party kept arguing that the crane expert was in charge and was negligent, because then it would become a case of late notification of the claim [which disentitles coverage]. The insurer said that the test in insurance cases is whether it was reasonable for the insured to believe that the facts give rise to a claim: one cannot allege he is negligent and not know that he was going to be sued. The insurer advised that it would not accept liability and the others should not view the crane expert as being insured. He had not heard anything to convince him otherwise.

Smith then personally spoke, referring to the fact that he had never spoken to such a large group of lawyers. He said the reason he walked under the crane was simple – there was no communication. If he had been told not to do it, he would not have done it. To the insurer, he advised that the insurance company had put his family through hell; for three years they have struggled. He said that there is a need to put in place a fund for people like him who are suffering.[58]

***

The parties articulate their opening positions, which reflect their views about the strengths of their case and the weaknesses of the others'. There is legal posturing, high demands and an emphasis on norms. The session tends to be competitive in terms of tactics and goals: parties seek to set the stage for a winner-take-all scenario.[59] Cognitive elements can be seen to be at play here, including the illusion of superiority and optimism, overconfidence, escalation of commitment, and Pruitt and Carnevale's negotiation scripts involving

---

58 In this particular case, the standard paradigm is extended to include multi-party defendants. However, this does not substantively impact phase one. Each party begins the negotiation with an articulation of their position.
59 The literature is laden with descriptions of the competitive, cooperative and problem-solving bargainer. For general discussion of these models see, for example, Roberts and Palmer, see note 45 at 134–42; D.G. Gifford, "A Context-based Theory of Strategy Selection in Legal Negotiation" (1985) 46 *Ohio St. L. J.* 41 at 44–57; Menkel-Meadow, see note 36 at 817–29; Williams, see note 25 at 53–8 (all discussing generally the models and descriptions of the competitive, cooperative and the problem-solving bargainer).

assumptions made about appropriate negotiating behaviour.[60] The latter point is reflected in the expressions of sympathy for Smith preceding hard-hitting denials of liability by the parties.

Each party takes turns to set out why it is that they are not responsible for the injury suffered by Smith. They speak of the law of negligence, and in particular issues of foreseeability and duties of care. They speak of the evidence of witnesses. They speak of the liabilities of others, but not of themselves. They are setting the stage here for the future discussions. With the exception of Construction Enterprises, which acknowledges that it may have some responsibility, the others do not acknowledge any fault.[61] The statements begin with a human sentiment of sympathy, but these expressions of sympathy are quickly buried in statements about the folly of Smith walking under a crane being lowered. In this introductory phase, we see the emphasis on legal positions and the expression of norms: in the former, it is the law of negligence that figures prominently; with respect to the latter, it is the norm of common sense – do not walk beneath a crane being lowered.

There is a competitive approach taken in this first session by the parties: they insist that they are not liable and therefore by implication will not be contributing to any offer.[62] There is posturing, vigorous dissent, and self-interest at play throughout this initial phase. Essentially, the parties seek to improve their bargaining power by a show of strength. They seek to hide any weakness or show of weakness. However, one cannot say it is this competitive approach that defines the phase, as suggested by Stevens, nor does it assist in determining the bargaining range, as characterized by Stenelo and Douglas.[63] The parties, excepting Construction Enterprises, are at zero in terms of their willingness to accept responsibility. No bargaining range can be ascertained at this time unless one defines bargaining range as including the implicit understanding that there needs to be movement for agreement.[64] That is not being suggested here.

As for Gulliver's developmental model, one could argue that elements of Gulliver's phase two, 'composition of agenda and definition of issues', are evident.[65] The parties in the case may have been defining issues – for example,

---

60 See M.H. Bazerman and M.A. Neale, *Negotiating Rationally* (New York: Free Press, 1993) at 2, 9–11, 56–61 with respect to escalation of commitment, overconfidence, and illusions of superiority and optimism; and Pruitt and Carnevale, see note 4 at 89 regarding negotiation scripts.
61 When seen in context, this acknowledgment is not surprising. Construction Enterprises was a corporate entity with a public profile. It was also the party with the deepest pockets, and it suggested some potential contractual obligation to Smith and Austen.
62 See note 59.
63 See generally, Stevens, see note 7 at 10–11, 57–96; Stenelo, see note 5 at 91–101; and Douglas, see note 20 at 72–3.
64 Douglas, see note 20 at 73.
65 Gulliver, see note 32 at 126–35.

the extent to which the crane falling was foreseeable and also the contributory negligence of Smith. The defining of issues, however, is not the primary aim of the phase here; rather, it is the articulation of the legal position and goal of establishing strength of conviction. This appears to overlap with Gulliver's third phase of 'establishing maximal limits to issues in dispute', during which expressions of strength are made and social, moral and personal faults of the others are expressed while promoting one's own faultless position.[66] There is a great divide between the parties which is illuminated during this initial phase, as suggested by Douglas and Gulliver.[67] There appears to be no possibility for agreement as the parties seem to be entrenched in their respective positions.[68] Williams' characterization of the first phase of 'orientation and positioning' is also relevant here.[69] Lawyers for the parties are communicating their client's opening positions through a competitive orientation to establish their positions as forcefully as they can.

This case provides a typical example of the first phase of the process, with its elements easily discernible. It should be noted, however, that the first phase may not always happen in the way it appears in this case; that is, in a sequential manner whereby each party takes turns to articulate their position. Although it generally occurs in this way, upon occasion it involves discussion of position statements, moving from point to point, party to party. No matter what the form, the outcome is the same. Parties state their positions, focusing on rules and norms. This introductory phase sets the stage for the next phase, 'information exchange'.[70]

Information exchange

During the information exchange phase, the parties disclose facts they believe are important for the furtherance of their position. They are clarifying their positions.

Case Study 2: Nuisance claim – the showering softballs[71]

The parties here are a residential landowner and the owners of a softball association whose pitches were located adjacent to the residential landowner's property.

---

66 Ibid. at 135–41.
67 Douglas, see note 20 at 72–3; and Gulliver, see note 32 at 137–9.
68 In fact, no agreement was reached in this negotiation; however, this does not detract from the example because this exchange is a common feature of the negotiations observed.
69 Williams, see note 25 at 79–81.
70 Some may say that the first phase is also about information exchange. However, there is a distinction. Phase one articulates that which the parties know already. It repeats the way in which they approach the dispute in the legal arena of the civil dispute.
71 An extended version of this case can be found in De Girolamo, see note 55.

The landowner, Marshall Hall, brought action against Maple Leaf Softball Association in nuisance for the invasion of his property by softballs. Both parties were represented by legal advisers. The Association's softball pitches and practice areas had been built a number of years before, on land that had been owned by Hall. Hall sold the land to the Association, knowing that softball pitches would be built on the land. After several years of living adjacent to the pitches, Hall made the allegation that the Association had changed the Association's original plan of development for the land, creating a nuisance as a result. Softballs were damaging his property and were a danger to his family. Hall was now looking to sell his remaining land to a developer for the construction of a large commercial complex. He said the continuing nuisance was a barrier to the sale and development of his land.

The parties gathered at the Association's Club House. The joint meeting room was the Members' Lounge, with vistas of the pitches. The private party meeting rooms were separated by a flight of stairs: the room housing Hall was dark and sombre, whereas the Association Team sat in the Manager's office located at the front of the building with its windows and impression of administrative productivity.

The parties set out their positions: Hall discussed the impact of the flying softballs on his property and the improper action of the Association. The Association stated that the softball situation was foreseeable when Hall sold his land for the development of the pitches, that it had a good defence in contract, and that it would not need to pay for the increasing litigation costs if the matter went to trial.

Once each had taken the opportunity to articulate their position, they began to discuss the facts of the dispute. This occurred with the parties directly in a brief session immediately following the articulation of their positions. It then occurred through the mediator in separate private meetings. During the face-to-face discussion, the parties discussed the events leading to the original sale of the land by Hall to the Association; in particular, they discussed the planning approval for the softball site, when it was approved and by whom. The Association's information was that Hall obtained the approval and sold the land with the planning approval. The purchase of additional property was also discussed and the amendment to planning approval as a result. Hall also raised the issue that a potential solution had been proposed by Hall – that of a netted structure to be placed around the property boundaries.

The next sessions of information exchange occurred through the mediator, where each party discussed their view of the case. Hall spoke of the history of the softball site, the Association's objection to Hall's current Planning Act application for approval of the large commercial development on Hall's current property due to safety concerns over flying softballs, the planning approval history for the softball site, the refusal of the Association to deal with either the problem or Hall, his attempts to deal with the problem, and the potential steps that could be taken to deal with the problem.

The exchange of information continued with the Association Team and the mediator. The discussion centred around the planning approval process, the extent to which softballs landed on Hall's property, the ability of the Association to deal with other neighbours living adjacent to the site, the steps already taken to prevent the softballs from hitting Hall's land, the potential new steps that could be taken, and the Association's own concerns over the intended development of Hall's property into a commercial building site.

The information exchange ended with a site visit to the pitches and practice areas, during which both parties pointed out the origin of the softballs from the site and the path of the softballs over to Hall's land. Hall pointed out where the commercial development would be, where the new buildings would be located on his land and where the softballs have landed on his property. The Association advised of the hitting areas and the pattern of the hill and ditch existing between the properties, which had been planted with trees to create a barrier between the properties.

***

In this second stage of the process, there is a focus on the facts of the dispute and evidentiary concerns. This differs from the first phase when there is more emphasis on the articulation of norms and rules supporting the positions. Here, the parties discuss facts and express what they believe is an appropriate way to resolve the dispute. They are not willing at this stage to accept another view of the facts, be influenced by their opponent's case or be willing to consider possible alternative ways to deal with the dispute other than their own stated options. Again, they appear to be overconfident of their positions. They use this phase to strengthen their bargaining position, hoping to influence the other party as to the merits of their view.

Strategically, they maintain vigorous opposition to their opponent's position and make vigorous statements of their own position. The parties are selective in the information they disclose; much of it is disclosed to support their position. Cognitively, they struggle with the same barriers as existed in phase one – that of overconfidence as well as a sense of superiority and optimism.[72] In addition, there is reliance on readily available information and a failure to look at matters from the opponent's perspective.[73] Wolfe's 'equity seeking' is also evident: Hall wanted an acknowledgment of his suffering over the years.[74] All of this serves to support the competitive tactics used during the phase.

---

72 Bazerman and Neale, see note 60 at 2, 60–1; M.A. Neale and M.H. Bazerman, "Negotiator Cognition and Rationality: A Behavioral Decision Theory Perspective" (1992) 51 *Organizational Behavior & Human Decision Processes* 157 at 160.
73 Pruitt and Carnevale, see note 4 at 85–8, 90–9.
74 P.Y. Wolfe, "How a Mediator Enhances the Negotiation Process" (2005) 46 *N.H.B.J.* 38 at 44.

This phase has no similarity in the Stevens, Stenelo, Douglas or Williams models, but some congruency in Gulliver's phase three, 'establishing maximal limits to issues in dispute', where he says that the phase is marked by "shows of strength and suggestions or forthright assertions of resoluteness and threat".[75] The difference may be in the aims of the phase: Gulliver says his phase is to determine where to set initial demands; here, the aim is to continue to strengthen bargaining power for later stages when proposals are suggested and tested.[76] The parties seek to lay what appears to be the defensive groundwork for the later stages in the negotiation, where they will need to shift their positions if they are to achieve agreement. In other words, they are not so concerned to persuade the other to move as to defend against movement. It appears to be a phase in which the parties seek to establish their firmness of position and reticence of retreat.

Testing of positions

The purpose of this phase is to establish the strengths and weaknesses of each case. By doing so, the parties determine where to place their first offer.

Case Study 3: The services contract – website malfunction

Entertainment Inc. is a website-based entertainment business with a turnover of £50 million per year. It sells theatre, film, concert, day trip and exhibition tickets through its website. In 2005, it contracted with IT Developer Inc. for the development of a new website for its business. The contract price was £2 million. Entertainment alleged that the website was defective and failed to provide what was contracted for. It further alleged that IT Developer's response was inadequate and so took steps to correct the deficiencies. As a result of IT Developer's breaches under the contract for the development and installation of a new website, Entertainment alleged that it sustained damages of £8 million. IT Developer defended on the basis that it provided the proper system and that Entertainment accepted the system upon its completion. It alleged that any deficiencies in the system lay at the feet of Entertainment for hiring staff unskilled in the use of the system. Furthermore, it did not advise IT Developer of the specific alleged deficiencies nor give IT Developer an opportunity to correct any deficiencies.

The fifth floor of the mediator's office provided the forum for this negotiation, with its friendly reception team welcoming the parties and ensuring they were well taken care of. The parties were cordial and friendly during their initial meeting.

---

75 For Gulliver, see note 32 at 137.
76 Gulliver, ibid. at 137–8.

Once positions were articulated and information exchanged, the parties were tested on their positions. This was done directly between the parties and through the mediator.

Entertainment was tested on its view that it was the David of a David and Goliath situation posed by this dispute. In other words, it was tested on its business position and its ability to deal appropriately with the website, given the lack of skill of its employees. It was also questioned about its decision to scrap the website developed by IT Developer 18 months after its installation and about the benefit it received from the website during the 18-month period. Entertainment was also questioned about its assertion that its team was able to rebuild the website within a three-month period, the fact that it rebuilt the website without giving IT Developer an opportunity to remedy the defects, and the fact that the damages could be limited to the cost of the rebuild. Difficulties with its loss-of-profit claim were made clear, as was the fact that IT Developer would not agree to pay the £8 million Entertainment was seeking in compensation.

As for IT Developer, the value received for payment made was questioned. It was also made clear to IT Developer that Entertainment would not accept the token payment IT Developer was inclined to offer, on the basis of its view of the strength of its position which it had maintained throughout the negotiation thus far. It was reminded that Entertainment had spent £2 million for a system it was no longer using. It was also reminded that IT Developer had acknowledged that there were some difficulties with the system, albeit minor difficulties. The value of the system needed to be considered by IT Developer, which it was failing to do. IT Developer was also challenged on its intent to calculate any compensation as a proportion of the profits it made from the contract with Entertainment. Throughout the testing of IT Developer, IT Developer threatened to cease the negotiations if Entertainment did not alter its view of its case.

***

The strengths of positions are tested in this phase. To a certain extent, this phase may be similar to Williams' second phase of 'argumentation', where he says that the parties work to reduce the distance between them, or to Douglas' second stage of 'reconnoitring the range', where the parties seek to establish a bargaining range.[77] The parties reduce the distance not by numbers, but by trying to undermine the other's confidence in their own case. As for establishing the bargaining range, they do so in their attempts to lower the expectations of their opponent's desired outcome and to increase the expectation of their opponent's view of *their* desired outcome. This stage continues to fall within Gulliver's stage three, 'establishing maximal limits to issues in dispute'.[78] Parties are continuing to thrust and parry what they perceive to be

77 Williams, see note 25 at 79–81; Douglas, see note 20 at 73.
78 Gulliver, see note 32 at 135–41.

strong positions. They have not yet begun to consider real potential outcomes. It is not until the movement into the next phase that shifts in positions occur.

The strategies used in this case include reliance on evidentiary issues relating to the proof of the positions, discussion of legal obligations and remedies, threats, and firm articulation of views and opinions regarding the merits of positions. These strategies continue to be of the same character as those used in phases one and two. Essentially, the parties engage in strategic distributive conduct: the unwillingness to accede to any form of compromise, the demand for unilateral concessions, the unrelenting hold on a positive view of one's case with the accompanying denial of weakness in any form, and the need to ensure that the pie is divided unequally – more for one than the other.[79] Within this phase, the escalation of commitment occurs to create a cognitive barrier when Entertainment made clear that it would not accept a token payment. Another example of such a barrier is in the inability of both parties to see the other's perspective: for example, from Entertainment's perspective the payment of £2 million for a system that did not provide the expected service, and from IT's perspective the lack of opportunity to correct the defect.

Shift in position

Critical to the negotiation process is the change that occurs to a party's self-assessment of its position. The move into the bargaining phase of negotiation demands this change. Given its ethereal quality, this shift in position is subtle and difficult to illustrate through case study analysis. However challenging, an attempt is made here.

Case Study 4: Management services contract – unpaid invoices

Personnel Inc. provided management personnel and other services to North Hill Limited from time to time under a project-based service contract. The parties had worked with each other over the course of several projects. Terry Smith had been an employee of Personnel and the project manager for the particular project at issue, but subsequently left its employ to become North Hill's employee. At the time of the negotiation, Smith was no longer employed by North Hill, but continued to provide services to North Hill through a consultancy agreement. It was implied by North Hill that his evidence would support North Hill's defence.

The issue in dispute related to unpaid invoices. Personnel alleged that an oral agreement had been entered into for the services of four employees at a set fee of £1,000 per day. Personnel alleged that those services were to be provided from March. During the same meeting at which the fee was

---

79 See note 59.

established for the employees, it was also discussed that Personnel would provide an assessment evaluation service for North Hill's administrative operations at a fee of £200,000. North Hill contended that the fees for the four employees were included in the £200,000 fee for the assessment evaluation service, and accordingly did not pay invoices submitted by Personnel in respect of the employee fees of £1,000 per day. Personnel commenced action against North Hill for payment of outstanding invoices.

The negotiation took place in the skyscraper offices of North Hill Limited. Meeting rooms were separated by employee workstations. The North Hill room was small and required a key to enter. Personnel was given a room with magnificent views of the London skyline. Personnel's CEO, Harry Johns, was in attendance for Personnel. Smith, together with a senior management employee, Joe Picton, was in attendance for North Hill.

After articulation of their positions, the parties exchanged information about the calculation of the invoice fee, the basis on which North Hill refused to pay the invoices at the fee charged, North Hill's calculation of fees owed, the documentary evidence relied upon by each party, the persons involved in the project, the nature of the services provided by Personnel, the circumstances surrounding the project for the assessment evaluation services, and the actual services provided to North Hill.

Testing of the positions began with North Hill being challenged on two documents: one which referred to a discussion between the parties regarding the fee to be charged for the assessment evaluation service (it was initially proposed to be £180,000 and was later changed to £200,000); and a second document which set out Smith's request for the payment of £4,000 in respect of one of the employees (which supported the fact that the invoice for this employee was not part of the £200,000, but was a separate fee for separate services).

The testing continued with Personnel when it was pressed for documents to establish the hours worked by the four employees.

North Hill was then challenged further on the fact that the invoices were provided for each month of March, April, May and June at £1,000 per day for the employees. When questioned as to what was done with the invoices upon receipt, North Hill could not respond. Discussion also occurred about the inability of North Hill to rely on the evidence of Gus St Clair, its representative at the first meeting between the parties, who was no longer able to testify. North Hill was also referred to a letter of intent with respect to the £200,000 assessment evaluation services – how could North Hill believe that the invoices it received for four months prior to receipt of the letter of intent were included in the £200,000 fee? The letter of intent was discussed at a meeting in July and it set out deliverables for the assessment evaluation service at a proposed fee of £180,000. Neither party had produced anything in respect of that service prior to the letter of intent. The decision to charge £200,000 was determined in the following month and a start date was established for the project.

Furthermore, North Hill was reminded that Terry Smith had raised a concern in March that four employees were being supplied to North Hill without the authorization of North Hill's Board of Directors (authorization of the expenditure was required), and that authorization was subsequently granted in August. It was reiterated to North Hill that it knew Smith had wanted four employees to provide services to North Hill and that North Hill had agreed to his request. At that point, North Hill's legal adviser said, *"Thank you for helping me with their position. I need to speak with my client. There is some scope for settlement...."* When the negotiation resumed, North Hill proposed an initial offer and the bargaining began.

***

Douglas states that the movement from her first phase, where parties are working to establish a bargaining range, to her second phase, where parties are seeking to determine the range, is difficult to distinguish because it is in the latter phase that judgments are made about the opponent's position and mutual willingness to move from stated positions.[80] The same subtlety is found here, with the data suggesting a shift occurring as a result of what has gone on in the process until this stage.[81] Druckman, in an exploration of turning points in international negotiation, sees the concept to be embedded within the chronology of a negotiation as an event that indicates movement

---

80 Douglas, see note 20 at 73–80.
81 'Turning points' in negotiation have been considered in other contexts: see, for example, S. Cobb, "A Developmental Approach to Turning Points: 'Irony' as an Ethics for Negotiation Pragmatics" (2006) 11 *Harv. Negot. L. Rev.* 147; and D. Druckman, M. Olekalns and P.L. Smith, "Interpretive Filters: Social Cognition and the Impact of Turning Points in Negotiation" (2009) *Negotiation J.* 13. These two studies acknowledge turning points as events that change the course of negotiation and explore their occurrence in relation to discourse analysis and social cognitive influences, respectively. Further still, the concept as a critical moment in negotiation has been explored. Transformations, moves and turns in social positioning and out-of-keeping acts are all seen as critical moments altering the direction of the negotiation. See, for example, L.L. Putnam, "Transformations and Critical Moments in Negotiations" (2004) *Negotiation J.* 275; D.M. Kolb, "Staying in the Game or Changing It: An Analysis of *Moves* and *Turns* in Negotiation" (2004) *Negotiation J.* 253; K.L. McGinn, E. Long Lingo and K. Ciano, "Transitions through Out-of-keeping Acts" (2004) *Negotiation J.* 171, respectively. Green and Wheeler, see note 32, say that critical moments must be recognizable during a negotiation, and C. Menkel-Meadow ruminates over their importance for negotiation research in "Critical Moments in Negotiation: Implications for Research, Pedagogy, and Practice" (2004) *Negotiation J.* 341. While I am not advocating the shift to be a critical moment in the sense as suggested by these scholars, it is a critical moment in the sense that the shift is needed for the negotiators to begin bargaining, as described above.

from one phase in the negotiation to another.[82] While it may be suggested that the shift in position is then not a separate phase in the negotiation process, but rather the result of the challenges made to the parties' positions, the data suggests otherwise. There is an intermediate step between phase three and phase five: the movement by the parties to begin to formulate, articulate and respond to bargaining proposals follows a change that occurs within the parties' assessments of their positions. This stage must occur before bargaining is contemplated.

The shift may come, as Gulliver suggests, as a result of information exchange and learning.[83] The parties have disclosed information about their position and have heard the articulation of the opponent's position. They have had an opportunity both to air their views and to receive information. They have been tested on the disclosure and their positions. They have learned about the dispute. Gulliver suggests that the cyclical exchange of information and learning leads to change and ultimately may avoid the necessity of bargaining.[84] While it is not advocated here that bargaining is avoided as a result of the information exchange (and indeed, the data does not support Gulliver's hypothesis in this regard), the information exchange and learning that takes place in the first three phases of the negotiation process prepares the parties to undergo a shift in judgment and negotiation behaviour. The shift leads parties to embark on a consideration of bargaining proposals, which forms part of a new stage in the process.

Although it is not always discernible when the shift occurs, the case study seeks to illuminate the subtlety. There is no one word that is exchanged, no one statement made, no movement of arms, no flapping of feet to signify when the change occurs. The shift is a culminating event, one that may take parties by surprise and surreptitiously lead them to the offer and counter-offer dance of bargaining proposals or one that occurs as a result of the rational assessment of information disclosed during the course of the process thus far.

This case study appears to fall into the latter category. We see that a change occurs after North Hill has articulated its position at the outset of the negotiation, has provided information to Personnel, has received information in turn, and has been tested on its position by both Personnel and the mediator. Something occurs to propel North Hill to initiate bargaining by making an initial offer. The actual cause of the event is known only to the party as it occurs within the privacy of its own internal deliberations. Suffice it to say, however it occurs, it occurs. It is an integral part of the negotiation process. Without this shift, the parties would not move from stated positions to

---

82 D. Druckman, "Turning Points in International Negotiation: A Comparative Analysis" (2001) 45 *J. Conflict Resol.* 519 at 520.
83 See generally, the discussion about the cyclical process of information exchange and learning in Gulliver, see note 32 at 83–120.
84 Ibid. at 71.

bargaining. Some may liken this shift to a movement from a competitive strategic approach, emphasizing self-interest, to a cooperative one where compromises are sought by each party in their attempt to resolve the dispute.[85] Alternatively, it may be seen as an instance where cognitive influences are at their lowest impact.

This shift in position needs to be experienced by only one of the parties before bargaining begins. It is what commences the bargaining. Here it is North Hill who makes the shift and opens the doors for settlement proposals. Personnel undergoes its own shift in the context of bargaining through its responses to North Hill's offers and its counter-offers to North Hill.

Bargaining proposals

At this stage, the parties are concerned with movement: they seek movement from the other and they consider the extent to which they are prepared to move in order to reach a solution. Concessions and compromise occur, alternatives are considered, a viable range is established, trading on issues is determined, and exchanges of proposals are made.

Case Study 5: Corporate liquidation – shareholder conduct

This case is about the action taken by a shareholder of a company that went into bankruptcy. The liquidator of the company, the Trustee, brought action against the former shareholder for allegedly removing £150,000 from the company accounts. The company ultimately filed for bankruptcy, and by the time of the liquidation had a £83,000 deficiency. The Shareholder denied the allegation, stating that the funds were removed to pursue new business opportunities for the company.

The parties were represented by lawyers. The negotiation was held at the offices of the Shareholder's solicitor. The Shareholder and his legal team were housed in a bright and spacious boardroom. The Trustee and his solicitor were given the stockroom.

It soon became clear in the negotiation that the central issue in the negotiation was the status of the original offer made by the Trustee early in the dispute. The Shareholder fixated on the offer, which became the foundation for his position. The fact that money had been taken from the company seemed to be a non-issue: the issue was how much would the Shareholder pay to the Trustee.

The Shareholder tested the position of the Trustee by referring to the initial offer made by the Trustee for payment by the Shareholder of £50,000 early

---

85 Stevens would suggest that this results in a new phase of the negotiation, one that moves from competitive strategies to cooperative strategies: Stevens, see note 7.

in the dispute. The Shareholder alleged that he had accepted the offer, but the Trustee had ignored his acceptance and instead raised the offer to £72,000, which was the revised value of the company deficiency at liquidation. The Shareholder invoked that initial offer and challenged the Trustee on it.[86] During the testing period (carried out by the mediator), the Trustee was challenged about its actions surrounding the withdrawal of the offer in the face of what appeared to be an acceptance by the Shareholder. Discussion of the legal status of the offer and acceptance occurred, as did the ability of the Shareholder to pay. The Trustee was adamant that the original offers made early in the dispute were not relevant and that in the current negotiation, it was seeking payment of £95,000 from the Shareholder. The Trustee continued to be tested on this position. Its subsequent agreement to compromise on this position and make an offer of £75,000 began the exchange of bargaining proposals.

The Shareholder was advised of the offer and was also advised that the Trustee had been firmly entrenched in the higher figure of £95,000 but had been challenged to reduce the amount. The Shareholder was concerned about the ability to pay the amount and raised the need for delayed payment terms. There was discussion about the value of real property against which funding could be obtained. The Shareholder's counsel mused on whether the drop from £175,000 to £75,000 in the Trustee's claim was a sign of its belief that its case was weak or whether it was in sympathy for the Shareholder. After some discussion, he wondered again whether it was because the Trustee was not as confident in its position as it had been at the beginning of the negotiation.

After some deliberation, the Shareholder counter-offered at £64,000 to be paid within a period of eight weeks to permit mortgage funding, with interest payable on the sum at the standard variable rate. The amount was inclusive of costs.

The Trustee was informed about the counter-proposal. Its legal adviser suggested that the parties split the difference between the two offers, with the Shareholder paying £70,000 and each party bearing its own costs. The Trustee wanted security for the payment in the form of a personal undertaking from the Shareholder. After some deliberation, the Trustee agreed that the offer suggested by its legal adviser be conveyed to the Shareholder.

The Shareholder was told that the Trustee's approach was to split the difference and informed of the need for the undertaking. He was also informed that if the Shareholder counter-offered at £69,000, the Trustee would go to trial.

---

86 One may argue that bargaining had begun with this initial offer by the Shareholder. However, the data suggests otherwise. As will be noted, there was much discussion with the Trustee about the history of the offers and the status of its original £50,000 offer. Bargaining did not begin until the parties were within what Stevens, see note 7 at 10, 97, and Stenelo, see note 5 at 101–6, refer to as the contract zone.

The Shareholder agreed to pay £70,000 but needed to discuss the terms of the security requested by the Trustee.

At that point, the solicitors for both parties met to discuss the security to be offered by the Shareholder for the payment. The Trustee wanted a charge on real property owned by the Shareholder. The Shareholder was against this because it would preclude the Shareholder from mortgaging the property further without the consent of his partner. The Trustee offered to refrain from registering the mortgage. The Shareholder suggested an equitable charge. The Trustee then suggested a judgment debt in the form of the Tomlin Order, which could be enforced as a judgment if the payment were not made.[87] The Shareholder agreed and an agreement in principle was reached.

***

This phase sees a shift from the competitive mode of the prior phases to a seemingly more cooperative approach as the parties seek to find an acceptable outcome. The bargaining proposals occur only after (i) the parties have made clear to their opponent their position and the firmness with which they believe in the strength of their position; (ii) parties have engaged in information exchange about their positions; (iii) they have been challenged about the strength and merit of their position; and (iv) a position shift occurs. In this case, the parties went through these stages to enter into the penultimate stage of the process: the exchange of offers and counter-offers. During this phase, the bargaining range is established and determined. The Trustee's first opening bid of £75,000 anchored the range, with the Shareholder's proposal of £64,000 setting the range.[88] There was an attempt by the Trustee to anchor the first offer at the much higher figure of £95,000 without regard to the history of the prior exchange between the parties. The Trustee was, however, persuaded to reduce the figure and thereby take the first step towards establishing a contract zone.

During this stage, parties re-evaluate their expectations, they assess their opponents' expectations, they speculate on the possible reactions to their offers, they formulate offers within the contract zone, and they postulate reasons why their offer merits acceptance. This phase appears to be a combination of

---

87 A Tomlin Order, under the Civil Procedure Rules, 1998 SI 1998/3132 for England and Wales, is a form of consent order staying proceedings on terms, also allowing parties to apply to the court for enforcement of the consent agreement without the need to initiate new proceedings. For an example of a Tomlin Order, see http://www.cedr.com/library/documents/settlement_agreement.pdf (accessed 22 June 2012).

88 You will note that the Shareholder's opening position of £50,000 is not considered as part of the bargaining proposal phase. It was a test by the Shareholder, an attempt to anchor the range as low to zero as possible. The data suggests that the Shareholder did not expect the Trustee to accept the offer, nor be persuaded by it. It seemed to be a tactical move to undermine the Trustee's confidence in its case.

three of Gulliver's phases: 'narrowing the difference', 'preliminaries to final bargaining' and 'final bargaining'.[89]

The difficulty of the phase, as many of the theorists state, is to know when the offer on the table is the final and best offer that will be made. For example, for Douglas, this represents the last stage of the negotiation process: it is during the final stage that parties need to decide whether the final offer is on the table.[90] Schelling refers to this period of bargaining as 'pure bargaining'. Concessions occur, according to Schelling, because one party believes that the other will not concede further and therefore he must concede if he wants to reach agreement. As Schelling states:

> 'I must concede because he won't. He won't because he thinks I will. He thinks I will because he thinks I think he thinks so ...' There is some range of alternative outcomes in which any point is better for both sides than no agreement at all. To insist on any such point is pure bargaining since one always *would* take less rather than reach no agreement at all, and since one always *can* recede if retreat proves necessary to agreement. Yet if both parties are aware of the limits to this range, *any* outcome is a point from which at least one party would have been willing to retreat and the other knows it! There is no resting place.[91]

Stevens says that this is pure bargaining because:

> any such outcome is a position from which at least one party would be willing to retreat for the sake of agreement, and this the other party knows. In such a situation, to insist upon any position other than that most favored by one's opponent is 'pure' bargaining in the sense that one would retreat if this were necessary to agreement.[92]

According to Stevens, Schelling says the reason why a party will concede is the belief that the other will not, and therefore to get to agreement requires the party's concession.[93]

The data supports the Schelling model of 'pure bargaining': at some point in the negotiation, the judgment must be made. Will my opponent concede further? If not, will I concede further for the sake of agreement? Another observation arising is that, generally, once the parties are in the bargaining phase of the process and have established the contract zone, a settlement will more than likely occur. It seems that if the parties have worked through the

---

89 Gulliver, see note 32 at 141–68.
90 Douglas, see note 20 at 80–1.
91 T.C. Schelling, *The Strategy of Conflict* (New York: Oxford University Press, 1975) at 22.
92 Stevens, see note 7 at 108.
93 Ibid.

prior phases of the negotiation and have managed to establish a contract zone without a party walking away from the negotiation table, the negotiation will reach agreement. This usually occurs in this phase; however, it may also occur earlier in the process. It is a moment in time and space when it is clear that one or both of the parties has understood what the dispute involves and that a settlement must be reached. It is when parties are prepared to coordinate their efforts to move towards agreement. Certainly, in the bargaining phase the parties move closer to each other's position, and sometimes, to the observer, the amount at which settlement will occur can be gleaned.[94]

While it could be said that the parties are engaged in a coordinated effort to reach resolution, they also continue to engage in some competitive moves such as bluffing, threatening and vigorous posturing in a bid to reduce the expectations of the other party. Indeed, the data suggests that even in their coordinated effort to reach agreement, their strategic approach remains highly competitive. The parties are balancing between two goals: to maintain bargaining strength and to reach agreement. On the one hand, in seeking agreement, they desire the most advantageous bargain they can get, and in this way they are at odds with each other. On the other hand, they both realize that there must be compromise to reach agreement. They struggle to manipulate who will compromise and by how much. They attempt to minimize their movements while demanding large concessions from their opponents.

Joint decision-making for final agreement

An agreement in principle is reached. The negotiation continues, however, as the parties work together to finalize the details of the agreement and to formalize its content in a signed settlement agreement.

Case Study 6: Employment dispute – the disabled worker

Lucy Shelley had been employed by a large corporation. She commenced a claim against her former employer alleging that she was discriminated against by reason of disability. She alleged that her performance, which had been highly rated, was rated poorly upon disclosure of her disability status, and that the company subsequently embarked on a course of conduct that

---

94 During the observations of the process, the mediator and I would often make a non-monetary 'wager' as to the amount at which a matter would be settled or the amount at which the first offer or counter-proposal would be set. More often than not, our estimates were accurate. Schelling refers to this when examining bargaining power and skill: is bargaining power or skill relevant when predictions of outcome can be made accurately, he queries: Schelling, see note 91 at 68–9. Menkel-Meadow, "Lawyer Negotiations", see note 48 at 377, says that the data of observed mediations suggests negotiators expect to compromise their claims in the middle of their two competing claims.

resulted in Shelley's exclusion from participating in certain corporate events including career advancement opportunities. The company, Riverdale Holdings, vigorously defended against the allegations of discrimination, particularly Shelley's damages claim for payment of a lifetime of income compensation she alleged she lost by reason of Riverdale's actions.

Both parties were represented by solicitors and both parties actively participated in the negotiation together with their solicitors. The negotiation took place at the offices of the solicitors for Riverdale. Boardrooms were large, refreshments plentiful and pens and pencils with the law firm's logo were available for the taking. This final phase of negotiation took place very late in the evening following a full day of mediation.

The parties agreed to a principal payment of £400,000 to be allocated in a tax-efficient manner, outplacement services and training, a letter of reference and payment of the mediation costs. Once the agreement in principle was reached, the parties embarked on fine-tuning the provisions. For example, there was discussion and negotiation on the tax aspect of the payment. There was a suggestion of splitting the payments into a payment for injury to personal feeling. Shelley wanted £50,000 to be tax-free and £30,000 to be apportioned to personal feelings. Riverdale was fine with the £50,000 tax-free payment but argued that the personal feeling allocation should be limited to £7,500. Shelley pointed out that the company had said it would make the payment in the most tax-efficient way. Riverdale retorted that it was subject to reasonableness. Shelley then suggested apportioning the payment to personal injury. Riverdale said that the tax rules did not permit such an apportionment; however, it would consider other suggestions by Shelley. On further consideration, Riverdale was willing to apportion £10,000 to personal feeling but nothing to personal injury because it was taxable as relating to employment. Shelley suggested £20,000 to personal injury subject to providing an indemnity to Riverdale in the event that the tax authorities found the payment to be taxable and penalized Riverdale. Riverdale refused on the basis that the payment was taxable and was not willing to avoid tax on it.

While this negotiation over the apportionment of the payment for tax efficiency was ongoing, the Riverdale legal team continued drafting the agreement, with review by Shelley's legal adviser. Some discussion also occurred relating to the payment date.

Another issue that arose dealt with the payment of legal costs. In Riverdale's view, the payment of legal fees was included in the overall payment of £400,000. For Shelley, the legal fees were a separate item and formed part of the agreement in principle. Miscommunication was responsible here for the misunderstanding. The parties became upset over the miscommunication and each party appeared to be adamant as to their position. Shelley threatened to walk away from the negotiation if the legal fees were not paid. Riverdale said that it had no more money to offer. Recriminations about each other's conduct were made. For a moment, there was a question as to whether the parties could continue to move towards agreement. In an effort to resolve the issue, the parties embarked on further bargaining over this issue, suggesting trade-offs of legal fees against an increase in the amount to be allocated to personal feeling. In the end, the parties each made some movement: Shelley reduced her claim for legal costs by £2,000 and Riverdale agreed to pay £6,000. A compromise was reached through concession-making.

All the while, drafting of the agreement continued. Once the legal fees were finalized, the parties concentrated on drafting details until the final moment was reached: the parties signed the agreement and parted for the day.

***

When the parties reach the point where they are at *idem* on principal terms such as the payment amount and payment date, the final stage of the negotiation process is entered into.[95] It is here that a cooperative effort is clearly evident. The parties work together to formalize the details of the agreement and the arrangements necessary for the agreement to be finalized.[96] The parties are generally no longer approaching the negotiation in a competitive mode; rather, the parties cooperate to get the deal done. This is particularly acute for the drafting of the written agreement. The whole agreement or portions of it are drafted, either jointly by the parties or one party takes the responsibility for preparing a first draft for comment by the other, which is what occurred in this case.

Once the first draft is prepared, there is joint discussion about its contents and any changes that need to be made to it. Cooperation typically reigns supreme during this period. This supports Stevens' view that negotiators are competitive in early stages and cooperative in later stages.[97] The difference here is that the data suggests a competitive strategic approach is taken throughout the phases of negotiation, with a suggested appearance of coordinated efforts occurring during the bargaining phase but which are really fuelled by competitive action and goals. It is only in the final phase that problem-solving and cooperation dominate. The domination, however, is dependent on the existence of an agreement on major terms, with ancillary terms to be determined.

---

95 Roberts and Palmer, see note 45 at 129–30, speak of the need to amend Gulliver's formulation of process (Gulliver moves from 'final bargaining' to 'ritual affirmation') to recognize the potential need for additional negotiation between the time that an agreement in principle is reached and an agreement in writing is executed.
96 One of the conditions of the mediations conducted during this ethnographic study requires all agreements achieved at mediation to be confirmed in writing. No agreement is reached until it is in writing and signed by the parties.
97 Stevens, see note 7 at 107–9.

For example, often issues arise and further negotiation is required on distinct points, as occurred here. They are discussed, and if necessary mini-negotiations are conducted of the issue, similar to the negotiation between Shelley and Riverdale. Two issues relating to the £400,000 payment were raised: the tax allocation of the payment and the payment by Riverdale of Shelley's legal costs. It appeared, at times, that the parties would not overcome the new disputes generated by these two issues and that the negotiation would not lead to resolution. However, the aim of both parties is not to lose the agreement that was reached in principle. Parties often strain to resolve any issues that arise during this phase.[98] Both problem-solving and competitive tactics are implemented during this phase. For example, when discussing the tax apportionment of the payment, joint problem-solving was evident: the parties considered how to make the payment most tax-efficient with reduced risk to the parties.

With respect to the issue of the legal costs, however, Shelley turned to competitive tactics, threatening to walk away from the deal if her costs were not paid. Cognitive barriers were in play once again. There was an escalation of commitment, as seen in phase one, an assumption made that any gain for one party was at the expense of the other party, rigid thinking about the issue, and arguably, a desire for equity: that is, a need for a recognition of suffering through payment of the legal fees. The payment of legal fees was an important issue for Shelley and one that she thought had been conceded earlier in the negotiation. That may have accounted for the competitive nature of the interaction. Ultimately, however, both parties compromised and resolved the issue. Given the fact that this remained the only outstanding issue to be resolved with other major items agreed, it is not surprising, and indeed it was expected, that parties would compromise to complete the agreement. Another instance, perhaps, of Schelling's pure bargaining.

Final agreement is reached when the parties sign the agreement, either in each other's presence or alone.[99] Any remaining steps to be taken, such as filing a court order, are delegated to the legal representatives of one of the parties to complete. Resolution is achieved and the parties depart, each with a copy of a signed agreement in hand. The negotiation has ended.

The processual arc

Theorists and others speak of the negotiation process as stages during which parties seek to explore bargaining ranges, to establish bargaining ranges, to uncover maximum limits, and to determine the contract zone.[100] From an

---

98 This is based on the data obtained from the mediations observed during the period of ethnographic fieldwork.
99 Recall the need for a signed written agreement as a condition precedent to agreement.
100 See earlier discussion herein about the phases of negotiation.

analysis of the six case studies, this is not what appears to occur in the phases; rather, the objectives of each phase seem to be (i) persuading as to the strength of positions, and (ii) the undermining of the opponent's positions. It does not appear that parties are interested in bargaining ranges until the bargaining proposal stage is reached. One may argue that the earlier phases help to establish a range through the information exchange that occurs. Parties are always assessing one another and are making judgments about the dispute, information to disclose, movements to make and offers to deliver. By doing this, they come upon the bargaining range for the negotiation, and it is within such a range that proposals are made. However, it cannot be said that a specific goal of the earlier phases is to set a range, as suggested by Douglas or Gulliver.[101]

The data suggests that the phases sit on a bi-directional plane, establishing the foundational elements of the process. The phases occur in what appears to be a sequential and cumulative manner. The process begins with each party *articulating their position*. This evolves into a period of *information exchange*, followed by *testing of positions*. These lead to a *shift in position*, which begins the *bargaining phase*. The next two phases – *bargaining proposals* and *joint decision-making* – are dependent on these phases. In other words, the bargaining proposal stage is not reached until the first four stages have occurred. And joint decision-making for final agreement does not occur until bargaining is completed. On this point, there is consensus with Gulliver's view that the negotiation process encompasses all phases of the proposed model, and that each phase must be completed for agreement to be reached.[102] Figure 4.1 illustrates the location of these phases on the bi-directional plane.

The first three phases, however, are not rigid in their movement. They can be fluid and can occur at any time during the negotiation process. For example, testing of positions can also occur during the phase of bargaining proposals. Articulation of positions and information exchange can occur throughout. Once introduced, the phases of the lateral plane (unilateral articulation of position, information exchange, and testing of positions) repeat, jump and superimpose themselves on this bi-directional plane. There is an underlying structure superimposed by its own elements: the structure is composed of six phases through which negotiators move to reach the conclusion of a negotiation. However, within that six-phase structure, the elements of the first three phases re-emerge and overlap with the other phases as the negotiation proceeds. They become part of a repetitive pattern, superimposed above and within the basic structure. The structure has echoes of Gulliver's hybrid

---

101 See earlier discussion: for Douglas, see note 20 at 72–81, and for Gulliver, see note 32 at 122–70.
102 Gulliver, ibid. at 174–7.

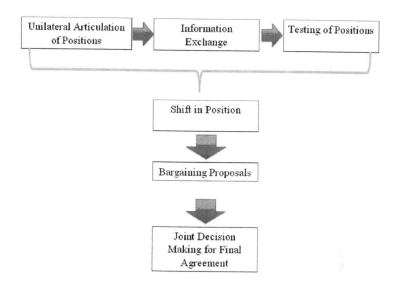

Figure 4.1 The six phases

model, although in compressed form.[103] Figure 4.2 illustrates the movement of phases of the processual arc.

Negotiation is a fluid and complex process, dependent on its participants. Its interactions occur within a normative and psychological context. Underlying the interactions is a structure that drives it to a conclusion. It is that structure which forms the process of negotiation. I have attempted to construct a model of negotiation suggested by an analysis of research data as a way to understand the real-life patterns of negotiating conduct and, by necessary implication, the patterns of a mediated negotiation. It is this negotiatory pattern that provides the foundation for mediation.

Summary

Theorists approach negotiation as a series of strategic moves, each of which is defined by the nature of the moves, or as irrational human behaviour due to cognitive realities affecting decision-making, or as a process of interactions.

---

103 Gulliver, see note 32 at 81–177, speaks of two models forming the process of negotiation: the cyclical model of information exchange and learning, and the developmental model of eight phases of negotiation. One may argue that the first three phases discussed here are cyclical in the nature of Gulliver's model. However, they are more than cyclical. In Gulliver's terms, they would form part of his developmental model and be cyclical within that developmental model.

108 Negotiated order

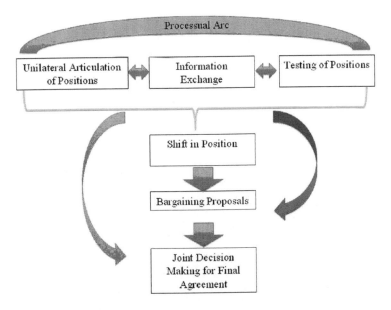

Figure 4.2 The processual arc

Arguably, negotiation is an amalgam of all three. The process involves social interaction. Cognitive influences inform the social interaction. Strategic moves occur within the process. Neither cognitive influences nor strategic moves alone, however, define the process. Strategy is not negotiation. It is one element of a process that *is* negotiation. Process provides the foundation to negotiation. Negotiation is a process undertaken for a specific reason – to achieve a desired outcome.

While there are a number of theoretical frameworks applied to the analysis of negotiation, it is the theories of the process analysers that resonate with this study. It is through their conceptual framework that an attempt has been made to illuminate a process that exists within a normative order affected by cognitive influences. A descriptive analysis was undertaken through case studies of negotiations conducted during a mediation process. The examination disclosed the existence of a six-phase bi-directional processual foundation, superimposed by a repetitive processual arc of phases interacting with one another within and during the process. The six stages disclosed by the data are: (i) unilateral articulation of positions; (ii) information exchange; (iii) testing of positions; (iv) shift in position; (v) bargaining proposals; and (vi) joint decision-making for final agreement.

5 The native voice

> ... the obstinacy with which I pursue the realisation of that part of nature which, falling before our eyes, gives us the pictures. So, the principle to develop – whatever our temperament or power in the presence of nature – is to give the image of what we see.
>
> Cézanne to Bernard, on the nature of the artist[1]

The artist may paint what he sees; he may paint what he interprets from what he sees; he may create anew. Cézanne suggests to Bernard that he strove to paint what he saw. This chapter strives to do the same. The ethnographer depicts what she sees during mediations she observed and experienced. Ethnographic data constructs the picture, resulting in the portrayal of mediated cases.[2] The portrayal reflects a combination of methods – Malinowski's scientific report through the medium of Turner's social dramas, replete with Geertz's thick description.[3]

The case study, in truncated form, was introduced in Chapter 4 to illustrate a suggested processual model of negotiation. Portions of cases were textualized, focusing on processual action. Generally and principally, the excerpts sought to illuminate the model, exposing the actions of each proposed stage of a negotiation. Such textualization was sufficient for the purposes of Chapter 4. It is not sufficient, however, for the exploration of mediator and party interactions in a mediated negotiation. The case study takes on fuller

---

1 This is an English translation provided by the Courtauld Gallery in London at an Exhibition of its Cézanne paintings in September 2008. A series of letters written by Cézanne to Emile Bernard late in Cézanne's life were also exhibited. This is an excerpt from one such letter written on 23 October 1905 in Aix.
2 See B. Malinowski, *Argonauts of the Western Pacific* (Long Grove: Waveland, 1984 edition) at 84, where he speaks of the ethnographer's task. In E.R. Galton, *Ripples From Peace Lake: Essays for Mediators and Peacemakers* (Victoria: Trafford, 2004) at 13, Galton describes his work as a mediator by analogy to art. One example he uses is that of the painter's canvas: he speaks of each mediation as a blank canvas, waiting to be filled in by him as mediator with the information he learns and the actions he takes during the course of the mediation.
3 See earlier discussion in Chapter 1.

shape in this and the following chapter. One may say that a holistic approach is taken to the social drama. More particularly, this chapter presents case studies of mediation set in real time,[4] although they are, in Gulliver's words, only an 'approximation to reality'.[5] The case studies are reconstructions of observed realities as experienced and deduced by the ethnographer.[6] Like Gulliver, I have endeavoured to report as accurately as possible, and because of that effort the case studies are not the creation of the observer.[7] To the extent that the observer observed the mediations, took copious notes to capture the moments reflected in the case studies and has textualized the observations, some may argue against the validity of this statement.[8] Despite the observer's role in this regard, the case studies remain the creation of the actors in the dramas themselves. Recall Turner and his emphasis on the social drama that takes place within the structure of the particular society he was studying. The actions and interactions of persons within that society created the social dramas he explored.[9] The dramas introduced in this chapter take place within mediation and they too arise from the actions and interactions of participants within that mediation. As such, they are not interpretive exercises.[10] This latter sentence, however, needs to be clarified, as all ethnography

---

4 See K. Kressel, "The Strategic Style in Mediation" (2007) 24 *Conflict Resol. Q.* 251 at 253, where he refers to Schon (1983). Schon stated that to improve professional activity there is a need to research the reality of professional activity. The case studies presented in this chapter and the following chapter seek to find the reality of mediator activity. However, it is interesting to note that Kressel's own use of 'vignettes', as he calls them, are said to be oversimplifications, the purpose of which is to highlight a certain aspect of a mediation; for example, see at 254. Query the extent to which such vignettes offer the reality of the mediation.
5 P.H. Gulliver, *Neighbours and Networks: The Idiom of Kinship in Social Action among the Ndendeuli of Tanzania* (London: University of California Press, 1971) at 358.
6 See Chapter 1 for discussion of the ethnographic approach.
7 Gulliver, see note 5 at 358, where he sets out what he seeks to achieve in his ethnographic account.
8 As noted in Chapter 1 at note 80, Clifford speaks of the textualization of ethnographic data: J. Clifford, "On Ethnographic Allegory" in J. Clifford and G.E. Marcus, eds, *Writing Culture: The Poetics and Politics of Ethnography* (Berkeley: University of California Press, 1986) 98, and see in particular at 115. See also Talal Asad, "The Concept of Cultural Translation in British Social Anthropology" in Clifford and Marcus, *Writing Culture*, 141 at 143–4, 159.
9 V. Turner, *Schism and Continuity in an African Society: A Study of Ndembu Village Life* (Oxford: Berg, 1996 edition). See for example at 93–4.
10 For interpretive exercises, see J. Krivis, *Improvisational Negotiation: A Mediator's Stories of Conflict About Love, Money, Anger – and the Strategies That Resolved Them* (San Francisco: Jossey-Bass, 2006); and Galton, see note 2, for example. They provide case studies that appear to be recreations of their experiences while mediating the disputes. In such case studies, it is unclear what portions actually occurred, what portions were created from

is an interpretive exercise to some degree.[11] They are not interpretative exercises in the sense that they are not an amalgam of many cases, nor have they been subjected to the observer's interpretation of language.[12] The language belongs to the parties themselves. *They* are the drama and it is *their* voice that strives to be heard. In the Malinowskian tradition, the intent of this textualization is to uncover the "objective realities of human thinking, feeling and behaviour".[13] In some way, the ethnography is one of listening: to observe what people say and what they hear.[14]

Such a method provides the context needed to access mediation and to glimpse the understandings that underlie it. How does the mediator present himself and the process of mediation to the parties who have come to him in conflict and about their conflict? How does the mediator see himself? How do the parties perceive him and the process? This chapter seeks to explore the relationships between mediator and process, mediator and parties, and between parties and process. It does so through the voices of the participants themselves. Through the mediator's own words, we will hear what she says to the parties about mediation and her role in this process and also what the mediator says to the researcher about the same thing. Also through their words, we will learn about the parties' opinions about process and mediator.

It is pedestrian to state the obvious: as noted earlier in Chapter 3, there is a vast literature in the mediation field, a literature that is filled with the views of academics, practitioners and researchers from many disciplines seeking to describe or prescribe the nature of mediation. What is lacking, however, are empirical studies of thick description about the statements and actions of mediators themselves before, during and after mediation.[15] We read what

---

information extraneous to the mediation itself (such as interviews), and what portions reflect an author's interpretations.

11 For example, Malinowski, see note 2 at 397; C. Geertz, "Thick Description: Toward an Interpretive Theory of Culture" in C. Geertz, *The Interpretation of Culture* (New York: Basic Books, 1973) at 20; V. Crapanzano, "Hermes' Dilemma: The Masking of Subversion in Ethnographic Description" in Clifford and Marcus, see note 8 at 74–5. For more detailed discussion of an analysis of the use of ethnography in this study, see Chapter 1.

12 It should be noted here that the notes were taken in a form of shorthand developed by the researcher. Pronouns, verbs and obvious words that may have been omitted in the writing have been added to complete phrases and ensure comprehension. However, any extraneous, newly created words are noted in square brackets.

13 Malinowski, see note 2 at 397.

14 Martin Forsey believes that ethnography encompasses a myriad methods; that it is not just about participant-observation. Ethnography is a broad concept that includes interviewing, video recording, for example. For him, ethnography is also about dialogue and listening. It should be defined by its purpose not its method, which is to uncover aspects of human existence. M.G. Forsey, "Ethnography as Participant Listening" (2010) 11 *Ethnography* 558, and in particular at 567.

15 Recall note 14 of Chapter 3 which provides examples of observational studies.

they have written about mediation and their practice.[16] It is now necessary to hear what they actually say to disputants about the process while within the process, their reflections on the process and the reflections of those around them, all with respect to the mediation they experienced *together*.

Three mediations are explored in this chapter. In particular, the chapter focuses on what the participants say about the process and about mediator action during five timelines and from three perspectives: (i) discussion with the mediator prior to the mediation day; (ii) introductory comments made to the parties by the mediator at the commencement of the mediation; (iii) comments made by the mediator to the researcher or to the parties during the mediation; (iv) post-mediation discussion with the mediator; and (v) views obtained after the conclusion of the mediation through telephone interviews with and questionnaires from party participants about the process and the mediator.[17] These timelines and perspectives are important because they contextualize the process from within the process. This ethnographic data, once presented, is then examined for illuminations of the underworld of mediation that exists beyond the contemporaneous world experienced by its participants in the moment of the drama. It is in this analysis that the cases take on significance and on which their explanatory power rests: their value

---

16 For example, in an empirical study conducted in 2009 by Kressel and Gadlin, mediators were interviewed about their participation in 18 cases through reflective case study conferences where the case and issues of concern for the mediator were discussed. The mediated cases were not observed nor parties contacted. See K. Kressel and H. Gadlin, "Mediating Among Scientists: A Mental Model of Expert Practice" (2009) 2 *International Association for Conflict Management* 308.

17 On this point (that is, regarding the views of the participants about the process and the mediator), a comment needs to be made regarding methodology. As indicated in Chapter 1, it was the Organization's policy that parties and lawyers be contacted after each mediation to obtain feedback about the mediation and mediator. One lawyer representative of each disputant would be contacted by telephone for a telephone interview and the parties would be sent a brief questionnaire. Not all parties completed the questionnaire and not all lawyers contacted were prepared to speak. To the extent that comments were obtained, they have been reported. The questionnaire, among other things, sought to ascertain the satisfaction levels of the participants on various aspects of the mediation process and the mediator. They were asked, again among other things, whether they were satisfied with the process of mediation, whether the process was as expected, whether they were satisfied with the outcome, and whether they were happy with the choice of mediator. Five possible levels were available for response: Extremely, Very, Yes, Fairly, No. With regard to the savings issues, the participants were asked whether there were savings in terms of management time, and legal and other costs. There were three possible levels available for response: Significant, Some, None. A list of questions used as a guide for the telephone interviews of the legal representatives can be found in Appendix B.

lies in the analysis that comes from the data, guided by theoretical constructs supported by the data.[18]

Case Study 7: Technology foul-up[19]

The case

The Claimant, HiWire Inc., is a designer, installer and management service provider for its customers' computer networks. The Defendant, Cavell Systems Limited, entered into a contract with HiWire for the creation of network services for Cavell's European organization. Contracts were entered into for the design, management, service and support of Cavell's central computer network. There was some dispute regarding the status of Cavell's back office[20] system and whether it would be sufficient for the operation of the European computer network to be provided by HiWire. Cavell alleged that the contract with HiWire was conditional on the existence of appropriate back office and back end[21] systems, which were to be developed by another company, not related to HiWire.

Cavell alleged that it served notice of its intention to cancel the contract due to the failure of the other company to develop an appropriate back office system. HiWire sought cancellation charges in the amount of £250,000, which it said were payable by Cavell. Cavell refused to pay the charges. HiWire took the position that the contract continued to be in force. It alleged

---

18 Clyde Mitchell explores the case study method, and in particular responds to the question of typicality or representative value, which he sees to be an inappropriate gauge of the value of the method. For him, its explanatory power is of value to the researcher, who then can analyse the case within a theoretical framework, using the data to support theoretical conclusions. See J. Clyde Mitchell, "Case and Situation Analysis" (1983) 31 *Sociological Review* 187, and in particular at 189, 191, 203–7. The three cases set out herein and in the following chapter were chosen for this explanatory power and the opportunities they offer for analytical commentary about mediator interventions and the mediatory process.
19 For the sake of anonymity, the names of the participants and selective details of the disputes in the case studies in this and the following chapter have been altered.
20 Back office is defined by Webopedia as follows: "The back office is generally considered to be the technology, services and human resources required to manage a company itself. Back office includes such systems as the IT, human resources and accounting departments. The back office is supported by a back end system." See Webopedia: Online Dictionary for Computer and Internet Technology Definitions: http://www.webopedia.com/TERM/B/back_office.html (accessed 10 July 2012).
21 Back end is defined by Webopedia as follows: "Back end systems are corporate systems that are used to run a company such as systems to manage orders, inventory and supply processing. Back end systems support the company's back office. This system collects input from users or other systems for processing." See Webopedia: Online Dictionary for Computer and Internet Technology Definitions:http://www.webopedia.com/TERM/B/back_end_system.html (accessed 10 July 2012).

that it confirmed the contract despite Cavell's repudiation. Cavell took the position that the contract was conditional and therefore subject to termination if the back office condition was not met.

The contract contained a dispute resolution clause requiring the parties to attend mediation prior to the commencement of litigation. The parties were sophisticated business entities, experienced with contractual disputes and their negotiation.

Discussion with the Mediator about the case prior to the mediation day

In the first conversation with the Mediator, the researcher was told by the Mediator, *"This is not an untypical case. The issue is whether there is a contract or not and what is the loss. One difficult issue involves Cavell's representative, who negotiated the contract and dealt with its cancellation. He has emotional face-saving issues, I suspect. It is hard to see more into it at this point.*

"I will ask the parties about their mediation experience today and will check out costs, timing and how they want to play it. If they are not experienced, I will get them to give sensible openings, and if they are experienced, they will know this."

The Mediator was asked about his approach to the mediation. He answered: *"Both want the opportunity to speak to each other, so we will have a good joint session. Cavell is turning up with a barrister, which is odd. They say contractually that their defence is strong and that the barrister is there to get the point across to HiWire. I think that means that they do not think their case is so strong. The joint session will be the opportunity to say why there is no contract and the other side to speak of the calculation of damages ... After that, we will just have to follow our noses to see the best way to proceed."*

The mediation day

In response to my prompting, the Mediator commented on his mediation style. *"I think of it afterwards. I see so many things during the opening that I tend to follow my instincts. I do not know what will come from it.*

"It is helpful to speak with the lawyers before the mediation. The problem with mediation is that it is a snapshot. The mediator sees five minutes from the whole day. I do not know the parties, what they bring with them. It is hard to have a preconceived plan. The best thing is that they are here.

"It is hard to be asked about legal positions. I do not have the papers; I did not meet the witnesses. I could give a quick view, but it would be unfair to the lawyers who worked on it for a long time. It can't be right."

First meeting with the HiWire Team

Upon entering the room, the Mediator said, *"I have come in to say hello and to talk about the basics. You provided an organized set of papers, thank you. I do not* know how this will pan out. I have spoken with the Defendant's solicitor. Some key things to know. This is your room. It is utterly private. You can tell me anything you like. It won't go beyond this room. There will be a bit of downtime. You may think – what is going on? I am trying to solve things.

"We will all meet together next door. I quite like, if it is OK with you, for both sides to say the key points. You may think they know {the points}, but it is good to say them again, especially with the clients there. It's not just to the lawyers. Listen to them. Is it a good point or not? And, say what you like."

When HiWire's solicitor, George David, said that he would not be too aggressive, the Mediator said, *"If you feel strongly about something, say it."*

In answer to the Mediator's inquiry as to whether they had any questions, David asked what they should do during the downtime. The Mediator responded, *"I could leave you with issues to think of. One issue is the amount of damages. It is better to put it out on the table sooner so that people can think about it."*

After some discussion about the contract and its mediation clause, the Mediator left the HiWire Team to speak with the Cavell Team.

First meeting with the Cavell Team

After a tardy arrival by the Cavell representatives, the Mediator met with the Team. Following introductions, the Mediator began. *"You have some experience with mediation. It is not a new process for you. You may speak freely here. It won't leave the room. This is a room where we can talk. There is downtime. Bear with it. It is part of the process. It is an essential part of it. I will spend time with both sides to find common ground. Hopefully, we will find some. I want a session to discuss the issues between you. You may think you know them, but it is helpful to hear the other side talk about key points.*

"There are two issues: the contract and what it is all about, and the amount of damages. I am keen to get them on the table and you can pick them off as appropriate. I encourage you to say something."

After Cavell's solicitor, Luke Alexander, said that he would set out the position briefly and anyone who thinks he is *"horribly wrong, will say it"*, the Mediator reiterated, *"I encourage you to speak. You may speak in groupings. There is value in discussion."*

Joint session

The Mediator led the HiWire Team into the joint meeting room. The Cavell Team arrived minutes later. Once all were seated, the Mediator began.

"Thanks to all for being here. This is the right place to start a round-table chat about the issues. I have had a chat with each of you. The rooms are confidential. They are private. I won't divulge what is said to the other side. The whole process is confidential and without prejudice, so you are able to speak freely. You now have an opportunity to listen to what the parties have to say. They will come up later.

"This is a voluntary process. I won't chain you to the wall. My hope is that a right frame of mind will resolve {the dispute}.

"*Both have authority to settle, I have been told. If you can go away with something better than litigation .... I am not a judge. It is not my job to give a view. I am a lawyer. I understand the issues, I have the background.*

"*I ask George David to set the scene from your perspective.*"

David, HiWire's solicitor, did as asked and spoke of HiWire's position, followed by Cavell's solicitor, Luke Alexander, on behalf of Cavell. When David then responded to Alexander's opening statement, the Mediator said, "*This is a good place to say that I want to meet privately with each. I will start with HiWire.*" And with that, the joint session concluded.

During the mediation

The Mediator commenced the private meetings with the HiWire Team. Generally, the day was spent alternating between Teams. The Teams did not meet again, with the exception of a brief meeting between the solicitors for each Team, a meeting that was ten minutes in length. This mediation was staccato. It consisted of short meetings, with the Mediator jumping from room to room. The longest meeting between Mediator and party was 40 minutes long and it was with the Cavell Team. Only two other meetings were nearly as long – another with the Cavell Team and one with the HiWire Team, both of which were 30 minutes in duration. The rest were roughly between 10 and 20 minutes in length. The parties reached settlement at the end of the day. The mediation day was approximately 7.5 hours in length. The Mediator spent 2.9 hours of the day with the HiWire Team, 2.5 hours with the Cavell Team, 0.6 of an hour in meetings with both parties present, and 1 hour alone. The parties spent approximately 0.4 hours drafting the settlement agreement.[22]

The Mediator, during a private moment, reflected on Cavell's suggestion that the parties continue the contract once the back office requirement is satisfied. "*Regarding the prospect of carrying on and joining hands, I will raise it without saying it came from the other side. Will they trust each other? People always say they can negotiate and work together again. In my experience, once people fall out, they stay out.*"

Interview with the Mediator after the conclusion of the mediation

When asked if he considered, prior to the commencement of the mediation, whether the mediation would result in a settlement, the Mediator stated, "*Yes, I did. I thought, in view of the amounts of money involved and the apparently*

---

22 It should be noted here that Luke Alexander (the Defendant Solicitor) had commenced drafting an agreement while proposals were being exchanged. Once a proposal was agreed, both parties' solicitors quickly worked together to finalize the agreement.

strong position HiWire was in on the contract, there was a likelihood that the parties would come to an agreement which might include future business. But, I certainly thought it would settle because the cost of litigation was fairly high."

As for his objectives going into the mediation, the Mediator said that it was *"to do my best to give the parties the most productive day I could with a view to assisting them, if possible, to solve their problems. Apart from this, I am absolutely open-minded. Sometimes, I am concerned about going in so open-minded."*

Regarding the Mediator's strategy, *"Strategy is the wrong word. I have an idea of what the issues are on which time needs to be spent. In some ways, having a strategy means having a conclusion in mind and I find it difficult in any mediation to have a strategy. I can see areas which will be difficult and I think how best to get them on the table and the timing of it. The more you have in mind what you think the issues are, the more you can get off course because the issues may not be what the parties think they are. Sometimes I am worried about going in with a blank mind. Is it good or bad?*

"Having a success rate is irrelevant. It is odd to talk about a success rate. It's not your settlement. I do not feel the parties need to settle. Of course I feel better if I get a deal, but I won't feel better if you think they will feel it is unsatisfactory. I find that by speaking with the solicitors beforehand, I get an inkling of what they think the issues and the difficulties will be and I start thinking of those and to the extent they match, then a strategy develops – how to bring a point up and get them to deal with it. For example, getting the lawyers speaking, or the financial people or groups together, but I can't start until I meet people because it could be the wrong strategy. I need to listen to them first and see who I am dealing with. It sounds like I just turn up and see which way the wind is blowing. It is like a toy box – which toy to play with. See who the playmates are and picking one. Some are better at ball games."

After reflecting for several moments, the Mediator described his mediation style, generally: *"Relaxed, open. It is a very difficult question because I do not see myself from the outside. I was thinking of this last week. One thing I do not do as a mediator is take a position, which I would do as a lawyer. One thing about mediation, which is quite difficult, is to act incisively without taking a position. The danger of taking a position is putting oneself in the process rather than getting the parties in the process.*

"The style I would like to have, but do not know if I have, is the ability to be incisive in a way that encourages the parties to come up with an idea. To scatter the seeds around rather than planting them in a particular spot. I am quite fearful of being dogmatic. I am trying to describe a style which caters for the need to direct the parties without obviously doing it."

With respect to his style in this particular mediation, the Mediator stated, *"With the HiWire Team, I felt that I was consciously encouraging them to continue with the progress, that they were making progress. Telling them they were making progress. I felt that encouragement was needed. As part of that, I was leading them to a conclusion. I was not aware where it would end. With Cavell, it was more a commercial understanding of what they wanted, and getting the Cavell representative to stay there."*

Participants' views about the mediation and the Mediator

Luke Alexander, Cavell's solicitor, was brief about the Mediator's style: *"It was quiet and understated, and I liked it."*

George David, HiWire's solicitor, was also positive: *"I thought he was very good. He was very calm, which is nice, and he was reasonable and thoughtful."* As for his strengths, *"He was very neutral. Being calm is a strength. And he was very well prepared."* The process did not provide any surprises for him: *"I have done a number of them and it proceeded as normal, really."*

HiWire's party representative responded to the Organization's questionnaire,[23] indicating that he was 'very' satisfied with the process of mediation, that it was 'as expected', and that he was 'happy' with the Mediator. There was 'some' savings in management time, and legal and other costs.

***

This Mediator first approaches the mediation on the basis of the legal nature of the dispute: it is about a contract and damages arising from its termination, yet there is a need for commerciality to achieve resolution. He says to the parties: prepare your damages calculation; put your issues on the table. At the same time, he seeks commonality and aspires for resolution. He hopes that the parties will achieve something better than what litigation could bring. There is a vacillation about the nature of mediation: is it informed by norms or by social processes? He is uncertain. He emphasizes the law and encourages parties to articulate their legal positions while insisting that there are opportunities for resolution, opportunities he will assist in finding. He sees the purpose of the joint session to be for the articulation of legal arguments. He provides the parameters for the discussion: the parties are to concentrate on two issues involving the contract and the damages claimed. As we will see later, this is in contrast to Case Study 9, where the Mediator stresses the need for commerciality and avoidance of rights' analysis.[24]

Despite all this talk about the legalities of the dispute, this Mediator asserts that he is not a judge and will not give an opinion about the dispute. It is not his job to do so, he says. It appears to be the lack of full knowledge of the dispute that seems to underlie this tenet. He sees his role as facilitator – he will help the parties find their settlement. He will help them find common ground and help to solve the problem. When the Mediator says that he is a facilitator, he is not referring to himself as a facilitator of the process. This is contrary to a common view of mediators as process facilitators in control of the process, while the parties are in control of the substance. This Mediator sees himself as a facilitator of settlement. Either he can get a deal, or he

---

23 Recall that the questionnaire sought to ascertain the satisfaction levels of the participants on various aspects of the mediation.
24 Discussion of Case Study 9 occurs later in this chapter.

cannot. He works towards this goal while stressing that it is the parties' settlement. He views mediator settlement rates as irrelevant because any resolution achieved is not his resolution; however, he does acknowledge that he 'feels better if I get a deal'. Ultimately, it is the 'deal' that is an indicator of achievement nonetheless.

The Mediator sees mediation as providing only a snapshot of the dispute. He does not have full knowledge of the case. He sees this as a difficulty which appears to impact his actions. This is one of the reasons why he refuses to give a view about the dispute. It is also a reason why he has no strategy going into mediation. He goes in with a blank canvas.[25] The Mediator says, given his state of ignorance about the parties, about the dispute and about their ambitions for the day, that he does not have a preconceived plan for the conduct of the mediation. As he describes it, he throws the seeds and sees where they grow. Yet, he does consider the legal positions of the parties before the commencement of the mediation and he does require the parties to deal with their legal positions early in the mediation. There is structure and the parties are advised of this structure early in the day. This, arguably, is a plan.

The Mediator is brief in his introduction of the process to the parties. He speaks of the confidentiality of the process and its without prejudice nature, as do other mediators.[26] Similarly, he tells the parties that, as a result of the private nature of the discussions, they should speak their mind to him and to the other side. Communication is important to the Mediator, both listening and talking. He differs, however, in requiring the parties to discuss the case and their respective views regarding the merits of their positions. He seems to see a need for this in order to set the stage for resolution, yet queries to what extent a discussion about merits will reflect a party's frankness of view as promoted by the Mediator to 'speak their minds'.

In addition to describing the confidentiality of the process, the Mediator refers to the process as voluntary. The parties can leave at any time. The Mediator also makes a specific point about 'downtime' in mediation. Parties need to be prepared for the extensive periods when they are alone, when they are waiting for the Mediator to attend to them. It is a necessary part of the process, he says. Given the brevity of his description of the process, it is curious that the Mediator should focus on this aspect of the process. Perhaps he is forestalling any suggestion that he is spending too much time with one party over the other.

There is no explicit discussion about mediator neutrality or impartiality.[27] Perhaps the assertion that he is not a judge and would not provide views, or the warning about 'downtimes', were implicit references.[28] Although the

---

25 Echoes here of Galton's analogy to the blank canvas, see note 2 at 13.
26 For example, see discussion in Case Study 9 below.
27 See discussion about neutrality and its place in the mediation lexicon in Chapter 3.
28 Heisterkamp, in his exploration of mediator conversational stances of neutrality, suggests that one way mediators define neutrality is by distancing themselves from adjudicative

Mediator did not expressly comment on neutrality, it is interesting to note that the Claimant Solicitor did. He described one of the Mediator's strengths as being 'very neutral'. So, one must ask, why was the Mediator silent on what many consider to be a fundamental characteristic of a mediator, including the Organization on whose panel the Mediator sat?[29] Unfortunately, the Mediator was not questioned directly on this point; we can only rely on the data that is available. That data is clear that no assurance was given to the parties, yet one of the parties felt it sufficiently to comment on its presence. The inevitable conclusion is that the Mediator's actions fed the party's view. This conclusion will be tested in the following chapter, when the focus of the ethnographic data is on the Mediator's actions in the case.

This case presents an example of a mediator who cannot easily describe his style. The Mediator feels that the answer requires an objective perspective that cannot be provided by him. He does, however, reflect on what he does not do. He does not act like a lawyer. He does not take positions, as would a lawyer. This is his view of himself. This reflective exercise uncovers a pivotal aspect of what he says is the mediator's role: 'to act incisively without taking positions'. To take a position is to place oneself in the process. This is unacceptable, he says. It is the parties who should be in the process, not the mediator. The suggestion here is that the mediator is external to the process and that mediator and process are separate. This accords with his view that it is the parties' settlement and therefore the parties' process: a mediator gives the parties the opportunity to generate ideas for resolution. Within the Mediator's view of the separateness between mediator and process there lies a contradiction. The Mediator says he strives to direct parties in an unobtrusive way. He hopes he has conducted the mediation in this way. Surely, however, to direct is to be within the process itself and thus be part of the process.

This view of his role suggests a manipulation of the parties by the Mediator. He seeks to direct the parties, but he does not want them to be aware of it. He is controlling their perceptions of his actions and hence his role. There appears to be a lack of transparency here. When something is hidden from view, it can take on an ominous tone. Is there something unsavoury about directing the parties in mediation? Why must the parties not be aware of what he is doing? The answers could be found in the Mediator's aim for the mediation: to give the parties the feeling that it is their settlement, and to direct in a non-directive way. Curiously, from the parties' perspective, the

---

functions of decision-making (although in his example they do this when describing to parties what it means to be 'neutral', which is not what occurred in this case as the Mediator did not refer to either neutrality or impartiality in his introduction to the parties). See B.L. Heisterkamp, "Conversational Displays of Mediator Neutrality in a Court-based Program" (2006) 38 *J. of Pragmatics* 2051 at 2056.

29 Recall discussion in Chapter 3 about neutrality and its treatment in the literature as well as its place within the Organization's philosophy.

Mediator was quiet, calm, reasonable and thoughtful. He did not appear to them to be directive. They were pleased with his efforts and the process. This is echoed in the view of the party representative for HiWire: he was satisfied with the Mediator as well, although interestingly, he was 'very' satisfied with the process. A distinction is made between process and Mediator, as seen in other mediations, with the party representative being 'very satisfied' with the process and 'happy' with the Mediator.[30] As for manipulation, for those in the process there was no sense of manipulation experienced by them. To the one outside the process, a question is raised about the seeming lack of express concern for the role of either neutrality or impartiality during the process, and the desire to direct without party knowledge.

Case Study 8: Partnership gone awry

The case

This was a case about endings – the end of a partnership relationship that began years ago. The Claimant, Robert Mitchell, had a 35-year relationship with the Defendant law firm partnership, Jarvis & Kimbourne Limited Partnership, first as an employee and subsequently as an equity partner. Mitchell became dissatisfied with the Partnership's new profit-share calculation and advised it of his intention to resign, which caused the Partnership to determine his entitlement on resignation. A Partnership Agreement dated 1995 set out the financial entitlement on retirement with respect to the calculation of goodwill and profit share. Mitchell and the Jarvis & Kimbourne partners entered into a negotiation to determine Mitchell's entitlement under the Partnership Agreement. A negotiated agreement was not reached and Jarvis & Kimbourne served notice to Mitchell of its intention to expel him from the Partnership for improper billing practices. He was suspended from the Partnership pending investigation. The Defendants (being the Partnership and six of its partners – Harris Jarvis, Anthony Kimbourne, Anna Ernest, Francis Michaels, Patrick Jordan and Andre Vincent) alleged that Mitchell not only refused to participate in the investigation of his billing practices, but also obstructed it.

The expulsion was subsequently confirmed. Mitchell then commenced legal proceedings against Jarvis & Kimbourne and the six partners. He claimed that the expulsion was unlawful, that he had been unfairly treated and that the Defendants discriminated against him in their conduct towards him. He sought payment of his share of profits arising from the Partnership, his share of goodwill (both of which were entitlements under the Partnership Agreement), and losses suffered from the discriminatory actions of the Defendants. It was alleged by Jarvis & Kimbourne and the partners that the claim for discrimination was added at the 'eleventh hour' to pressure

---

30 Case Studies 8 and 9 offer the same distinction. This is examined later in the chapter.

them to settle. The partners were outraged by Mitchell's conduct; Mitchell was hurt and angry by their conduct.

Discussion with the Mediator about the case prior to the mediation day

The Mediator said that this was a case of the new guard versus the old guard partners and summarized the dispute. The partners were not happy with Mitchell's work-in-progress. They alleged that he was not billing, not collecting and not posting invoices. They believed that he was not in control of his practice and a decision was made to expel him. The Mediator advised that under the Partnership Agreement, if a partner is expelled, the expelled partner is not entitled to goodwill. However, if a partner retires, the partner is entitled to a share of goodwill plus accumulated capital. Mitchell spoke of retirement, but no notice of retirement was given. Despite this, the parties attempted to negotiate the terms of retirement. When agreement was not reached, the Defendants chose to expel Mitchell from the Partnership. They did so without providing reasons and prior to the completion of an investigation. The Defendants were required to withdraw the expulsion because due process was required. Once the investigation was completed, the expulsion was reinstated. In the Mediator's view, if Mitchell had been unlawfully expelled, he would be entitled to compensation in respect of capital and goodwill.

The Mediator pointed out that no partnership accounts were produced and therefore he did not know what Mitchell would be entitled to receive. The Mediator was requested by Mitchell's solicitor to obtain documents, which he agreed to do. He would inform the Defendants that it would be useful to have the accounts if they wanted to settle. The documents were necessary to determine the claim. If they were not available, the ability to get a settlement would become more difficult, he advised. Unless Mitchell were to see the documents, his valuation of the goodwill at £600,000–£800,000 would remain and he would be entitled to capital.

The Mediator further said, *"I don't know if the partners could get into the same room. I will see each separately first. Then, to plenary. I will see if they are prepared to negotiate face to face. Shuttle is not as effective. It is purely because it is repeating things and not getting the message across right.*

"Whatever your assumptions are at the beginning, they will change throughout the day. I do not believe in midnight {endings}. It is not the way to settle."

The Mediator concluded by stating, *"Negotiation is a process. Mediation is a process in the negotiation. We are not beginning to bargain. They are already doing it and we are just the tools for it."*

The mediation day

When we met at the mediation premises, I asked the Mediator to describe his style generally. *"I meet them at the knees,"* he said. When queried as to what this

meant, the Mediator stated that he *"will bring them down to size. I have a road map that I tell the parties: 60 per cent of their time is spent with the mediator; that leaves two hours for bargaining and two hours for drafting the agreement. Also, all mediators have to be somewhat evaluative. The parties expect it. Watch for my neutrality because I empathize with Mitchell. I know how it feels to be in a partnership."*
With that, we entered the Mitchell meeting room.

First meeting with the Mitchell Team

After the introductions, the Mediator began. *"Mediation is an informal process. You can take your jacket and tie off, but not your shirt! If we speak of a ten-hour mediation, 60 per cent is spent briefing the mediator. I have reviewed the documents over the weekend, but you have lived with it longer. There is truth and what you present. The mediation day is as follows: 60 per cent, or six hours, for trading information, two hours for drafting the agreement. That means that at 3 p.m. we start bargaining. What time would you like to leave? After lunch we will have an idea if we are making progress. My sense is that the parties will need a resolution. My gut says that no one will win and to go forward will be costly. We need to find a way through it. Mediation is an informal procedure. If you feel under pressure, tell us. If you need someone to hold your hand, get one but you should have raised it earlier. Everything said to me is confidential. I have Alzheimer's. I will forget it as I leave. Keeping confidentiality is important. We need a signed settlement agreement before there is agreement. Parties can step away at any time. I will speak with the lawyers from time to time. You can tell anyone anything I say."*

After this introduction to the process, the Mediator invited Mitchell to tell him about the dispute. *"Give me the story."*[31]

Mitchell, having been invited to speak, did so. He gave the history of his relationship with Jarvis & Kimbourne and the individual partners. Once information about invoicing was received, the Mediator turned to the opening joint session, and in particular inquired of Mitchell whether he would speak and what his plans were. When the Claimant Solicitor, Max Elliot, said that he was prepared to speak, but perhaps Mitchell would as well, the Mediator said to Mitchell, *"It would be good for you. You may want to rehearse."* In response to Mitchell's comment that he *"does not rehearse"*, the Mediator said, *"This is a negotiation. Set out what you lost: ask, is this fair? It is a time to say that this is what you have done rather than being accusatory. I use the word 'rehearse' so that you know what to say and make it hard to defend. Your message is that if you were expelled, there was no cause because there was no loss suffered by the Partnership."* The Mediator

---

31 It should be noted at this point that the Mediator had not spoken with the parties prior to the mediation day due to scheduling issues. Time was spent in the first meetings with each party discussing the details of the case from each of their perspectives, more so than usual. As a result, these early private pre-joint session meetings took the form of the early private meetings that would have followed joint sessions and which were typical of mediations observed.

continued on this issue later in the session: *"Under the Agreement, the Partnership can terminate with cause if there is damage to the Partnership, not to the individual partners. You {Mitchell} need to point out that there was no loss to the Partnership. Your big argument is that the expulsion is without cause."*

The Mediator concluded with reference to the joint session. *"It would be more powerful for you to speak than your solicitor. Speak of the damage to you and that there is no damage to the firm. This is subject to legal advice and the fact that you know them {the partners}, I do not. I will speak to them and then we will have the joint meeting. If possible, let's get you speaking directly with them, but six against one is hard. I may get the lawyers talking. This is a flexible process. By 3 p.m. I will want to know where we are going."*

First meeting with the Jarvis & Kimbourne Team

On entering the Jarvis & Kimbourne room, the Mediator dealt with administrative matters first. He then described the process.

"Mediation is an informal process. We already have our jackets off. I see ties coming off as well, but keep your shirts on! The Partnership Agreement speaks of a neutral adviser. I am not an adviser. I am not evaluative. Lawyers are here. This dispute needs to be resolved. There will only be losers. It will be messy. It has been built up. We will get through it. What time do you want to go?" asked the Mediator. *"I turn into a pumpkin,"* continued the Mediator. *"After 9 p.m. people get testy. 60 per cent of the time during mediation is spent briefing the mediator. I have gone through the bundle of documents, but I won't know as much as is known in the room. The underlying issues are not in the bundle. As I said, 60 per cent of the time in mediation will be spent with the mediator, two hours to get an agreement. If we want to finish by 7 p.m., then terms need to be agreed by 5 p.m. I started at 8:30 a.m. with the others. By lunch, we will know. I am not fixed in a routine. I am flexible, but most mediations follow this process. This can be done if the parties want it to be done. I will assess at 3 p.m. and break then. This is not to pressure you, but if we put a framework on it, people will work to it.*

"Everything I hear is confidential. What I hear here stays here. I have Alzheimer's when I leave the room. I forget. I may want to meet with the lawyers separately or with each partner separately. The rule of confidentiality applies to the mediator but you can share the information. Sometimes the mediator needs information. Mediation can be nerve-racking but less so than arbitration or court proceedings. If you feel under pressure, please let me know. That is in a nutshell what mediation looks like. There is no agreement until it is in writing. Any suggestion is not binding until it is in writing. You can change your mind and no reason need be given. If we do not have this, you would get into positional bargaining.

"Tell me about the history. I've read the bundle, but you tell me about it." And thus the Defendants were invited to tell their story.

After learning about the dispute and asking questions about the Team's position, the Mediator turned to the conduct of the opening joint meeting. *"Who will speak?"* asked the Mediator. The Defendant Solicitor, Daniel Rose, replied that he would, but would be brief. The Mediator then said, *"I want to* concentrate on the cause no cause issue. The rest is capable of being sorted. I have been there where parties have lost faith in each other. He may genuinely believe he hasn't cheated you. I do not know your system." Discussion then followed about the Defendants' invoicing system and legal position.

The Mediator concluded the session by saying, "It is important to do the plenary {the opening joint session}. The aim is to get the parties talking. I may get Mitchell to speak to you as a group or individually. A right proposal at a bad time may be appropriate to raise now {sic}. I wish I had a time machine. Let's see how it goes. I will prepare the room."

Second meeting with the Mitchell Team

The Mediator referred again to the issue of cause and the invoices. Much discussion ensued over the invoicing issue and how to frame the actions of Mitchell.

Joint session

The Mediator invited the Jarvis & Kimbourne Team to the joint meeting room and then invited the Mitchell Team into the room. He welcomed the parties.

"Thanks for coming. I have met with each side. If progress is to be made, it will be because the parties are talking directly. You know about confidentiality, that nothing is binding until it is in writing. This is important to know. If the mediation goes to midnight, I turn into a pumpkin. We will break into groups and you may suggest the same if you want. I am trying to ensure that there are no surprises.

"I am entitled to decide who goes first." And with that, he asked Mitchell to begin. Mitchell spoke of his history with the law firm, his billing practice, the fact that the Partnership suffered no loss as a result of the billing practice and the impact of the Defendants' conduct on him.

The Defendants spoke through Rose, countering the position. The lawyers also bantered about the legal merits of the case.

In bringing the joint session to a close, the Mediator said, "You each have different views. We won't be able to resolve it here. At the end of the day, we need to resolve it."

The joint session ended.

During the mediation

After the conclusion of the joint session, the Mediator met privately with the Mitchell Team, followed by a meeting with the Jarvis & Kimbourne Team. Thereafter, the processual structure of the day became somewhat curious. After this meeting with the Jarvis & Kimbourne Team, Daniel Rose became a prime player within that team. He would meet privately with the Mediator throughout the course of the day to discuss the Defendants' positions and offers. He would seek out the Mediator. The Mediator would meet with the Jarvis & Kimbourne Team after a meeting with the Mitchell Team and this meeting would be invariably followed by a visit from Rose to report on the Defendants' position.

A joint session between the legal teams of both parties occurred later in the day at the behest of the Mediator for the purpose of discussing their respective views about litigation risk.

If one looks at the road-map of this mediation, as the Mediator termed it, one would see that the mediation was broken down into brief slots of time during which the Mediator met with one of the parties or waited for a party's deliberation. Offers came early in the day, with the Mediator raising the issue of offers immediately after the joint session. It was in his second meeting with the Mitchell Team, within one hour after the joint session, that the first offer was formulated and delivered to the Jarvis & Kimbourne Team. Approximately seven offers were exchanged until agreement in principle was reached, approximately 11 hours after the mediation began. A further 3.5 hours was spent on drafting the written agreement. The day ended at 11:15 p.m., 14.6 hours after it started. The Mediator spent 3.7 hours with the Mitchell Team; 0.2 hours with Max Elliot alone; 2.4 hours with the Jarvis & Kimbourne Team; 1.3 hours with Daniel Rose alone; 1.1 hours in joint sessions; and 2.8 hours alone.[32]

The comments below were made during the course of the day.

I asked the Mediator during the mediation about his objectives entering the mediation. He said, *"I felt the Defendants were bullying Mitchell and I wanted to stop the expulsion because I think it was unfair in equity. Mitchell was not treated properly and I thought I would try to get the negotiation started. We have six partners: two are strong and have a 'do not care' attitude and are ready to crush Mitchell. I did care. Two are far more pragmatic. And two are uncomfortable and want to get a deal done. My objective was to get the suspension stopped and get the discussion going. These were met."* After the conclusion of the mediation, the Mediator described his objectives as follows: *"To see if I could get the parties to speak to each other and agree on a compromise to resolve the dispute."*

During an early meeting with the Mitchell Team when speaking of Mitchell's demands for settlement, the Mediator said that he would speak with the Jarvis & Kimbourne Team to find out what it needs. He said, *"There may be shuttling – I do not like doing it."*

In private to me before continuing to shuttle between parties, the Mediator reflected on the process: *"The process is predictable. The timing and the amounts are not. People do not want to hear it because they want to be unique and at the same time it is important to know that this is part of the process and this is what happens. There is a general tendency in negotiation that each exchange takes twice as long for half as much, so it takes longer as it goes along for smaller movements and then it speeds up at the end."*

When reviewing the dispute resolution clause in the Partnership Agreement and its reference to the appointment of a 'neutral adviser' with the Jarvis &

---

32 The timelines here are slightly askew. The time during the brief sessions following the acceptance of Mitchell's offer was not recorded accurately. Accordingly, there is a margin of error in the computations of approximately 0.5 hours, give or take.

Kimbourne Team, the Mediator said to the Team, *"No one ever accused me of being a neutral adviser."*

The Mediator made reference to his role in the mediation to the Mitchell Team. He wondered whether the Defendants had considered all the arguments surrounding litigation risk. He suggested that Max Elliot discuss it with the Jarvis & Kimbourne Team because, he said, *"It is not up to me to make the point."*

Later, the Mediator commented to me also about his consideration of settlement when preparing for the mediation. *"As for whether I thought about settlement as an objective, it did not start as an objective. I just wanted to see if I have enough pieces to get us there. It was lucky that we have counsel here who want to get it resolved."*

Interview with the Mediator after the conclusion of the mediation

In answer to the inquiry whether, prior to conducting the mediation, he considered the possibility of settlement, the Mediator said, *"Yes, I did when I was reviewing the documents because it is not pleasant for the practice and the public to have someone with over 35 years of service to be tossed out after a ten-minute meeting. It is not good for morale or for client retention. You need to find a better way. Mitchell could bring the house down. He could tie the house for months. It was not an embarrassment, rather the time the partners would have to devote to give his money back. I did not believe the Defendants when they said they did not have to give the money back. A judge would not buy it. It would hurt the firm. Therefore it had to be settled. This is how I read it."*

In the Mediator's view, the mediation was of benefit to the parties because *"it put control into their hands away from litigation and enabled them to arrive at their own settlement rather than receive an imposed settlement. I suspect they won't ever do this again. It was a learning experience and it cost them."*

When asked to describe his style generally, the Mediator replied, *"I would love to know. I cut them at the knees. I am interventionist, evaluative. My sense is that the market has matured. It is the experienced mediator who will do more than listen and explore. I do it in a way to get people to explore. I do not care about settlement rates. My role is to create an environment to make the parties want to settle. If the parties are being silly, then I do find a way to knock them. For example, if a totally unwarranted position is taken by a solicitor, I need to figure out a way to deal with it. I may have the party speak directly to the other party. They need to be challenged and they may not like it.*

"In this mediation, there was no chopping off at the knees. It was not really what I did. That is bravado. If they have an unsupported position, I do challenge. I do not take it on board personally. I do sleep {at night}. When I negotiate as a negotiator, I will consider the WATNA and BATNA and will walk beyond it.[33] *I expect the*

---

33 BATNA is a negotiation acronym introduced by Roger Fisher and William Ury. It stands for Best Alternative to a Negotiated Agreement. Fisher and Ury speak of BATNA as an

parties to do it, to do their homework. Here, I was interventionist and evaluative. In a way, yes, I was not permitting discussion on areas like discrimination. I told them not to do it. Regarding evaluation, the discussion of what happened in July, I asked Mitchell, 'What did you do to make them frustrated?' I asked the Defendant Partner Harris Jarvis the same thing, 'Why are you frustrated?' It was more than reality testing. Think of the consequences and come to the table. In calculating the settlement price of £480,000 and working it out with the Defendants' solicitor, although I was outmanoeuvred by him ... I was evaluative in the settlement amount. I could see where they were halving it, so I told them to cut to the chase."

The Mediator offered a view on the relationship between mediation and negotiation: *"You can negotiate without a mediator, but you cannot mediate without a mediator."*

Participants' views about the mediation and the Mediator

Daniel Rose, the Jarvis & Kimbourne solicitor, said that the mediation *"followed a universal pattern. It was effective, long-winded – the longer we stayed, the more there was to do."* Was he happy with his Mediator? *"Absolutely. He grasped the issues and put the parties to work as required."* As for the Mediator's strengths, *"He is a good communicator – he is very good at communicating. He formed a view regarding the appropriate outcome and worked towards it. He spent less time with us, which meant that he was working hard to move the other side's position."* Rose described the Mediator's style as *"relaxed, quietly spoken and helpful"*.

Max Elliot, Mitchell's solicitor, had a similar reaction to the mediation process. *"It was pretty similar to ones I have done. There was nothing new. It is an effective but excruciating process, or rather, an excruciating process, but effective."* Regarding the Mediator, *"I thought he was good. Not every mediator does what he did. He spent time before the mediation with us and heard from the client in his own words how he felt about the case. He was keen for him to make the opening statement rather than me, and I thought it was effective and worked well. The Mediator was excellent. He did a really good job of always appearing to be sympathetic and on my client's side. My client found it reassuring and put a lot of trust in him. The Mediator worked very, very hard on getting a deal. It was a nice combination of approachability and gravitas."* As for his style, *"It was very measured and conciliatory. I did not get the impression that he would bang heads or shout. He is persistent, measured and worked very hard to get a settlement. He was tenacious."*

One of the Defendants returned a completed questionnaire. He indicated that he was 'very' satisfied with the process, 'satisfied' with the outcome and

---

important element in negotiation and one that parties must consider prior to commencing negotiation in order to properly assess options available for resolution. See generally, R. Fisher, W. Ury and B. Patton, *Getting to Yes: Negotiating Agreement Without Giving In* (New York: Penguin, 1991). The acronym BATNA spawned others such as WATNA, also referred to by the Mediator. It stands for Worst Alternative to a Negotiated Agreement.

'happy' with the Mediator. He noted that there were 'significant' savings in terms of management time, and legal and other costs.

***

The Mediator creates an illusion. Right from the beginning, he describes the case in legalistic terms, referring to the Partnership Agreement and entitlements thereunder. He narrows the issues and focuses the parties on those issues. He tells the parties what is to be discussed in the joint session. Focus on cause, he says. In this way, he takes charge of the dispute. It becomes his dispute: he is concerned about the circumstances surrounding Mitchell's retirement from the Partnership; he is concerned about the impact of litigation on the Jarvis & Kimbourne reputation and business; and he is sympathetic to Mitchell. On this latter point, he goes as far as assuming that Mitchell has entitlements, with the only unknown being quantum.

Despite this preoccupation with rights and obligations under the Partnership Agreement, the Mediator tells Mitchell privately, and the parties jointly, that the dispute must be settled. He takes a surprising turn at the end of the joint session. Recall that he orchestrated the joint session to focus on cause allegations and termination entitlements under the Partnership Agreement. At the end of the session, he announces that no agreement will be reached on these issues and, despite this, the dispute must still be resolved. It is as though he were directing the parties to a cathartic experience: talk about your rights and defend your actions. It is the proverbial 'get it off your chest'.[34] This time, however, it is not about hurt feelings, it is about legal positions. Once having done this, the Mediator moves on. For him, it is time to negotiate.

The theme of mediation as a negotiation is recurrent in this case study. The Mediator explicitly notes this to the researcher and to Mitchell. To the Jarvis & Kimbourne Team he is not as explicit, but speaks in terms suggestive of negotiation: for example, he talks about the impact of proposals. He expects the parties to prepare for the negotiation in the same manner as he would prepare; that is, considering BATNAs and WATNAs. He sees negotiation as the process within which mediation occurs. Interestingly, this seems to suggest that it is a process distinct from negotiation. This is further reinforced when the Mediator says that the parties had begun to bargain prior to the mediation and he is there to further it. Recall too that he says negotiation can occur without a mediator but a mediation cannot occur without a mediator.

Communication as part of negotiation is important to the Mediator. He speaks of 'shuttle diplomacy' and says that it is not effective because

---

34 Mediation literature is prolific about the benefit of mediation in providing disputants the opportunity to be heard and validated. The transformative literature sees this as empowering. See discussion in Chapter 3 and also at note 49 below.

miscommunication can result when parties speak through a third party. The Mediator prefers parties to speak directly to one another and it is his objective to achieve this. This will lead to resolution, he says. This accords with his characterization of mediation as a negotiation. In negotiation, parties bargain directly. More particularly, as he explains, it is his objective to get the parties to talk with each other and agree on a compromise. Communication is the key to resolution. Or, at the very least, it is the key to progressing the negotiation. The Mediator believes the negotiation should occur directly between the parties rather than through the mediator. He tells the parties that he does not like to shuttle between parties. This view is contrary to the prevalent use of private meetings in commercial mediation and mediator preference as suggested by the ethnographic data.[35] It is also contrary to what occurred in this mediation. Out of a 14.6-hour day, the parties were together and communicating directly for 1.1 of those hours; all other communication, including bargaining proposals, was conveyed through the Mediator, reflecting a common pattern throughout these cases.

Rules of confidentiality assist the function of communication, says the Mediator. They encourage the parties' participation in the dialogue. Furthermore, the declaration that the parties are not bound by their communication until a written agreement is signed also encourages parties to speak. Such encouragement is the intention of the rules.

These rules help form the underlying structure of mediation. Mediation is an informal flexible process, says the Mediator. It is a flexible process with structure. The road-map provided by the Mediator about the process categorizes the day into time periods. The Mediator acknowledges that it does not sound as though the process is flexible when he describes its structure, but asserts that his experience supports the characterization.[36] He conveys strict timelines to the day: he wants to finish within a business day. He stresses that he does not like late nights. This advice seems to box the dispute, the parties and the mediation into slices of time. It appears to be a technique of control: the Mediator is making clear his expectations for the day. They are all there

---

35 Some mediators state that they prefer direct communication between parties, but like this Mediator, they revert to the private meeting soon after the joint session is completed. Here, lawyers were put together again during the process, but the parties were not. The majority of mediators of my village, however, see value in the private meeting and prefer it.

36 The mediation day did not proceed as noted by the Mediator. Bargaining, for example, commenced soon after the joint session: by 1 p.m. the first offer had been made by the Mitchell Team. Bargaining continued until 7:25 p.m. when an agreement in principle was reached. The majority of the day was spent bargaining and almost similar time spent drafting and exchanging information: approximately, 30 per cent was spent on information exchange, 49 per cent on bargaining, and 24 per cent on drafting (recall note 32, where it is stated that computations are slightly skewed). This differs from the Mediator's figures of 60 per cent for information exchange, two hours for bargaining, and two hours for drafting.

for a purpose, which is to resolve the litigation. This is to be done within the confines of the day created and prescribed by the Mediator. As previously stated, the Mediator takes charge of the dispute. Process and mediator fuse.

This Mediator is more self-aware than other mediators. He was concerned about his 'neutrality' because he felt empathy for Mitchell. This was an honest acknowledgment, particularly since he projected a sympathetic air to the Mitchell Team. Although aware of the concern for 'neutrality', curiously this Mediator did not discuss neutrality with the parties other than referring the Jarvis & Kimbourne Team to the dispute resolution clause in the Partnership Agreement, which described his role as being a 'neutral adviser'. All he says in this respect is that he is not an adviser. Later, again to the Jarvis & Kimbourne Team and with reference to the same clause, he says that he is not a 'neutral adviser'. Nothing further was said about neutrality.

When speaking of his style to the researcher, the Mediator is explicit. He is evaluative, directive, interventionist and bullying when necessary. It is clear that he is not afraid of taking a view. He does so before he meets the parties and also when he introduces himself and the process to the parties. The Mediator has firm opinions about the impact of the dispute on the parties and the difficulties faced by the parties about their legal position. He makes these opinions known. He believes that this is appropriate for a mediator of experience because mediation is more than just facilitating through listening and exploration. His goal is to get a deal and he will do what he thinks is necessary to move the parties to that goal. In describing his style, he uses a physical analogy of cutting people off at the knees. Later, he says this is bravado, but the statement is made twice. It is how he perceives himself. He is creating a particular persona. He is silent about his style and role to Mitchell, and most intriguing, he tells the Jarvis & Kimbourne Team expressly that he is not an adviser nor evaluative. Why should he hide a style to which he so fervently aspires? It is suggestive of manipulation: hiding how one will conduct the mediation. How can the parties be aware of what they will be subjected to when a mediator tells them one thing, but may do another?

The party perspective is illuminating. Both solicitors found the process frustrating: in particular, its tedious pace. They were wholly satisfied with the Mediator, however. The solicitors saw the Mediator as an active force in the mediation, moving the parties to resolution. For them, he was responsible for getting a deal. Recall that the Mediator told the Jarvis & Kimbourne Team that he was not evaluative: this accords with Max Elliot's view of him. Elliot did not see him as evaluative; rather, he describes the Mediator as conciliatory and non-directive. He also said that the Mediator was not a type to bang heads. This is consistent with the Mediator's description of his actions in this particular mediation, but not of his style generally. The Mediator said that there was no need to challenge here. This chapter does not explore the Mediator's actions during the mediation, so comment is not made in this regard here. This will be examined in Chapter 6. As for the party representative, interestingly and yet again, we see a party representative being more satisfied with the process than with the mediator.

Case Study 9: The fishing logo

The case

The Claimant, Angler Co-Operative Ltd, had been the exclusive licensee of the Defendant, HighLander Fishing Co. Ltd logo, for the manufacture and supply of its fishing equipment and sporting apparel. A well-known and respected angler had developed the brand, and as such, products bearing his logo were popular and sold well in the worldwide marketplace. Angler Co-Operative had been the sole licensee of the logo for over 15 years pursuant to a written licence agreement (the 'Agreement') which provided for, among other things, the payment of royalties on the sale of the products. The Agreement had been automatically renewed after its initial term; however, the royalty calculation soon became an issue between the parties.

In its action, Angler Co-Operative alleged that as a result of the inability to come to terms on the calculation of the royalty, it decided to manufacture fishing equipment and sporting apparel under its own private brand. When it learned that HighLander had given the logo's licence rights to another company, Angler Co-Operative alleged that HighLander was in breach of the Agreement, which prevented the licensing of the logo during an 18-month sell-off period. Angler Co-Operative further alleged that the new licensee had advised Angler Co-Operative's major supplier that Angler Co-Operative was not permitted to use the logo, which led to the supplier's refusal to supply necessary products to Angler Co-Operative. Angler Co-Operative sought injunctive relief to permit its continued use of the HighLander brand. It alleged that it had a period of time after the termination of the Agreement within which to continue selling products bearing the HighLander logo, and also the right to continue manufacturing products that had been ordered prior to the termination of the Agreement. The injunction was denied.

HighLander defended the claim on the basis of estoppel regarding the appointment of the new licensee. It alleged that Angler Co-Operative was aware of the appointment and consented to it. As for the continued use of the logo by Angler Co-Operative following the termination of the Agreement, it was HighLander's position that Angler Co-Operative had the exclusive right to manufacture for a 12-month period following the termination but not for an 18-month period, as sought by Angler Co-Operative. It also alleged that orders submitted prior to the termination date were not legitimate. It counterclaimed, alleging trademark infringement and passing off. It also sought payment of outstanding royalty fees, and accounting and domain name transfer.

The parties had engaged in settlement negotiations after the judicial hearing for injunctive relief. Offers and counter-offers had been exchanged, but no settlement had been reached. A mediation was scheduled to deal with the impasse. The party representatives were confident, charming businessmen with strong views and personalities.

Discussion with the Mediator about the case prior to the mediation day

In a telephone conversation with the Mediator prior to the mediation, the Mediator commented on the mediation. The mediation looked, he said, *"straightforward. The issues are not complex. It is a pure contractual dispute. Yes, there will be views on interpretation but the number of issues is not great. The parties' interests are limited to some issues. I will speak to them later and try to flesh it out."* As for the potential for settlement, he said, *"The case may or may not settle."*

When asked about his style, the Mediator was unable to comment. He said, *"I can't describe it. Other people have, though, and my biography sets out those comments. I don't know myself.*

"I don't know how I will approach it: I need a better view of where the parties are coming from. My sense is that HighLander is very well advised, that it has put on its thinking hat. It has advanced a very good defence and has taken a strategic view on the counter-claim. I think that Angler Co-Operative initiated a claim that it may now regret because it will be thrown into a trial in three months. It has an early decision against it which may not be reflective of what will happen at trial, but it is there. Litigation takes on a life of its own. I will just see what stance the parties are taking and I will try to flush out the real interests. I think Angler Co-Operative is worried about the royalty payment and wants to sell as many products as possible. There will likely be a horse-trade on how many products it can sell and how this will interact with the royalties."

And finally, the Mediator mentioned that he knows one of the lawyers for HighLander. The lawyer is *"sensible and experienced and will have told HighLander that it would be sensible to do a deal, to regularize the marketplace".*

First meeting with the HighLander Team

This meeting began with the introduction of an unexpected issue regarding the Mediator's prior work with the HighLander solicitor, Michael James.[37] Angler Co-Operative's solicitor, Lee Benjamin, raised an allegation of conflict of interest. An email had been sent to the Mediator that morning advising

---

[37] The prior work between the Mediator and James was described by both individuals. To the Mediator and the HighLander Team, James said that they had litigated a case opposite one another; they mediated a case as legal representatives opposite one another; and James acted as assistant mediator in one of the Mediator's prior mediations. The Mediator informed the Angler Co-Operative Team that he and James litigated a case at the bar and that James acted as an assistant mediator to the Mediator in a prior mediation. The Mediator also said that he has kept in touch with James on a professional basis since meeting him when he was a junior lawyer, but does not see him much.

the Mediator of Angler Co-Operative's concern that the Mediator had worked with James in other cases. It should be noted that the email also stated that the Mediator's integrity was not being questioned. The HighLander Team also received a similar email.

James explained his prior relationship with the Mediator and the process that led to the Mediator's selection by the parties. The Mediator commented that this was *"a storm in a teacup. If I was not comfortable, I would not mediate, but Angler Co-Operative needs to feel comfortable. ... I am here to try to settle. If they don't have trust in me, it won't settle. I will have a chat with them."*

However, prior to speaking with the Angler Co-Operative Team about its concern, the Mediator described the mediation process to the HighLander Team. *"It is an informal, non-binding, private meeting. Nothing you say today, carried to the other side, will be used outside here."* The HighLander party representative, Lewis Jacob, asked what 'non-binding' meant. The Mediator replied, *"There is no agreement until a document is signed, by either your solicitor, counsel or me. No one leaves until it is signed. At one mediation, someone left without signing and they later backed out."*

The Mediator then told the HighLander Team about his experience as an angler – a bad angler at that – and his knowledge of the fishing brand and fishing season. Thereafter, he continued with his description of the process. *"When we start the mediation, I will spend time privately with you to understand your priorities, things that you care deeply about and those you care less deeply about. I need to evaluate that and develop a shopping list. I will do the same with Angler Co-Operative."*

The Mediator left the HighLander Team to speak with the Angler Co-Operative Team.

First meeting with the Angler Co-Operative Team

The Mediator told the Team that he had discussed the concern raised in Lee Benjamin's email with the HighLander Team. Benjamin immediately said, *"It is not an issue for us; we are not suggesting anything less than impartiality from you."* The Mediator responded, *"From your perspective, if I did not feel comfortable, I would tell you."* He then proceeded to advise of the history of his relationship with Michael James.[38] *"It does not trouble me, but it is a very important issue."* The Claimant party representative, Dominic Gerald, said that this was the first time he had become aware of the issue and he was happy to proceed. After some further discussion about the mediator selection process, the Mediator said, *"If you're comfortable, I am."*

The Mediator described the process to the Team. *"It's informal. I am not here sitting as a judge. The process is completely informal. The parties are acting sensibly.*

---

38 See description of this relationship as told by the Mediator at ibid.

The rules of engagement I will say in the joint session. There are few rules. It is a flexible procedure. Ultimately, it is your day, but I will make suggestions on how to move forward. I do not want to keep you until midnight. I want to help you reach a deal. If we reach a stage where we can't, I will tell you. Ultimately, it depends on you and HighLander."

One of the Team members asked whether there is a structure to the process although it is informal. The Mediator replied, "We start all together. Introductions are made. I will draw attention to points in the mediation agreement, telling you what they mean. I will reiterate confidentiality. We will spend time with each party saying what they would like to say to the other side. It should be productive and constructive. I will then spend time in private. What you say in the room does not go to the other side. Frankness helps. Do not play me. If I know what you want, I can help you achieve it. I do sit as a judge from time to time, but I stress that I am not here as a judge. I do not hear the evidence. I am not judging who is right or wrong. I will give my views but they are provisional and of no value at all.

"I am an angler – a bad angler – I fish enough to know your brand and their brand. I do not buy it. I have understood how the fishing season works, except this year is odd. I think we're fishing later in the year now." He then discussed that he would be fishing in the north of Scotland while on holiday.

Dominic Gerald talked about his relationship with Lewis Jacob and the history of the negotiations between them. The Mediator, in concluding the session, spoke again about the joint session. *"Let's give each side the opportunity to say what they need to say. I would like to keep the opening statements to 20 minutes. Bear in mind, you can eyeball the other side and say what you want. Get it off your chest, the commercial and the emotional. It can apply to all. I do not want to spend the entire morning in joint session. Let's get into private session."*

Second meeting with the HighLander Team

The Mediator entered the HighLander room saying, *"First crisis averted. There was some misunderstanding by Lee Benjamin. Dominic Gerald said immediately that he had no trouble."* With that, he proceeded to advise that the conflict of interest issue had been resolved.

Lewis Jacob asked who would be making the opening statement on behalf of Angler Co-Operative. In response, the Mediator said, *"I think it will be Dominic Gerald. It is not to be a legal analysis. Do what you want. This is the one chance to eyeball them before going to court. Take advantage of it and say what you want. Be commercially constructive. Get it off your chest. Keep it to 20 minutes."* The Mediator then advised that the Angler Co-Operative Team would go first because it initiated the action.

Joint session

The parties entered the room, shook hands with one another and introduced themselves.

The Mediator began by stating that the mediation agreement had been signed and gave copies to each party. *"Thank you for appointing me and agreeing to come to the mediation. We have resolved the issue that arose overnight and everyone is comfortable continuing. I have no difficulty and everyone is OK with it."*

The Mediator then gave a description of his law practice. He continued, *"My role today is different from my day-to-day practice. I have practised for several years as a mediator. As a mediator, my role is to facilitate, not judge. My intention is not to judge, and I cannot because I haven't heard all the evidence. A Chancery Division judge will decide who is right and wrong. The advantage today is complete flexibility. There is no right or wrong. Each will receive the benefit of mediation. The essence of mediation is that neither will be entirely happy, but you will reach something that you will live with. In litigation one party will be unhappy, and even the winner will be unhappy.*

"Regarding the rules of the game, it is informal. We are on first names basis. Leave it to me to judge how to move matters along. Regarding the mediation agreement, whatever discussion of information occurs today is private and confidential. It cannot be used for any purpose except for the mediation. Bear this in mind. We will have private meetings. Anything you tell us will not go outside the room. I encourage parties to be frank so I can help you achieve your objectives. I won't disclose to the other side unless you authorize me to. I will invite parties to deliver a short opening. All can participate. Limit it to 20 minutes. It is the one time to eyeball each other and say what you want to. Put anything forward. There is one rule. No interruptions. I will adopt a yellow card system. Because Angler Co-Operative is the claimant, I will suggest that it goes first."

Thus, the joint session began.

Once the Angler Co-Operative Team finished, the Mediator confirmed it had nothing further to add and then invited the HighLander Team to speak. At the conclusion of its opening, the Mediator asked whether any other Team members wished to add anything. *"It is clear that Angler Co-Operative is itching to respond and debate. Unless you have a firm desire, then let's go ahead."* When Lee Benjamin said that he had three points to make, the Mediator told him to *"be brief"*. As soon as he finished, the Mediator concluded the joint session as follows: *"Thanks for keeping it brief. It is after noon, so I will spend time separately {with each party}. Do not attribute importance to how long I spend or with whom. Use the time productively. Read a book, take a stroll, but leave your mobile number."*

With these words, the Mediator met privately with the Angler Co-Operative Team in the joint session meeting room after HighLander decamped to its private room.

During the mediation

Following this joint session, the Mediator met with the Angler Co-Operative Team for approximately an hour. He met with the HighLander Team immediately thereafter. This was followed by private meetings alternating between

Angler Co-Operative and HighLander until an agreement in principle was reached. The parties spent about two and a half hours drafting the agreement, with active Mediator participation.

The mediation day was approximately 10.5 hours in length, with Mediator time spent as follows: 3.4 hours with the Angler Co-Operative Team; 2.9 hours with the HighLander Team; 1.3 hours in joint session with both teams; 0.5 hours alone; and 2.4 hours drafting the written settlement agreement. There were four separate meetings with Angler Co-Operative after the joint session, and five sessions with HighLander.

During the time the agreement was being drafted, Dominic Gerald and Lewis Jacob met and chatted amicably. There was much laughter between them. They insisted that the researcher take a photo of them together, stating, *"This is what mediation is all about."* One of the solicitors said, *"It shows the continuation of a relationship."*[39]

Interview with the Mediator after the conclusion of the mediation

The Mediator's objectives for this mediation were to *"build trust and confidence, and to figure out if there was an issue, particularly with respect to the conflict issue. This helped me because Dominic Gerald did not know it, but it built trust with Gerald as a result. It was a silly move. It was an inexperienced solicitor and a Scottish lawyer applying Scottish principles here to conflict {of interest} issues."*

The Mediator does consider whether the dispute will settle: *"Yes, I do consider it. I look at the papers and usually think that there will be difficulty, but here I did not think that with this case. I would have been disappointed if I did not settle because it did not seem that they were far apart, but I could have been surprised by the mediation. I could turn up at the day and be surprised by something. Here I did not know Angler Co-Operative's solicitor, but it was good that I knew HighLander's solicitor. His presence was good news. He is sensible and pro-mediation. He is a professional friend. It influenced my view on the issue."*

When asked to describe his style generally, the Mediator responded, *"In this mediation, I don't know. I don't think a mediator can answer. I genuinely do not go in with a predetermined view of what I would do. I just knew I would make a joke about being a poor angler. Let it all sail over you and go with what seems right."* As for his style during this mediation, he said, *"Things about this mediation would have influenced what I did. I did not need to be analytical of the claims. I did not need to push very hard on the desirability of a solution. I never needed to deal with risks. I never had to make a cost-risk analysis. I have never had to do it in a mediation. This was the first time. It was moving along nicely and I did not need to*

---

39 Interestingly, the agreement was about the termination of the relationship. There was no future business contemplated beyond what was necessary for the termination of the contractual arrangement that existed between the parties.

rock the boat. I had two parties who wanted to settle here." Further, he stated, "I did not need to do reality checking with the parties. Any half-decent mediator could do this one." As for his good relationship with the parties and particularly Dominic Gerald, the Mediator stated, "Any mediator would have got on with Gerald. It is a mediator's job to get along with the parties – that is what mediation is all about."

Participants' views about the mediation and the Mediator

Lee Benjamin, Angler Co-Operative's solicitor, said that the mediation was similar to others he had attended. There were no surprises from the process. *"I expected more leading from the Mediator but he was not prepared to give it. He was at pains to be even-handed, which can become quite vexing. There was endless to-ing and fro-ing. It is an inherent problem with the process. We did not get led. It is a matter for the mediator to persuade. I know it flies in the face of the remit of mediation: for the mediator to see the strengths and weaknesses of the parties, the ability to sum up and focus the mind of the parties, to conduct shuttle diplomacy. It can be a frustrating experience."*

Benjamin continued: *"I was genuinely happy with the Mediator."* As for his strengths, *"He was very easy-going, he was quick to get a grip on the situation. He was a keen angler and this aided more than anything else – more than skill. Dominic Gerald is extremely difficult to deal with. He took the Mediator seriously; he felt that the Mediator understood the industry. If he did not understand it, Gerald would have walked out by lunchtime. He established a common interest in fishing and they had mutual acquaintances as well. The Mediator knew the Scottish north. It was luck, who was to know."*[40]

In an email sent directly to the Mediator following the mediation, Benjamin also commented about the mediation process: *"If you were wrong about anything, I think you might have underestimated the extent to which both sides could be content at the end of a successful mediation."*

In another email, sent by another member of the Angler Co-Operative legal team, a comment was made that parties had to set aside any desire to be in control: *"The mediation process requires the parties to put such inclinations to one side in order to reach a genuine compromise."*

A member of HighLander's legal team thought that the process *"worked very well. It did what I would expect it to do. It was like the others I attended. I was very happy with the Mediator."* Although he could not recall the Mediator's style specifically, he said, *"The Mediator managed to make it feel sufficiently informal. He was businesslike, he was there to do a deal and he did it in the end."* The solicitor also commented about the process and the Mediator's role in an email sent directly to the Mediator: *"I am pretty confident that this is one*

---

40 It was pure luck that this Mediator was a keen angler: his curriculum vitae did not disclose this detail nor was the specific fishing experience requested by the parties.

which would not have settled by other means and I have no doubt that you were able to strike the right note in your private sessions with each of HighLander and Angler Co-Operative, and have no doubt that the 'right note' will have been quite different for each party!"

One of Angler Co-Operative party representatives responded to the Organization's questionnaire. The lead representative was 'extremely' satisfied with the process, and 'very' satisfied with outcome and 'very' happy with the choice of mediator. The process was 'very' much what he expected. The second Angler Co-Operative party representative was 'very' satisfied with the process, 'happy' with the mediator, and 'satisfied' with the outcome. 'Significant' savings in management time, and legal and other costs were noted. The process, for him, was 'as expected'.

One of the HighLander party representatives also responded. In his response he indicated that he was 'very' satisfied with the process, that it was 'as expected', and he was 'fairly' satisfied with the outcome. He reported 'significant' savings in management time, and legal and other costs. He was 'extremely' happy with the Mediator. The representative also noted, *"First-class mediator. Feel mediation should be obligatory in all litigation. Shame it did not happen earlier."*

***

Similarities and inconsistencies could be the title of this commentary: the similarities of discourse to that of other mediations were anticipated; the inconsistencies within the mediation itself were not. Commencing with the similarities, we see a desire for freedom of expression from the parties. The Mediator implores them to be frank and to 'eyeball' the other. Be emotional, he tells them. Get it off their chest. But, he also tells them to be productive and constructive, somehow undermining the advice for them to speak their mind. Furthermore, he restricts them by saying that he wants to keep the joint session brief with the intention of moving into private meetings quickly.[41] This is confirmed in the joint session when he firmly tells HighLander to be brief in response, and when thanking the parties for their brevity. As it turned out, the joint session was not as brief as the Mediator intended: it lasted 1.3 hours rather than the 0.7 hours he requested.

The Mediator speaks of frankness in communication. His concern for frankness is not solely directed to the parties' communication with the others; he asks them to be frank with him and he tells them not to 'play' him. The suggestion here is of manipulation by the parties of the mediator. He says that he can only help them if they are open with him. He needs to find out their objectives in order to help them achieve those objectives.

---

41 Recall that the Mediator told each party to limit their opening statements to 20 minutes.

The Mediator tells the parties that he is not a judge and will not opine on what is right and wrong. He is there to facilitate their dialogue for resolution. He does not say what facilitation involves. He merely uses the word 'facilitate'. He does say to the Angler Co-Operative Team, however, that he sits as a judge and he will give his views on matters, which it is free to accept or reject as it sees fit. This seemingly accords with his assertion that the mediation is about the parties; it is their day. Yet, he sees a need to tell one party that he sits as a judge and he tells both parties that he will be in control of the day. He will determine how to move matters forward. He tells them what to speak about and for how long.

The issue of the 'conflict of interest', as coined by the parties including the Mediator, is another example of mediator-centredness. This was a concern about the Mediator's status as a non-aligned third party. The Angler Co-Operative Team was concerned about the Mediator's prior work relationship with Michael James. This suggested a compromise of mediator neutrality. Although the Mediator understood that the party needed to be satisfied with the Mediator's neutrality, the Mediator appeared to be patronizing about it. It was a 'storm in a teacup'. He belittled the concern to the other party. He did so because he felt that if he were comfortable with the situation, then the party should also be comfortable. The Angler Co-Operative Team should trust him to be neutral because if *he* felt that he could act in the face of a prior relationship with a member of the opposite party, nothing else mattered.

Two interesting observations arise from this interaction. First, the Mediator made positive comments about the skills of James prior to the mediation; for example, that the lawyer would be sensible and that HighLander is well advised. James' mere presence led the Mediator to believe that a settlement could be reached. Whether this impacted the way the Mediator conducted the mediation is not within the scope of this chapter. The point is raised to illustrate that the concern raised by the Angler Co-Operative Team was genuine and supportable. The Mediator played lip-service to the concern, focusing instead on his own view regarding the state of his neutrality, or using the folk discourse of the parties, regarding the existence of a 'conflict of interest'. Second, the words used by all participants in referring to this 'storm in a teacup' were 'conflict' and 'conflict of interest', with the exception of Lee Benjamin who raised the concern. He expected 'impartiality' from the Mediator. Despite the concern raised by Benjamin, the Mediator did not discuss this seemingly fundamental aspect of his role; he did not describe himself as a neutral or impartial third party; he did not assure the parties that he would be neutral or impartial; and he did not explain what it means to be neutral or impartial. Their meaning was assumed. Even with respect to their own native discourse, no one explained, defined or clarified what was meant by 'conflict of interest' or its impact on the mediation. A legalistic label was given and used by the legal players in the mediation. It also generated an assumed understanding.

As for his style or strategy, the Mediator is nonchalant about both. It is interesting that he uses the words interchangeably. On style, he cannot comment. He leaves it for others to comment. This is suggestive of a lack of reflection on his craft.[42] On strategy, he has none and he does not believe that mediators should go into mediation with a plan. His only plan was to make use of his experience as an angler. As for his strategy in this mediation, the Mediator was of the view that he did not challenge the parties nor was an active participant in the mediation. He felt there was no need because the parties were intent on settlement, suggesting that his presence was not necessary to help them reach a resolution.

Perhaps the Mediator felt this way because of his relationship with the parties. Rapport appears to play an integral role in this mediation.[43] Rapport took on the mantle of the angler. The common joint hobby of the Mediator and the parties took on a particular significance here. Lee Benjamin is quite clear on this: the fact that the Mediator was a keen angler was crucial to Dominic Gerald. It created a bond between the Mediator and Gerald. It lent gravitas to the Mediator and his authority. The Mediator knew this. He played the role of avid angler with purpose. It was strategic on his part. He spoke of his interest, experience and knowledge of the industry with both teams before the joint session. He placed himself within the playing field of the parties as an insider of the industry, speaking their language. It was part of relationship-building. For this Mediator, it is what mediation is all about. As he states, *"It is a mediator's job to get along with the parties."* Rapport insinuates itself in mediation through the mediator's efforts. It gives confidence to the mediator and to the parties.

As for the process itself, mediation is described as a private, informal meeting, where nothing is binding until it is in writing and signed. The Mediator tells the parties that his role is to help them get a deal. Although prior to the mediation he thinks of the dispute in legal terms, commerciality is the aim for the day. Mediation as negotiation is paramount here. He uses negotiation-speak: approach the dialogue commercially, not legally; it is not binding; it is confidential; it is without prejudice.

The parties see mediation in this frame as well. Michael James said that the Mediator was there to do a deal and he achieved it. Lee Benjamin also viewed the mediation through the negotiation lens. For him, the Mediator was not sufficiently active and did not persuade. Interestingly, this solicitor

---

42 M.D. Lang and A. Taylor, *The Making of a Mediator: Developing Artistry in Practice* (San Francisco: Jossey-Bass, 2000). Lang and Taylor speak of the need for mediator self-reflection as a prerequisite to achieving artistry in practice. For example, see at 51, 120, 240.

43 Rapport is a word that is much used by the mediation community. For the purposes of this chapter, the following definition is used: "a close and harmonious relationship in which there is common understanding". See *The Concise Oxford English Dictionary*, at: http://www.oxfordreference.com (accessed August 2012).

recognizes that this role is contrary to common mediation practice, which he described as a mediator seeing the parties' strengths and weaknesses, summing up and focusing their minds, and conducting shuttle diplomacy. This is what he believed his Mediator did; he would have preferred something more, something different. Despite this, he was pleased with the Mediator's performance.

Another contradiction arises here: Benjamin sees the process as frustrating; he sees the Mediator as effective. A distinction is made between process and mediator by a mediation participant. The three party representatives also see a distinction between mediator and process in terms of satisfaction levels, not as happy with process as mediator or vice versa. It is, however, a distinction without boundaries. The Mediator speaks of controlling the day; it is more than that. He creates the process as the day progresses. There is no process without him.

Summary

In this chapter, an image of mediation is created through the voices of its participants. What do the participants tell us about mediation? Some themes emerge.

There is a significant focus on communication and the need to be frank, forthright and clear so that each participant may understand the nature of the dispute and its impact on the party. Yet, it must be remembered that the majority of party communication during mediation occurs in private meetings with the mediator, not with the other party. The suggestion here is that only with full and unfettered communication *with the mediator* can a resolution be achieved, and it can only be reached through mediator involvement. It also suggests a lack of transparency regarding the process and the mediator's intended actions.

The lack of transparency and the inconsistencies in what is said to parties compared to what is said to the researcher as gleaned through the observations are intriguing. The parties are often kept in the dark about this process called mediation and about the mediator who embodies the process. An example is found with the issue of neutrality: despite the prevalence of the concepts of neutrality and impartiality in the description of mediation activity in the literature and in the Organization's training material and mediation model, there is little, if any, discussion of either concept with parties.[44] Parties are not assured about neutrality or impartiality, yet mediation is said to involve a neutral third party. Mediators are aware of a need to be 'neutral' or 'impartial', but do not see the need to assure the parties of this. This is the case even when a party raises a concern about mediator neutrality.[45]

---

44 See notes 27, 28 and 29 above.
45 Recall the 'conflict of interest' issue of Case Study 9.

Intriguingly, the parties, generally, continue to see the mediator as 'neutral' or as being 'impartial'.[46]

Rather than speaking expressly about neutrality or impartiality, the mediators speak of the fact that they are not judges, they will not make decisions, and they will not provide a view on the merits of legal positions. They talk about helping the parties with their attempt to resolve their dispute. It is for the parties to make decisions on views they take about the dispute. They describe mediation as a negotiation, one that is facilitated by them. The focus is on the deal. In the initial meetings with the parties, they emphasize the need for commerciality for resolution.[47] They encourage offers early in the process and they discourage long days.

It is clear that the mediators see themselves as the dealmakers.[48] They imply that they are facilitators of the process, but this is only a façade. They speak of the necessity for full communication, of parties being responsible for the outcome, of the need to hear each other's views, and of the importance of getting things off their chest. Yet, in the midst of this remains the deal – for mediators and parties alike. For mediators, mediation is all about the deal rather than the process. They explicitly describe themselves as facilitators of settlement. The processual goal is to find the deal. The mediator's goal is to find the deal. The mediator is there only to do the deal and it is the deal that is important.

It is important for parties too. Parties want mediators to deliver on what can be said to be, for them, the promise of mediation. This is not the Bush and Folger transformative promise, but the commercial promise of a compromise agreement.[49] For the parties, mediation is not about empowerment, continuing

---

46 In these case studies, an exception may be found with the Claimant Solicitor's view in Case Study 8, who said that the Mediator was sympathetic to the Claimant.
47 This statement is not intended to suggest that the mediators do not consider the legal positions of the parties or the legal issues in the dispute. To the contrary, the mediators are aware of the legal issues and deal with them in different ways. However, it is not the intent of this chapter to examine the role of law in mediation.
48 Deborah Kolb, in her examination of federal and state labour mediators in the United States, categorized federal mediators as 'orchestrators' and state mediators as 'dealmakers'. The 'dealmakers' saw their aim to be to make a deal. The 'orchestrator', on the other hand, saw himself as a facilitator of dialogue. See, for example, D.M. Kolb, "Roles Mediators Play: State and Federal Practice" (1981) 20 *Industrial Relations* 1 at 4. Although the word 'dealmaker' is being used here, it does not imply that the mediators of this study are 'dealmakers' in the same manner as are the mediators of the Kolb study. In fact, the mediators of this study see themselves both as dealmakers (in the ordinary usage of the term) and as facilitators (as used by mediation literature).
49 R.A. Baruch Bush and J. Folger, *The Promise of Mediation* (San Francisco: Jossey-Bass, 1994). For the authors, transformation is used to describe a process leading to empowerment of and recognition by parties in a dispute. Transformation occurs on the attainment of these two states of being: "Empowerment is achieved when disputing parties experience a

relationships, or gaining an understanding of the other party's view. It is about finding a solution to end their dispute. The parties see the process of mediation as a way to find a settlement, to create order from disorder. They look to the mediator to deliver on this promise.

This paramount concern for agreement confirms a view of mediation as an intervention auxiliary to negotiation rather than as an autonomous process.[50] Its process is dependent on the negotiation aims of its participants. Mediator 8 expressly refers to the negotiatory shape of the mediation process. The other two, Mediators 9 and 7, are not as direct in linking mediation to negotiation. They speak only in general terms: mediation is informal, it is non-binding, it is private. This suggests a vision of a process distinct from negotiation. Yet, their articulated characteristics of mediation are similar to those of negotiation. For them, the goal of mediation is the goal of negotiation: to find common ground, to compromise and to find a mutually acceptable resolution to the dispute. Ultimately, for all, the essence of mediation is negotiation. It is the underlying foundation on which the participants proceed in the search for an agreement. Mediation depends on negotiation to provide its processual shape.

Process is briefly described to the parties. The informality of the process is almost always noted without any articulation of what is meant by informality. The characterization of mediation as informal suggests that process is fluid and changeable at the whim of the parties. In reality, it is at the whim of the mediator only. In this regard, the parties are expressly advised that the mediator is in control of the process and will dictate what occurs and when. Although the parties are given a brief sense of the general structure of joint and private meetings and a need to draft an agreement if a deal is reached, they remain ignorant of the actual processual shape of the day. That knowledge remains with the mediator. It is the mediator who crafts the process from the moment she engages with the parties. The mediator sees a need to be responsive to the parties in conducting the mediation. The process the mediator directs is determined by her perceptions about party needs and mediator goals.

The participants themselves, including mediators, see a distinction between mediator and process. The mediators speak about being in control of the process, referring to process as something that is independent from them. The mediator in Case Study 7, for example, is specific about this. He says that

---

strengthened awareness of their own self-worth and their own ability to deal with whatever difficulties they face, regardless of external constraints. Recognition is achieved when, given some degree of empowerment, disputing parties experience an expanded willingness to acknowledge and be responsive to other parties' situations and common human qualities." See at 84–5.

50 S. Roberts and M. Palmer, *Dispute Processes: ADR and the Primary Forms of Decision-making* (Cambridge: Cambridge University Press, 2005) at 173.

a mediator is to remain outside the process; it is for the parties to be in the process. The legal representatives, when pleased with the mediator, are often critical about the process. They see mediators as responsible for getting a deal, actively engaging in the dispute in a non-directive and non-confrontational way. Yet, they find the process frustrating. Although generally satisfied with process and mediator, the parties themselves are not as satisfied with the mediator as they are with the process. These distinctions between process and mediator made by the participants suggest that participants may not understand the nature of the relationship between mediation and mediator. At a minimum, the distinctions suggest that participants do not share the same vision for what the process is and what they expect it to be.

The internal views of the participants and the external view of the observer regarding mediator and process collide. The case studies suggest that it is difficult to distinguish between the mediation process and the mediator. 'How can we know the dancer from the dance?'[51] Yeats' poetic question encapsulates perfectly the conundrum of the fluidity of the merger of mediator and process. When one examines the mediators' descriptions of their approaches, objectives, and role within mediation, it appears that process and mediator cannot be distinguished.[52] In the way the mediator speaks about the mediation and his intentions in relation to it, it becomes evident that he *is* the process. As stated above, the mediator is responsible for every stage of the process; he defines it. Mediator 8 described succinctly the relationship between process and mediator: there cannot be mediation without a mediator. Mediator and mediation are fused.

We learn that mediators do not appear to think in terms of strategy when approaching mediation, at least not to the extent that they wish to be either self-aware about it or wish to disclose it. They tell parties that they cannot state definitively what will occur during the day beyond the fact of joint session and private meetings. That is all the parties are aware of. They do not know how long the joint session will last, whether there will be others and with whom, what the mediator will say to them in private, when offers will be made. They do not know what will be required of them beyond the joint session, other than to be patient during the time when the mediator is not with them.

---

51 William Butler Yeats, 'Among School Children'. Many thanks to Professor Simon Roberts for recalling this line from Yeats' poem.
52 Although not with specific reference to the dichotomy between mediator and process that is being discussed here, Folger raises a somewhat analogous point when he suggests that the institutional context within which mediation occurs shapes the process according to the institution's values and vision so that process reflects the institution's image. J.P. Folger, "'Mediation Goes Mainstream' – Taking the Conference Theme Challenge" (2002–03) 3 *Pepp. Disp. Resol. L. J.* 1 at 4.

Despite denials of strategic planning, the case studies suggest the contrary. There is a strategy, albeit an unacknowledged, unarticulated one. One might call it a *laissez-faire* approach to strategy, but a strategy nonetheless. Mediators consider the issues, the information that must be disclosed, the barriers to resolution and the anticipated needs and reactions of the parties. This raises a baffling observation. The mediators in these social dramas claim they have no pre-planned strategy. They convey an image of someone who dives headlong into the lake, not knowing whether leeches will stick to his body, whether weeds will entangle his limbs, or whether an undertow will take him further out from the shore. A reactive rather than proactive picture emerges. This contradicts the literary portrayal of the mediator as having a defined, articulated role. What is the benefit in such a disempowering claim? It is unclear.

Similarly, the self-ascribed inability to describe one's style of mediating also runs contrary to the many styles suggested by the literature as glimpsed in Chapter 3. Recalling this survey of mediator interventions, the use of the facilitative and evaluative nomenclature became typical in the literature exploring mediator styles together with the Bush and Folger transformative approach to mediation, and more recently, Winslade's narrative mediation.[53] These primary approaches have been augmented by other developments, including strategic and insight mediation, for example.[54] Despite these developments, the facilitative/evaluative divide still lives on in the nomenclature of mediator practice.[55] To recap from the earlier discussion about the

---

53 See discussion about mediator interventions under the heading 'Mediator vision' in Chapter 3. For examples of the categorizations of these approaches as primary approaches, see S.N. Exon, "The Effects that Mediator Styles Impose on Neutrality and Impartiality Requirements of Mediation" (2007–08) 42 *U.S.F. L. Rev.* 577; and B. Jarrett, "The Future of Mediation: A Sociological Perspective" (2009) *J. Disp. Resol.* 49.

54 Again, see discussion about mediator interventions under the heading 'Mediator vision' in Chapter 3. Regarding insight mediation, see in particular, C.A Picard and K.R Melchin, "Insight Mediation: A Learning-centered Mediation Model" (2007) *Negotiation J.* 35; and regarding strategic mediation, see in particular, K. Kressel, "The Strategic Style in Mediation" (2007) 24 *Conflict Resol. Q.* 251.

55 See E. McDermott and R. Obar, "'What's Going On' in Mediation: An Empirical Analysis of the Influence of a Mediator's Style on Party Satisfaction and Monetary Benefit" (2004) 9 *Harv. Negot. L. Rev.* 75 for an overview of the literature on the facilitative/evaluative dichotomy. For a discussion of mediation as both evaluative and facilitative, see R. Birke, "Evaluation and Facilitation: Moving Past Either/Or" (2000) *J. Disp. Resol.* 309; and K.M. Roberts, "Mediating the Evaluative-facilitative Debate: Why Both Parties are Wrong and a Proposal for Settlement" (2007–08) 39 *Loy. U. Chicago L. J.* 187. Golann sees mediators moving along the facilitative/evaluative grid: D. Golann, "Variations in Mediation: How – and Why – Legal Mediators Change Styles in the Course of a Case" (2000) *J. Disp. Resol.* 41; and D. Golann and M.Corman Aaron, "Using Evaluations in Mediation" in

facilitative and evaluative mediator, an evaluative mediator is often described as one who gives an opinion on the legal merits of the parties' positions, assesses the strengths and weaknesses of positions, makes suggestions for resolution, controls the discussion between parties, and focuses on legal outcomes and rights. A facilitative mediator, on the other hand, is described in terms of gentle intervention: one who supports and guides, who does not opine, advise or propose solutions, but instead focuses the parties on determining the strengths and weaknesses of their case through information exchange and self-assessment, and helps the parties come to their own solution.[56] These terms are often invoked by the mediators in these case studies.

For example, to the parties the mediators say that they will not advise or guide. They say that they will not be evaluative or directive or provide a view.[57] They say that they are there to facilitate their settlement of the dispute. Interestingly, however, they tell the researcher that they are evaluative, they challenge parties on their positions, and their objective is to find a settlement. They seek to direct without party awareness. Despite such clear language to the researcher as to how they intervene in a dispute, we hear in this chapter from Mediators 9 and 7 that they cannot comment on their style. They say that it is up to those who experience their interventions to describe their style. The unwillingness to articulate an approach or style taken to mediation suggests a cavalier attitude, or at best a naivety, to the practice and to the needs of mediation participants.

Mediators use rapport as a strategic tool to build a relationship with the parties, to instil party confidence in their actions, and to create a perception of mediator support for them to allow the mediator to confront them about the dispute. Ultimately, through relationship-building, mediators manipulate the parties into accepting their active involvement in the negotiation of a resolution to their dispute. Mediators promote an image of a benign intervener, one who will help the parties find *their* way to resolution. Their intentions are the opposite: *they* will actively *move* the parties to resolution.

AAA Handbook on Mediations (American Arbitration Association/Juris, 2010) at 327–41. See D.J. Della Noce, "Communicating Quality Assurance: A Case Study of Mediator Profiles on a Court Roster" (2008) 84 *N.D. L. Rev.* 769, in which she examines the manner in which court-roster mediators are asked to categorize their styles as facilitative, evaluative or transformative: specifically, at note 33 therein, Della Noce offers a description of each orientation according to the literature.

56 Descriptions of the evaluative and facilitative mediator are plentiful. The descriptions given of evaluation and facilitation that follow are not controversial and are based on a general reading of the literature in this area, beginning with Riskin and other writings cited in Chapter 3 and herein.

57 The exception here is Mediator 9: he tells the parties that he will give a view, but it is up to them whether to accept it.

In addition, by advising the parties that control of the dispute rests with them, that the day offers an opportunity for full and frank communication and resolution of the dispute, the mediator appears to be empowering the parties. Mediators encourage the parties to speak of how the dispute has affected them and say that it will be powerful to do so. What is the purpose of this empowerment? Is it to empower the parties or is it to empower the mediator? The usual understanding in the literature is that the purpose is to empower the parties. The data suggests otherwise: it is the mediator who is empowered by the parties' empowerment. The mediator sees her ability to reach a resolution of the dispute to be dependent on the parties' confidence and trust in her. She creates trust and confidence through their empowerment. It is this trust and confidence that empowers the mediator to do what is necessary to achieve resolution.

6 The mediation quintet
Hidden identities

> One face, one voice, one habit, and two persons –
> A natural perspective that is and is not.
> The Duke, *Twelfth Night* (V.i.216–17)[1]

> I am not what I am.
> Viola, *Twelfth Night* (III.i.143)

Chapter 5 introduced three disputes and their dramatis personae. During their performance, we heard what mediators say to parties during the course of mediation. In particular, we heard how they perceive mediation and how they perceive themselves in that mediation. We also heard from the disputing parties about their reactions to mediator and process. The aim was to give audience to the native voice, and in so doing, to expose it. Once exposed, the words achieve significance.

In this chapter, the consideration of real-life patterns of interaction takes centre stage. The three case studies of Chapter 5 are revisited to emphasize the separation of voice and action, and to seek their interconnectedness. This chapter focuses on mediator and party interaction throughout the process. The data of the observed mediation is pivotal in liberating the transformations undertaken by a mediator in the quest for the mediatory goal.

Who is this figure of mediator? What does she tell us of the mediated process? The prescriptive and descriptive narratives of the mediation literature about mediator role, goal and actions are cast aside – a new narrative emerges from the chaos of the real-life patterns explored in these case studies.[2]

---

1 William Shakespeare, *Twelfth Night, or, What You Will* (New York: Signet, 1965).
2 The discussion in this opening section of the chapter relating to the mediator's shifting identities resulting from mediator interactions during mediation will be published in D. De Girolamo, "A View from Within: Reconceptualizing Mediator Interactions" (2012) 30(2) *Windsor Y. of Access to J.* (in press), in which the analysis is made in relation to a case not explored in this or the previous chapter. The article also briefly canvasses some of the mediator literature discussed earlier in Chapter 3 herein.

150 *The mediation quintet*

Gulliver comes close to describing the interactions of the mediator when he said that the mediator becomes *a* party in the negotiation, but Gulliver does not go far enough. He refers to the initial dyad of the two-party negotiation becoming a triad with the introduction of the mediator. By deconstructing the mediation process through case study analysis, it is apparent that Gulliver's triad may be an oversimplification.

Through the data, we will see that the mediator becomes a party to the negotiation, as stated by Gulliver and Roberts;[3] that she takes on the party reality, as suggested by Benjamin;[4] and that the relationship between the mediator and parties is not extrinsic to the negotiation, as envisioned by Bowling, Hoffman and de Bono.[5] She moves between and beyond what Roberts and Palmer refer to as "two analytically distinct forms of intervention": a minimal intervention that facilitates communication and an active direct intervention that includes evaluation and advice.[6] The mediator is not only at the centre of a process parties have chosen to assist with the resolution of their dispute: she ultimately defines the process.

Beginning from the premise that mediation is a facilitated negotiation within the Organization's mediation framework,[7] mediators must intervene in such a way as to impact the negotiation. The data suggests that a mediator does so by assuming the identity of five personas at various times during the process. She is not only a mediator in the intervention; she is also a party negotiator and a party adviser. For example, in a two-party dispute with Party A and Party B, the mediator takes on the following five identities:

1 that of her own self as mediator when with the parties;
2 that of Party A when confronting Party B or when empathizing with Party A;
3 that of Party B when confronting Party A or when empathizing with Party B;
4 that of Party A's adviser when with Party A; and
5 that of Party B's adviser when with Party B.

---

3 See discussion in Chapter 3 and in particular, P.H. Gulliver, *Disputes and Negotiations: A Cross-Cultural Perspective* (New York: Academic Press, 1979) at 213–14; M. Roberts, *Developing the Craft of Mediation: Reflections on Theory and Practice* (London: Jessica Kingsley, 2007) at 154.
4 R.D. Benjamin, "The Constructive Uses of Deception: Skills, Strategies, and Techniques of the Folkloric Trickster Figure and Their Application by Mediators" (1995) 13 *Mediation Q.* 3 at 5–6.
5 D. Bowling and D. Hoffman, "Bringing Peace into the Room: the Personal Qualities of the Mediator and Their Impact on the Mediation" (2000) *Negotiation J.* 5 at 11–12; E. de Bono, *Conflicts: A Better Way to Resolve Them* (London: Harrap, 1985) at 124.
6 S. Roberts and M. Palmer, *Dispute Processes: ADR and the Primary Forms of Decision-Making* (Cambridge: Cambridge University Press, 2005) at 155–6.
7 See discussion about the Organization's mediation framework in Chapter 3.

The mediation quintet 151

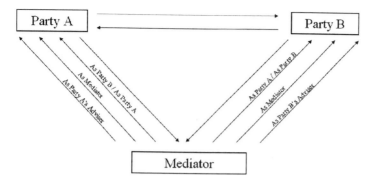

Figure 6.1 Mediator interactions

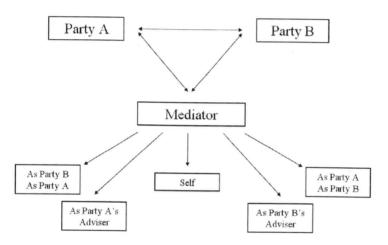

Figure 6.2 Mediator identities

Figure 6.1 highlights the interactions and Figure 6.2 highlights the five identities.

At the beginning of mediation, a mediator does what is expected of every mediator. In the pre-mediation meetings with the parties and at the joint session, he is describing the process and his role in the process. The mediator is acting as *self* – he is explaining the process, the parties' involvement in that process and his own position within the process. He is the third-party intervener selected to help the parties to negotiate a resolution to their dispute. This is not the only time he acts as *mediator* during the course of a mediation. The mediator identity emerges throughout the process when the mediator may be, among other things, describing and controlling the process, setting the agenda, determining the issues, exploring facts and interests, relaying information including offers, considering the other side's perspectives, and moving parties to conclusion. This is one identity.

Another identity is as *party*. There are two aspects to party identity: that of opponent and that of party proper. As opponent, for example, in the two-party dispute between parties A and B, the mediator takes on the identity of Party B to negotiate directly with Party A. The same occurs with Party B: the mediator takes on the identity of Party A and negotiates directly with Party B. In this identity, the mediator may undermine a party's factual position on issues, he may articulate a contrary view on evidentiary points or refute them totally, he may refer to weaknesses of articulated positions, he may argue the other party's case against the party or he may make demands. These interventions are distinct from *mediator* interventions. With these interventions, the mediator steps into the negotiation as a *party* against a *party*.

As *party*, however, the mediator is not only a party adversary; she also assumes direct party identity. For example, when with Party A, on occasion, she becomes Party A, articulating Party A's interests, concerns and demands: in essence aligning herself with Party A as a member of Party A. A similar occurrence arises when with Party B. In this form, the mediator may agree with party demands, articulate party interests, seek ways to protect party concerns, or criticize the other party and its position. These actions result in the disappearance of the mediator persona, leaving in its wake, a fortified *party* voice.

These identities evolve further into one of *party adviser*. When discussing the case with Party A, the mediator becomes A's adviser, recommending courses of action, formulating offers and responses, opining on merits and giving legal advice. This also occurs in her discussion with Party B. In this persona, the mediator enters the realm of expert consultancy, sharing her professional expertise with the parties for the parties.[8]

The mediator is mediator; the mediator is party; the mediator is party adviser. The mediator is much more than *a* party to the negotiation – she does much more than assist or facilitate a party with their negotiation, or actively negotiate on behalf of an unable party. The mediator wears the mask of these additional personas throughout the course of mediation. The mediation becomes *her* negotiation; she becomes party and party adviser. The quintuple identity of the mediator emerges, creating a mediation quintet and thus defining the process.[9]

The case studies highlight the changes in mediator identity when interacting with the parties throughout the mediation. The changes are fluid, alternating from one to another in a single session and throughout the sessions. They occur with each party and occur frequently.

---

8 Roberts and Palmer, see note 6 at 155.
9 It is within the context of a two-party dispute paradigm that the quintet is created: the mediator takes on the identity of two parties, two advisers and retains his own.

Case Study 7: Technology foul-up

We remember that the back office system of the Defendant, Cavell Systems Limited, was not properly installed, leading to Cavell's termination of its contract with the Claimant, HiWire Inc., for the design, installation and management support of Cavell's central computer network. Debate focused on the conditionality of the contract and Cavell's obligations thereunder.[10]

Joint session (10:35 a.m.–10:55 a.m.)

After the Mediator discussed the process and his role, he invited the HiWire solicitor, George David, to speak.

David relied on the customer order form as setting out the terms of the contract between HiWire and Cavell, explicitly stating that the contract was not a conditional one. HiWire performed its obligation, it sought information from Cavell in furtherance of the contract, and Cavell cancelled the contract. When the contract was cancelled, HiWire says, Cavell asked for and was given the cancellation charges. On receiving the amount, Cavell then said that it would not pay it. A breach of contract resulted.

Cavell's solicitor, Luke Alexander, argued that the contract was conditional on the back office services being installed by a third-party service provider. Alternatively, even if a breach of contract occurred, no work had been carried out under the contract, therefore no loss was suffered. Additionally, HiWire did not provide standard terms and conditions which were to form part of the contract. As for Cavell's request for the amount of the cancellation charges, it alleged that it was willing to cover lost costs, but not lost profit for the three-year contract term as sought by HiWire.

The parties clarified the factual points on which they relied. Both parties said they were at the mediation to reach a settlement, if one could be reached. At this exchange, the Mediator brought the joint session to a close by saying, *"It is a good place to say I want to meet privately with each. I will start with HiWire."*

First meeting with the HiWire Team (10:55 a.m.–11:07 a.m.)

During this meeting, HiWire reiterated its position on the facts and the law. The Mediator inquired about the facts. After specifically inquiring whether the contract was a typical one for services, the Mediator asked, *"From a common-sense perspective, would it have been necessary to sort out the back office because it needed to have been dealt with internally first, and then, your system?"* HiWire's representative, Todd Preston, talked about this aspect of the services to be provided to Cavell. He spoke of HiWire's losses and the work it had carried out.

---

10 For a full case description, see Chapter 5.

The Mediator, during this exchange of information, said, *"Their point is that some key points are missing {from the contract}: {for example}, the cut-off date – that was an important date because they needed the time period to go forward. Is there any relevance to this argument?"* Further discussion ensued about the contract terms and HiWire's position in respect of the breach. David said that HiWire did not accept the repudiation and the contract remained alive. The Mediator concluded the session by stating that it was *"helpful. The background was useful. I will chat with them. I will be at least 30 minutes."*

First meeting with the Cavell Team (11:07 a.m.–11:45 a.m.)

The Mediator began by asking whether anything surprised Cavell about the joint session. When the Defendant representative, Joseph Simeon, said that he found Preston's body language to be negative, the Mediator said, *"It elicited the instruction from HiWire's solicitor, so it was helpful to hear why they are here.*[11] *Their comments were helpful. You were the key people at the time, but they said that the documents do not say it. Are the people still around? Who?"* The discussion then centred on the contract negotiation, Cavell's evidence in that regard and the event leading to the cancellation of the contract.

Discussion then moved to the start date of the contract. Simeon advised that the contract was not to begin until the back office support was completed. The Mediator said, *"I did not see the names of the people who were at the meeting in the documents."* Simeon noted there had been a change in ownership at the HiWire business. The Mediator pointed out, *"Preston did not have involvement."* Alexander interrupted and said, *"I could make a larger point of the entire agreement clause. You can't stop parties having a verbal agreement that is conditional. All three people at the meeting say the same thing."* In reply, the Mediator stated, *"Being the devil's advocate – you would be saying the same thing – that the contract was signed, the terms were there and there was no conditional term. That is part of the lawyers-speak to say this. That is the backdrop of the case, and if it had not been there, you would have sorted it out. You have three witnesses. In 24 months you would be at trial, there are costs in time. That is the backdrop."* The Mediator inquired about Cavell's business, its knowledge about HiWire and its relationship with HiWire. When Simeon spoke of the failure of the third-party provider to install the back office system, the Mediator asked, *"It wasn't appropriate to find an alternative to {the third party}?"* Simeon said it was not appropriate, and explained why.

The Mediator raised the issue of invoicing, pointing out, *"they invoiced you"*. Only once, replied Simeon. *"On the basis the contract is still running – it is the basis on which they are dealing with things,"* the Mediator stated. Later he mused,

---

11 The Mediator is referring to the solicitor's reiteration that his Team is at the mediation to resolve the dispute despite the comments made by the Team about the strength of its contractual position.

"*They seem to be leaving the contract open, which seems odd.*" The Mediator continued: "*They say you are in breach of contract and they haven't accepted the breach. The contract is still running and they are entitled to invoices.*" When Simeon asked, "*How can they say it is still running?*" "*They are willing and able,*" replied the Mediator. There was further discussion about HiWire's legal position and its claim.

The Mediator then summarized the issues: "*Your team says everything is conditional, yet we have a contract on the other hand.*" "*Undated,*" reminded Simeon. "*Yes, undated, and you say you signed it because they wanted the paperwork to organize the {work},*" continued the Mediator. "*Yes, I signed it because they needed it for the {work},*" replied Simeon. "*You didn't have to sign it, then,*" responded the Mediator. Simeon continued to explain the circumstances surrounding the signing of the contract and considered the impact of HiWire's position on the contract continuing. The Mediator concluded the meeting, saying that he wanted to speak to HiWire about the points raised.

Second meeting with the HiWire Team (11:55 a.m.–12:25 p.m.)

The Mediator began, "*It was very useful. I picked up from the other side, the project and the plan. This was part of a program, as you said. They have organized their business over 100 cities. It is not the most exciting business they are in. They have a lot of offices in many countries. They coordinate the work and invoice centrally from head office. Their position on the contract is very strong, as indicated to you in correspondence and the meeting today. Everyone on the team knew everything was conditional on everything fitting into place. Cavell will rely on Felix Kingston {a former HiWire employee}, who used to be with HiWire. They have spoken and he will say it was conditional.*"

HiWire countered this with a list of its own witnesses. David wondered, "*Why was it {the condition} not documented? Why wasn't it in writing? Why did they sign the document?*" The Mediator replied, "*They will say, look at the start date. It is not in because it would be put in when all systems were in place. This is one example. It is not inconsistent.*" David replied, "*But it is not consistent with ours.*" The Mediator retorted, "*Yes, but that is what each says. In the commercial context, it is how a judge will look at it. What did the parties intend?*" The HiWire Team replied that the entire agreement clause protects them. The Mediator queried, "*Why would he have signed it, from his point of view?*" The Mediator asked Preston to explain what happens after a contract is signed and what would occur if the contract was given a start date of today. After some discussion about the status of the contract, the Mediator said, "*It was just a thought to me because they have a need for a system.*"[12]

The Mediator questioned what would occur if a settlement were not reached, inquiring when a trial would be held. He then reminded HiWire

---

12 The Mediator is referring to the start date of the contract. His 'just a thought' refers to the possibility of continuing the contract.

about the evidence of Felix Kingston, one of the people who negotiated and signed the contract. He also inquired about the communication between the parties during the period between signing the contract and its cancellation; specifically, whether there had been any meetings. *"There were lots of telephone conversations, emails seeking information,"* replied Preston. *"They told me of one meeting,"* said the Mediator. Preston said, *"Yes, we would have had meetings with suppliers. {Others} were there. We could not deliver until the back office was working. The problem is that we would not have discussed the condition."* The Mediator responded, *"I can see the room for confusion. You just said that you could not deliver until the back office was done."*

Preston then reiterated the lack of a condition in the documents, stating that pricing would have differed had there been conditionality. The Mediator, after further talk on this point, asked whether he could tell Cavell that there is another form of contract that is used when conditional arrangements are entered into, because in his view, *"it needs to come out"*. Preston replied, *"We would have given them different pricing."* *"It would have taken into account the risk,"* added the Mediator.

The Mediator shifted the discussion to figures, in particular, the claim, information about HiWire's position, and the possibility of future business with Cavell. Discussion veered to the contract terms again and whether Cavell had a different understanding from HiWire's. David opined to the HiWire Team that, although there may be a gentlemen's agreement, a written agreement with set terms is necessary. The Mediator interjected, *"From your perspective, you would want a contract filled in. In business, people move on thinking they have an understanding, but here it was not there."* Preston replied, *"It is too fundamental here to have an understanding. I would sack the person."* *"Here, the top person signed,"* replied the Mediator. *"He should have known better,"* retorted Preston.

The session finished soon after, with the Mediator stating, *"I usually like to leave a task, but you've already done the work."*

Second meeting with the Cavell Team (12:25 p.m.–12:55 p.m.)

This next meeting began with a discussion about Felix Kingston and the circumstances surrounding the execution of the contract, with the Mediator teasing out information from Simeon. When Simeon said that the signing took place at his office, the Mediator said, *"So, the documents would be brought there. Their information is that there is nothing in the file about a condition. If it had a condition, the contract would be different, the fee would be different, and the commission to the sales person would be different. It goes to the fact that it was not conditional. These are evidentiary points, so each side builds up the evidence on each side. This is their position on it."*

The Mediator inquired whether Cavell would be willing to consider future business opportunities with HiWire. When Simeon replied in the affirmative on the basis that it would be conditional on the installation of the back office support, the Mediator said, *"To be on their side, they would want a time, within a reasonable time to deal with the back office and then proceeding as originally planned. Is this realistic?"* Simeon confirmed Cavell's willingness to contract with HiWire. The Mediator: *"Surely it would be fine with them because your organization is a good one to do business with. I will explore it with them. Putting that to one side and the contractual position to one side because you have your advice, I think it is conceded it would have been better if the conditional provision was in there, and they would concede it would be better if it had a start date."*

The Mediator discussed numbers. He reiterated HiWire's offer to accept one-half of its original claim of £468,000 in settlement and reminded the Cavell Team, *"You haven't responded to it other than saying it is horrendous, which is how you felt."* When the Mediator inquired about Cavell's response to the offer, Simeon spoke of continuing the contract. The Mediator asked, *"What would you need to tie up now – the conditionality. They would want a realistic timeframe."* *"24 months,"* responded Simeon. The Mediator added, *"Everything is suspended until 2009. If you have an effective back-up, HiWire would implement, and if you do not have it, then all bets are off. From their perspective, how would they know you were proceeding {with the back office}?"*

Talk followed about the shape of Cavell's proposal for continuing business with HiWire, including a payment in the event the relationship did not continue. When Simeon said payment under the new contract would be due as areas are serviced, the Mediator noted, *"Is this a defect in the original agreement? There is no reference in there regarding the {various cities} to kick in over time, just as there was no condition."* And further, *"With the benefit of hindsight in a witness box, you would say that the conditional provision should have been in writing."* He explained his action in challenging Simeon by stating, *"I am just putting to you what you would be facing if you go forward; you are a sophisticated businessman."*

The Mediator summarized the proposed offer and asked whether there was anything else Cavell thought HiWire would want in it. Before leaving the room, Alexander referred the Mediator to a provision in the contract in support of the proposition that if any cancellation charge were owed, it would be restricted to the sum of the minimum quarterly charge. The Mediator said, *"Perhaps, you would say it would override the standard terms because it is specific and overrides the general, as a lawyer."*

The meeting concluded. The Mediator suggested they have their lunch and said he will be with the HiWire Team for 30 minutes.

Third meeting with the HiWire Team (12:55 p.m.–1:05 p.m.; 1:20 p.m.–1:35 p.m.; 1:40 p.m.–1:42 p.m.)

The Mediator began by referring to the legal point Alexander made: any cancellation charge is limited under the contract to £28,000, the minimum quarterly commitment under the contract. He set out Cavell's offer for either continuation of the contract on new terms or payment of £44,000 as a lump sum with no continuing relationship.

When Preston said that the Team would consider the offer, the Mediator said, *"I have one point to make. At the initial meeting, Felix Kingston was there and he was there for the company and he says what they said he sets {out in the statement}."* Preston was not interested in this point, asserting he had already provided his view on Kingston's evidence. David then reiterated that HiWire has a signed document, to which the Mediator responded, *"The reason why it is signed is to get {the equipment} in it."*[13] *"We know that,"* replied David. The Mediator retorted, *"It is best to get everything on the table and you can chuck off what you do not like."* With that statement, the Mediator left the room to permit the HiWire Team some time to deliberate in private.

When the Mediator re-entered the room, the HiWire Team responded to Cavell's argument regarding the limitation of damages to the minimum quarterly commitment in the event of cancellation, arguing that this is a minimum payment fee owing in respect of each named site and an additional fee in respect of additional sites. The Mediator countered, *"Do you accept it does not say that {in the contract} and there is room for argument?"* Although David acknowledged the ambiguity, he reaffirmed the clarity of the rest of the contract and pointed out that the argument was only raised today. The Mediator replied, *"That is what litigation is all about."*

The HiWire Team proceeded to explain why Cavell's offer to continue the contract on new terms was not viable. It also stated that the sum of £44,000 was insufficient to cover its costs and loss of profit margin. When it said that it did not want to disclose its profit margin, the Mediator said, *"If this went to trial, the profit element would have to come out."* Later he added, *"In their shoes, they will say, what have you actually suffered – legal fees, setting up the lines. Regarding the rest, you are employing people anyway, doing other business, so it is unfair to put it on us. It is not for me to say it is a right or wrong figure; it is just my job to make sure you thought about it."*

The Mediator left the room to permit private deliberation by HiWire. During this brief interlude, the Mediator told the Cavell Team that HiWire was considering Cavell's proposal and its response to it. After a few minutes the Mediator re-entered the HiWire room.

HiWire advised the Mediator of its offer, and the session ended.

Third meeting with the Cavell Team (1:42 p.m.–1:45 p.m.)

The Mediator spoke: *"I appreciate that serious consideration is going on, you are continuing to give a lot of thought. About the future, the problem is not with the concept, but how it would work out. If it quoted a conditional contract, the pricing would reflect it so it could not resolve it immediately; head office would be involved to figure out pricing; they would want a minimum amount of locations. I think it was unrealistic but they*

---

13 The Mediator is referring to the requirement of a signed contract for the installation of certain equipment.

want to build it in. Although they liked the idea, and would like to do business with you, 24 months is a long time; the discussion was along those lines. They could discuss it, but not today because they need data. They like the second option better. They had a couple of responses to the £28,000 limitation: their view is that there is a £28,000 minimum each three months and for new sites, and it was not raised before."[14] The Mediator then explained the calculations supporting the numerical offer. Cavell requested time to consider the offer. The Mediator left the room.

First meeting with Luke Alexander (1:55 p.m.–2:10 p.m.)

Alexander came to the Mediator to discuss Cavell's reaction to the HiWire offer. He spoke about the gap between the parties and that the gap did not appear bridgeable. The Mediator urged him not to think that and stated what he saw the problem to be: *"The problem is that he {Joseph Simeon} signed the document and he is a businessman."* When Alexander countered with the evidence of those attending the meeting, the Mediator challenged, *"He said he trusted them, but he hadn't met them."*

The Mediator told Alexander to formulate a counter-proposal, reminding the solicitor that *"they won't negotiate against themselves"* and that the *"conditional offer is not attractive for anyone"*.

Fourth meeting with the HiWire Team (2:10 p.m.–2:20 p.m.)

The Mediator told the HiWire Team that Cavell was not prepared to discuss its offer further, but pointed out that it had not left the mediation yet. *"Let's see if there is a way out of it; I am sitting in the middle. They feel it's not realistic enough."* Preston said, *"They should come back with a figure."* *"I agree with you,"* replied the Mediator.

The Mediator then suggested that David speak with Alexander to convey the need for an offer from Cavell. *"Tell him that you are here to settle, that you are not prepared to negotiate against yourself. There is some flexibility, but you need to have a figure from them – there are some costs. To proceed without a response, you can't do that. I could say it, but it would not be the same. You carry with you the Company's instruction. It won't do harm. There is a log-jam, and this is the solution."*

First meeting between the HiWire and Cavell solicitors (2:25 p.m.–2:35 p.m.)

The Mediator introduced the session: *"It is useful to have both together without the clients. I think you pretty well understand the legal issues, how long to get to court, the legal costs and the client time. I think there is a desire to reach a solution, but proximity is the issue."*

---

14 This represents the minimum quarterly contract payment referenced in the prior session.

With that, the solicitors engaged in a dialogue about the offers, the presence of their clients at the mediation, the calculation of losses suffered, the need for disclosure of HiWire's profit margin, and litigation risk. Alexander wanted Cavell to give its bottom line and avoid 'salami-slicing'. David was not keen and the discussion became positional with neither solicitor wishing to make a suggestion on an offer. The Mediator said, *"I have a couple of ideas, but I will speak to you separately about it. There is no use in doing it together. Share comments with your room."* The meeting ended as Alexander demanded David's bottom line once again.

Fifth meeting with the HiWire Team (2:35 p.m.–2:50 p.m.)

David reported the outcome of his discussion with Alexander to the Team. At the Mediator's request, he then considered the various litigation scenarios available to HiWire. The Mediator, in commenting on the second option where HiWire would accept the breach and sue for damages, stated, *"Yes, but you need to discount it for getting it now so the second option is more real."* The Mediator then asked about HiWire's weak points, summarizing at the conclusion of the discussion: *"It's an upside of £200,000 with a downside of £140,000. They will say that £180,000 is not much of a discount."*[15] In response to David's comment that the parties are not very far apart and that it is *"not as bleak as they say"*, the Mediator stated that *"Alexander has a job to do."*

Further discussion took place about profit margins and legal costs. David said that he was *"anxious to move it forward"* to which the Mediator replied, *"I think that you have made the points very well and I will take it back to the Team. It was said very competently."* The Mediator then suggested that the bottom line be disclosed to him: anything above £80,000 would make the HiWire Team happy. The Mediator assured the Team he would not disclose the figure and concluded the meeting by saying to David, *"His comments would have gone well."*

Fifth meeting with the Cavell Team (2:50 p.m.–3:05 p.m.)

When the Mediator went into the room, he commented on the utility of the meeting between the two solicitors. He then asked, *"Could you share figures with me?"* Simeon replied, *"No, I am happy with the figures."* The Mediator continued, *"They have reiterated they are here to settle. He has authority to settle. There is a margin for movement but they are not going to negotiate against themselves and you are not giving appropriate risk in terms of costs. There is some margin, but they haven't given me a bottom line and I haven't asked for it. To move it*

---

15 £180,000 is the offer presented by the HiWire Team to the Cavell Team, which was discussed at the meeting between the solicitors David and Alexander before this particular meeting. The Mediator is making a statement regarding the fact that the figure is only 10 per cent less than the most HiWire believes it could win at trial.

forward, you need another figure. You feel £180,000 is their best case, yet they say it is not. Their costs would be £120,000 with £40,000 out of pocket." Simeon replied, "They aren't giving anything." Alexander added, "Their best case is £160,000 yet they want £180,000." The Mediator pointed out, "They are thinking of ways to put it. They have costs incurred." Alexander retorted, "I am interested in them saying they incurred £60,000. How could five meetings bring it to £60,000?" The Mediator: "There were internal meetings, they did not tell you. They liaised with third parties to get the system in place."

Simeon said he was not prepared to offer anything further from his prior offer of £44,000, given the HiWire offer of £180,000, but also said he might go to £60,000. The Mediator warned him of trial costs. Simeon saw little change in HiWire's position: "They offered £220,000 and now £180,000, it's bullshit." The Mediator replied, "They spent £20,000 on legals now." Further debate occurred about Cavell's response to the £180,000 offer and whether any offer would be made. Ultimately, the figure of £66,000 was agreed as Cavell's counter-offer.

Sixth meeting with the HiWire Team
(3:10 p.m.–3:15 p.m.; 3:25 p.m.–3:35 p.m.)

The Mediator began: "They haven't gone as far as I want. They are difficult. They take the view of an irrecoverable element of £40,000 so they keep thinking you are at the top point. They will move up a bit. They will do a contract as per this morning or £66,000." The HiWire Team asked for some time to consider the offer, after inquiring about the Mediator's view whether this was Cavell's final position. The Mediator said, "I was going to say it, but how could I possibly say it? I do not know it. There is a point where people say enough. They have looked at the best case and that is where they are."

On the Mediator's return to the room, the HiWire Team attempted to support its costs and losses, ending with the statement, "They are not plucked out of air." The Mediator retorted, "But they are not wrong to say that it is not forensic accounting." David introduced HiWire's counter-offer of £100,000, saying, "We are not saying, there is no leeway." The Mediator replied, "It is a significant move; sensible and realistic." The Mediator then worked with the HiWire Team to determine how to explain the offer to Cavell. The Mediator left to speak to Cavell.

Sixth meeting with the Cavell Team *(3:35 p.m.–3:40 p.m.)*

The Mediator began: "£60,000 of expenses can and will be justified, including the following items: original central line costs – {they were} put in and {are} functional – were a minimum of £10,000 – they don't have the exact costs; project management; engineer fees; commitments made to suppliers filled through other work; those are the key ingredients. They are appreciative of the increase {to the Cavell offer}. They are prepared to reduce significantly their figure to reflect where they want to be. They would settle at £100,000, net of VAT. It is cutting it as tightly as they are able, taking the profit, taking the realities regarding where they want to end up. And they are hopeful that you would look at it as an acceptable figure, recognizing that it is not what each side wants."*

The Mediator left the room to allow Cavell to deliberate privately.

Second meeting with Alexander (3:45 p.m.–3:50 p.m.)

Alexander again came to the Mediator to deliver Cavell's position. Cavell was interested in reinstating the offer of a continuing contract, or alternatively, payment of an increased amount of £80,000, to be made over time. After the Mediator warned the solicitor that the staggered payment could be interpreted as Cavell experiencing financial difficulties, the meeting ended.

Seventh meeting with the HiWire Team (3:53 p.m.–3:55 p.m.)

The Mediator delivered the Cavell offer. HiWire was interested in why the payments had to be staggered and asked the Mediator to inquire of Cavell.

Seventh meeting with the Cavell Team (3:55 p.m.–3:57 p.m.)

Cavell advised of its reason for the staggered payment: to provide for an opportunity for the parties to work out a new contractual arrangement.

Eighth meeting with the HiWire Team
(3:57 p.m.–4:05 p.m.; 4:07 p.m.–4:10 p.m.)

The Mediator told the HiWire Team about Cavell's position. They discussed the viability of negotiating a new contract and HiWire's reaction to the staggered payment plan. The Team wanted a few minutes of privacy to consider the offer.

After re-entering the room, HiWire told the Mediator its counter-offer. The Mediator repeated it and left the room to take it to the Cavell Team.

Eighth meeting with the Cavell Team (4:10 p.m.–4:15 p.m.)

The Mediator relayed HiWire's counter-offer of an immediate payment of £80,000, or alternatively, a payment of £70,000 now and £20,000 in 18 months, with no provision for the negotiation of a new contract. Cavell responded with £80,000 to be paid in 90 days, during which time the parties would see if they could negotiate a new contract, failing which they could walk away. Cavell continued to be keen about negotiating a new contract with HiWire. The Mediator said, *"It puts them to the test."* As for how to reduce such a commitment to writing, the Mediator suggested, *"Within 90 days, both parties use best endeavours to negotiate a working agreement."* Alexander argued, *"Best endeavours is without legal obligation."* The Mediator retorted, *"Best endeavours is a high test in my experience."* Alexander was persuaded, but suggested the language should be *"reasonable efforts".*

The Mediator took the offer to the HiWire Team.

Ninth meeting with the HiWire Team (4:15 p.m.–4:33 p.m.)

After putting the Cavell offer to HiWire, the Mediator said, *"They are keen to negotiate a contract, and if you do, then you have an ongoing relationship, and if you do not, then you get £80,000."* Much discussion ensued over the viability of negotiating a new deal given HiWire's lack of confidence in Cavell due to the past circumstances of their relationship. The Mediator asked, *"Could you not draft something that would give you scope without binding you?"* When David insisted that payment of the £80,000 be made now and could be built into the new price if a new contract is agreed, the Mediator queried, *"What message will it send if you do not want to tie the £80,000 with the new contract?"* Later, *"They are putting it as giving a real opportunity to do a new deal."* And further, *"I think he wants to see if you could negotiate {a deal}. There is no reason why not to try it. The {current} deal fell through not because of HiWire."*

Preston considered it further, and agreed to give it a chance: *"£80,000 now, 90 days to do a deal, give credit {for the £80,000 if a deal is reached} and if we do not do a deal, both parties walk away."* The Mediator noted, *"You are bringing the payment up front."* David explained that HiWire is out of pocket on costs. The Mediator suggested, *"Credit the invoices for the ones given, and I do not think VAT is applicable, so, it would be 'VAT if applicable'."*[16] Some discussion occurred about the VAT implication. The session ended soon thereafter.

Ninth meeting with the Cavell Team (4:33 p.m.–4:40 p.m.)

"We're not quite there," began the Mediator. He set out HiWire's offer. Discussion ensued about HiWire's desire for a new agreement and the date for the payment. Cavell came to the view that HiWire was not interested in a new contract and thus concentrated on the payment aspect of its offer. A new offer was formulated dealing with an accelerated payment period, credit for invoices submitted and VAT. The Mediator was instructed to give it to HiWire.

Concluding meetings (4:40 p.m.–5:10 p.m.)

HiWire accepted Cavell's offer with some tweaking. Alexander drafted the agreement and the two solicitors worked on the drafting details together. Once the written agreement was completed, the Mediator reviewed it and the parties executed it. Parties shook hands and left the premises. The mediation ended.

***

---

16 Here, the Mediator is adding terms to the offer: he is suggesting a way to deal with the invoices already delivered to Cavell and any VAT obligation.

It is difficult to immediately see this Mediator. His voice is straining to be heard above those of the parties. Perhaps it is because of a subtle and seemingly non-intrusive manner. He appears almost invisible, yet there is a sophistication of layered interventions in the conduct of the mediation that becomes unravelled the deeper one looks into it.

In Chapter 5, the Mediator says that he would like to direct parties without the parties' awareness. The data discloses the Mediator's success in this regard. The parties are directed by the Mediator's interactions with them through his various identities. Recall David's remarks that the Mediator is 'very neutral'; Alexander says he is very 'quiet' and 'understated'. These views do not conform to the data.

This Mediator takes on the quintet of identities. For example, during his first meeting with the HiWire Team he is both adviser and mediator in his actions: as *adviser* in helping to formulate arguments in HiWire's favour and as *self* in trying to elicit information from HiWire. In the subsequent meeting with the Cavell Team, the Mediator adds the third dimension: he acts as *HiWire* in challenging Cavell's assertion that the contract was conditional. He specifically relies on contract terms to counter Cavell's arguments. He is also adviser when answering the query posed by Simeon as to how HiWire could argue that the contract was continuing, information arguably better suited for Simeon's solicitor to provide given the intrinsic legal nature of the inquiry. The Mediator further blends these two distinct voices with that of *mediator*, when learning about the circumstances of the dispute.

In his second series of meetings with the parties, the Mediator spends most of his time as the opposing party and as mediator, with a brief performance as adviser at the end of each session. Let's examine more closely his identity as opposing party. The Mediator, after giving information to HiWire about the Cavell business, speaks as *Cavell*, remarking on the strength of its position and the evidence supporting that position: *"Their position on the contract is very strong, as indicated to you in correspondence and the meeting today. Everyone on the team knew everything was conditional on everything fitting into place. Cavell will rely on Felix Kingston, who used to be with HiWire. They have spoken and he will say it was conditional."* When HiWire counters with the question as to why the contract does not state that it is conditional, the Mediator replies, *"They will say, look at the start date. It is not in because it would be put in when all systems were in place. This is one example. It is not inconsistent."*

In these examples, this Mediator prefaces his statements by referring to Cavell as though to reaffirm that *he* is saying merely what Cavell has said. Later in the day, he prefaces arguments with phrases such as *"devil's advocate"* or *"from their view"*. Whatever the preface, it is one that seeks to convince the parties that he is not challenging the party, but rather making the party aware of the other's position. He seeks to put distance between the intervention and the party for whom the intervention is made. Despite this aim, however, the existence of this qualifier is irrelevant. The Mediator may indeed use prefaces such as these to qualify his statements when taking on the position of the opposing party to challenge the other, but that does not detract from the nature of the intervention. The Mediator intervenes as adversary; he argues as adversary. It seems that the use of a qualifier (whether as preface, during or at the end of a statement) is to soften the intervention. It acts as a shield. Superficially, it seems to work; parties do not recoil from the Mediator as they might if the opposing party had confronted them directly.

Stripped bare, however, it is the party voice that is heard through the mediator intervention. It is the opposing view that is projected in a confrontation with the party. We see it over and over again. For example, in the second meeting with the Cavell Team, the Mediator becomes *HiWire*, asserting why the contract was not conditional: *"If it had a condition, the contract would be different, the fee would be different, and the commission to the sales person would be different. It goes to the fact that it was not conditional. These are evidentiary points, so each side builds up the evidence on each side. This is their position on it."* The Mediator qualifies his statements by asserting that he is stating HiWire's position, but this does not disguise a party challenge. In the third meeting with HiWire, the Mediator is *Cavell* when he says, *"I have one point to make. At the initial meeting, Kingston was there and he was there for the company and he says what they said he sets {out in the statement}."* Another qualifier, another challenge. Despite the Mediator's attempt to temper his intervention, it does not hide the Cavell voice that is heard.

It is clear that the Mediator enters the negotiation not only as mediator, the individual retained by the parties to help them to negotiate a resolution; he is *the* negotiator, negotiating directly with the parties as party. This may not be unusual – indeed, there are references in the literature to the parties negotiating through a mediator – that the mediator becomes a participant in the negotiations between the parties. The key, however, is that he is not any negotiator; he is *the* negotiator for *the* party *against* the party. This occurs despite his attempts to couch the negotiation with language that seeks to separate him from the party. On the surface, it appears that he is successful in this; however, the data discloses that which is beneath the surface. The data discloses that which the participants cannot see, or possibly do not want to see, and in fact do not see.[17]

What is intriguing about the second session with the HiWire Team is the introduction of what appears to be the expansion of the party identity – as *party* when with party. In other words, the identity is not as opposing party, but as *the* party with whom the Mediator is physically present. The identity is marked by a sympathetic view of the position espoused by the party or a criticism of the other. The result appears to be a disappearance of the distinction

---

17 Recall in Chapter 5 the parties generally view the Mediators of all three case studies as being non-directive, neutral interveners, or not sufficiently interventionists. This particular Mediator was described as "quiet, understated, calm, reasonable, thoughtful and very neutral".

between party and third-party intervener. We see this in the second meeting with the HiWire Team. The Mediator is not defendant against claimant; he is not claimant adviser, nor is he mediator. He becomes *claimant* with claimant. It occurs in two instances in this meeting. When the Mediator begins the session, he begins as mediator, reciting information about the Cavell business as told to him. He adds commentary, however, during his description: "*It is not the most exciting business they are in.*" Further in the meeting, when Preston talks about the fact that pricing would have been different if the contract had been a conditional one, the Mediator says, "*It would have taken into account the risk.*" One might argue that the first comment is irrelevant and meaningless, and the second is merely a summary by a mediator to a party to confirm his understanding of the party's case. However, the data suggests they are more than this.

Beginning with the latter example, Preston says only that a different form of contract would have been used for a conditional contract. It is the Mediator who takes the information a step further and connects the new contract pricing with risk protection. He speaks with *party* voice. It is information belonging to the party, but not yet enunciated by the party. He does not act as adviser in making this logical connection; he is not advising on a course of action or on an issue. He is merely stating what, for HiWire, is an important consideration in its defence of the Cavell assertion on the status of the contract between the parties. As such, it can be seen to be a party reflection and therefore a shift in identity. As for the first comment regarding Cavell's not-so-exciting business, the comment is an editorial one – it serves no purpose but to seemingly undermine Cavell in HiWire's eyes and to connect the Mediator closer to HiWire; in essence, to identify the Mediator as a member of the HiWire Team.

This alignment with HiWire occurs again later in the process. In the fourth meeting with the HiWire Team, the Mediator becomes *party* – not as Cavell to counter HiWire, but as *claimant* with claimant. In this example, he sympathizes with the HiWire position over the lack of an offer from Cavell. Preston says, "*They should come back with a figure.*" The Mediator replies, "*I agree with you.*" To that end, he arranges a meeting between solicitors so David can explain the need for an offer from Cavell if bargaining is to begin. The Mediator's status as *party* ends and as *adviser* begins when he tells David what David should say to ensure an offer is delivered. The Mediator's identification with HiWire leads to the next step in the process: that of a meeting, the aim of which is to persuade Cavell to engage in the bargaining proposal phase of the negotiation.

This expansion of the party identity does not rest solely in the guise of claimant. It occurs much later with the Cavell Team, in the eighth Cavell Team meeting. Cavell speaks of its desire to negotiate a new contract with HiWire and suggests linking payment to a period of time during which the parties would attempt to negotiate new terms. The Mediator signals his agreement to the idea, as well as suggested sympathy for Cavell's position in his remark, *"It will put them to the test."* Putting HiWire to the test is an adversarial move, suggesting a forcing of decision-making. The Mediator, soon after, moves into an *adviser* role, suggesting language to create a contractual obligation on HiWire to negotiate that contract.

This identification with party is both separate from that of *party adviser* yet similar in that it represents another aspect of alignment with the parties. It presents another facet of mediator identity as *party*, further illustrating the chameleon residing in the third-party intervener.

Case Study 8: Partnership gone awry

We revisit the ending of a partnership. Allegations of improper behaviour and the negotiation of rights arising under a Partnership Agreement take centre stage in this *mise-en-scène*.[18]

First pre-mediation meeting with the Mitchell Team (8:40 a.m.–9:35 a.m.)[19]

The Mediator introduced himself and the process. He also asked the Claimant, Robert Mitchell, to tell him about the case. As noted in Chapter 5, Mitchell spoke of his relationship with the partners Jarvis, Kimbourne, Ernest, Michaels, Jordan and Vincent, and his history with the Partnership. He talked about the various compensation formulas, his acquisition of goodwill in the Partnership over the years, the invoicing system at the Partnership, and the events leading to his resignation including the negotiations regarding the calculation of payments due on resignation from the Partnership. Once he had concluded, the Mediator questioned Mitchell about his family and his financial needs. The Mediator pointed out that litigation is costly. He then requested information about invoicing, saying, *"When I was in practice we would do it all the time for interim billing – we'd issue credit notes and then issue one in full in the end."* The Mediator asked specific questions while Mitchell described his procedure.

The Mediator turned to the joint session, questioning who would be speaking. When the Claimant Solicitor, Max Elliot, said that he was prepared to speak, but perhaps Mitchell would as well, the Mediator said to Mitchell, *"It would be good for you. You may want to rehearse."* In response to Mitchell's comment that he *"does not rehearse"*, the Mediator said, *"This is a negotiation. Set out what you lost; ask, is this fair? It is a time to say that this is what you have done rather than being accusatory. I use the word 'rehearse' so that you know what to*

---

18 See Chapter 5 for a full case description.
19 This Mediator did not have an opportunity to speak with the parties before the mediation. The pre-mediation meetings therefore were more detailed than usual in terms of fact-finding.

say and make it hard to defend. Your message is that if you were expelled, there was no cause because there was no loss suffered by the Partnership.[20]

When Mitchell said that he had a statement from another partner referring to the Defendants' wrongdoings in relation to expenses and a statement from a forensic accountant, the Mediator suggested, *"I would not use it. These kinds of things happen. A forensic accountant would look at that and the invoices."* When Mitchell insisted, *"I would raise it as something for them to see,"* the Mediator said, *"Park it."* Mitchell continued to insist: *"It would be more damning to the Partnership."* The Mediator replied, *"I understand that there is no loss {from Mitchell's invoicing}. The Partnership is an entity on its own. Under the Agreement, it can terminate a partner with cause if there is damage to the Partnership, not to the partners individually. You need to point out that there is no loss to the Partnership. Your big argument is that the expulsion is without cause."*[21] Further discussion ensued about the invoices and the Defendants' reliance on termination for cause.

The Mediator discussed the litigation process, remarking on the fact that all types of assertions are made in litigation and that parties need to develop a thick skin when it comes to facing a barrister whose job is to provoke. Mitchell said that he *"will fight to the bitter end"*. The Mediator responded, *"Make notes. Why is it important? The crux of the case – is it right to take away money paid by you? May 16 is crucial – you are not that far apart and then you get a letter expelling you. So, what happened? How is your relationship with the individual defendants?"* Discussion followed about the relationship.

The Mediator asked Elliot to explain the legal situation with respect to Mitchell's rights under the Partnership Agreement. When Elliot spoke of the changes made to the calculation of profit, the Mediator stated, *"There is a counter-argument – use the same basis for consistency. Do not worry about that because there is a formula for goodwill and the ratio is the only question – is it 30 per cent or 50 per cent? Profit share is what it is. It falls by the wayside if there was a lawful expulsion. I see bits and pieces. If this goes to trial, it will be examined in detail. Get it out of the way because there will be no winners."* Talk continued about the litigation process. The Mediator concluded the session by speaking of the joint session and Mitchell's preparation for it.

First pre-mediation meeting with the Jarvis & Kimbourne Team (9:45 a.m.–10:40 a.m.)

The Mediator spoke of the mediation process and his role in it. He then asked the Defendants to speak to him about the history of the dispute. During the discussion, the Mediator asked questions of the partners, getting the facts

---

20 This discussion between the Mediator and the Mitchell Team is also found in Chapter 5.
21 Ibid.

surrounding the dispute. On the issue of the invoices and Mitchell's expulsion from the Partnership, the Mediator said, *"If a partner is not pulling his weight, it is clear he has to go, but the issue is, is there cause? Goodwill is dependent on it. Looking at the invoice issue, most were paid. What is the impact?"* One of the Defendant partners, Harris Jarvis, replied, *"Loss of trust."* The Mediator replied, *"I understand that – that is a big thing."* And when Jarvis continued to talk about Mitchell's behaviour that led to a loss of trust, the Mediator said, *"To me that is a big thing."* Jarvis agreed that it was a big thing. When Jarvis further told the Mediator that the invoices were not sent out, the Mediator said, *"He said they got billed."* Jarvis pointed out that they were billed, but several months later. Jarvis wondered, *"Why raise invoices without sending them to the client? Who does that?"* The Mediator replied, *"I could not understand that."*

Further discussion ensued about the invoicing procedures and Mitchell's billing history. Jarvis reiterated the loss of trust suffered by the Partnership; the Mediator reminded him that *"the issue is the expulsion with cause"*, and spoke of the need to concentrate on the cause issue. The Mediator said, *"I want to concentrate on the cause no cause issue. The rest is capable of being sorted. I have been there where parties have lost faith in each other. He may genuinely believe he hasn't cheated you. I do not know your system."*[22]

Again, the Jarvis & Kimbourne Team spoke of the Partnership's invoicing procedure, with the Mediator asking questions about it: *"Would you not notice {Mitchell personally inputting the invoices}; do you not cost WIP {work-in-progress} against the invoices; was the WIP written off?"* The Mediator then asked the Defendant Solicitor, Daniel Rose, about his assessment of the legal issues. On concluding, Rose said, *"There is a risk to all: they may have to pay versus Mitchell getting nothing and having his name blackened."* The Mediator replied, *"Currently, he has nothing."*

Second pre-mediation meeting with the Mitchell Team (10:50 a.m.–11:10 a.m.)

Although Mitchell was absent from the room, the Mediator advised Elliot, *"I will hold the plenary. I went through it with them. Cause is the issue and the invoices will be raised again. Mitchell may want to say he never intended to deceive. It may be bad practice. And, some acknowledgment regarding the concern over creating an invoice and not billing. If it were an employment situation, it would not be cause, but with a Partnership..."* The Mediator was interrupted by Mitchell's arrival. Elliot asked the Mediator to repeat what he had just said so that Mitchell would hear it from the Mediator. The Mediator repeated, *"I was speaking of the opening. Regarding the issue why the invoices were raised but not delivered, I heard that you*

---

22 This discussion between the Mediator and the Jarvis & Kimbourne Team is also found in Chapter 5.

spoke with {your assistant} and assumed they would be delivered. An acknowledgment that it was not done to deceive because their concern is deception – an acknowledgement may break the ice." In response to the question as to the meaning of 'acknowledgment', the Mediator said, *"That you never intended to deceive and to explain that they were delivered later."*

When Mitchell pointed out that all the invoices were delivered, the Mediator retorted, *"Some were delivered late."* Elliot questioned his client about the invoices raised by Jarvis & Kimbourne as improper and asked whether they were sent out at the time they were created. Mitchell said that the Jarvis & Kimbourne Team is referring to credit notes, not invoices. The Mediator added, *"What about the other schedule? If you go back to the schedule – if you are in a position to say that the invoice was raised and you can say whether it was delivered or not, say it. If it was delivered three or four weeks later, then it was not delivered. Then say it was not delivered. Say it was because of your practice – not to deceive. It may break the ice."* Later, *"If you raised them in advance and did not deliver them, say so."* The Mediator suggested that Mitchell go through his response to the invoices with Jarvis & Kimbourne, since Mitchell hadn't yet done so.

Elliot inquired about the other Team's concern regarding the invoices. The Mediator replied, *"They say that it affected profit-sharing. The big question is, why was it done – to deceive, because Mitchell was inefficient? I'm not saying he is inefficient; it does not matter. It is the issue whether you want to do it. If you do not, fine."* Mitchell said that his assistant sent out the invoices. The Mediator: *"Maybe you need to say that – your {assistant} is sending them out. Still, it is your responsibility as a boss. But it was not your intention to deceive."*

The discussion turned to a transcript of a meeting at which the invoices were discussed, and in particular, a reference that the assistant did not create the invoices. Elliot asked the Mediator, *"Do you read the {transcript} of the expulsion as slightly self-serving?"* The Mediator replied, *"Oh, how could you say that – I could not."* Again, when Elliot referred to the transcript's reference to the [assistant] not being responsible for creating the invoices, the Mediator said, *"There are two different things: you raised the invoice but the {assistant} was to send them out. You did not finish it off to send out, but it was not done with the intention to deceive. It is just a matter of saying you did not follow up."*

Elliot suggested to Mitchell that he explain each invoice with the Jarvis & Kimbourne Team. When Mitchell said he would do so *"if it serves a purpose; I do not want to go through the motions,"* the Mediator said, *"They say they asked for it and did not get it. If it enables us to move forward because they need it, do it. We can't go back in time – if I found a way, I would patent it. We are trying to go back in time – I do not think it's a problem, let's go through it, but go with Jarvis in a separate situation, not in the opening. I will say after the opening, I will ask Jarvis and Mitchell to stay, with the solicitors as flies on the wall. You can tell him that this {the letter} was prepared at the time but you didn't go through it. Deliver it with a message that you were not intending to deceive."* The session then ended.

Joint session (11:10 a.m.–12:00 p.m.)

The Mediator introduced the session and invited Mitchell to speak. Mitchell spoke of his history with the law firm, the changes to the Partnership Agreement in relation to goodwill and profit-sharing, the invoicing issue and his explanation for the invoicing, the decision to leave the firm, the negotiation of the goodwill and profit share on leaving, and the expulsion. Once he finished, Rose spoke for the Jarvis & Kimbourne Team. He spoke to the invoice issue and the impact of Mitchell's act on the calculation of profit share. He spoke of the fact that there were two views as to what occurred in the Partnership – Mitchell's and the Team's – and they would not come to a consensual view on it. He talked about coming to the mediation with the intention to do a deal on the basis of *"a risk and cost-benefit analysis; it is not commercial; it is not principle"*. He set the stage for a negotiation rather than discussing the merits of the Team's position. In his view, *"We are a long way apart on the issues, not so far on the money. £300,000 is not a lot. We won't persuade each other on risk. We hope this is the way for discussion. I am happy to discuss the merits but it would not be time well spent."*

A debate followed between solicitors about the very merits that Rose did not wish to discuss. They argued about the issue of the invoices and Mitchell's expulsion, with Jarvis entering the fray at the end. At that point, the Mediator turned to Mitchell and asked, *"Do you want to say anything? Keep it cool."* Mitchell replied, *"There is no reason not to be cool – my anger has passed."* He then reiterated his view about the invoices.

When Jarvis stepped in to counter Mitchell's comments, the Mediator concluded the session stating, *"You each have different views. We won't be able to resolve it here. At the end of the day, we need to resolve it.*[23] *It is not worth going through the invoices. I will adjourn this session right now. It was useful to set this out on the table. Let's work out what we can do."* Turning to the Jarvis & Kimbourne Team, he said, *"Hopefully, by 1 o'clock, I will come to see you."*

First meeting with the Mitchell Team (12:10 p.m.–12:25 p.m.)

The Mediator started the session: *"How do you feel?"* Mitchell replied, *"I prepared myself for a long day. On his reading, I am very surprised by him saying that they are here to negotiate. I am not sure it is their view."* The Mediator said, *"Sure it is ... In mediation, often, one side had put forward offers which were refused then but now are willing to accept. What I heard was that they are willing to negotiate goodwill. It may be dressed up as litigation risk. They are acknowledging cause {is an issue}. For him {Rose}, the issue is proportionality. They may not be happy with the invoices, but is it fair to remove all goodwill? We should build on it. I can imagine what it is like for you – going in to discuss profit share and {thinking} you will be*

---

23 These concluding statements are also found in Chapter 5.

bashed again. So you just hear profit share. Jarvis is saying, let's talk about the invoices and then I'll bash you."

When Mitchell expressed doubt whether the Jarvis & Kimbourne Team was really interested in reaching a deal, the Mediator reassured him, saying, *"There is a process to go through to reach resolution."* He then began to discuss litigation risk, BATNAs and WATNAs. He asked Elliot if he had worked them out, and then proceeded to do so for the Team. In doing so, the Mediator established a settlement range and other necessary terms for settlement such as payment of costs, timing of payments and release from restrictive covenants. On this latter point, the Mediator suggested that Mitchell would *"agree he will not take work away from the firm, but if an existing client wants help, he will tell them that he is not intending to set up practice"*. When Mitchell said that he wanted the opportunity to work, but did not want the firm's clients, the Mediator said, *"Be practical about it – you are already out for several months and you do not want the clients anyway. Do not look into what is less likely because it creates fear and doubt."* The discharge of a loan (owed by Mitchell for the benefit of the Partnership) was also discussed, about which the Mediator said that he *"did not think it will be an issue."*

The session concluded shortly thereafter.

First meeting with the Jarvis & Kimbourne Team (12:25 p.m.–12:35 p.m.)

On entering the room, the Mediator asked, *"How to move to the next stage?"* There was some discussion of first offers. Jarvis then said, *"I do not think Mitchell told the truth to his solicitor."* The Mediator replied, *"Does he really understand the issue? He speaks of loss as none, yet he does not get the 'improper' aspect."* *"He doesn't understand it,"* said Jarvis. *"That is what I am saying,"* replied the Mediator. Rose added, *"Maybe he doesn't understand the issue or he does know and there is no innocent explanation available. The risk is what the court will assess."* The Mediator continued, *"There is a higher proportion {of risk} if he is doing it fully dishonestly. It is maladministration here. He underestimated the impact on the Defendants. I understand your perspective. I believe that your duty does not end with giving an invoice to {an assistant}. The responsibility to get it out is on the partner. It could be very bad working habits. Let's take your case. He is deceiving you but does not see it as wrong because there is no financial loss. You could spend a lot of time on it."* Jarvis said, *"I do not want to. His lawyer doesn't know all the details."* The Mediator replied, *"His lawyer is not stupid. I do not agree with Rose."*

After some discussion about the case, Rose raised the issue of who would make the first offer. The Mediator replied, *"In negotiation, people fuss about the first offer. In my experience, it is good as long as it is in the ballpark because it brings them down. If you are looking at £500,000 and £1 million – I am just using those figures – and you go in with £560,000, they will come way below £1 million."* Rose suggested numbers on goodwill and profit share. The Mediator left the Team to consider the numbers.

First meeting with Rose (12:40 p.m.–12:45 p.m.)

Rose came to speak with the Mediator. He asked whether the other side would put forward the first offer. The Mediator told him that he did not speak with the other Team. Rose then told the Mediator what Jarvis & Kimbourne and the partners were prepared to offer for goodwill since it was the larger issue and the parties are not far apart on the other issues. The Mediator asked him to give numbers for the other aspect of the claim as well because *"sometimes getting agreement on the small items gets the discussion going"*. Rose left to further consider the details of the offer they would be prepared to make.

Second meeting with the Mitchell Team (12:45 p.m.–1:00 p.m.)

The Mediator spoke with the Mitchell Team while the Jarvis & Kimbourne Team was formulating its first offer. He spoke of negotiation theory, preparing Mitchell for the first offer by stating, *"Remember, you are in insult zones when you start negotiating."* He then spoke of the shape of negotiations in general.

The Mediator went over the parties' positions on the numbers. Elliot described Mitchell's position regarding settlement and the terms of any offer. He gave figures for both profit share and goodwill.

The session ended after some discussion about present value discounts and the Mediator left the room with an offer from the Mitchell Team.

Second meeting with the Jarvis & Kimbourne Team (1:00 p.m.–1:05 p.m.)

The Mediator relayed Mitchell's view on the items in dispute such as profit share, tax and loan payments, and restrictive covenants. As for the goodwill, the Mediator said, *"On goodwill, the difference between the two of you is turnover. It is not big. The big difference is 30 per cent versus 50 per cent. I am not arguing the point because I do not understand it."* He then gave Mitchell's offer for goodwill of £700,000, stating it was *'less insulting'*. With that, he left the room.

Second meeting with Rose (1:30 p.m.–1:50 p.m.)

Rose spoke privately with the Mediator for the second time. He explained the Jarvis & Kimbourne Team counter-offer and asked whether it was necessary to justify the numbers *"because it is pure horse-trading"*. The Mediator suggested that he could go back to Mitchell and tell him why the Team was not meeting his figure. At this point, Rose informed the Mediator that the Jarvis & Kimbourne Team had documentary evidence of a personal nature that would embarrass Mitchell if the matter proceeded to a hearing. The documents would be disclosed and would cause Mitchell personal upset. Rose said that he did not want the Mediator to disclose the existence of the documentary evidence to the Mitchell Team, but wanted the Mediator to be aware of it to avoid any surprises later in the mediation.

Third meeting with the Mitchell Team
(2:00 p.m.–2:15 p.m.; 2:30 p.m.–2:35 p.m.)

The Mediator described the Jarvis & Kimbourne counter-offer. Mitchell was disappointed at what he believed was a low offer. The Mediator said, *"Like you, they would prefer to settle. Like you, I would like that parties reach settlement. This will take three or four times. There is a pattern to these and Elliot knows."* He asked them whether they wanted to think about the offer. Both Mitchell and Elliot thought that the parties were too far apart. Mitchell asked if anything was offered for the discrimination claim. The Mediator said the Team would not [respond] to it. When Elliot said that Mitchell had a strong claim on discrimination, the Mediator said, *"You won't get anywhere. It is highly inflammatory; it will bring damage to them and to you."*

The Mediator suggested that they deal with the profit share aspect of the claim and try to get agreement on that number before dealing with the goodwill portion of the claim on the basis that agreement on profit share may lead to agreement on the goodwill. The Mitchell Team was not in agreement with this proposed strategy. The Mediator left the room to let the Team consider its response to the Jarvis & Kimbourne counter-offer.

After a brief period of time, the Mediator re-entered the room.

Elliot introduced the offer by referring to the strength of Mitchell's case. Once the offer was tabled, the Mediator questioned the party about the strength of the case, asking about the outcome of the invoice issue. When Elliot said that Jarvis & Kimbourne should have given Mitchell a chance to remedy the default on expulsion, the Mediator replied, *"Obviously, they will need to prove it happened."* Elliot spoke again of the strength of the case on the failure to provide a remedy. The Mediator asked, *"What is the damage suffered?"* It was agreed that the Mediator would relay the offer to Jarvis & Kimbourne.

Third meeting with the Jarvis & Kimbourne Team
(2:35 p.m.–2:55 p.m.)

The Mediator described Mitchell's offer. He then asked about the public nature of the proceedings. A discussion followed about Mitchell's entitlement to goodwill, with the Mediator reiterating Mitchell's view of the value of the goodwill and that it is dependent on the percentage used to calculate it: 30 per cent versus 50 per cent. There was some debate on this point. Rose noted that Mitchell did not discount his offer to take into account litigation risk.

Rose queried whether the Team should disclose the embarrassing documentary evidence against Mitchell. The Mediator replied, *"I do not know if it will get you anywhere. I do not know if he would continue, if his family knows. It is a Damocles sword, useful only if it is swinging and someone knows it is swinging."*

I don't know the details. I don't know if it is relevant. I don't know if it will come out in court. I don't know if it is a stunner or a killer." Rose said, "It is not relevant if the family knows." The Mediator continued, "It may be relevant to the community. I just do not know. It could go either way. We are here to do a commercial deal." Rose replied, "Let's put it aside but how do we deal with him?" The Mediator said, "Bring up the litigation risk when we need to. Also, in his view, he paid out money for the goodwill. And on proportionality, assuming the invoices were done, is expulsion a fitting {outcome} for it?" Jarvis said, "Yes. When drawing up the agreement, it was that £500,000 to get, so today £320,000 is not different from what had been offered because it is less costs."[24] The Mediator retorted, "Yes, but he has his costs. I do not know what a judge would say – will a judge see it as fair?" Anna Ernest piped in, "Under the agreement, it appears black and white." The Mediator said, "Judges will do what they think is fair and proper. Your solicitor can say this better."

The Mediator left the room to give the Team time to consider its position. As he was leaving, he mentioned that the issue of goodwill needs to be dealt with as well as litigation risk. He also suggested that payment over time might be helpful.

Third meeting with Rose (3:15 p.m.–3:36 p.m.)

Rose once again sought out the Mediator to relay to him the Jarvis & Kimbourne Team counter-proposal. He prefaced the offer by stating that the partners *"want to do a deal"*. He then described the offer for the profit share portion of the claim and explained the reason for the figures. When Rose told the Mediator the offer for the goodwill was £350,000, the Mediator said, *"I thought you would go to £390,000."* When Rose asked, *"Why – we already went up from £200,000 to £320,000."* The Mediator replied, *"Because I think you need to break £400,000."* Rose explained the calculation supporting the figure, including the application of litigation risk to the formula set out in the Partnership Agreement. The Mediator asked about the length and cost of proceedings. Rose said that costs would be in the range of £150,000 to £200,000. The Mediator then gave his view of costs, saying, *"I thought about £200,000 for costs. At the end of the day, {to} win costs of £80,000 – then you put the discount in – you need to break £400,000. He needs to come down and you need to go up."*

There was further discussion about the numbers. The Mediator asked if the Jarvis & Kimbourne Team was prepared to make a lump-sum payment. He then concluded the meeting by telling Rose that he might arrange a meeting between the two solicitors. Rose retorted that Elliot wouldn't persuade him or his client, and he would not persuade Elliot. The Mediator replied, *"This is*

---

24 Jarvis is referring to the fact the partners had offered to pay Mitchell the amount for goodwill at the time of his resignation before the expulsion notice was served. Their offer of goodwill was now at £320,000.

not an arguing session. It would be a listening session if we do it. I sometimes put clients together and sometimes the solicitors together." With that, the meeting ended.

Fourth meeting with the Mitchell Team (3:36 p.m.–3:50 p.m.)

The Mediator described the Jarvis & Kimbourne offer, beginning with, *"There is a little bit of progress, but not much more."* He concluded with a reference to the proceedings between the parties, *"I don't know whether Rose knows about your ability to bring action. Maybe you should just discuss it; not argue it. It is not up to me to make the point."* The Mediator then asked about the costs of proceeding. Elliot replied that it would be in the range of £140,000 to £200,000. The Mediator said, *"My thought is the same. Forty per cent are irrecoverable and there is the time involved. Even if you won, you would not recover £80,000. You need to bring the goodwill under £600,000. I know it will take a lot to move under £600,000 and the same for them to go up from £400,000. There is a big gap here."*

There was discussion about the numbers for profit share. The Mediator suggested that Elliot discuss his perception of litigation risk with Rose and hear Rose's perception. The Mediator said, *"You may need to discuss your perception of risk with Rose and his with you so you both can discuss it with your clients. ... They made another shift but it is not enough, but it is a shift. Shall we continue? If you want to speak with Rose, I will {arrange it}. It may not feel like it, but it is a step forward."* With that, the meeting ended.

First meeting between Rose and Elliot (3:55 p.m.–4:16 p.m.)

The Mediator set the tone for the meeting by stating, *"This is a discussion only, not an argument."* The two solicitors then explained their respective views of litigation risk attendant on the case, including the legal merits of each of their positions. The Mediator interrupted on several occasions to remind them that they are not to debate the points – they are to explain them and to listen to the other's explanation. The meeting ended with Rose stating he was not giving up on getting a deal done.

First meeting with Elliot (4:30 p.m.–4:35 p.m.)

Max Elliot came to the Mediator to talk about the case. He spoke of percentage entitlements accruing to Mitchell. The Mediator said, *"You may think I am just arguing their case. Look at the figure. The calculation to £480,000 started at £700,000 at 80 per cent with an 80/20 per cent litigation risk and £70,000 in costs. I am only raising it with you. You need to find a way to bridge the gap and to identify the litigation risk."*[25] Elliot told the Mediator that he might require

---

25 The calculation of the litigation risk is described in the meeting with Mitchell following this meeting.

help with litigation risk. The Mediator then asked him if there was any concern with full disclosure if the proceedings continue. The meeting ended with Elliot saying that he would take Mitchell through the calculation on the figures, which he said *"may inform the debate"*.

Fifth meeting with the Mitchell Team (4:35 p.m.–5:05 p.m.)

The Mediator began the session with a discussion about litigation risk. *"I will do a litigation risk analysis. {Let's say you have} £700,000 of goodwill. On the litigation risk, the highest a lawyer would give you is 80 per cent because even if it is a 100 per cent case, there is still a risk on what a judge will do, so 80 per cent is the best. Eighty per cent of £700,000 is £550,000, which is a reassessment of a very good case. Do not take it from me, look to your solicitor. If I had a £20,000 claim, it would cost me that in legal fees. Here, there are £200,000 of legal fees of which 30–40 per cent is irrecoverable. Therefore, if you win on everything, you will get £480,000. You may say that you haven't spent £200,000, but the litigation risk is still there. This is where it lands."*

Mitchell engaged in a debate over the calculation of litigation risk. The Mediator pointed out that the claim had not been fully documented and new information would come up if the matter proceeded. The Mitchell Team retorted that it had all the information already – there was no loss and the partners did not follow the requirements of the Agreement for the expulsion procedure. The Mediator replied, *"There is a debate when the one-month period started, but I am not putting forward their case. I need to reality test."* To this, Mitchell replied, *"I am being done."* The Mediator confirmed, *"Yes, you are being done."*

The Mediator questioned Mitchell whether there were any documents that may be found in his computer that could be harmful as part of the risk assessment. Mitchell began talking about how much he was giving up to get a solution and asked the Mediator what he would do if he were in his shoes. The Mediator replied, *"Looking at this, I would want to get on with life. At what cost, litigation? If the claim is £800,000 and I could get £500,000, I would take it. That is me. The number is not £500,000 – I am sucking it out of air. I would want to spend time with my family. Litigation will consume life. You lose control of life."* Mitchell said, *"This is bullying."* The Mediator responded, *"No, the lawyers will bully you."* He then continued to talk about the effect of litigation on life and talked about his own experiences with litigation. He concluded, *"You need to balance out what you want to do in life and you won't be happy with it."*

Discussion then centred on the formulation of a counter-proposal. There was some discussion as to whether the Jarvis & Kimbourne Team would be willing to add something for costs. The Mediator said on the latter point, *"Check it out and you may need to reframe it as something else because costs are always a problem."* Mitchell uttered, *"This is frustrating."* The Mediator responded, *"Yes, and this is the good time. It will get a lot worse. Litigation is a lot worse than this. You need to refute allegations which take a lot of time."* Further discussion occurred about the vagaries of litigation.

They discussed the restrictive covenants and whether they should be included in the offer: Elliot wanted to raise it now, whereas the Mediator suggested leaving it until the end. An offer was formulated. Mitchell took the Mediator's suggestion that the costs be hidden in the numbers for the portion of the profit share calculation which was still in dispute (a portion had been previously agreed). As the Mediator said, "*I will say you still want £130,000 not £70,000. It sounds better ... I'm taking the £70,000 and putting it in somewhere and it looks reasonable.*" Once the numbers were confirmed, Mitchell said, "*I've conceded quite a bit.*" The Mediator replied, "*They think they've conceded.*" "But they were at £600,000," retorted Mitchell.[26]

The Mediator left the room.

Fourth meeting with the Jarvis & Kimbourne Team (5:10 p.m.–5:25 p.m.)

Rose began with an argument against Elliot's interpretation of the Partnership Agreement wherein Elliot alleged that Mitchell had to be terminated from the Partnership within one month after becoming aware of the breach. Rose said that Mitchell had to be terminated within one month after the Partnership meeting. The Mediator replied, "*I think he was saying that you need to do something within 30 days, but I am not your lawyer.*"

The Mediator inquired about the meeting where the 50 per cent rate was to be reduced to 30 per cent. The Defendants said that it was never done. The Mediator said, "*This indicates maybe the intention the rate was 50 per cent.*" Jarvis replied, "*We asked him to do the calculation but he didn't do it – we had to.*"

The Mediator set out Mitchell's offer, talked about the need to do a deal and left the room, leaving the Team to deliberate on the offer.

Fourth meeting with Rose (short time after 5:25 p.m.–5:35 p.m.)

Rose came to the Mediator and told him about his Team's counter-proposal. When he said the offer for goodwill was £390,000, the Mediator asked, "*You won't break £400,000?*" Rose explained why they were not prepared to at that moment, but would once Mitchell reduced his demand. The Mediator then inquired about costs. When that received a negative response, the Mediator told Rose that he did ask Mitchell "*if he was comfortable there is nothing he is worried about in the disclosure*". There was some discussion whether the embarrassing documentary evidence should be disclosed. The decision was not to disclose it. Rose continued to talk about the Defendants' offer, adding that he did not understand why they continued to see litigation risk at 80 per cent. The Mediator said, "*Because historically he received an offer at £600,000.*"

The meeting ended.

---

26 It was Mitchell's evidence that the partners originally offered £600,000 for goodwill.

Sixth meeting with the Mitchell Team (5:40 p.m.–5:55 p.m.)

The Mediator pointed out Rose's response to the one-month notice requirement raised by Elliot. Elliot was not surprised and reiterated his view.

The Mediator then described the Defendants' offer: *"They have come back. We are not at the end of the road although you may think so. They were at £350,000 for goodwill, £70,000 for [the portion of] profit share [in dispute] and no to costs. I spoke with Rose. If you change your £130,000 to £110,000, they will come up. They are there because you did not move. They are at £390,000 for goodwill. They did not break £400,000, but my sense is that they will. The gap [between you] was £500,000; now it is £210,000. My sense is that they will go at £480,000/£490,000. I do not know what happened on 16 May when you were at £390,000 and they at £350,000 for [total] profit share, and you were at £700,000 for goodwill and they were at £600,000. Maybe they misread you. It was such a small gap, why not discuss it further? Suddenly, they stopped all discussion. I raise it now because it could happen again."*

The other elements of the offer were discussed including a payment schedule, restrictive covenants and costs. The Mediator reiterated on a couple of occasions his view that the Jarvis & Kimbourne Team would move on goodwill. Elliot asked whether it would be a struggle to get the Defendants to £490,000. The Mediator said, *"Yes, it will be a struggle. It could be brutal. You may say, cut to the chase and go to £490,000. I say, do not speak to them yet about it."* As to whether the Jarvis & Kimbourne Team would move from £70,000 on the profit share component, the Mediator said, *"I suspect if you move from £130,000 they will move. If you say it's costs, they won't move."*

Mitchell asked for time to consider a response. The Mediator said, *"This is a good point. We are negotiating."*

The meeting ended.

Second meeting with Elliot (6:05 p.m.–6:10 p.m.)

Elliot explained the offer: £110,000 for profit-sharing and £560,000 for goodwill, to be paid over two years. In response to Elliot's comment that *"it is getting quite close"*, the Mediator said that he couldn't *"fathom what happened"*. Elliot asked him whether he could speak with the partners about it. The Mediator said, *"I think one said, do not give another penny and I don't think it was Jarvis. I think there are two in there who do not care for Mitchell. They feel so strongly that any concession is giving too much. Look at the bidding. Why not come in at £400,000? They need to jump now."* The meeting ended shortly after.

Fifth meeting with the Jarvis & Kimbourne Team (6:10 p.m.–6:20 p.m.)

The Mediator began immediately with Mitchell's counter-proposal. The Mediator then turned to the Team's offers. *"You are moving £30,000 each time.*

Do you want to accelerate it?" Rose said, *"We want to do a deal. If we say that a deal is between £380,000 and £560,000, the chaps will deal with it."* The Mediator replied, *"It takes twice as long for a small gain. I turn into a pumpkin at midnight. If you have a number in mind, get there sooner, not through three offers."* Rose said, *"But, if I give you a number, don't come back and say that you need more."* The Mediator retorted, *"I know what my WATNA is. Will the alternative be better than what is on the table?"*

The Mediator asked what happened in May over the £600,000 offer. Each of the partners provided an explanation. The Mediator concluded, *"We are where we are. I told him not to repeat the same mistake. You know him better than I do. At the end of the day, you need to do a deal. Think of a number to close the deal. He may reject it and I may come back and say I need more."*

Rose said they would return with a serious offer.

Fifth meeting with Rose (short time after 6:20 p.m.–6:35 p.m.)

Rose set out the Jarvis & Kimbourne offer of £420,000 for goodwill, paid over two years,[27] and £80,000 for the portion of profit share in dispute. He said that it was a larger figure than they intended to offer because of what the Mediator had said to the Team, but that they were at *"squeeze room"*. The Mediator asked whether the number was £430,000. Rose said, *"Yes, it could be that, or if we are at midnight, we may be prepared to go at £450,000."* With that comment, the meeting ended.

Seventh meeting with the Mitchell Team (6:35 p.m.–6:50 p.m.)

The Jarvis & Kimbourne offer was relayed and explained. Mitchell immediately proposed a counter-offer of £510,000 for goodwill, paid over three years. The Mediator made some comments about the Defendants' offer, advising that the payment over two years rather than five years is an advantage. Mitchell reiterated his offer.

As for the amount for profit share, the Mediator reminded Mitchell, *"£130,000 was my number for legals. They say £70,000 is the proper profit share, so you got an extra £10,000."* The Team commented further on the offer and the elements of its proposal, saying it had made large concessions. The Mediator told the Team, *"We are into doing the final bits and pieces. It is at this time, with little movement. I am concerned they will reject it. That is why I am asking and am hesitant."* Mitchell reiterated: *"£510,000 over three years is a concession."* The Mediator replied, *"They came back with £420,000 over two years. What is the interest factor?"* The Mediator agreed with Mitchell's assessment of interest at £20,000.

---

27 Under the Partnership Agreement, payment is to be made over five years.

Mitchell confirmed the amount sought for profit-sharing. Armed with Mitchell's offer, the Mediator left the room.

Sixth meeting with the Jarvis & Kimbourne Team (6:50 p.m.–6:55 p.m.)

The Mediator told the Team about Mitchell's offer. There was some discussion about its elements. Rose asked, *"Is there squeeze room?"* The Mediator replied, *"I honestly don't know, but I don't know where your squeeze room is either. We have reached the point where we are going slower and slower."* Jarvis asked, *"If we split the profit in the middle, will it work?"* *"Yes, probably,"* replied the Mediator. With that, the Mediator left to allow the Team to consider its response.

Sixth meeting with Rose (7:00 p.m.–7:02 p.m.)

The Jarvis & Kimbourne offer for goodwill was increased to £450,000 payable in two years; the profit share figure remained at £80,000. Rose told the Mediator that there was a bit of squeeze room on the profit share if the £450,000 was accepted, but not on goodwill.

Eighth meeting with the Mitchell Team (7:05 p.m.–7:10 p.m.)

The Mediator began, *"About the loan, it will be repaid. They won't move on the £80,000. They have moved from £420,000 to £450,000, payable over two years. I suspect there is flexibility over the payment terms, but I do not think over the amount. Your last position was £510,000. I know where it should be – I think it should be £480,000 and I am not just splitting {the difference}."* Elliot said, *"You know because they discussed it with you."* The Mediator retorted, *"I have not discussed this number with them. We are now tweaking. Just because I think £480,000 is the right number does not mean others will think it, and it does not mean it's right."*

When Mitchell said that he felt £500,000 was not unreasonable, the Mediator replied, *"I do not think I'll get there. I am not sure I will get to £480,000. I do not think I will get more."* The decision was to offer £480,000 for goodwill and £90,000 for profit-sharing.

Seventh meeting with the Jarvis & Kimbourne Team (7:10 p.m.–7:15 p.m.)

"I stuck my neck out," began the Mediator. *"Three or four bids prior, I told them the number should be £480,000 with litigation risk. They stuck with £500,000. Now they will go to £480,000, if you want to close it now."* One of the partners, Anthony Kimbourne, asked, *"Did they say £480,000?"* The Mediator replied, *"I told them £480,000 a while ago. It is not splitting the difference: it was based on litigation risk and it was my number."*

The Team wanted time to reflect.

Seventh meeting with Rose (short time after 7:15 p.m.–7:20 p.m.)

Rose once again delivered the Defendants' counter-offer on his own. He offered £460,000 for goodwill and £90,000 for profit share, stating that Mitchell wins on the profit share. The Mediator said, *"I'm the one who hammered them to £480,000."* Rose replied, *"You hammered us too."* The Mediator retorted, *"But they were prepared to pay £600,000."* Rose said, *"No, they were not. This is to move beyond the halfway. This is something to let him shake hands and win the battle. There is a deal here to do. I know he will do the deal."*

The session ended.

Ninth meeting with the Mitchell Team (7:22 p.m.–7:25 p.m.)

After the Mediator relayed the Jarvis & Kimbourne latest proposal, there was much angst in the room over Mitchell's response. Mitchell decided to split the difference for goodwill and offer £470,000, and accept the £90,000 for profit share.

Eighth meeting with the Jarvis & Kimbourne Team (7:25 p.m.–7:37 p.m.)

The Mediator told the Team that Mitchell was splitting the difference on the two numbers and was offering £470,000 for goodwill. Anna Ernest said, *"Let's split the difference and offer £464,000."* The Mediator retorted, *"No, don't go there."* They agreed to the offer. The Mediator left the room to tell the Mitchell Team of the acceptance of its offer.

Concluding meetings (7:37 p.m.–11:15 p.m.)

Elliot took the lead in drafting the agreement. He had commenced writing the agreement while the negotiation was ongoing. Rose attended the Mitchell room to discuss the various drafts of the agreement. There was some clarification on tax issues, and other administrative details that were worked out. They worked together on some of the language of the agreement. The Mediator went through a draft of the agreement with the solicitors, making suggestions to it and giving some advice on the settlement terms. Each party signed a copy of the agreement in private. Copies were made and exchanged. One of the partners attended in the Mitchell room to bid goodbye to Mitchell. Mitchell did not bid goodbye to the others. The mediation ended.

***

Recalling the Mediator's voice in Chapter 5, we hear this Mediator telling the parties he is not an adviser and he is not evaluative. We hear him tell the researcher that he is an interventionist and he does evaluate. He says mediation is more than just listening and exploring. These views, together with his view of mediation as a negotiation, prepare us for his actions in this mediation. He is interventionist. He is an evaluator. He does more than listen and explore. He is a negotiator. He is self-aware and willing to act expressly to lead the parties to a place where he assumes they want to be. They chose him to assist with the resolution of their dispute. He works for that goal. It is a goal he sees as necessary for these parties and a goal he believes they want for themselves. It is the *raison d'être* for this Mediator. All his energies are applied to the fulfilment of this goal.

The Mediator sympathizes, empathizes, argues, persuades and cajoles the parties to resolution. He speaks frankly in stating that resolution is his goal – not for himself, but for the parties. He has a firm view of this: he sees risks for both if they proceed to trial. It is with this firmly held belief that this Mediator acts. What is interesting to note is that although not all mediators expressly articulate such goals or methods, they act in a manner similar to this Mediator. The difference is in cognitive awareness: the others appear to intervene with their actions either without self-awareness of the extent and nature of their interventions or by masking both their intent and nature.[28]

In looking at the patterns of mediator interactions, this Mediator shows an immediate alignment with the Mitchell Team. He negotiates with the Jarvis & Kimbourne Team as *Mitchell* from his first meeting with the Jarvis & Kimbourne Team. With Mitchell, his identity as *Jarvis & Kimbourne* appears briefly in his second and third meetings, but does not appear resoundingly until the fifth meeting when the parties are in the bargaining proposal phase of their negotiation. The Jarvis & Kimbourne Team is faced by the *Mitchell* voice almost immediately into the process.

In his first pre-mediation meeting with the Mitchell Team, the Mediator acts as *mediator* in describing the process, getting information about the case and history of events, and in discussing the litigation process. The Mediator slips into a *party* frame of reference when he speaks of his own experience with invoicing, talking about taking the same approach to invoicing as did Mitchell. He illustrates his empathy with Mitchell's position here, stepping into the shoes of *Mitchell* himself to draw an affinity between himself and Mitchell. In doing this, he moves beyond the mediator intervention of validating parties' feelings: he is agreeing with party action and giving strength to Mitchell rather than helping him feel heard.[29] There is a loss of third-party voice as a result. He also acts as *adviser* when giving a view on whether to

---

28 For example, Mediator 9 appears to lack self-awareness of the nature of his interventions and the roles he takes on, whereas Mediator 7 attempts to excuse his interventions by reminding the parties that he is merely vocalizing what was told to him. This is examined further in the analysis of their respective cases.
29 Validation is a tool used by mediators to acknowledge feelings, experiences and the like. It helps to ensure that a party has been heard. See, for example, J. Macfarlane *et al.*, eds, *Dispute Resolution: Readings and Case Studies* (Toronto: Emond Montgomery, 2010) at

retain a forensic accountant, the approach to the profit calculation, and in explaining to Mitchell the basis of the Jarvis & Kimbourne case and how to counter it. On this latter point, he advises Mitchell to argue that there is no loss to the Partnership because termination of a partner under the Partnership Agreement can only occur if there is damage to the partnership. These interactions suggest a mediator propping up a claimant, giving him confidence in his negotiation, and supporting him in the battle against his opponent.

In the following pre-mediation meeting with the Jarvis & Kimbourne Team, the usual *mediator* activity of describing the process and seeking the history of the case occurs. However, the Mediator soon launches into a challenge in the guise of *Mitchell*. He challenges the Jarvis & Kimbourne action in expelling Mitchell from the Partnership: *"If a partner is not pulling his weight, it is clear he has to go, but the issue is, is there cause? Goodwill is dependent on it. Looking at the invoice issue, most were paid. What is the impact?"* When the Jarvis & Kimbourne Team later remarks that the invoices had not been sent out, the Mediator retorts that they had been billed.

During these interludes as *claimant*, however, the Mediator also slips into the voice of *defendant*. When Jarvis replies that the impact of the invoice issue is a loss of trust, the Mediator commiserates by stating, *"I understand that – that is a big thing."* And again, when Jarvis says of the invoices, *"Why raise invoices without sending them to the client? Who does that?"* The Mediator acknowledges the difficulty: *"I could not understand that."* These latter interactions show a mediator who is sympathetic to Jarvis, assuming a *party* voice. The Mediator then continues his intervention as *adviser* when he then tells the Jarvis & Kimbourne Team to concentrate on the cause issue because that is the foundation of its case.

After these brief interludes of party-aligned identification, the Mediator becomes *claimant* once again, pushing the Jarvis & Kimbourne Team on the issue of the invoices, attempting to undermine its defence: *"Would you not notice {Mitchell personally inputting the invoices}; do you not cost WIP against the invoices; was the WIP written off?"* This seems to be in aid of disclosing the Team's weaknesses in its insistence that it suffered loss from the manner in which Mitchell administered the invoices. A further example of the *claimant* voice comes at the end of the session when the Mediator counters the Jarvis & Kimbourne assertion that Mitchell would lose everything if he proceeded with his action. The Mediator says, *"Currently, he has nothing,"* suggesting Mitchell has nothing to lose and therefore will be strong in his position.

This easy movement between identities continues during the second pre-mediation meeting with the Mitchell Team. The Mediator points out that invoices were delivered late in retort to Mitchell's assertion that all invoices

315–16; C. Menkel-Meadow, L. Love and A. Schneider, *Mediation: Practice, Policy, and Ethics* (New York: Aspen, 2006) at 168–9.

had been delivered. After this brief moment as *defendant*, the Mediator vacillates between *adviser, claimant* and *self* identities. As *adviser*, he discusses how Mitchell should deal with the invoices; in particular, the fact they were not delivered and there had been no intention to deceive. He slips into a combined *adviser* and *opposing party* identity when suggesting to make clear to the Jarvis & Kimbourne Team that Mitchell's assistant had sent out the invoices while at the same time noting they remained his responsibility as partner. Further shifts occur when we hear the *party* voice in agreement with Elliot's view that the transcript of the expulsion meeting was self-serving, and *mediator* voice when conveying the Jarvis & Kimbourne concern that the invoices affected profit-sharing and the intent to place the party representatives together after the joint session.

As the mediation progresses, the Mediator uses these five identities as necessary to further the negotiation. At times, he is only *mediator*, conveying information without commentary; or he is *adviser*, advising how to respond to offers and formulating those offers; or he is *opposing party*, when delivering offers with rationales to support their elements or countering arguments on issues raised; or he is *party with party*, sympathizing with a view or being critical of the other party. In this case, the shifts to opposing party are prevalent during the early and middle stages of the negotiation, with movement to *adviser* and *mediator* functions predominating in the latter stages, excepting the final meetings with the Jarvis & Kimbourne Team when the *opposing party* voice re-emerges to challenge it to increase its offer.

The data suggests Mediator awareness of his shifting identities. In the second meeting with the Jarvis & Kimbourne Team after the joint session, the Mediator conveys Mitchell's offer, pointing out that the parties are not far apart on one aspect of the offer, noting the difference lies in the percentage for calculation: *"On goodwill, the difference between the two of you is turnover. It is not big. The big difference is 30 per cent versus 50 per cent. I am not arguing the point because I do not understand it."* Note his assertion that he is not arguing the point. This suggests he is aware he is arguing for a party as the party. He is stepping out of the role, however, to make clear that he cannot retort as he would normally, due to his lack of understanding. I suggest that had he the understanding he says he lacks, he would have continued as *claimant* in spinning Mitchell's offer as an attractive one.

This is further highlighted in the first meeting with Elliot. The Mediator challenges Mitchell's position on goodwill as *Jarvis & Kimbourne* but prefaces the challenge by anticipating a reaction to the challenge: *"You may think I am just arguing their case. Look at the figure. The calculation to £480,000 started at £700,000 at 80 per cent with an 80/20 per cent litigation risk and £70,000 in costs. I am only raising it with you …."* And once again, in the following meeting with the Mitchell Team in response to the Team's assertion that Jarvis & Kimbourne did not follow the appropriate notice procedure for expulsion: *"There is a debate when the one-month period started, but I am not putting forward their case. I need to reality test."* To this, Mitchell replies, *"I am being done."*

The Mediator confirms, *"Yes, you are being done."* He stresses that he is not arguing the Jarvis & Kimbourne points or putting forward its case, yet he is doing these very things. He is like Mediator 7 in this regard, but with much more vigour in both the denial of the act and the act itself.

"I need to reality test." This is a common phrase used by mediators similar in tone to the Mediator's phrase in Case Study 7 that he will be devil's advocate. In this case, the common phrase of 'needing to reality test' is invoked. This is how mediators describe their challenges to the parties and how they would characterize their assumption of the parties' identities during the course of these mediations. The data suggests that mediators hide behind this label of reality testing when they are doing exactly what this Mediator and Mediator 7 say they are not doing; that is, putting forward the other side's case. We have seen it throughout these cases. They are doing it under the guise of reality testing, which does not change the nature of the action. The use of the labels seems to be a way to gain acceptance from the parties to engage in the negotiation with them and against them. It is a tool used to mask the actions of the mediator and arguably to help maintain the perception of 'impartiality' and 'neutrality' that is an undercurrent running beneath the process.

Case Study 9: The fishing logo

This dispute about anglers and their products returns for further examination. We recall the parties negotiating the end of their long-standing licence agreement for the exclusive use of a fishing logo in the manufacture and supply of fishing equipment and sporting apparel.[30]

Joint session (10:50 a.m.–12:05 p.m.)

In his opening statement, the Claimant Solicitor, Lee Benjamin, summarized the legal position of the Claimant, Angler Co-Operative, regarding the provisions of the Agreement: the Defendant, HighLander, was in breach of the Agreement by appointing a new licensee. As a result, Angler Co-Operative was entitled to continue using the HighLander brand for the manufacture and sale of new stock for a further 18-month period after termination. Benjamin discussed his view of the viability of the defence and took issue with HighLander's mediation statement.

Once he concluded, the Claimant representative, Dominic Gerald spoke. Gerald spoke about the history of the licence arrangement between Angler Co-Operative and HighLander, emphasizing that HighLander did nothing to protect Angler Co-Operative's entitlements under the Agreement over the

---

30 See Chapter 5 for a full case description.

years, and suffering as a result. He also spoke about the impact of the appointment of the new exclusive licensee on Angler Co-Operative's business.

The Defendant Solicitor, Michael James, in his opening statement, referred to Angler Co-Operative's agreement to the appointment of a new licensee and the 'sell-off' period under the Agreement. With respect to the latter, HighLander's position was that the Agreement permitted Angler Co-Operative to continue selling stock-on-hand for a period of only 12 months after the termination of the Agreement. It was not for an 18-month period and it did not include new stock. Some dialogue occurred regarding each position until the Mediator concluded the session.

The Mediator did not engage in the dialogue between Angler Co-Operative and HighLander.

First meeting with the Angler Co-Operative Team (12:05 p.m.–12:50 p.m.)

The Mediator entered the room and asked, *"How will we settle this?"* When Gerald replied that it came down to money and HighLander should either write a cheque or Angler Co-Operative would manufacture the 200,000 pieces that have been ordered but not yet manufactured, the Mediator retorted, *"You do not have the fabric."* When Gerald said they had the alternative of manufacturing the stock under their own brand, the Mediator said, *"It is purely a question of trademark whether you can use it. Could they prevent you using the Angler Co-Operative brand?"*[31] Discussion continued about the difference between the two brands and which brand Angler Co-Operative wished to sell. The Mediator sought information about the brand preference and the minimum royalty payment required to be paid for use of the HighLander brand. He asked about HighLander's counter-claim for an inspection of Angler Co-Operative's books: *"Is it to get a few quid more?"* When the Angler Co-Operative Team spoke of its view of such a demand, the Mediator said, *"I do not sense enthusiasm from James {for this claim}."*

The Mediator asked what Angler Co-Operative would do if the parties did not reach settlement that day; specifically whether the products would be manufactured notwithstanding the litigation. When Benjamin said, *"If Angler Co-Operative loses, it will lose money. If HighLander loses, it will be severely compromised with the licensee and the launch will be buggered; it will be out of the market for years, it will be sued by {others} ... And, the brand will be in turmoil."* The Mediator replied, *"Yes, I can see it."* After some talk about HighLander's interests, the Mediator said, *"I am not sure that I want a proposal*

---

31 Recall from the case description in Chapter 5 that Angler Co-Operative manufactured fishing equipment and sporting apparel under its own private brand as well as under the HighLander brand.

now because I want to talk to them. You need to decide – money or garments. I need to tease out of them what they are thinking of."

Discussion then ensued about the Angler Co-Operative brand and Angler Co-Operative's intention to manufacture under its own private brand. This first meeting ended with the Mediator telling the Angler Co-Operative Team that it needed to think about what it wanted out of a settlement, and that he would speak with the HighLander Team to *"tease out of them what they would do"*. He concluded with two similar statements: *"Let's see what they have to say,"* and *"Let's see what deal they are thinking of."*

First meeting with the HighLander Team (12:50 p.m.–1:55 p.m.)

The Mediator began this meeting stating, *"After the joint session, you've heard the legal arguments, so the question is how to settle it. You've had good legal advice. There are risks to you and them. What sort of settlement would you like to see? I could see a couple of ways to structure it."* The Mediator explored the issue of outstanding royalty payments. He said, *"The ideal is to pay something, knowing that you do not want to pay them anything. A sum is owed by them, £320,000 for 2006, and there is a sum to buy out their claim.*[32] *2007 is divided into two – there are certain rights. Is there any advantage to you to renegotiate the position for 2007 that could assist, or am I barking up the wrong tree?"* In response, the Team spoke of Angler Co-Operative's outstanding order for the manufacture of 160,000 additional garments.[33] In relation to this order, the Mediator queried, *"This is a puzzle that was raised when you {James} and I spoke. There is no claim for specific relief."* James agreed. The Mediator then said, *"It makes sense to do a cash deal and have no more sales of the HighLander brand stock. It is not in anyone's interest."*

After a discussion about Angler Co-Operative's relationship to the HighLander brand, the Defendant representative, Lewis Jacob, suggested that Gerald felt strongly aligned to the brand, that money was not the issue, and that it was an 'ego thing' with him. The Mediator replied, *"Yes, there is an ego issue here. He sees himself closely associated with the brand."* Some additional dialogue followed about Gerald's history with the brand. The Mediator said, *"I have good and bad news. The good news is that he {Gerald} wants a settlement. The bad news is that he is prepared to fight a principle. He has a huge amount of respect for you. He is a highly intelligent man who is creative. What you told me, I expected to hear. A cash deal is the ideal. Have you formulated something to take to them?"* Jacob described prior settlement offers made to Angler Co-Operative involving payment of the royalties and legal fees. The Mediator responded,

---

32 Recall that part of the HighLander counter-claim was for payment of outstanding royalty payments; Angler Co-Operative alleged that the royalty payments were improperly calculated or not due.

33 This reflects a portion of the allegedly 200,000 outstanding orders.

"But the discussion was on the royalty with legal costs to each own account. That is a long way off what it will take to settle."

The HighLander Team discussed the Angler Co-Operative inventory of brand products, their sale in the various regions and Angler Co-Operative's outstanding orders. The Mediator opined on the price that Angler Co-Operative would receive for each product: *"He won't make £100 per garment."* Jacob replied, *"The figure is £40 maximum."* They discussed Angler Co-Operative's orders for Scandinavia and whether it was 24,000 in volume, as believed by HighLander, or more. The Mediator said, *"What would you like me to do? I could give a proposal for cash or products. I think that Angler Co-Operative will say the amount {for orders} is above 24,000."* Again, the HighLander Team queried the price Angler Co-Operative could receive for the products in the various markets and whether it could have such a large outstanding order. The Mediator interrupted: *"It is difficult for you to interpret documents. If you want to put forward a proposal, then say, 'if you can prove the orders in Scandinavia, we will pay for those.'"* When the HighLander Team again questioned the veracity of the orders, the Mediator said, *"The only way to take this forward – you will formulate a proposal but you need binding orders in Scandinavia."*

As for where Angler Co-Operative could sell the products, the Mediator said, *"He will say this – I do not know this because he hasn't said it – under the contract, he can sell anywhere so he needs compensation."* Jacob replied, *"I do not care if he sells what is in stock anywhere. The problem is the 160,000."*[34] The Mediator: *"I realize that. I can see the different view on the 160,000. On his view, he can take in 160,000 and sell anywhere. This is to anticipate a problem. Let's get the ball rolling – cash or selling products in Scandinavia subject to conditions. I am happy to put either or both."* Jacob was not interested in pursuing this. The Mediator then raised the prior offer made by the HighLander Team: *"Angler Co-Operative is to pay £320,000 in royalties, 24,000 sales in Scandinavia, each bearing their own costs and Angler Co-Operative can sell its existing stock. Is it worth putting this forward now to get the ball rolling?"*

Jacob reminded the Mediator about the three restrictions on selling that he raised earlier. The Mediator summarized them: goods are not to be sold to another retailer, they are not for export and they are not to be sold via the internet. James then queried, *"How to deal with a trust issue, that he will only sell 24,000?"* The Mediator replied, *"You can provide for it contractually, but the question is how to police it. I cannot think of a way to police it. If he intends to hide, you can't find it."* James said, *"I want to flag it now because you can't do anything if you learn he is selling more."* He suggested sending a letter to all manufacturers. The Mediator said, *"Whether that does any good, James has made a good point."* Jacob asked, *"Won't there be a contract?"* The Mediator suggested, *"Make it part of the settlement,"* which Jacob thought might work. In response, the Mediator

---

34 A portion of the total of 200,000 outstanding orders is being referenced here.

said, "Right now these are good points but raise them at the drafting stage. As a starting point, shall we start with this, but I am quite confident he will say no." And further, "Let me put that to them, which I am sure they will have something to say and I will come back with a flea in my ear. Let me see what it provokes – hopefully a counter-offer ... maybe I am completely wrong. He appears very wealthy and may give it a shot."

Second meeting with the Angler Co-Operative Team (1:55 p.m.–3:27 p.m.)

Upon entering the room, the Mediator began, "*I tried to get something on the table. You may not like it. They pointed to the last offer. They are prepared to reinstate it subject to qualification.*"

He proceeded to set out the offer. Much discussion occurred over the calculation of sales and royalties arising from various regions, and a possible counter-offer by Angler Co-Operative. The Mediator reacted to the offer proposed by Angler Co-Operative: "*What I will have to do is prove to them the loss is proved – establish what orders you are walking away from and the profit.*" When discussing the sale of products in Scotland, the Mediator said, "*My sense is that they won't let you sell anything in Scotland except for existing stock.*" In answer to Gerald's question about selling in Ireland, the Mediator said, "*They won't agree Ireland; Scandinavia is the one area they are receptive to.*" On an offer, the Mediator suggested, "*Best thing to do ... you want the £144,000 loss, in cash, in dollars, in Scandinavian sales, you don't care which ... Put it to their option.*"[35] After Gerald confirmed he would not pay a minimum royalty, only a real royalty, the Mediator suggested that Angler Co-Operative say to HighLander, "*We will not pay a royalty for 2007 – you buy back our position for Scotland and Ireland.*"

With respect to the conditions for sale required by HighLander, in response to Gerald's response that it would be best efforts only, the Mediator said, "*They may say you can have orders if the customers agree to terms.*" When Gerald reiterated he was willing to agree to best efforts, the Mediator replied, "*The trouble with it is, we'll be here in six months to argue it.*" Further discussion occurred with respect to the formulation of Angler Co-Operative's proposal. The Mediator warned the Angler Co-Operative Team that he did not believe HighLander would accept the proposal, but he also said he did not think HighLander would walk out.

When formulating a proposal, the Mediator advised the Angler Co-Operative Team that he would have to be prepared to take the HighLander Team through its calculations, saying, "*There is enough distrust that they will

---

35 The £144,000 loss is the value of the orders from outside Scandinavia which the Highlander Team is not prepared to permit Angler Co-Operative to manufacture and sell.

want to be taken through it." Gerald retorted that he did not have all the necessary documents for costing. The Mediator said, *"If you are asking for some level of compensation, they will want to be satisfied about costs."* The Angler Co-Operative Team said it would come up with something. Benjamin said that if the Mediator goes in with a number, they cannot go higher and there remain two possibilities: they agree or HighLander goes lower. The Mediator said, *"What we are hearing from Benjamin is valid. They will not bite the hand; they will come back with a counter-offer. No one is totally happy after a mediation. You are arguing over a run-off and there is nothing more at the end of the year."* When the Team speculated on HighLander's reaction, the Mediator said, *"I will see what I can do. They may not do a deal at this level, but we need to start somewhere."*

Some further comments were made about the offer and the extent of the information to be disclosed to the HighLander Team by the Mediator. For example, Gerald pointed out that his business suffered a loss in the range of £4 million as a result of the appointment of the new licensee. The Mediator responded, *"There is no claim in the proceedings for it,"* to which the Team said there would be. Gerald also mentioned possible orders from England. The Mediator inquired whether *"this would cause angst to the Defendant?"* On hearing Benjamin's affirmative answer, the Mediator said, *"I'm inclined not to mention England because it is antagonistic, unless you tell me to."* Gerald said, *"It is the easiest place to sell."* The Mediator retorted, *"But it is in their backyard."* The meeting concluded with further comment from the Team about orders increasing as time passes.

Second meeting with the HighLander Team
(3:27 p.m.–4:00 p.m.)

"I've been gone a long time," began the Mediator. *"We need introductions again! You gather that it was not easy and they were not overwhelmed by your proposal. Strong feelings are coming out of the room and they have competing views. It took some time to get through the process. You may or may not like it, but at least you get a proposal. You need to understand where they are coming from. They have a different contractual view regarding their entitlement. This is the starting point. I am looking at this not where we are today, but where we will be next week. It is fluid. They have expressions of interest from Scandinavia and Scotland. If they take the litigation route, they will be successful. If they give up today, they are giving up set orders and prospective orders."* And with that introduction, the Mediator set out Angler Co-Operative's proposal.

The HighLander Team picked at the proposal. The Mediator answered questions regarding the calculations, saying, *"I said I would anticipate you would want a breakdown of the costs. They can give it."*

On the conditions regarding the sale of products, the Mediator said, *"In principle, Angler Co-Operative does not have difficulty with it, but how to deal with it. So I suggested to Gerald that he would sell on the basis that the customer would agree; for example, Angler Co-Operative to give a commitment to procure the commitment."*

When James replied, *"He can't because they are already on the internet,"* the Mediator retorted, *"That is not your problem, because if the settlement has a condition in it, they cannot sell it, and it is your problem because you can't police it."*

As for the royalty payment, Jacob said that the obligation is in the contract and they have been paying it. The Mediator said in response, *"They said that there wasn't one in the contract."* When Jacob confirmed there wasn't one in the last two years, but they carried on in the same way, the Mediator inquired, *"In those years, you invoiced?"* *"Yes, we invoiced them, but it was not an issue because the amount was always over,"* replied James. The Mediator said, *"There is some argument on either side; maybe a horse-trade {is necessary}."*

The HighLander Team worked on the formulation of a counter-proposal. When it suggested that it wanted Angler Co-Operative to speak with its Scandinavian customers regarding agreement to the three restrictive conditions of sale, the Mediator said, *"It is up to him what he puts in the contract and the risk he is willing to take. By asking the question, you will surface a problem ... The disadvantage of raising it now is, if he says no, there will be alternatives and he will say that he wants to be able to sell products."* A further suggestion was made to hold a portion of the settlement monies in escrow to ensure Angler Co-Operative's commitment to the restrictive conditions. The Mediator said, *"You can say it but I do not think {it's needed}; they are good for the money."* Jacob said, *"Yes, they are rich, but what sanction is there to ensure payment?"* The Mediator replied, *"It depends on the way the agreement is drafted. If Angler Co-Operative gives an undertaking to the court and then breaches, then ..."* James interrupted, *"Jail, contempt of court."*

Further discussion occurred about the products to be sold by Angler Co-Operative. The Mediator summarized the HighLander offer and concluded the meeting.

Third meeting with the Angler Co-Operative Team (4:00 p.m.–4:30 p.m.)

In answer to Gerald's *"How did we get on?"* the Mediator said, *"We're not there and are a long way off. On the money, they want the minimum royalty. They are not happy about the legal costs. They took a very pragmatic approach. Take the difference between what you want and they want and split it."*

When questioned about the calculation of the offer, the Mediator explained the offer. On the point of the loss of the 22,000 orders and how much HighLander was willing to compensate for it, the Mediator stated, *"The biggest issue is the 22,000 units because last week you told him you are doing business for no profit."*[36] When Gerald replied, *"I said I was making less profit,"* the

---

36 The 22,000 orders are those from Ireland and Scotland, which HighLander refused to permit Angler Co-Operative to manufacture and sell.

Mediator said, *"He interprets it as no profit."* Further discussion occurred about the calculations, and the Team complained that not all losses were accounted for. The Mediator stated, *"You won't get a full shopping bag today; only if you take it to trial and win."*

Gerald began formulating a counter-offer using words such as *'non-negotiable'* on various items sought and advising that he would go to court rather than negotiate further. Summarizing the various elements of the offer and, in particular, confirming the intent to pay royalty on the existing stock, the Mediator told the Team, *"They will want to know the stock figure when they are drafting {the settlement} agreement."* Gerald replied, *"I did not want to bring it up because then there would be negotiation on it."* *"But I think the way it will be drafted, it will be set out as an ongoing liability,"* retorted the Mediator. Upon Gerald confirming the offer and stating that he will go to court if it doesn't settle, the Mediator said, *"I will tell them 'no further negotiation'. This will help in a way because it helps with the horse-trading."*

Third meeting with the HighLander Team
(4:30 p.m.–4:45 p.m.; 4:55 p.m.–5:15 p.m.)

On entry into the HighLander room, the Mediator said, *"Good news. Final position, non-negotiable. We've reached the end of the road. They shifted quite a lot. I always counselled against saying it, it is Gerald's position and he is prepared to walk on it."* After outlining the main points and Gerald's position on the points, the Mediator continued to talk about the sale of products: *"There is a big concession: Gerald is prepared to waive Norway, which is a substantial part of the loss of profit because it is a recent order and he can say no to the customer. Regarding Ireland, he will either deliver or you compensate lost sales of £40,000, which are more or less the same as the royalty coming from Scandinavia of £46,000. Each cancels out."* On the domain names, the Mediator advised that Gerald would transfer them. When James said they should just cancel them, the Mediator suggested, *"Isn't it better to keep them rather than have someone else get them?"*

The Mediator then spoke of the final elements of the offer, *"and no more auditing. He is fed up with your auditors – although I am sure your auditors are delightful."* To which Jacob interjected, *"He was never audited. No one attended in 11 years!"* The Mediator ignored the interjection and continued, *"When you look at it, there's lots of progress. I am told that it is the last offer and if the deal is not made, he will go out."*

After reiterating the terms of the offer, Jacob inquired, *"Can we write it so it has serious consequences?"* The Mediator replied, *"I think it is possible to draft it in such a way that he does not have permission unless he procures it {the customer commitment to the restrictive sale conditions}."* When Jacob raised payment issues, the Mediator said, *"I am sure that you can put it in the drafting. You are raising issues that will come up in drafting."*

The HighLander Team requested a few minutes to deliberate privately.

When the Mediator re-entered the room, James gave the Team's response to the offer: *"We are there, provided we can write it to obtain a commitment from Scandinavia regarding the three {restrictive sale} conditions. Therefore £216,000 to exchange hands, from them, £268,000 less £30,000 less £22,000 with payment within a period of ..."*[37] *"Raise this now?"* interjected the Mediator. James said, *"Stick it in the document."* The Mediator said, *"It will provoke an argument."* After determining that it should be dealt with now, James then raised the issue of the procurement of the transfer of the domain name from Angler Co-Operative and a third-party owner. The Mediator said, *"I suggest you draft it. Draft it in the Tomlin Order with the undertaking in the main body, with the terms in the schedule, plus permission to apply for enforcement.*[38] *I could draft it but I am a slow typist."*

With respect to other points to cover in the offer, James said that Angler Co-Operative should undertake not to interfere with the new licensee. The Mediator replied, *"Cover it in the settlement agreement."* The Mediator pointed out, *"We did not discuss confidentiality and the press."* A little later, *"We could put it in the agreement."* When James queried whether they should raise the timing of the payment now, the Mediator said, *"If it is a deal-breaker, raise it, but if not, leave it to the agreement."* When Jacob insisted that it be raised now, the Mediator said, *"It will provoke discussion."* Further, *"There will be a number of drafting issues; deal with it as you go."*

James requested the Mediator to return to the room after conveying the offer to Angler Co-Operative to *"help draft"*. In answer to Jacob's inquiry, *"Is it best to have the Mediator do it?"* the Mediator said, *"I can. I have in the past, but I think James should do it."*

Fourth meeting with the Angler Co-Operative Team (5:15 p.m.–5:40 p.m.)

The Mediator began: *"Subject to a couple of points, the devil will be in the drafting. Two issues are not a problem, I think – you procure the third party {consent with the domain name} because evidence in court says you have the power to do it."* When Gerald suggested that Angler Co-Operative did not have control over the third party, the Mediator said, *"In one of the witness statements, you suggest you could make things happen."* Gerald replied, *"I promise, I did not."* The Mediator moved to the next point, *"On the timing of payment, £216,000 within 14 days of settlement."* *"{Payment} is normally due in January,"* replied Gerald.

---

37 The figure of £268,000 represents royalty payments allegedly owed by Angler Co-Operative less the value of lost sales from booked orders. The other amounts, which are deducted, reflect amounts previously agreed and dealt with prior to the mediation.
38 As described in Chapter 4, a Tomlin Order under the Civil Procedure Rules, 1998 SI 1998/3132 for England and Wales, is a form of consent order staying proceedings on terms, also allowing parties to apply to the court for enforcement of the consent agreement without the need to initiate new proceedings.

The Mediator reverted to the third-party issue once again, *"Regarding the witness statement, it is the third statement where you explain the cock-up on the website."* He then read out the relevant provision. When Gerald again demurred, the Mediator suggested that he *"undertake to use best endeavours with a letter asking {the third party} to do it"*. Gerald agreed and the Mediator turned to the issue of the timing of the payment. He also reminded the Angler Co-Operative Team, *"There will be some points to debate in the drafting. I do not think they will take anyone by surprise."* He told them James had begun drafting and he *"will help him"*. A few administrative details were then sorted. The Mediator left the room saying, *"I need to see these guys, where are we."*

Concluding meetings (5:40 p.m.–8:20 p.m.)

The drafting of the agreement followed. Gerald wanted to leave the mediation and leave it to his advisers to draft the agreement. The Mediator told him that he could leave as long as he gave authority to his legal team to sign the agreement. The Mediator told the HighLander Team of Gerald's desire to leave. They did not want him to leave, so Jacob suggested he take him out for a drink. Gerald and Jacob chatted while the Mediator worked with James to draft the settlement agreement.

During the drafting session with the HighLander Team, the Mediator was actively involved in drafting the agreement, making suggestions for inclusion in the agreement including the specific language. He asked if there were any tax issues. *"Don't you want a full release clause?"* he asked. James responded, *"Yes."* James also wanted Angler Co-Operative to acknowledge the new licensee. The Mediator suggested wording: *"Angler Co-Operative undertakes not to bring any claims against {the new licensee}."* He queried, *"Is that wide enough?"* On the HighLander point that it did not want Angler Co-Operative to be selling other products, the Mediator replied, *"I suggest, 'Angler Co-Operative has no authority to sell any other products other than those set out'."* As for the labelling of the products, the Mediator suggested, *"Not for sale outside Scandinavia."* As for whether the label should be sewn into the garment, the Mediator said, *"Yes, you would likely want that."* James drafted the wording for the provision dealing with the transfer of the domain name by Angler Co-Operative and the Mediator said, *"Add 'forthwith'."* He then asked what HighLander required from a confidentiality clause. When James suggested, *"The terms of settlement to be confidential,"* the Mediator added, *"The terms of settlement and detail of the dispute between the parties."* James said that HighLander needs to be able to say something to its new licensee. The Mediator replied that an agreed statement was required. The drafting continued in this vein, with the Mediator advising the HighLander Team on drafting issues and working with it to create a written agreement.

Once the agreement was drafted, it was given to the Angler Co-Operative Team for review. Some further details were discussed and agreed. The atmosphere was jovial. The Mediator, Gerald and Jacob spoke of their next fishing trips.

The parties worked together to confirm the agreement in principle. The agreement was signed and the parties said goodnight to one another. The mediation ended.

***

As with the Mediator in Case Study 7, the Mediator is silent during the opening joint session. He lets the parties speak and does not participate in the dialogue until his first meeting with the Angler Co-Operative Team, during which the *HighLander* voice is immediately heard. The Mediator challenges Gerald on his assertion that he had 200,000 orders for garments. The Mediator says, *"You do not have the fabric."* Thereafter, he quickly becomes Angler Co-Operative's *adviser* regarding its ability to use the HighLander brand and shifts just as easily to a *mediator* stance when he asks questions to obtain information.

The Mediator is somewhat ambivalent in these identities. For example, towards the end of this first session with Angler Co-Operative, the Mediator remarks on the lack of enthusiasm HighLander has for its counter-claim. Is this statement made as an adviser, as a mediator, or as party? I would suggest that it is made as *Angler Co-Operative*, assessing the strength of the HighLander case. This is further supported by the Mediator's purpose in leaving the Angler Co-Operative Team to speak with HighLander: *"to tease out of them what they would do"*. His use of the word 'tease' suggests an intent to approach HighLander not as a mediator or an adviser, but as the very *party* against whom HighLander is in dispute. This view is further supported by the inherent lack of impartiality in these two comments – their words suggest an alignment with Angler Co-Operative.

The shift between *party*, *adviser* and *mediator* continues throughout the mediation and during meetings with both parties. The movements are quick, instantaneous and as fluid as seen in the prior cases. This is particularly acute in the Mediator's first meeting with the HighLander Team. The Mediator starts with questions about settlement and HighLander's goals for the day. He continues by suggesting options for settlement. So far, he acts as *self*, doing the job expected of him. He becomes HighLander's *adviser* when he points out Angler Co-Operative's failure to specifically plead the value of the outstanding booked orders and also when he recommends a particular course of action: *"It makes sense to do a cash deal and have no more sales of the HighLander brand stock. It is not in anyone's interest."* With regard to this latter point, he implies that it is not in HighLander's interest for Angler Co-Operative to continue to market the HighLander brand, whereas Angler Co-Operative desires it. Recall that it was HighLander who terminated the Licence Agreement, not Angler Co-Operative. This apparent protection of HighLander's interest helps to underscore the *adviser* voice here rather than the more benign voice of *mediator*.

The ambivalence described above occurs again in this session when the Mediator agrees with HighLander's opinion that Angler Co-Operative is strongly aligned to the HighLander brand and that money is not at the core of the dispute; rather, it is Gerald's ego. The Mediator replies, *"Yes, there is an ego issue here. He sees himself closely associated with the brand."* It is difficult to categorize this statement either as falling into mediator-speak or adviser-speak. The Mediator once again seems to become the *party* itself – he aligns himself to the *HighLander* view, resulting in a unified perception of Angler Co-Operative's motivations in the dispute. Just as quickly, he shifts to embody the voice of *Angler Co-Operative* to advise HighLander of the Angler Co-Operative desire to settle the case, yet its willingness to fight a principle. He softens this challenge by referring to the great respect held by Gerald for Jacob, and referencing Gerald's creativity and intelligence, all seemingly to persuade HighLander as to the strength of Gerald's commitment to his claim. Without pausing for breath, we hear the Mediator as *adviser*: *"A cash deal is the ideal."* And, switching equally as quickly to the *Angler Co-Operative* voice in response to the HighLander demand for the payment of outstanding royalty fees and legal costs, he states: *"But the discussion was on the royalty with legal costs to each own account. That is a long way off what it will take to settle."*

For the rest of this session, the Mediator moves between *adviser* and *mediator*, working to guide HighLander in the formulation of a settlement proposal, anticipating Angler Co-Operative's reaction and HighLander's needs. He considers what HighLander requires, particularly in relation to the protection of the HighLander brand. He acts as *self* when summarizing the terms of the offer and noting the intent of the first offer is to instigate a counter-offer.

When relaying the offer to the Angler Co-Operative Team, the Mediator acts as *HighLander*. He does so in a way that is not immediately obvious: *"I tried to get something on the table. You may not like it. They pointed to the last offer. They are prepared to reinstate it subject to qualification."* The key to the voice is the way in which the Mediator prefaces the difficulty in convincing HighLander to make the offer in the first place, reminiscent of negotiating ploys and bluffs made by competitive bargainers. He steps into the shoes of the *opposing party* once again in order to remove any expectation of selling products in England, and further in response to Angler Co-Operative's proposal to use best efforts regarding conditions of sale: *"They may say you can have orders if the customers agree to terms."* Later, he challenges Angler Co-Operative's claim for losses suffered by reason of the appointment of the new licensee stating, *"There is no claim in the proceedings for it."*

The Mediator moves to *adviser* mode between these moments of party voice. He tells Angler Co-Operative it must be able to prove the existence of orders and the loss of profit suffered; he suggests the position to take on the royalty payment for 2007; and towards the end of the session, cautions Angler Co-Operative against disclosing the existence of orders from England for fear of antagonizing HighLander. He does not, however, forget his *mediator* identity during these episodes: he talks about the willingness of HighLander to accept the Angler Co-Operative proposal and his view that HighLander will not terminate the negotiation; he anticipates the HighLander reaction to the offer; he prepares Angler Co-Operative for a response to the reaction; and he speaks of the need to resolve the dispute.

The following meeting with the HighLander Team begins with the Mediator as *Angler Co-Operative*. He sets out the Angler Co-Operative offer, explaining how Angler Co-Operative arrived at the offer. Again, the Mediator prefaces the offer with the difficulty encountered in developing the offer. He builds up the importance of the proposal by suggesting that its mere existence is something to be gratified by. He explains the extent to which Angler Co-Operative will suffer by the proposal in terms of lost expected sales. He also talks about Angler Co-Operative's firm belief in the strength of its legal position. In so doing, the Mediator is preparing the way to negotiate the Angler Co-Operative proposal against HighLander. He is prepared to answer questions as to its calculations and points out Angler Co-Operative's willingness to accede to conditions on the sale of products. The Mediator quickly becomes *HighLander's adviser* when HighLander responds to the Mediator's suggestion that Angler Co-Operative can commit to procuring customer agreements. James responds by saying that it is too late for such a term given the sale of the items on the internet. Despite the presence of James in the room, the Mediator retorts, *"That is not your problem, because if the settlement has condition in it, they cannot sell it, and it is your problem because you can't police it."*

The Mediator acts as *Angler Co-Operative* when challenging HighLander on the requirement to pay invoices. HighLander notes the requirement, but the Mediator rebuffs the requirement, stating there is no such obligation in the contract. HighLander agrees, but says payment has been made notwithstanding. The Mediator seeks to uncover another weakness by asking whether the royalty fee has been invoiced in the past. This exchange pits Mediator against HighLander – not as mediator against defendant, but as *party claimant* against defendant. The Mediator acts as though *his* interests are at stake. Yet, *his* interests become *HighLander's* interests soon after. After HighLander suggests one way of dealing with the conditions to the sale, the Mediator cautions it against the plan, suggesting that raising the issue could lead Angler Co-Operative to make other demands contrary to HighLander's interests. Unmistakably, he is here an *adviser* seeking to protect his client.

The following sessions with each of the parties disclose an emerging pattern. At the beginning of each private meeting, the Mediator speaks as *party*: he delivers proposals as *party*. To HighLander, he becomes *Angler Co-Operative* to deliver Angler Co-Operative's counter-offer. To Angler Co-Operative he becomes *HighLander*. The data discloses that he does this in every private meeting but one.[39] Some may argue that this is the mediator

---

39 The Mediator does not take on this mantle in his first meeting with HighLander. It should also be noted that in the first meeting with Angler Co-Operative, although he does invoke the voice of HighLander when challenging Angler Co-Operative, it is not in the context of delivering an offer, which occurs in the subsequent meetings.

function; that is, to deliver messages between parties, particularly offers. The Mediator in each of these meetings, however, is doing more than just conveying the information of an offer. He is setting the stage for the conveyance. He speaks of feelings and views. He talks about the rationales behind the proposals and he challenges reactions to them. He defends the proposals. He tries to pre-empt further negotiation. In other words, he speaks to persuade just as negotiating parties speak to persuade.

The Mediator acts as *self* during these sessions as well. He is there as *mediator* when he reminds Gerald he will not get everything he wants in a settlement because that is the nature of mediation. He is there as *mediator* when he puts a positive spin on the progress of the negotiation while at the same time suggesting that its end has come. He says to HighLander about Angler Co-Operative's proposal, *"When you look at it, there's lots of progress. I am told that it is the last offer and if the deal is not made, he will go out."* This is an attempt to focus the party to see the offer for what it is: a movement to resolution, one that must be taken to achieve that resolution. One might argue that the Mediator is taking on *party* voice in threatening to walk out of the negotiation. The data suggests otherwise: here we have the Mediator guiding the process to conclusion by his announcement that parties have both engaged in movement but that one party is no longer willing to move further. He is assisting with the recognition of the final offer, which Schelling refers to as the moment of pure bargaining.[40]

The Mediator also continues as *adviser* in these sessions when he suggests responses to proposals and later participates in the drafting of the agreement. On this latter point, the concluding sessions see a remarkable engagement by the Mediator. He sits as *HighLander's adviser*, making explicit suggestions benefiting HighLander on the content of the agreement. For example, he queries whether the release language is broad enough, he says products should be clearly listed to ensure no others are sold, he suggests labelling to ensure products are not sold out of Scandinavia, he recommends the transfer of the domain name be made 'forthwith', and he ensures all details of the agreement remain confidential.

In recalling the Mediator's words about his work, this Mediator begins the day by stating that he does not know how he will approach the mediation because he does not go into mediation with a predetermined view of what he will do. He speaks of his role as being facilitative, impartial. He speaks of being 'impartial' and 'even-handed'. The data discloses little evidence of this, as particularly noted not only in the multiple shifts to *party* identity but also in the concluding meetings where HighLander's interests are paramount. In the post-mediation interview, he reflects that this mediation did not require

---

40 See discussion in Chapter 4; in particular see, T.C. Schelling, *The Strategy of Conflict* (New York: Oxford University Press, 1975) at 22; and C.M. Stevens, *Strategy and Collective Bargaining Negotiation* (New York: McGraw-Hill, 1963) at 108.

him to press hard for resolution or to press the parties on the risks of litigation. He suggests that his role was a minimal one. As he puts it, anyone could have conducted this mediation. A consideration of the case, however, discloses a mediator who is actively engaged with the parties and the negotiation of their agreement. It discloses a mediator who acts contrary to what he perceives himself to be and to do. He is not facilitative in the Riskin worldview,[41] nor does he *not* press the parties: he takes on the negotiation directly *as party* together with an *advisory* and *mediatory* role.

Summary

The literature is filled with references to the facilitative, the evaluative, the transformative mediator, to name a few. We learned in our introduction to the mediators in Chapters 1 and 5 that they seek more than just a distributive outcome: they seek the integrative outcome; they hope for improved communication; they encourage empowerment and recognition. They are not one-dimensional actors who fit within a preconceived notion of what mediation is and what a mediator does. Reliance on the terminology of the literature may preclude an understanding existing beyond the terminology. The ethnographic method provides an expanded scope for discovery. It lets us see that their interactions move beyond labels; indeed, they move beyond mediator and party understandings. It lets us see what they want to do and how they do it. Labels mean nothing to them. The focus is on their goals and principles and the manifestation of these goals and principles in their actions.

This chapter suggests another way of *seeing* what mediators do and the impact on process. It offers an opportunity to move beyond labels that may categorize, stigmatize or stagnate theoretical and practical developments. We step away from such categorizations of mediator action, and in so doing, the actions speak for themselves to enable a clarity of view regarding the interactions that occur at mediation, particularly between parties and mediator. The interest is to discover patterns that emerge from the observations of mediation in action. The analysis offers a conceptualization that seeks to 'tell it like it is'.

The case studies explored in this chapter suggest identities emerging in response to a need for resolution. In Chapter 5 we heard that mediators see themselves as dealmakers: mediation is about the deal rather than the process. The parties, too, come to mediation in search of agreement for the resolution of their dispute. The quest for agreement encourages the fugitive nature of mediation. Mediators 'morph' into whatever persona is required to persuade parties to resolution. Parties permit this morphing. The mediator becomes

---

41 See discussion in Chapter 3; in particular see L.L. Riskin, "Understanding Mediators' Orientations, Strategies, and Techniques: A Grid for the Perplexed" (1996) 1 *Harv. Negot. L. Rev.* 7; and L.L. Riskin, "Decisionmaking in Mediation: The New Old Grid and the New New Grid System" (2003–04) 79 *Notre Dame L. Rev.* 1.

the *party*, the *party adviser* and the *third-party intervener*. He takes on five identities, forming a quintet of mediator behaviour. This quintet describes the observed interactions of a mediator. Mediation depends on the interactions to effect change in the parties for movement to negotiated order. At the core of these interactions are these fluid, ever-changing identities assumed by mediators. These identities create the persona we call *mediator*. The quintessence of mediation is uncovered: the quintessence of mediation lies in the fugitive nature of the mediator and the unification of mediator and process.

In Chapter 5, the line between process and mediator begins to blur. I suggest that the identities assumed by the mediator create the process of mediation; in other words, process is dictated by the mediator's mode of confrontation with parties. This is better understood when recalling that mediation is a negotiation. The processual shape of negotiation was examined in Chapter 4. Six phases of the negotiation process emerged from the data. These negotiation phases are party-centric: party interactions define each phase. In mediation, the dyad of a bilateral negotiation becomes a triad due to the addition of the mediator to the process. Mediation is mediator-centric. The mediation process is created by the mediator's decisions and actions. We see this in each of the cases.

Due to the constant movement of mediator identity, it is with some difficulty that one defines 'mediation'. At times, it is a facilitated negotiation where the mediator assists parties with their negotiation as a third-party intervener. It can also be expert consultancy, a phrase coined by Roberts and Palmer,[42] where the mediator is party adviser; or it can take on the shape of empathetic counselling, with the mediator taking on party concerns and interests. Yet at other times, it is a direct negotiation between parties where the mediator negotiates directly against the parties, each in their turn.[43] During all times, the mediator is at the centre of the drama. The mediator's interactions ultimately define the process. Mediator and process are so entwined that their beginnings and ends merge. Superficially, one might argue that there is a process of mediation. We have seen the Organization's mediation framework and we have reviewed the definitions of mediation in

---

42 Roberts and Palmer, see note 6 at 155.

43 In her examination of community mediation programmes, Garcia suggests that mediators replace parties in the negotiation by stepping into their shoes to confront the other party with arguments not suggested by the replaced party – in other words, stepping outside the four corners of the negotiation between the parties in making arguments or taking positions not raised by the parties. In the research conducted leading to this view, Garcia illustrates the replacement with aggressive and coercive interventions by mediators, interventions which are, arguably, expressly beyond a mediatory mandate. In the commercial and civil context, the shift is subtle: it is a recurring pattern of action which led to the 'sighting' of the shift. See A. Garcia, "The Problematics of Representation in Community Mediation Hearings: Implications for Mediation Practice" (1995) 22 *J. Soc. & Soc. Welfare* 23.

the literature in Chapter 3. What the literature does not discuss is the impact of the fugitive nature of mediator identity on the process of mediation. It is this fugitive quality that renders the generic descriptions of the mediation process futile in providing an insight into mediation. It is this fugitive quality of mediator identity that begets the fugitive identity of mediation.

One outcome disclosed from the data is the lack of mediator self-awareness regarding the nature of mediator actions. This is not unusual: studies have shown that there is no agreement on the meaning of words used to describe mediator interventions such as evaluative, facilitative or transformative, for example.[44] The mediators of Case Studies 9 and 7 typify this. These mediators see themselves as facilitators, believing that they are merely helping the parties with *their* process. Mediator 7's comment that he does not take positions as lawyers would because it would put him in the process rather than getting the parties in the process, is illustrative of this lack of self-awareness. Contrary to his view, these mediators put themselves *in* the process. Mediator 9 is somewhat disingenuous when he states that he did not have to press hard for a resolution – the data contradicts him in this regard. It discloses active encouragement, involvement and confrontation.

There exists a dichotomy between the interventionist and the facilitator. This was first hinted at in Chapter 5 and is developed significantly in this chapter. The dichotomy exists on two levels: within mediator and within party. At the mediator level, we see that the mediators appear to fall into one of two categories: those who see themselves as interventionists, willing to be actively engaged with the parties in the search for resolution, and those who see themselves as facilitators, believing themselves to be mindful of boundaries separating them from the parties and from the parties' dispute. This dichotomy exists in words only; mediator actions belie the existence of this dichotomy. All the mediators are interventionists. Those who believe they are facilitators are deluding themselves. And those who see themselves as interventionists are deluding the parties by refusing to make clear their nature. This is where the dichotomy appears within parties. As we learn in Chapter 5,

---

[44] Picard learns that there is no agreement on the meaning of the words 'evaluative' and 'facilitative' among mediators: they use the words to describe their approach to their practice, yet these words mean different things to different people. See, C. Picard, "Common Language, Different Meaning: What Mediators Mean When They Talk About Their Work" (2002) *Negotiation J.* 251 at 261–2, 264. Della Noce also examines the use of labels in court roster mediator descriptions of mediator activity, concluding that labels of mediator actions such as evaluative, facilitative or transformative do not disclose what it is that mediators actually do, nor are their descriptions as used by mediators consistent with the label attached to the term. See D.J. Della Noce, "Communicating Quality Assurance: A Case Study of Mediator Profiles on a Court Roster" (2008) 84 *N.D. L. Rev.* 769 at 808, 819–22; and D.J. Della Noce, "Evaluative Mediation: In Search of Practice Competencies" (2009) 27 *Conflict Resolution Q.* 193 at 195–6.

the parties do not appear to see the extent to which mediators intervene in their negotiation: they see them as neutral, even-handed, non-directive or insufficiently interventionist. Despite mediator promises that they will not advise, evaluate, judge or decide, the parties engage fully with each of the mediator personas they encounter, and they do so without a realization of the nature of the interaction.

Is this lack of realization the result of steps taken by mediators to hide the nature of their interventions? The data suggests it is. Mediators use labels to mask their actions. We hear them say that they will 'reality test' the parties, or they will play 'devil's advocate'; that is, they will challenge the parties' views on their cases.[45] If an intervention is challenged by a party, the mediators defend their intervention as reality testing, suggesting that this is typical mediator conduct and therefore acceptable. Or, they excuse their confrontations by invoking the name of the other party; they confront because the other party will confront, not because *they* are confronting. In doing this they are deflecting party awareness from the true nature of their intervention. The cases suggest that they do this in order to maintain an image of 'neutrality' or 'impartiality'. As stated earlier in the chapter, whatever label is used, it does not change the very nature of their interventions. Labels can mask the nature of actions and they can support mediator mythology.[46]

One may argue that reality testing or playing devil's advocate reflects a normal part of the mediator repertoire. The case studies suggest that the actions of the mediators go beyond reality testing or playing devil's advocate – at times, the mediators lose their mediator persona and take on the opposing party identity to progress the negotiation. They are not just facilitative mediators who say they are merely playing devil's advocate, nor are they

---

45 During the ethnographic fieldwork, mediators who described themselves in non-evaluative terms often described their interventions as 'reality testing' or 'playing devil's advocate'. See also, for example, D.E. Noll, "Mediation: The Myth of the Mediator as Settlement Broker" (2009) 64 *J. Disp. Resol.* 42 at 44, 47. Della Noce suggests that 'playing devil's advocate' is evaluative behaviour: see Della Noce, "Evaluative Mediation", ibid. at 203.

46 For discussions about the mythology of mediation, see S.S. Silbey, "The Emperor's New Clothes: Mediation Mythology and Markets" (2002) *J. Disp. Resol.* 171, and D.J. Della Noce, R.A. Baruch Bush and J.P. Folger, "Clarifying the Theoretical Underpinnings of Mediation: Implications for Practice and Policy" (2002–03) 3 *Pepp. Disp. Resol. L. J.* 39, for example. The effect of labelling is also discussed in S. Oberman, "Style vs. Model: Why Quibble" (2008–09) 9 *Pepp. Disp. Resol. L. J.* 1. For a discussion about labels used by mediators to hide the nature of their actions as engaging in the practice of law, see J.M. Nolan-Haley, "Lawyers, Non-Lawyers and Mediation: Rethinking the Professional Monopoly from a Problem-Solving Perspective" (2002) 7 *Harv. Negot. L. Rev.* 235. See also J. Kidner, "The Limits of Mediator 'Labels': False Debate between 'Facilitative' versus 'Evaluative' Mediator Styles" (2011) 30 *Windsor Rev. Legal & Soc. Issues* 167, in which she focuses on the evaluative and facilitative dichotomy and the impact that labelling has on party choice and party participation in the process.

evaluative mediators whose actions include reality testing. They become part of the negotiation between the parties as a party. These are catchwords used to mask the nature of the intervention. The mediator is negotiating as principal under the guise of mediator parlance and he is permitted to do so by the authority bestowed upon him by the mediator mantle. The use of the phrases provide an insight into the mediators' perceptions of their own activities: the phrases constrain the perception into an acceptable image of the third-party intervener and his permitted actions. To the mediators' thinking, they are merely doing what is expected of all mediators; that is, to challenge the parties. This begs the question of what truth lies beneath the phrases. The data suggests the assumption of party identity in the shape of adversary negotiating directly against party.

One cannot escape the effect of the fugitive identities on either of the concepts of neutrality or impartiality as used by mediators. As stated earlier, for purposes of this study, I refer to these concepts as referencing a term of separation between mediator and party and use instead the word 'equidistance' to signify a mediator's concern for 'neutrality' or 'impartiality'.[47] In other words, a mediator is said to operate at equidistance from each party. It is clear on an analysis of each of the cases studied in this chapter that the mediators do not remain at equidistance from each party. For example, when one examines the interventions in Case Study 9, one sees a distinct overall favouritism to the Defendant, HighLander, whereas in Case Study 8 there appears to be a pro-Claimant mediator stance in favour of Mitchell. With Mediator 7, the favouritism shifts from party to party and there is no singular bias noted for one party or another. As a result of their shifting identities, these mediators are constantly altering the distance between themselves and parties: the distance lessens or increases in direct relation to the identity assumed. Kolb suggests that this is neutrality – as long as the mediator aligns himself to parties in equal proportion, neutrality is maintained. This is because, says Kolb, the mediator is expressing a mutual support towards the parties, and if done well, neutrality is maintained in the eyes of the parties.[48] An interesting idea and one supported by the data, but one that does not fit within the traditional concept of mediator neutrality as generally accepted. As Kolb describes, it is "an ironic form of neutrality".[49] This ability to exercise

---

[47] Recall in Chapter 5 that the mediators do not describe what it means to be 'neutral' or 'impartial' to either the parties or the researcher when invoking these terms. It is not the intent of this study to explore these concepts in any significant manner except to the extent that they are affected by the quintet of identities assumed by mediators. See discussion in Chapter 3 for a brief description of the terms 'neutrality' and 'impartiality' as used in this study.

[48] D. Kolb, "To be a Mediator: Expressive Tactics in Mediation" (1985) 41 *J. of Soc. Issues* 11 at 19–20.

[49] Ibid. at 19.

a non-neutral stance while maintaining a neutral perception reflects one aspect of the mediator's power: parties accept the intervention having this perception. The data certainly confirms this as the perception of the parties – they experience a neutral mediator in their world-view of the mediation.

The mediators themselves, although not expressly speaking of neutrality to the parties, suggest an awareness of its implications for the process: they all stress to parties that they are not judges and will not offer views of what is right and wrong; the mediator in Case Study 8 is concerned about his neutrality, he says, because he empathizes with one of the parties; the mediator in Case Study 9 sees himself impartial in the wake of a relational issue despite a party's concern; and they all say they do not have a predetermined view of the case. They *suggest* that they carry a mantle of neutrality; even in the time they spend with the parties, we see they spend roughly the same amount of time with each party during the course of the mediation.[50] The mantle, however, is of gossamer – in their interactions as they shift between identities, the mediators cannot be neutral, impartial or remain equidistant from the parties. Despite this, and intriguingly, the integrity of the process is maintained to all within the process.

Ultimately, hidden identities are at the core of this process called mediation.

---

50 In Chapter 5, we learn the following: Mediator 7 spent a total time of 2.9 hours with the Claimant Team and 2.5 with the Respondent Team during the mediation; Mediator 8 spent 3.9 hours with the Claimant Team and 3.7 hours with the Respondent Team (this time includes the time spent with each party's solicitor in private as well); and Mediator 9 spent 3.4 hours with the Claimant Team and 2.9 hours with the Respondent Team. Marginally slightly more time was spent overall with the Claimant Team – an interesting observation and one that could be the subject of further research and consideration.

7 Epilogue

The fugitive identity of mediation – negotiations, shift changes and allusionary action

> To paint a small picture is to place yourself outside your experience. However, to paint the larger picture, you are in it. It isn't something you command.
>
> Mark Rothko[1]

> I reduced painting to its logical conclusion and exhibited three canvases: red, blue and yellow. I affirmed: it's over. Basic colours. Every plane is a plane and there is to be no representation.
>
> Aleksandr Rodchenko, on his triptych *Pure Red Colour, Pure Yellow Colour, Pure Blue Colour*[2]

Mediation "still represents an elusive, fugitive label, presently resorted to all too easily and with little precision in the context of contemporary transformations in the management of disputing": so say Roberts and Palmer.[3] Marian Roberts disagrees, stating, "These reflections [of her referenced mediators] cast doubt on the accuracy of the picture of the imprecise and 'fugitive' nature of mediation [with reference to the previous quote]. On the contrary, a clear, consistent and coherent view, based on practice experience across fields, emerges about the nature and purpose of mediation."[4] The data of this ethnographic study supports the Roberts and Palmer fugitive label in what appears to be the illusory process of mediation; all is not what it seems or is said to be.

Mediation is a process wholly integrated with the negotiation process. At its core is a social process in which actors engage to seek a desired goal. As stated earlier in this study, mediation offers an additional contextual layer to

---

1 M. Rothko, quoted in the Tate Modern's Gallery Guide for its exhibition, *Rothko: The Late Series*, 26 September 2008–1 February 2009.
2 A. Rodchenko, quoted in the Tate Modern's Gallery Guide for its exhibition, *Rodchenko & Popova: Defining Constructivism*, 12 February–12 May 2009.
3 S. Roberts and M. Palmer, *Dispute Processes: ADR and the Primary Forms of Decision-Making* (Cambridge: Cambridge University Press, 2005) at 153.
4 M. Roberts, *Developing the Craft of Mediation: Reflections on Theory and Practice* (London: Jessica Kingsley, 2007) at 93.

parties' negotiations. The third-party mediator is invited into the negotiation. She then creates the process called mediation. The mediator defines the process by her actions within that negotiation.

A mediator is a negotiator. He is not, however, a neutral negotiator.[5] He becomes part of the negotiation process together with the parties who invited him to the negotiation. He negotiates *with* party *against* party. A mediator is an adviser. He is not, however, a neutral adviser. He advises *as* party *for* party. At other times, the mediator is a non-aligned facilitator. He may be impartial or neutral, or neither. As facilitator, he guides the parties through the negotiation process. A mediator's role is not solely about listening to the parties, helping them to communicate with each other or guiding them through an integrative problem-solving exercise. He also engages fully in the negotiation, moving between various states of being separate from, aligned with or against a party. He is the supreme participant in the process: he is mediator; he is party; he is adviser. By approaching mediator interactions in terms of these identities, the nature of the interactions become clearer than they would otherwise be by merely using terminology that indicates that a mediator is evaluative, facilitative, transformative and the like. The identities suggest that new relationships are created with the parties in the process. It is no longer a relationship of the distant third-party intervener; it is also a relationship of adviser, adversary and supporter. These identities posit the mediator in the very centre of the mediated negotiation, where he is embedded in the negotiation moves of the parties.

In taking on the identity of these personas, the mediator quintet becomes more than just the guiding force of mediation – it becomes its *raison d'être*. It is the quintessence of mediation.

Perceptions of mediation are in a state of flux. The mediator sees her role to be one of facilitator guiding parties in a process that seeks to resolve their dispute. The mediator says that she is there for the parties, yet not responsible for their destiny. She says she cannot take an active role in the process: she does not have the information necessary; she is not a judge and it is the party's responsibility to determine the outcome of the process. The mediator seeks an active role in a passive way; that is, she wants to remain outside of the dispute while guiding the parties through the dispute. Mediators are interested in settlement for the parties but also in concepts of empowerment, recognition, self-determination and effective communication. They advocate a model that comprises all this – they do not advocate a model of evaluation. They are directive but want to be facilitators. The process is the tool to achieve this. The mediator determines the process.

For the parties, the mediator is the neutral third party who has been asked to help them resolve their conflict. They see him as a non-threatening,

---

5 Recall the discussion in Chapter 3 about the mediator as negotiator.

non-bullying, non-evaluative intervener; he is the eye in the centre of the storm. They see a distinction between the mediation process and the mediator, often finding the process frustrating where they find the mediator excellent; or the process excellent and the mediator merely satisfactory.

The data creates a third perception of a mediator who cannot be separated from the process, of a mediator who becomes consumed in the process with the parties, and of a mediator who becomes party, adviser and third-party facilitator as the need arises.

The moniker of neutral or impartial third-party intervener has no place in the mediator's lexicon. Yet, it remains within the party's. Parties sense neutrality and impartiality despite mediator silence about neutrality or impartiality. An interesting observation arises here. Why are mediators silent on what some would argue is a fundamental trait of mediators?[6] Curiously, however, their silence does not impede a perception of neutrality by the parties, despite the actions taken by mediators during the course of the process and in particular the shifting identities they assume. By the very nature of the mediator's changes, neutrality is impacted. Where is neutrality when the mediator becomes party with party, empathizing with the party or criticizing the other? Where is neutrality when the mediator engages in negotiation combat against a party? The answer must lie in the labels used by the mediators: they insist that they are merely 'reality testing' or playing 'devil's advocate'. They hide behind such labels to mask the nature of their interactions. These labels are ways to say something which to mediators and parties alike may seem unpalatable. The mediator is negotiating the deal *for* the party and *against* the party. The labels, arguably, permit the charade. And as a result, parties are accepting of the mediators' actions, and indeed, praise their actions.

The impact of a mediator's action is to depersonalize the negotiation. The mediator becomes an advocate in each room, an advocate who is interested in reaching agreement. Parties hear from a mediator that which they are not willing to hear from the other participants. It means more coming from the mediator because he has depersonalized the communication in that he stands apart from the dispute in the parties' eyes. He is both intervener and party without history to the dispute and without connection to the participants.

I suggest that 'depersonalized' is a concept distinct from neutrality and impartiality. Depersonalization is what allows the quintet to flourish. It gives the mediator the permission to take on the quintuple identity. Throughout it all, the parties see the mediator as self, even when he is not acting as self. Although he acts not only as self but also as party and as party adviser, the mediator lacks a perceived emotional attachment to the dispute, and as such can be said to engage in depersonalized advocacy. For the parties, it appears that this is sufficient to meet their requirements of neutrality and impartiality.

---

6 The concepts of neutrality and impartiality have been explored in Chapters 3, 5 and 6.

Whether it is sufficient for the purposes of professionalism, institutionalization and justice, remains to be seen.

I began this study by referring to a need to separate mediation from the law in order to study it in relation to the law. That which has come to light in this research is a social interaction that relies on the rules, norms and structures of the world it is positioned in. Depersonalized advocacy straddles the normative and processual divide. The mediations take place within a particular western common-law system of dispute resolution: the cases are either in the throes of litigation or litigation has been threatened. The sword of Damocles hangs over the participants. This presents one structural layer to mediation.

Another layer is that of a public view of mediation as an informal, non-binding, non-adjudicatory process in which a 'neutral' third-party intervener assists parties with the resolution of their dispute. Within these structures is the social interaction of competing interests, which may or may not lead to the attainment of order. Rules and structures fuel the social interaction. Depersonalized advocacy allows the mediator to participate directly in the social interaction that takes place. The mediator uses elements of rules, norms and structures to negotiate with party and against party. For example, he uses the norms relating to public understanding of what mediation is and what it involves to elicit the trust and confidence from the parties to permit him to engage in a direct negotiation with them. He applies rules and norms both as expert consultant and negotiator to the social interaction. He is conscious of the external and internal structures within which he is engaging, relying on both the sword and the 'mediation' label ascribed by the parties, to direct the process. The social interaction between parties and between mediator and party retains, at its heart, the desire to attain or protect party self-interest in coming to negotiated order. The participants to the process strive for social order but do so while invoking the norms and rules of the structures within which they are engaging.

Implications

What does this mean for the field? A new understanding of mediation emerges from the ethnographic data – mediation is spawned from negotiation and lives only through negotiation. It is at times the well-known facilitated negotiation and it is at times a direct negotiation where the third-party intervener merges with party to become party. The mediator *is* the process as a result of the changes in identity he assumes: he chooses when the mediation becomes a facilitated negotiation or direct negotiation.

Negotiation is a critical element of the mediation world. The data suggests ignorance of this element on the part of the participants. The nature of the interactions between party and mediator is unseen by all participants. Mediator, party and legal representative alike are blind to the nature of the interactions and the changes that result from those interactions. They are accepting of the interactions, often praising them. Ultimately, they are accepting of the direct engagement by the mediator in the negotiation of their dispute.

This leads to a need for the reconceptualization of the process called mediation and for an acknowledgment of a mediator's active engagement in the interaction between parties and with parties. Negotiation remains the anchor of mediation: to recognize mediation as anything more is to subvert its true nature. The emergence of mediator identities lays bare a process that remains, in its essence, a negotiation between parties whose structure contains the presence of a chameleon.

This raises questions about the impact of this new reconceptualization on issues of neutrality and impartiality, stated to be fundamental elements of mediation; about the role of transparency in mediation and the extent to which mediator interventions are not seen for what they are, yet accepted for that which they are not; about the extent to which mediators are qualified to engage in negotiations with and against parties; and about the efficacy of a process that portrays itself as something more than what it is.

From a broader perspective, the focus on mediator identity and the shifts that take place during negotiations between parties in dispute may impact the way disputes in other contexts are approached. This study focused on the commercial mediation taking place in a large Anglo-European metropolis at one moment in time: its findings, however, resonate across disputes, boundaries and restrictions of time. Explorations of mediated interactions from the perspective suggested by this study may offer an alternative context within which to approach conflict and its resolution, on both a domestic and an international level.[7]

Limitations to this study

Like all ethnographic studies, the limitations to a study such as this lie in the context of the study. Here, the frame is the commercial mediation conducted through a mediation agency located in a city of the United Kingdom. It is a

---

[7] For example, Block and Siegel use an identity analysis for mediation of international disputes: they look at conflict from a cultural identity perspective. Parties come to the table with different identities (which are cultural in nature such as religious, language, ethnic identities). To improve the possibility of reaching resolution, a common identity shared by the parties needs to be uncovered. A mediator assists in focusing the parties on the common identity, and does so, in particular, when the mediator shares the parties' common identity. The conflict is then seen through the perspective of the common identity, leading to an improved probability of resolution. Although the study focuses primarily on the cultural identities of the parties and the place of commonality in conflict to ease such conflict, its argument suggests that the concept of mediator shifting identities, albeit not from a cultural identity point of view, may be applicable to a macro-level of analysis. See R. Block Jr and D.A. Siegel, "Identity, Bargaining, and Third-party Mediation" (2011) 3 *International Theory* 416.

mediation with its own framework and with mediators trained according to the philosophy of the mediation agency. As such, it provides a snapshot of one type of dispute resolution process.

Another limitation is the extent to which the researcher was not privy to all communications during the process. Recall that the first contact by the mediator with the parties is outside the ambit of this study. Also unknown are the communications that occurred intra-party during the mediation: mediator and researcher were not privy to those discussions. Additionally, in terms of participant information, not all participants responded to the questionnaire or the request for a telephone interview. To the extent that data was obtained, it was examined. However, fuller participation would have assisted in further illuminating the party experience.

A limitation can be found in the ethnographic method itself.[8] It must be accepted that the method brings controversy. However, this is not a study on the ethnographic method. It is a study of mediation through the clarity of view offered by the ethnographic method. Some aspects of criticism, though, must be acknowledged. For example, the textualization of the data, although aspiring to provide objective reporting, does involve subjective decisions as to the data to be included in the reporting and therefore can be subject to criticism. The transcription is also an issue in terms of the interpretation of the words, not capturing all the words or correctly and which words to focus on.[9] These are issues of textualization that have been recognized and effort made to ensure as accurate a portrayal as is possible within the reality of human frailty. Enslin suggests another limitation: the dialogue may not reflect the speaker's view of the narrative, raising the question whether it is interpreted in a manner in which it was intended to be heard.[10] The interpretation of the data and its limitations are a matter I leave for others to determine.

Another challenge relating to the data lies in the number of case studies presented here. Quite frankly, I struggled with the number of cases to be reported. I would have liked to include more (recognizing a propensity towards the view that more is better), but ultimately, the limitations of space and the desire to render fuller accounts of the mediation experiences dictated the number of cases that were presented. Further and similarly, the decisions

---

8 See Chapter 1 for discussion of the methodology.
9 For example, Cecile B. Vigouroux conducted a study in which she examined the transcription of several minutes of a video by a research team as well as the speakers in the conversation. She noted how interpretations of the words uttered differed among them, illustrating how different people hear different things and interpret them differently, even the speakers themselves; see C.B. Vigouroux, "Trans-scription as a Social Activity" (2007) 8 *Ethnography* 61.
10 Enslin considers the role of ethnography and its outcome in the practical life of women in Nepal as it impacts their place in political organization. In so doing, she suggests that dialogue may not always reflect a speaker's view of the narrative; E. Enslin, "Beyond Writing: Feminist Practice and the Limitations of Ethnography" (1994) 9 *Cultural Anthropology* 537 at 561.

regarding the use of the data and their analysis raise questions regarding the extent to which the data presented here and corresponding analysis can be generalized for broader application. Some hold that findings must be generalized to be valuable; others eschew generalizations favouring an ethnographic snapshot of phenomena to uncover patterns of disputing behaviour. Either way, the importance lies in the manner in which the study has advanced knowledge of the phenomena under observation. In the end, it was the story I was interested in – the story conveyed by the participants in their journey to negotiated order and what the story tells us about the journey.

It was difficult at times to step away from the lawyer or mediator lens I brought to the study and to see the mediation for what it is: a social process by which participants seek to create order. With this comes the potential of bias regarding process, participants and outcome.[11] To overcome this, I sought to be self-aware during the mediation sessions, recalling my purpose for attendance, and I recorded, to the extent my hand permitted, the discourse verbatim to lessen interpretive guesses, which leads me to another limitation. The sessions were not electronically recorded and as such the data relies on the researcher's ability to have manually recorded the discourse.

A further limitation to the work is the lack of cultural perspective on the dispute process. The study assumes a monolithic participant identity. For example, gender implications were not considered: the majority of participants in this study were male (as a result of the randomness of the selection). As such, gender considerations could not be part of the study.

What next?

Given the limitation of space, many issues could not be canvassed in this study, but have been left for another day. Justice, for example, figures prominently in my mind. What do these parties feel about justice? Do they feel that it is an important consideration in the process? Do they feel that they received justice? Or, is justice not applicable in the process – that only satisfaction of outcome and satisfaction of process are relevant? Do ideas and experiences of justice differ between the subjective universe of the party and the objective goals of the researcher? What place does substantive justice have

---

11 With regard to this issue of bias, the parties looked to the lead mediator for guidance and the mediators conducted the process at their discretion. This was consistent throughout the study, with the exception of one mediation when the lead mediator became ill and could not continue. The parties requested that I take over from the lead mediator and conduct the mediation. The experience as lead mediator in that case was clearly different from that experienced in my participant-observer role as assistant mediator and external researcher. As lead mediator, I was not able to 'see' as clearly the interactions that were ongoing because I was immersed in the process itself, focusing fully on my role as mediator and on the parties and the dispute. Such was not the case as assistant mediator and researcher: I am not aware of any bias imposed on the process by those roles.

in mediation? Must mediation remain in the world of procedural and popular justice alone? I noted early in the study that not all parties left mediation willing to encounter the other party with whom they had just resolved their dispute. Rancour continued to exist. Why? Is this indicative of a perceived lack of justice? A review of the ethnographic data from a justice analytical framework may add further knowledge about the place of justice in private social ordering.

Connected to this search for justice in mediation is a need to examine further the relationship between the normative and processual order that leads to resolution. For example, an in-depth study would be compelling for an examination of: the extent to which participants rely on rules and norms throughout each stage of the process to invoke social order; the role of law in mediation, a process that is arguably outside of the law;[12] and whether social order can be attained without reference to the law and its normative order in an environment where mediation has become part of a civil justice programme. These issues invite further analysis.

Recognizing that gender is not an element of this study, consideration of the male/female voice of third-party intervener raises another area for research. Four of the 38 mediators observed were female. Observations of additional female mediators would permit a comparative study to be carried out which could test the various hypotheses in the literature that the female voice and negotiating patterns differ from those of male negotiators.[13]

As mentioned earlier, the role of neutrality and impartiality is another area requiring further research in light of the reconceptualization of mediation. To what extent does mediator neutrality and impartiality, or the lack thereof, impact mediation? We see in this study that the parties felt that neutrality and impartiality were present; the data suggests otherwise. What is the significance of this for questions relating to the existence of, absence from or need for neutrality or impartiality in mediation?

The place of power in mediation is challenged: traditionally, it is to reside with the parties. The process is to give parties power to deal with their dispute as they deem fit. The shifting identities confer additional power to the mediator, which in turn permits the shifts. There is a circularity of

---

12 The role that rules and norms play in mediation was examined in relation to an exploration of the meaning of legal culture where the impact of rules and norms on a social process of negotiation was examined; see D. De Girolamo, "Seeking Negotiated Order Through Mediation: A Manifestation of Legal Culture?" (2012) 5 *J. Comp. Law* 118, and also in D. Nelken, ed., *Using Legal Culture* (London: Wildy, Simmonds & Hill, 2012) 153. The issue regarding the relationship of law to mediation needs to be examined further, particularly in view of the extent to which mediation has become part of civil justice systems and is offered as a method by which disputes are to be resolved in lieu of adjudication.

13 See for example, D. Tannen, *You Just Don't Understand: Women and Men in Conversation* (New York: Ballantine, 1990).

cause and effect. The mediator is the guiding spectre of the process – he is the process. Power over the dispute and its trajectory to resolution is given to the mediator by the parties, enabling him to negotiate for them, with them and against them. The various identities of the mediator can be a tool of control.[14] Mediators speak of the parties being in control, empowered to take responsibility for their dispute and its resolution. Their actions belie the message: mediators exert control over the negotiation by taking part in the negotiation directly yet implicitly. A question then arises: to what end? What is the mediator gaining by exerting such control? The impact of these shifting identities needs to be explored.

Another area for consideration is the role of the party legal representative in the mediated negotiation. To what extent did the representative's presence obscure the party voice or take control away from the party or further ensure that rules did not stray far from the discourse?

The issue of professionalization of mediator professionals is also impacted by this study, and in particular, questions of qualification and training. Given the direct and principal role played by a mediator in the mediated negotiation, issues of ethics, codes of standards, negotiation skills and mediator awareness must be made subject to further research scrutiny.

Coda

It is my belief this study has shown that the field has not yet exhausted the learning for those who are interested in achieving greater clarity about a process of social ordering in a western normative context. It is my hope that this ethnographic study about mediation has shed light on that which may have been obscure, and on that which we do not see in ourselves for ourselves:

> To see ourselves as others see us can be eye opening. To see others as sharing a nature with ourselves is the merest decency. But it is from the far more difficult achievement of seeing ourselves amongst others, as a local example of the forms human life has locally taken, a case among cases, a world among worlds, that the largeness of mind, without which objectivity is self congratulation and tolerance a sham, comes. If interpretive anthropology has any general office in the world it is to keep reteaching this fugitive truth.[15]

---

14 Laura Nader explores international river disputes for a power analysis of negotiation, finding that negotiations about river rights are an exercise of control by the dominant players. She says that negotiation must be examined from a framework of control, arguing that a macro-level of exploration requires that the social structure of the negotiation process must be examined. See L. Nader, "Civilization and its Negotiations" in S.F. Moore, ed., *Law and Anthropology: A Reader* (Malden, MA: Blackwell, 2005) at 332.

15 C. Geertz, *Local Knowledge* (New York: Basic Books, 1983) at 16.

Appendix A
Interview protocol for mediators post-mediation

Pre-mediation stage
1 What did you think the case was really all about?
2 What were the issues?
3 What did you think was needed for a settlement to be achieved?
4 What were your objectives going into the mediation?
5 What was your strategy going in?
6 Did you consider whether you would settle the dispute?

Mediation session
7 What were the barriers to settlement?
8 Were you surprised about the outcome?
9 What were the participant roles in this mediation?
10 What was the most important thing that happened in the mediation?
11 What is your impression of how each party experienced the mediation?
12 Was mediation of benefit to the parties? In what way?
13 How would you describe the interactions among the parties?
14 Did the parties' interactions assist or impede the mediation?
15 Why did it/did it not settle?
16 How would you describe your style generally?
17 How would you describe your style in this particular mediation?
18 Was this case suitable for mediation?

The law and mediation
19 What role did law have in this mediation?
20 Was it a barrier? Why?
21 Did the parties rely on the law to further their position?
22 Would it have benefited the parties to have an evaluation conducted on their legal position?
23 Was there any way to remove law as an element of this mediation?

24 Did the parties benefit from having their solicitors at the mediation?
25 Do you feel that being a lawyer/non-lawyer was helpful to this dispute?
26 Do you feel that knowledge of the law was needed here?
27 What is the role of the private meeting?
28 What do you see your role to be during the private meeting?

Appendix B
Interview guideline for participants post-mediation[1]

Mediation process

- What are your overall thoughts about the process?
- What surprised you about the process?
- Regarding the timing of the mediation, was it the right time to mediate?

Thoughts about the Mediator

- How would you describe this Mediator's style?
- What were the Mediator's strengths?
- What could he/she have done differently/better?
- Why did you choose this Mediator?
- Were you happy with this Mediator?
- Would you use this Mediator again?

---

1 I list here only the questions that are relevant for this study: that is, questions relating to the mediation process and mediator. Other questions were also asked relating to the Organization's services which are not listed here.

Bibliography

R. Abel, "Law, Anthropology and Mediation: Mediation in Pre-capitalist Societies" (1983) 3 *Windsor Y.B. Access Just.* 175.
ADR Chambers UK, www.adrchambers.co.uk/mediation (accessed 27 August 2012).
M. Alberstein, "The Jurisprudence of Mediation: Between Formalism, Feminism and Identity Conversations" (2009) 11 *Cardozo J. Conflict Resol.* 1.
M. Alberstein, "Forms of Mediation and Law: Cultures of Dispute Resolution" (2007) 22 *Ohio St. J. Disp. Resol.* 321.
N. Alexander, "The Mediation Metamodel: Understanding Practice" (2008) 26 *Conflict Resolution Q.* 97
J.J. Alfini, "Mediation as a Calling: Addressing the Disconnect Between Mediation Ethics and the Practices of Lawyer Mediators" (2007–08) 49 *S. Tex. L. Rev.* 829.
J.J. Alfini, "Evaluative versus Facilitative Mediation: A Discussion" (1996–97) 24 *Fla. St. U. L. Rev.* 919.
J.J. Alfini, "Trashing, Bashing and Hashing It Out: Is This the End of 'Good Mediation'?" (1991) 19 *Fla. St. U. L. Rev.* 47.
E. Anderson, "The Ideologically Driven Critique" (2002) 107 *Am. J. of Sociology* 1533.
J.R. Antes, J.P. Folger and D.J. Della Noce, "Transforming Conflict Interactions in the Workplace: Documented Effects of the USPS REDRESS™ Program" (2001) 18 *Hofstra Lab & Emp. L. J.* 429.
T. Asad, "The Concept of Cultural Translation in British Anthropology" in J. Clifford and G.E. Marcus, eds, *Writing Culture: The Poetics and Politics of Ethnography* (Berkeley: University of California Press, 1986) 141.
H. Astor, "Mediator Neutrality: Making Sense of Theory and Practice" (2007) 16 *Soc. & Legal Studies* 221.
K. Avruch, "Of Time and the River: Notes on the Herrman, Hollett, and Gale Model of Mediation" in M.S. Herrman, ed., *The Blackwell Handbook of Mediation: Bridging Theory, Research, and Practice* (Oxford: Blackwell, 2006) 384.
R. Axelrod, *The Evolution of Cooperation* (New York: Basic Books, 1984).
M.H. Bazerman and M.A. Neale, *Negotiating Rationally* (New York: Free Press, 1993).
M.H. Bazerman, M.A. Neale *et al.*, "The Effect of Agents and Mediators on Negotiation Outcomes" (1992) 53 *Organizational Behavior and Human Decision Processes* 55.
R. Bean, *England People Very Nice* (London: Oberon Books, 2009).
R. Behar, "Ethnography and the Book That was Lost" (2003) 4 *Ethnography* 15.

S.R. Belhorn, "Settling Beyond the Shadow of the Law: How Mediation Can Make the Most of Social Norms" (2005) 20 *Ohio St. J. Disp. Resol.* 981.

H.S. Bellman, "Some Reflections on the Practice of Mediation" (1998) *Negotiation J.* 205.

R.D. Benjamin, "The Constructive Uses of Deception: Skills, Strategies, and Techniques of the Folkloric Trickster Figure and Their Application by Mediators" (1995) 13 *Mediation Q.* 3.

L. Bernstein, "Private Commercial Law in the Cotton Industry: Creating Cooperation Through Rules, Norms and Institutions" (2000–01) 99 *Mich. L. Rev.* 1724.

L. Bernstein, "The Questionable Empirical Basis of Article 2's Incorporation Strategy: A Preliminary Study" (1999) 66 *U. Chi. L. Rev.* 710.

L. Bernstein, "Social Norms and Default Rules Analysis" (1993–94) 3 *S. Cal. Interdisc. L. J.* 59.

R. Birke, "Evaluation and Facilitation: Moving Past Either/Or" (2000) *J. Disp. Resol.* 309.

S. Blake, J. Browne and S. Sime, *A Practical Approach to Alternative Dispute Resolution* (Oxford: Oxford University Press, 2012).

R. Block Jr and D.A. Siegel, "Identity, Bargaining, and Third-party Mediation" (2011) 3 *International Theory* 416.

S. Blount White *et al.*, "Alternative Models of Price Behavior in Dyadic Negotiations: Market Prices, Reservation Prices, and Negotiator Aspirations" (1994) 57 *Organizational Behavior & Human Decision Processes* 430.

P. Bohannan, *Justice and Judgment Among the Tiv* (London: Oxford University Press, 1957).

J.B. Boskey, "The Proper Role of the Mediator: Rational Assessment, Not Pressure" (1994) 10 *Negotiation J.* 367.

D. Bowling and D. Hoffman, eds, *Bringing Peace Into the Room: How the Personal Qualities of the Mediator Impact the Process of Conflict Resolution* (San Francisco: Jossey-Bass, 2003).

D. Bowling and D. Hoffman, "Bringing Peace into the Room: The Personal Qualities of the Mediator and Their Impact on the Mediation" (2000) *Negotiation J.* 5.

A. Bradney and F. Cownie, *Living Without Law: An Ethnography of Quaker Decision-Making, Dispute Avoidance and Dispute Resolution* (Aldershot: Dartmouth, 2000).

M.J. Brannan, "Once More With Feeling: Ethnographic Reflections on the Mediation of Tension in a Small Team of Call Centre Workers" (2005) 12 *Gender, Work and Organization* 420.

D. Brenneis, "Law, Anthropology and Mediation: Official Accounts: Performance and the Public Record" (1983) 3 *Windsor Y.B. Access Just.* 228.

P. Brooker and A. Lavers, "Mediation Outcomes: Lawyers' Experience with Commercial and Construction Mediation in the United Kingdom" (2005) 5 *Pepp. Disp. Resol. L. J.* 161.

Burchell v. Bullard et al. [2005] EWCA Civ 358.

R.P. Burns, "Some Ethical Issues Surrounding Mediation" (2001–02) 70 *Fordham L. Rev.* 691.

S.L. Burns, "Pursuing 'Deep Pockets': Insurance-related Issues in Judicial Settlement Work" (2004) 33 *J. of Contemporary Ethnography* 111.

S.L. Burns, "'Think Your Blackest Thoughts and Darken Them': Judicial Mediation of Large Money Damage Disputes" (2001) 24 *Human Studies* 227.

S. Lee Burns, *Making Settlement Work: An Examination of the Work of Judicial Mediators* (Aldershot: Ashgate Dartmouth, 2000).

S. Burns, "The Name of the Game is Movement: Concession Seeking in Judicial Mediation of Large Money Cases" (1998) 15 *Mediation Q.* 359.

R.A. Baruch Bush and J. Folger, *The Promise of Mediation* (San Francisco: Jossey-Bass, 1994 and 2005).

R.A. Baruch Bush, "'What Do We Need a Mediator For?' Mediation's 'Value-added' for Negotiators" (1996–97) 12 *Ohio St. J. Disp. Resol.* 1.

R.A. Baruch Bush and S.G. Pope, "Changing the Quality of Conflict Interaction: The Principles and Practice of Transformative Mediation" (2002–03) 3 *Pepp. Disp. Resol. L. J.* 67.

J. Butterworth, *Jerusalem* (London: Nick Hern, 2009).

E.S. Cahn, "Book Review: An Anthropologist Examines the Lawyer Tribe" (2005) 17 *Yale J. L. & Human.* 291.

N.R. Cahn, "Book Review: Speaking Differences: The Rules and Relationships of Litigants' Discourses" (1991–92) 90 *Mich. L. Rev.* 1705.

P. Caplan, ed. *Understanding Disputes: The Politics of Argument* (Oxford: Berg, 1995).

B.N. Cardozo School of Law, "Should Mediators Evaluate? A Debate Between Lela P. Love and James B. Boskey" (1999–00) 1 *Cardozo Online J. Confl. Resol.* 1.

P.J.D. Carnevale, "Strategic Choice in Mediation" (1986) 2 *Negotiation J.* 41.

P.J.D. Carnevale, D.E. Conlon and K.A. Hanisch, "Experimental Research on the Strategic-choice Model of Mediation" in K. Kressel, D.G. Pruitt and Associates, eds, *Mediation Research: The Process and Effectiveness of Third Party Intervention* (San Francisco: Jossey-Bass, 1989) 344.

G. Carter Bentley, "Maranao Mediation and the Reproduction of Social Hierarchy" (1983) 3 *Windsor Y.B. Access Just.* 270.

Paul Cézanne, Letter to Emile Bernard, 23 October 1905, Aix. English translation provided by the Courtauld Gallery in London at an exhibition of Cézanne paintings in September 2008.

L. Charkoudian et al., "Mediation by Any Other Name Would Smell as Sweet – Or Would It? The Struggle to Define Mediation and Its Various Approaches" (2009) 26 *Conflict Resol. Q.* 293.

O.G. Chase, *Law, Culture, and Ritual: Disputing Systems in Cross-cultural Context* (New York: University Press, 2005).

Civil Procedure Rules, 1998 SI 1998/3132, rules 1.4(1), 1.4(2)(e), 26.4(1) and 44.3(5).

Civil Procedure Rules, 1998 SI 1998/3132, Tomlin Order: for example, see http://www.cedr.com/library/documents/settlement_agreement.pdf (accessed 22 June 2012).

J. Clammer, "Approaches to Ethnographic Research" in R.F. Ellen, ed. *Ethnographic Research: A Guide to General Conduct* (London: Academic, 1984) 63.

B. Clark, *Lawyers and Mediation* (London: Springer, 2012).

B. Clark, "Mediation and Scottish lawyers: Past, Present and Future" (2009) *Edin. L. R.* 252.

The Right Hon Lord Clarke of Stone-cum-Ebony, Justice of the Supreme Court, "The Future of Mediation", speech given at the Second Civil Mediation Council National Conference, Birmingham, 8 May 2008 (as then Master of the Rolls). Available at: www.judiciary.gov.uk/Resources/JCO/Documents/Speeches/mr_mediation_conference_may08.pdf (accessed 22 August 2012).

J. Clifford, "Introduction: Partial Truths" in J. Clifford and G.E. Marcus, eds, *Writing Culture: The Poetics and Politics of Ethnography* (Berkeley: University of California Press, 1986) 1.

J. Clifford, "On Ethnographic Allegory" in J. Clifford and G.E. Marcus, eds, *Writing Culture: The Poetics and Politics of Ethnography* (Berkeley: University of California Press, 1986) 98.

J. Clifford and G.E. Marcus, eds, *Writing Culture: The Poetics and Politics of Ethnography* (Berkeley: University of California Press, 1986).

S. Cobb, "A Developmental Approach to Turning Points: 'Irony' as an Ethics for Negotiation Pragmatics" (2006) 11 *Harv. Negot. L. Rev.* 147.

S. Cobb, "Creating Sacred Space: Toward a Second-generation Dispute Resolution Practice" (2000–01) 28 *Fordham Urb. L. J.* 1017.

S. Cobb and J. Rifkin, "Practice and Paradox: Deconstructing Neutrality in Mediation" (1991) 16 *Law & Soc. Inquiry* 35.

J.R. Coben, "Gollum, Meet Smeagol: A Schizophrenic Rumination on Mediator Values Beyond Self-determination and Neutrality" (2004) 5 *Cardozo J. Conflict Resol.* 65.

J. Comaroff and J.L. Comaroff, "Ethnography on an Awkward Scale: Postcolonial Anthropology and the Violence of Abstraction" (2003) 4 *Ethnography* 147.

J. Comaroff and J.L. Comaroff, "Occult Economies and the Violence of Abstraction: Notes for the South African Postcolony" (1999) 26 *American Ethnologist* 279.

J. Comaroff and J.L. Comaroff, "Response to Moore: Second Thoughts" (1999) 26 *American Ethnologist* 307.

J.L. Comaroff and S. Roberts, *Rules and Processes: The Cultural Logic of Dispute in an African Context* (Chicago: University of Chicago Press, 1981).

J.L. Comaroff and S. Roberts, "The Invocation of Norms in Dispute Settlement: The Tswana Case" in I. Hamnett, ed., *Social Anthropology and Law* (London: Academic Press, 1977) 77.

The Concise Oxford English Dictionary, http://www.oxfordreference.com (accessed August 2012).

R.J. Condlin, "'Every Day and in Every Way We are All Becoming Meta and Meta,' or How Communitarian Bargaining Theory Conquered the World (of Bargaining Theory)" (2007–08) 23 *Ohio St. J. Disp. Resol.* 231.

R.J. Condlin, "Bargaining in the Dark: The Normative Incoherence of Lawyer Dispute Bargaining Role" (1992) 51 *Md. L. Rev.* 1.

J.M. Conley and W.M. O'Barr, "A Classic in Spite of Itself: The Cheyenne Way and the Case Method in Legal Anthropology" (2004) 29 *Law & Soc. Inquiry* 179.

J.M. Conley and W.M. O'Barr, "Back to the Trobriands: The Enduring Influence of Malinowski's Crime and Custom in Savage Society: Bronislaw Malinowski" (2002) 27 *Law & Soc. Inquiry* 847.

J.M. Conley and W.M. O'Barr, *Just Words: Law, Language and Power* (Chicago: University of Chicago Press, 1998).

J.M. Conley and W.M. O'Barr, "Legal Anthropology Comes Home: A Brief History of the Ethnographic Study of Law" (1993–94) 27 *Loy. L. A. L. Rev.* 41.

J.W. Cooley, "Mediation Magic: Its Use and Abuse" (1997–98) 29 *Loy. U. Chi. L. J.* 1.

J.W. Cooley, "A Classical Approach to Mediation – Part I: Classical Rhetoric and the Art of Persuasion in Mediation" (1993–94) 19 *U. Dayton L. Rev.* 83.

J.W. Cooley, "A Classical Approach to Mediation – Part II: The Socratic Method and Conflict Reframing in Mediation" (1993–94) 19 *U. Dayton L. Rev.* 589.

F. Cownie, A. Bradney and M. Burton, *English Legal System in Context* (Oxford: Oxford University Press, 2007).

D. Cornes, "Commercial Mediation: The Impact of the Courts" (2007) 73 *Arbitration* 12.

V. Crapanzano, "Hermes' Dilemma: The Masking of Subversion in Ethnographic Description" in J. Clifford and G.E. Marcus, eds, *Writing Culture: The Poetics and Politics of Ethnography* (Berkeley: University of California Press, 1986) 51.

V. Crapanzano, *Tuhami: Portrait of a Moroccan* (Chicago: University of Chicago Press, 1980).

R.A. Creo, "Mediation 2004: The Art and the Artist" (2003–04) 108 *Penn St. L. Rev.* 1017.

R.S. Dampf, "The Two Sides of Mediation: Tips from the Mediator: Of Sticks and Stones" (1997) 45 *L. A. Bar J.* 138.

E. de Bono, *Conflicts: A Better Way to Resolve Them* (London: Harrap, 1985).

D. De Girolamo, "Seeking Negotiated Order Through Mediation: A Manifestation of Legal Culture?" (2012) 5 *J. Comp. Law* 118, and in D. Nelken, ed., *Using Legal Culture* (London: Wildy, Simmonds & Hill, 2012) 153.

D. De Girolamo, "A View from Within: Reconceptualizing Mediator Interactions" (2012) 30 (2) *Windsor Y.B. Access Just.* (in press).

D. De Girolamo, "The Negotiation Process: Exploring Negotiator Moves Through a Processual Framework" (2013) 28(2) *Ohio St. J. Disp. Resol.* (in press).

D.J. Della Noce, "Evaluative Mediation: In Search of Practice Competencies" (2009) 27 *Conflict Resol. Q.* 193.

D.J. Della Noce, "Communicating Quality Assurance: A Case Study of Mediator Profiles on a Court Roster" (2008) 84 *N. Dak. L. Rev.* 769.

D.J. Della Noce, "From Practice to Theory to Practice: A Brief Retrospective on the Transformative Mediation Model" (2003–04) 19 *Ohio St. J. Disp. Resol.* 925.

D.J. Della Noce, *Ideologically Based Patterns in the Discourse of Mediators: A Comparison of Problem-solving and Transformative Practice*, Dissertation submitted to the Temple University Graduate Board in partial fulfilment of the requirements for the degree Doctor of Philosophy, May 2002.

D.J. Della Noce, "Mediation Theory and Policy: The Legacy of the Pound Conference" (2001–02) 17 *Ohio St. J. Disp. Resol.* 545.

D.J. Della Noce, R.A. Baruch Bush and J.P. Folger, "Clarifying the Theoretical Underpinning of Mediation: Implications for Practice and Policy" (2002–03) 3 *Pepp. Disp. Resol. L. J.* 39.

D.J. Della Noce, J.P. Folger and J.R. Antes, "Assimilative, Autonomous, or Synergistic Visions: How Mediation Programs in Florida Address the Dilemma of Court Connection" (2002–03) 3 *Pepp. Disp. Resol. L. J.* 11.

H.S. Desivilya and M.R. Elbaz, "Do Mediators Walk the Talk? A Study of Israeli Mediators" (2008) 63 *Disp. Resol. J.* 63.

H.S. Desivilya *et al.*, "Implicit Theory of Mediation Practice: The Relationships between Mediators' Gender, Professional Background and Construal of Mediation Practice", paper submitted to the 17th Annual Conference of the International Association for Conflict Management, June 2004, Pittsburg, PA.

Directive 2008/52/EC of the European Parliament and of the Council of 21 May 2008, Article 3(b).

A. Douglas, "The Peaceful Settlement of Industrial and Intergroup Disputes" (1957) 1 *Conflict Resol.* 69.

A. Douglas, "What Can Research Tell Us About Mediation?" (1955) 6 *Labor Law J.* 545.

D. Druckman, "Intuition or Counterintuition? The Science Behind the Art of Negotiation" (2009) *Negotiation J.* 431.

D. Druckman, "Turning Points in International Negotiation" (2001) *J. Conflict Resol.* 519.

D. Druckman, M. Olekalns and P.L. Smith, "Interpretive Filters: Social Cognition and the Impact of Turning Points in Negotiation" (2009) *Negotiation J.* 13.

M. Duneier, "What Kind of Combat Sport is Sociology?" (2002) 107 *Am. J. of Sociology* 1551.

D. Dyck, "The Mediator as Nonviolent Advocate: Revisiting the Question of Mediator Neutrality" (2000) 18 *Mediation Q.* 129.

R.F. Ellen, J. Clammer and R. Firth eds, *Ethnographic Research: A Guide to General Conduct* (London: Academic, 1984).

R.C. Ellickson, *Order Without Law: How Neighbors Settle Disputes* (London: Harvard University Press, 1991).

H. Englund and J. Leach, "Ethnography and the Meta-narratives of Modernity" (2000) 41 *Current Anthropology* 225.

E. Enslin, "Beyond Writing: Feminist Practice and the Limitations of Ethnography" (1994) 9 *Cultural Anthropology* 537.

European Code of Conduct for Mediators, Article 2: http://ec.europa.eu/civiljustice/adr/adr_ec_code_conduct_en.pdf (accessed 29 July 2012).

E.E. Evans-Pritchard, *The Nuer: A Description of the Modes of Livelihood and Political Institutions of a Nilotic People* (New York: Oxford University Press, 1969).

S.N. Exon, "The Effects that Mediator Styles Impose on Neutrality and Impartiality Requirements of Mediation" (2007–08) 42 *U. S. F. L. Rev.* 577.

S.N. Exon, "How Can a Mediator Be Both Impartial and Fair? Why Ethical Standards of Conduct Create Chaos for Mediators" (2006) *J. Disp. Resol.* 387.

P. Field, "The Unreliable Narrator?" (Review Essay) (2011) *Negotiation J.* 387.

R. Fisher, W. Ury and B. Patton, *Getting to Yes: Negotiating Agreement Without Giving In* (New York: Penguin, 1991).

J. Folberg and A. Taylor, *Mediation: A Comprehensive Guide to Resolving Conflicts Without Litigation* (San Francisco: Jossey-Bass, 1984).

J.P. Folger, "'Mediation Goes Mainstream' – Taking the Conference Theme Challenge" (2002–03) 3 *Pepp. Disp. Resol. L. J.* 1.

J.P. Folger, "Mediation Research: Studying Transformative Effects" (2001) 18 *Hofstra Lab & Emp. L. J.* 82.

J. P. Folger and T.S. Jones, eds, *New Directions in Mediation: Communication Research and Perspectives* (Thousand Oaks: Sage, 1994).

M.G. Forsey, "Ethnography as Participant Listening" (2010) 11 *Ethnography* 558.

R.F. Fortune, *Sorcerers of Dobu: The Social Anthropology of the Dobu Islanders of the Western Pacific* (London: Routledge, 1963).

J.C. Freund, *The Neutral Negotiator: Why and How Mediation Can Work to Resolve Dollar Disputes* (New Jersey: Prentice-Hall Law & Business, 1994).

L.L. Fuller, "Mediation – Its Forms and Functions" (1970–71) 44 *S. Cal. L. Rev.* 305.

E.R. Galton, *Ripples From Peace Lake: Essays for Mediators and Peacemakers* (Victoria: Trafford, 2004).

A.C. Garcia, "Negotiating Negotiation: The Collaborative Production of Resolution in Small Claims Mediation Hearings" (2000) 11 *Discourse & Society* 315.

A. Garcia, "The Problematics of Representation in Community Mediation Hearings: Implications for Mediation Practice" (1995) 22 *J. Soc. & Soc. Welfare* 23.

P.J. Gardner, "A Conversation with Leonard L. Riskin" (2005) 46 *N. H. B. J.* 5.

C. Geertz, *Local Knowledge* (New York: Basic Books, 1983).

C. Geertz, "Thick Description: Toward an Interpretive Theory of Culture" in C. Geertz, *The Interpretation of Culture* (New York: Basic Books, 1973).

C. Geertz, *The Interpretation of Culture* (New York: Basic Books, 1973).
H. Genn, *Judging Civil Justice* (Cambridge: Cambridge University Press, 2010).
H. Genn, "Solving Civil Justice Problems: What Might be Best?" Scottish Consumer Council Seminar on Civil Justice, 19 January 2005.
H. Genn, *Court-based ADR Initiatives for Non-family Civil Disputes: The Commercial Court and the Court of Appeal*, Lord Chancellor's Department, Research Series, 2002.
H. Genn, *Central London County Court Pilot Mediation Scheme: Evaluation Report, 1998*, Lord Chancellor's Department, Research Series, 5/98.
H. Genn et al., *Twisting Arms: Court Referred and Court Linked Mediation Under Judicial Pressure* (May 2007) Ministry of Justice Res Ser 1/07, Ministry of Justice, London.
D.G. Gifford, "A Context-based Theory of Strategy Selection in Legal Negotiation" (1985) 46 *Ohio St. L. J.* 41.
D. Gladwell, "Alternative Dispute Resolution and the Courts" (1 May 2004) *CCN* 1 (27).
D.W. Golann, "Is Legal Mediation a Process of Repair or Separation? An Empirical Study and Its Implications" (2002) 7 *Harv. Negot. L. Rev.* 301.
D. Golann, "Variations in Mediation: How – and Why – Legal Mediators Change Styles in the Course of a Case" (2000) *J. Disp. Resol.* 41.
D. Golann and M.C. Aaron, "Using Evaluations in Mediation" (book chapter) in *Mediating Legal Disputes: Effective Strategies for Lawyers and Mediators* (American Bar Association, 2009) 327.
S.B. Goldberg and M.L. Shaw, "The Secrets of Successful (and Unsuccessful) Mediators Continued: Studies Two and Three" (2007) *Negotiation J.* 393.
J.H. Goldfien and J.K. Robbennolt, "What if the Lawyers Have Their Way? An Empirical Assessment of Conflict Strategies and Attitudes Toward Mediation Styles" (2006–07) 22 *Ohio St. J. Disp. Resol.* 277.
M. Goodale, "A Life in the Law: Laura Nader and the Future of Legal Anthropology" (2005) 39 *Law and Soc'y Rev.* 945.
M. Goodale, "From the Trenches and Towers: Commentary: The Globalization of Sympathetic Law and its Consequences" (2002) 27 *Law & Soc. Inquiry* 595.
G. Goodpaster, "Rational Decision-making in Problem-solving Negotiation: Compromise, Interest-valuation, and Cognitive Error" (1992–93) 8 *Ohio St. J. Disp. Resol.* 299.
D. Greatbatch and R. Dingwall, "Selective Facilitation: Some Preliminary Observations on a Strategy Used by Divorce Mediators" (1989) 23 *Law & Soc'y Rev.* 613.
G.M. Green and M. Wheeler, "Awareness and Action in Critical Moments" (2004) *Negotiation J.* 349.
M. Greenberg, "Mediating Massacres: When 'Neutral, Low-power' Models of Mediation Cannot and Should Not Work" (2003–04) 19 *Ohio St. J. Disp. Resol.* 185.
A. Griffiths, "Reconfiguring Law: An Ethnographic Perspective from Botswana" (1998) 23 *Law & Soc. Inquiry* 587.
P.H. Gulliver, *Social Control in An African Society: A Study of the Arusha: Agricultural Masai of Northern Tanganyika* (London: Routledge, 2000 edition).
P.H. Gulliver, "Anthropological Contributions to the Study of Negotiations" (1988) *Negotiation J.* 247.
P.H. Gulliver, *Disputes and Negotiations: A Cross-cultural Perspective* (New York: Academic Press, 1979).

P.H. Gulliver, "On Mediators" in I. Hamnett, ed., *Social Anthropology and Law* (London: Academic Press, 1977) 15.

P.H. Gulliver, *Neighbours and Networks: The Idiom of Kinship in Social Action among the Ndendeuli of Tanzania* (London: University of California Press, 1971).

Halsey v. Milton Keynes General NHS Trust [2004] EWCA Civ 576.

M. Hammersley, *What's Wrong with Ethnography? Methodological Explorations* (London: Routledge, 1992).

R.G. Hann et al., *Evaluation of the Mandatory Mediation Program*, submitted to the Civil Rules Committee: Evaluation Committee for the Mandatory Mediation Pilot Project (Queen's Printer, 2001).

C.M. Hanycz, "Introduction to the Negotiation Process Model" in C.M. Hanycz, T.C.W. Farrow and F.H. Zemans, *The Theory and Practice of Representative Negotiation* (Toronto: Emond Montgomery, 2008) 41.

C.M. Hanycz, "Strategic Negotiation: Moving Through the Stages" in C.M. Hanycz, T.C.W. Farrow and F.H. Zemans, *The Theory and Practice of Representative Negotiation* (Toronto: Emond Montgomery, 2008) 67.

C.M. Hanycz, "Through the Looking Glass: Mediator Conceptions of Philosophy, Process and Power" (2004–05) 42 *Alberta L. Rev.* 819.

C. Harper, "Comment – Mediator as Peacemaker: The Case for Activist Transformative-narrative Mediation" (2006) *J. Disp. Resol.* 595.

C.B. Harrington and S.E. Merry, "Ideological Production: The Making of Community Mediation" (1988) 22 *Law & Soc'y Rev.* 709.

R.E. Hartley, *Alternative Dispute Resolution in Civil Justice Systems* (New York: LFB Scholarly Publishing LLC, 2002).

B.L. Heisterkamp, "Conversational Displays of Mediator Neutrality in a Court-based Program" (2006) 38 *J. of Pragmatics* 2051.

D.A. Henderson, "Mediation Success: An Empirical Analysis" (1996) 11 *Ohio St. J. Disp. Resol.* 105.

D.R. Hensler, "Our Courts, Ourselves: How the Alternative Dispute Resolution Movement is Re-shaping Our Legal System" (2003–04) 108 *Penn. St. L. Rev.* 165.

D.R. Hensler, "Suppose It's Not True: Challenging Mediation Ideology" (2002) *J. Disp. Resol.* 81.

D.R. Hensler, "In Search of 'Good' Mediation: Rhetoric, Practice, and Empiricism" in J. Sanders and V. Lee Hamilton, eds, *Handbook of Justice Research in Law* (New York: Kluwer Academic, 2001).

M.S. Herrman, ed., *The Blackwell Handbook of Mediation: Bridging Theory, Research, and Practice* (Oxford: Blackwell, 2006).

D. Hoffman and D. Ash, "Building Bridges to Resolve Conflict and Overcome the 'Prisoner's Dilemma': The Vital Role of Professional Relationships in the Collaborative Law Process" (2010) *J. Disp. Resol.* 271.

R. Hollander-Blumoff, "Just Negotiation" (2010–11) 88 *Wash. U. L. Rev.* 381.

M.E. Holmes, "Optimal Matching Analysis of Negotiation Phase Sequences in Simulated and Authentic Hostage Negotiations" (1997) 10 *Communication Reports* 1.

C. Honeyman, "Bias and Mediators' Ethics" (1986) *Negotiation J.* 175.

In Place of Strife, The Mediation Chambers, www.mediate.co.uk/what_is_mediation/index.html (accessed 27 August 2012).

C. Izumi, "Implicit Bias and the Illusion of Mediator Neutrality" (2010) 34 *Wash. U. J. L. & Pol'y* 71.

J. Jacob, *Civil Justice in the Age of Human Rights* (Aldershot: Ashgate, 2007).
JAMS, www.jamsadr.com/mediation/defined.asp (accessed 27 August 2012).
JAMS, http://www.jamsadr.com/adr-mediation/ (accessed 29 July 2012).
JAMS, http://www.jamsadr.com/mediators-ethics/ (accessed 29 July 2012).
B. Jarrett, "The Future of Mediation: A Sociological Perspective" (2009) *J. Disp. Resol.* 49.
G.T. Jones, "Fighting Capitulation: A Research Agenda for the Future of Dispute Resolution" (2003–04) 108 *Penn St. L. Rev.* 277.
T.S. Jones, "A Taxonomy of Effective Mediator Strategies and Tactics for Non Labour Management Mediation" in M.A. Rahim, ed., *Managing Conflict: An Interdisciplinary Approach* (New York: Praeger, 1989) 201.
R.F. Kandel, "Situated Substantive Expertise: An Ethnographic Illustration and a Proposed Standard of Practice for Mediators" (1998) 15 *Mediation Q.* 303.
N.H. Katz, "Enhancing Mediator Artistry: Multiple Frames, Spirit, and Reflection in Action" in M.S. Herrman, ed., *The Blackwell Handbook of Mediation: Bridging Theory, Research, and Practice* (Oxford: Blackwell, 2006) 374.
J. Katz, "From How to Why: On Luminous Description and Causal Inference in Ethnography (Part 2)" (2002) 3 *Ethnography* 63.
J. Katz, "From How to Why: On Luminous Description and Causal Inference in Ethnography (Part 1)" (2001) 2 *Ethnography* 443.
J. Kidner, "The Limits of Mediator 'Labels': False Debate Between 'Facilitative' Versus 'Evaluative' Mediator Styles" (2011) 30 *Windsor R. of Legal & Soc. Issues* 167.
T.W. Kheel, *The Keys to Conflict Resolution: Proven Methods of Settling Disputes Voluntarily* (New York: Four Walls Eight Windows, 1999).
D.M. Kolb, "Staying in the Game or Changing It: An Analysis of *Moves* and *Turns* in Negotiation" (2004) *Negotiation J.* 253.
D.M. Kolb, "To Be a Mediator: Expressive Tactics in Mediation" (1985) 41 *J. of Social Issues* 11.
D.M. Kolb, "Strategy and the Tactics of Mediation" (1983) 36 *Human Relations* 247.
D.M. Kolb, *The Mediators* (Cambridge, MA: MIT Press, 1983).
D.M. Kolb, "Roles Mediators Play: State and Federal Practice" (1981) 20 *Industrial Relations* 1.
D.M. Kolb and Associates, eds, *When Talk Works: Profiles of Mediators* (San Francisco: Jossey-Bass, 1994).
D.M. Kolb and K. Kressel, "The Realities of Making Talk Work" in D.M. Kolb and Associates, eds, *When Talk Works: Profiles of Mediators* (San Francisco: Jossey-Bass, 1994) 459.
K.K. Kovach, "Mediation" in M.L. Moffitt and R.C. Bordone, eds, *The Handbook of Dispute Resolution* (San Francisco: Jossey-Bass, 2005) 304.
K.K. Kovach, "The Vanishing Trial: Land Mine on the Mediation Landscape or Opportunity for Evolution: Ruminations on the Future of Mediation Practice" (2005) 7 *Cardozo J. Conflict Resol.* 27.
K.K. Kovach, "Mediation for Mediators? If You Talk the Talk, You'd Better Walk the Walk: An Examination of How Dispute Resolvers Resolve Disputes" (1996) 11 *Ohio St. J. Disp. Resol.* 403.
K.K. Kovach and L.P. Love, "Mapping Mediation: The Risks of Riskin's Grid" (1998) 3 *Harv. Negot. L. Rev.* 71.
K. Kressel, "The Strategic Style in Mediation" (2007) 24 *Conflict Resol. Q.* 251.

K. Kressel, "Mediation Revisited" in M. Deutsch and P.T. Coleman, eds, *The Handbook of Conflict Resolution: Theory and Practice* (San Francisco: Jossey-Bass, 2006) 726.

K. Kressel, "Mediation" in M. Deutsch and P.T. Coleman, eds, *The Handbook of Conflict Resolution: Theory and Practice* (San Francisco: Jossey-Bass, 2000) 522.

K. Kressel and H. Gadlin, "Mediating Among Scientists: A Mental Model of Expert Practice" (2009) 2 *International Association for Conflict Management* 308.

K. Kressel and D.G. Pruitt, "Conclusion: A Research Perspective on the Mediation of Social Conflict" in K. Kressel, D.G. Pruitt and Associates, eds, *Mediation Research: The Process and Effectiveness of Third Party Intervention* (San Francisco: Jossey-Bass, 1989) 394.

K. Kressel, D.G. Pruitt and Associates, eds, *Mediation Research: The Process and Effectiveness of Third Party Intervention* (San Francisco: Jossey-Bass, 1989).

K. Kressel and D.G. Pruitt, "Themes in the Mediation of Social Conflict" (1985) 41 *J. of Soc. Issues* 179.

J. Krivis, *Improvisational Negotiation: A Mediator's Stories of Conflict About Love, Money, Anger – And the Strategies That Resolved Them* (San Francisco: Jossey-Bass, 2006).

A. Kydd, "Which Side Are You On? Bias, Credibility and Mediation" (2003) 47 *Am. J. of Pol't Science* 597.

H.A. Landsberger, "Interaction Process Analysis of Professional Behavior: A Study of Labor Mediators in Twelve Labor-management Disputes" (1955) 20 *Am. Sociological R.* 566.

M.D. Lang and A. Taylor, *The Making of a Mediator: Developing Artistry in Practice* (San Francisco: Jossey-Bass, 2000).

D.A. Lax, and J.K. Sebenius, *The Manager as Negotiator: Bargaining for Cooperation and Competitive Gain* (New York: Free Press, 1986).

K.N. Llewellyn and E.A. Hoebel, *The Cheyenne Way: Conflict and Case Law in Primitive Jurisprudence* (Norman: University of Oklahoma Press, 1941).

L.P. Love, "The Top Ten Reasons Why Mediators Should Not Evaluate" (1996–97) 24 *Fla. St. U. L. Rev.* 937.

L.P. Love and J.W. Cooley, "The Intersection of Evaluation by Mediators and Informed Consent: Warning the Unwary" (2005–06) 21 *Ohio St. J. Disp. Resol.* 45.

M.J. Lowy, "Law, Anthropology and Mediation: Law School Socialization and the Perversion of Mediation in the United States" (1983) 3 *Windsor Y.B. Access Just.* 245.

J. Macfarlane, "Culture Change? A Tale of Two Cities and Mandatory Court-connected Mediation" (2002) 2 *J. Disp. Resol.* 241.

J. Macfarlane, "Why Do People Settle?" (2001) 46 *McGill L. J.* 663.

J. Macfarlane, *Court-based Mediation of Civil Cases: An Evaluation of the Ontario Court (General Division) ADR Centre* (Toronto: Queen's Printer, 1995).

J. Macfarlane et al., eds, *Dispute Resolution: Readings and Case Studies* (Toronto: Emond Montgomery, 2010).

K. Mackie, "Breakthrough: Overcoming Deadlocked Negotiations" in C. Newmark and A. Monaghan, eds, *Butterworths Mediators on Mediation* (Haywards Heath: Tottel, 2005) 106.

K. Mackie et al., *The ADR Practice Guide: Commercial Dispute Resolution* (Haywards Heath: Tottel, 2007).

B. Malinowski, *Argonauts of the Western Pacific* (Long Grove: Waveland, 1984 edition).

B. Malinowski, *Crime and Custom in Savage Society* (London: Routledge, 2002 edition).

W. Mansell, B. Meteyard and A. Thomson, *A Critical Introduction to Law* (London: Cavendish, 2004).

G.E. Marcus, "Contemporary Problems of Ethnography in the Modern World System" in J. Clifford and G.E. Marcus, eds, *Writing Culture: The Poetics and Politics of Ethnography* (Berkeley: University of California Press, 1986) 165.

G.E. Marcus, "Afterword: Ethnographic Writing and Anthropological Careers" in J. Clifford and G.E. Marcus, eds, *Writing Culture: The Poetics and Politics of Ethnography* (Berkeley: University of California Press, 1986) 262.

P.M. Mareschal, "What Makes Mediation Work? Mediators' Perspectives on Resolving Disputes" (2005) 44 *Industrial Rel.* 509.

D.E. Matz, "Mediator Pressure and Party Autonomy: Are They Consistent with Each Other?" (1994) 10 *Negotiation J.* 359.

B.S. Mayer, "What We Talk About When We Talk About Neutrality: A Commentary on the Susskind-Stulberg Debate" (2012) 95 *Marquette L. R.* 859.

B.S. Mayer, *Beyond Neutrality: Confronting the Crisis in Conflict Resolution* (San Francisco: Jossey-Bass, 2004).

E.P. McDermott and R. Obar, "'What's Going On' in Mediation: An Empirical Analysis of the Influence of a Mediator's Style on Party Satisfaction and Monetary Benefit" (2004) 9 *Harv. Negot. L. R.* 75.

C.A. McEwen and R.L. Wissler, "Finding Out if It is True: Comparing Mediation and Negotiation Through Research" (2002) *J. Disp. Resol.* 131.

K.L. McGinn, E. Long Lingo and K. Ciano, "Transitions Through Out-of-keeping Acts" (2004) *Negotiation J.* 171.

A.K. Mehotra, "Law and the 'Other': Karl N. Llewellyn, Cultural Anthropology, and the Legacy of the Cheyenne Way" (2001) 26 *Law & Soc. Inquiry* 741.

C. Menkel-Meadow, "Chronicling the Complexification of Negotiation Theory and Practice" (2009) *Negotiation J.* 415.

C. Menkel-Meadow, "Why Hasn't the World Gotten to Yes? An Appreciation and Some Reflections" (2006) *Negotiation J.* 485.

C. Menkel-Meadow, "Critical Moments in Negotiation: Implications for Research, Pedagogy, and Practice" (2004) *Negotiation J.* 341.

C. Menkel-Meadow, "Remembrance of Things Past? The Relationship of Past to Future in Pursuing Justice in Mediation" (2004) 5 *Cardozo J. Conflict Resol.* 97.

C. Menkel-Meadow, "Mothers and Fathers of Invention: The Intellectual Founders of ADR" (2000) 16 *Ohio St. J. Disp. Resol.* 1.

C. Menkel-Meadow, "Whose Dispute is it Anyway? A Philosophical Defense Of Settlement" (1995) 83 *Geo. L. J.* 2663.

C. Menkel-Meadow, "Lawyer Negotiations: Theories and Realties – What We Learn from Mediation" (1993) 56 *Mod. L. Rev.* 361.

C. Menkel-Meadow, "Pursuing Settlement in an Adversary Culture: A Tale of Innovation Co-opted or 'The Law of ADR'" (1991–92) 19 *Fla. St. U. L. Rev.* 1.

C. Menkel-Meadow, "Toward Another View of Legal Negotiation: The Structure of Problem-solving" (1983–84) 31 *U.C.L.A. L. Rev.* 754.

C. Menkel-Meadow, L. Love and A. Schneider, *Mediation: Practice, Policy, and Ethics* (New York: Aspen, 2006).

S.E. Merry, "From the Trenches and Towers: Commentary: Moving Beyond Ideology Critique to the Analysis of Practice" (2002) 27 *Law & Soc. Inquiry* 609.

S.E. Merry, "Crossing Boundaries: Ethnography in the Twenty-first Century" (2000) 23 *PoLAR* 127.

S.E. Merry, "Sorting Out Popular Justice" in S.E. Merry and N. Milner, eds, *The Possibility of Popular Justice: A Case Study of Community Mediation in the United States* (Ann Arbor: University of Michigan Press, 1993) 31.

S.E. Merry, "Culture, Power, and the Discourse of Law" (1992) 37 *N.Y.L. Sch. L. Rev.* 209.

S.E. Merry, "Book Review: The Culture of Judging" (1990) 90 *Colum. L. Rev.* 2313.

S.E. Merry, "Varieties of Mediation Performance: Replicating Differences in Access to Justice" in A.C. Hutchinson, ed., *Access to Civil Justice* (Toronto: Carswell, 1990) 257.

S.E. Merry and N. Milner, *The Possibility of Popular Justice: A Case Study of Community Mediation in the United States* (Ann Arbor: University of Michigan Press, 1993).

S.E. Merry and S.S. Silbey, "What Do Plaintiffs Want? Re-examining the Concept of Dispute" (1984) 9 *Just. Sys. J.* 151.

E. Mertz, "From the Trenches and Towers: Editor's Introduction: Current Illusions and Delusions about Conflict Management – In Africa and Elsewhere" (2002) 27 *Law & Soc. Inquiry* 567.

N. Milner, "From the Trenches and Towers: Commentary: Illusions and Delusions about Conflict Management – In Africa and Elsewhere" (2002) 27 *Law & Soc. Inquiry* 621.

J. Clyde Mitchell, "Case and Situation Analysis" (1983) 31 *Sociological Review* 187.

R. Mnookin, "Why Negotiations Fail: An Exploration of Barriers to the Resolution of Conflict" (1992–93) 8 *Ohio St. J. Disp. Resol.* 235.

R. Mnookin and L. Kornhauser, "Bargaining in the Shadow of the Law: The Case of Divorce" (1979) 88 *Yale L. J.* 950.

The Model Standards of Conduct for Mediators, http://www.americanbar.org/content/dam/aba/migrated/dispute/documents/model_standards_conduct_april2007.authcheckdam.pdf (accessed 29 July 2012).

M.L. Moffitt, "Schemediation and the Dimensions of Definition" (2005) 10 *Harv. Negot. L. Rev.* 69.

C.M. Moore, "Why Do We Mediate" in J.P. Folger and T.S. Jones, eds, *New Directions in Mediation: Communication Research and Perspectives* (Thousand Oaks: Sage, 1994) 195.

C.W. Moore, *The Mediation Process: Practical Strategies for Resolving Conflict* (San Francisco: Jossey-Bass, 1996).

S. Falk Moore, "Debate: Reflections on the Comaroff Lecture" (1999) 26 *Am. Ethnologist* 304.

P. Morgan, *Frost/Nixon* (London: Faber & Faber, 2006).

L. Mulcahy, "The Possibilities and Desirability of Mediator Neutrality – Towards an Ethic of Partiality?" (2001) 10 *Soc. & Leg. Stud.* 505.

L. Nader, "Civilization and its Negotiations" in S.F. Moore, ed., *Law and Anthropology: A Reader* (Malden, MA: Blackwell, 2005) 332.

L. Nader, *The Life of the Law: Anthropological Projects* (Berkeley: University of California Press, 2002).

L. Nader, "When is Popular Justice Popular?" in S.E. Merry and N. Milner, eds, *The Possibility of Popular Justice: A Case Study of Community Mediation in the United States* (Ann Arbor: University of Michigan Press, 1993) 435.

L. Nader and E. Grande, "From the Trenches and Towers: Current Illusions and Delusions about Conflict Management – In Africa and Elsewhere" (2002) 27 *Law & Soc. Inquiry* 573.

L. Nader and E. Grande, "From the Trenches and Towers: Reply: Current Illusions and Delusions about Conflict Management – In Africa and Elsewhere" (2002) 27 *Law & Soc. Inquiry* 631.

P. Naughton, "Mediators are Magicians: A Modern Myth?" (2003) *Society of Construction Law* 1.

M.A. Neale and M.H. Bazerman, "Negotiator Cognition and Rationality: A Behavioral Decision Theory Perspective" (1992) 51 *Organizational Behavior & Human Decision Processes* 157.

The Right Hon Lord Neuberger of Abbotsbury, President of the Supreme Court (then Master of the Rolls) "Has Mediation had its Day?" Gordon Slynn Memorial Lecture, 10 November 2010, *The Expert and Dispute Resolver* (published by the Academy of Experts), Winter 2010, Vol. 15 No. 3, 8.

K. Newman, "No Shame: The View from the Left Bank" (2002) 107 *Am. J. of Sociology* 1577.

C. Newmark and A. Monaghan, eds, *Butterworths Mediators on Mediation: Mediator Perspectives on the Practice of Commercial Mediation* (Haywards Heath: Tottel, 2005).

M.E.R. Nicholson, "Law, Anthropology and Mediation: Modern Mediator in Cross-cultural Perspective" (1983) 3 *Windsor Y.B. Access Just.* 204.

J.M. Nolan-Haley, "Lawyers, Non-lawyers and Mediation: Rethinking the Professional Monopoly from a Problem-solving Perspective" (2002) 7 *Harv. Negot. L. Rev.* 235.

J.M. Nolan-Haley, "Court Mediation and the Search for Justice Through Law" (1996) 74 *Wash. U. L. Q.* 47.

D.E. Noll, "Mediation: The Myth of the Mediator as Settlement Broker" (2009) 64 *J. Disp. Resol.* 42.

D.E. Noll, "A Theory of Mediation" (2001) 56 *Disp. Resol. J.* 78.

S. Oberman, "Style vs. Model: Why Quibble" (2008) 9 *Pepp. Disp. Resol. L. J.* 1.

S. Oberman, "Mediation Theory vs. Practice: What Are We Really Doing? Re-solving a Professional Conundrum" (2005) 20 *Ohio St. J. Disp. Resol.* 775.

M. Palmer, "Controlling the State? Mediation in Administrative Litigation in the People's Republic of China" (2006–07) 16 *Transnat'l L. & Contemp. Probs.* 165.

M. Palmer, "The Revival of Mediation in the People's Republic of China: (2) Judicial Mediation" in W.E. Butler, ed., *Yearbook on Socialist Legal Systems 1988* (New York: Transnational Books, 1989).

M. Palmer, "The Revival of Mediation in the People's Republic of China: (1) Extra-judicial Mediation" in W.E. Butler, ed., *Yearbook on Socialist Legal Systems 1987* (New York: Transnational Books, 1988).

D.R. Papke, "How the Cheyenne Indians Wrote Article 2 of the Uniform Commercial Code" (1999) 47 *Buffalo L. Rev.* 1457.

G. Paquin and L. Harvey, "Therapeutic Jurisprudence, Transformative Mediation and Narrative Mediation: A Natural Connection" (2001–02) 3 *Fla. Coastal L. J.* 167.

J. Paquin, "Avengers, Avoiders and Lumpers: The Incidence of Disputing Style on Litigiousness" (2001) 19 *Windsor Y.B. Access Just.* 3.

D.E. Peachy, "What People Want From Mediation" in K. Kressel, D.G. Pruitt and Associates, eds, *Mediation Research: The Process and Effectiveness of Third Party Intervention* (San Francisco: Jossey-Bass, 1989) 300.

C.A. Picard, "Exploring an Integrative Framework for Understanding Mediation" (2004) *Conflict Resol. Q.* 295.

C.A. Picard, "Common Language, Different Meaning: What Mediators Mean When They Talk About Their Work" (2002) *Negotiation J.* 251.

C.A. Picard, *The Many Meanings of Mediation: A Sociological Study of Mediation in Canada*, Executive Summary of Doctorate Dissertation and Doctoral Dissertation, Carleton University, August 2000.

C.A. Picard and M. Jull, "Learning Through Deepening Conversations: A Key Strategy of Insight Mediation" (2011) *Conflict Resol. Q.* 151.

C.A. Picard and K.R. Melchin, "Insight Mediation: A Learning-centered Mediation Model" (2007) *Negotiation J.* 35.

L. Pirandello, *Six Characters in Search of an Author*, a new version by Rupert Goold and Ben Power (London: Nick Hern Books, 2008).

M.L. Pratt, "Fieldwork in Common Places" in J. Clifford and G.E. Marcus, eds, *Writing Culture: The Poetics and Politics of Ethnography* (Berkeley: University of California Press, 1986) 27.

S. Prince, "ADR after the CPR: Have ADR Initiatives Now Assured Mediation an Integral Role in the Civil Justice System in England and Wales?" in D. Dwyer, ed., *The Civil Procedure Rules Ten Years On* (Oxford: Oxford University Press, 2009) 321.

D.G. Pruitt and P.J. Carnevale, *Negotiation in Social Conflict* (Buckingham: Open University Press, 1993).

D.G. Pruitt, et al., "Long-term Success in Mediation" (1993) 17 *Law and Human Behavior* 313.

D.G. Pruitt, et al., "Process of Mediation in Dispute Settlement Centers" in K. Kressel, D.G. Pruitt and Associates, eds, *Mediation Research: The Process and Effectiveness of Third Party Intervention* (San Francisco: Jossey-Bass, 1989) 368.

L.L. Putnam, "Transformations and Critical Moments in Negotiations" (2004) *Negotiation J.* 275.

R.W. Rack Jr, "Thoughts of a Chief Circuit Mediator on Federal Court-annexed Mediation" (2002) 17 *Ohio St. J. Disp. Resol.* 609.

H. Raiffa, *The Art and Science of Negotiation* (Cambridge, MA: Harvard University Press, 1982).

T. Relis, *Parallel Worlds of Disputes and Mediation*, thesis submitted for PhD in Law, London School of Economics and Political Science, June 2005.

A. Riles, "From the Trenches and Towers: Commentary: User Friendly: Informality and Expertise" (2002) 27 *Law & Soc. Inquiry* 613.

A. Riles, "Representing In-between: Law, Anthropology, and the Rhetoric of Interdisciplinarity" (1994) *U.Ill. L. Rev.* 597.

L.L. Riskin, "Decision-making in Mediation: The New Old Grid and the New New Grid System" (2003–04) 79 *Notre Dame L. Rev.* 1.

L.L. Riskin, "Mediation Quandaries" (1996–97) 24 *Fla. St. U. L. Rev.* 1007.

L.L. Riskin, "Understanding Mediators' Orientations, Strategies, and Techniques: A Grid for the Perplexed" (1996) 1 *Harv. Negot. L. Rev.* 7.

K.M. Roberts, "Mediating the Evaluative-facilitative Debate: Why Both Parties are Wrong and a Proposal for Settlement" (2007–08) 39 *Loy. U. Chi. L. J.* 187.

M. Roberts, *Developing the Craft of Mediation: Reflections on Theory and Practice* (London: Jessica Kingsley, 2007).

S. Roberts, "'Listing Concentrates the Mind': The English Civil Court as an Arena for Structured Negotiation" (2009) 29 *Oxford J. Legal Stud.* 457.

S. Roberts, "Order and the Evocation of Heritage: Representing Quality in the French Biscuit Trade" in K. von Benda-Beckmann and F. Pirie, eds, *Order and Disorder: Anthropological Perspectives* (New York: Berghahn Books, 2007) 16.

S. Roberts, "After Government? On Representing Law Without the State" (2005) 68 *Mod. L. Rev.* 1.

S. Roberts, "Settlement as Civil Justice" (2000) 63 *Mod. L. Rev.* 739.

S. Roberts, "Alternative Dispute Resolution and Civil Justice: An Unresolved Relationship" (1993) 56 *Mod. L. Rev.* 452.

S. Roberts, *Order and Dispute: An Introduction to Legal Anthropology* (Harmondsworth: Penguin, 1979).

S. Roberts and M. Palmer, *Dispute Processes: ADR and the Primary Forms of Decision-making* (Cambridge: Cambridge University Press, 2005).

E.M. Rock, "Mindfulness Meditation, the Cultivation of Awareness, Mediator Neutrality, and the Possibility of Justice" (2005) 6 *Cardozo J. Conflict Resol.* 347.

A. Rodchenko, quoted in the Tate Modern's Gallery Guide for its exhibition, *Rodchenko and Popova, Defining Constructivism*, 12 February–12 May 2009.

R. Rosaldo, "From the Door of his Tent: The Fieldworker and the Inquisitor" in J. Clifford and G.E. Marcus, eds, *Writing Culture: The Poetics and Politics of Ethnography* (Berkeley: University of California Press, 1986) 77.

W.H. Ross Jr, "Beliefs of Mediators and Arbitrators Regarding the Effects of Motivational and Content Control Techniques in Disputes" in M.A. Rahim, ed., *Managing Conflict: An Interdisciplinary Approach* (New York: Praeger, 1989) 209.

M. Rothko, quoted in the Tate Modern's Gallery Guide for its exhibition, *Rothko: The Late Series*, 26 September 2008–1 February 2009.

R. Rubinson, "Client Counselling, Mediation, and Alternative Narratives of Dispute Resolution" (2003–04) 10 *Clinical L. Rev.* 833.

Rules of Civil Procedure, RRO 1990. Reg. 194 (as am.), Rule 24.1.

D. Sally, "Yearn for Paradise, Live in Limbo: Optimal Frustration for ADR" (2003–04) 108 *Penn St. L. Rev.* 89.

V.A. Sanchez, "Back to the Future of ADR: Negotiating Justice and Human Needs" (2002–03) 18 *Ohio St. J. Disp. Resol.* 669.

F.E.A. Sander, "Achieving Meaningful Threshold Consent to Mediator Style(s)" (2007–08) 14 *Dispute Resolution Magazine* 8.

F.E.A. Sander and L. Rozdeiczer, "Matching Cases and Dispute Resolution Procedures: Detailed Analysis Leading to a Mediation-centered Approach" (2006) 11 *Harv. Negot. L. Rev.* 1.

N. Sargent, C. Picard and M. Jull, "Rethinking Conflict: Perspectives from the Insight Approach" (2011) *Negotiation J.* 343.

C.A. Savage, "Culture and Mediation: A Red Herring" (1996) 5 *Am. U. J. Gender & L.* 269.

R. Scaglion, "Law, Anthropology and Mediation: The Effects of Mediation Styles on Successful Dispute Resolution: The Abelam Case" (1983) 3 *Windsor Y.B. Access Just.* 256.

T.C. Schelling, *The Strategy of Conflict* (New York: Oxford University Press, 1975).

E.W. Scherwin, *Mediation, Citizenship Empowerment and Transformational Politics* (West Port: Praeger, 1995).

A.K. Schneider and C. Honeyman, *The Negotiator's Fieldbook: The Desk Reference for the Experienced Negotiator* (Washington: American Bar Association, Section of Dispute Resolution, 2006).

J.K. Sebenius, "Review Essay: What Can We Learn from Great Negotiations?" (2011) *Negotiation J.* 251.

J.K. Sebenius, "Negotiation Analysis: From Games to Inferences to Decisions to Deals" (2009) *Negotiation J.* 449.

Series, "From the Trenches and Towers" (2002) 27 *Law & Soc. Inquiry* 567.

J.R. Seul, "How Transformative is Transformative Mediation? A Constructive-developmental Assessment" (1999–2000) 15 *Ohio St. J. Disp. Resol.* 135.

J.G. Shailor, *Empowerment in Dispute Mediation: A Critical Analysis of Communication* (West Port: Praeger, 1994).

W. Shakespeare, *Twelfth Night, or, What You Will* (New York: Signet, 1965).

R.K. Sherwin, "Lawyering Theory: An Overview – What We Talk About When We Talk About Law" (1992) 37 *N. Y. L. Sch. L. Rev.* 9.

S. S. Silbey, "The Emperor's New Clothes: Mediation Mythology and Markets" (2002) *J. Disp. Resol.* 171.

S.S. Silbey, "Mediation Mythology" (1993) *Negotiation J.* 349.

S. Silbey and S. Merry, "Mediator Settlement Strategies" (1986) 8 *Law & Soc'y Pol'y Review* 7.

D. Spencer and M. Brogan, *Mediation Law and Practice* (Melbourne: Cambridge University Press, 2006).

D. Spenser Underhill, "The English Courts and ADR – Policy and Practice since April 1999 (Part II)" (2005) 16 *Eur. Bus. L. Rev.* 183.

D. Spenser Underhill, "The English Courts and ADR – Policy and Practice since April 1999" (2003) 14 *Eur. Bus. L. Rev.* 259.

J.W. Stempel, "The Inevitability of the Eclectic: Liberating ADR from Ideology" (2000) *J. Disp. Resol.* 247.

J.W. Stempel, "Identifying Real Dichotomies Underlying the False Dichotomy: Twenty-first Century Mediation in an Eclectic Regime" (2000) *J. Disp. Resol.* 371.

L.G. Stenelo, *Mediation in International Negotiations* (Malmo, Sweden: Nordens boktryckeri (Studentlitteratur), 1972), trans. E.C. Coble.

C.M. Stevens, *Strategy and Collective Bargaining Negotiation* (New York: McGraw-Hill, 1963).

J.B. Stulberg, "Must a Mediator be Neutral? You'd Better Believe it!" (2012) 95 *Marquette L. R.* 829.

J.B. Stulberg, "Facilitative Versus Evaluative Mediator Orientations: Piercing the 'Grid' Lock" (1997) 24 *Fla. St. U. L. Rev.* 985.

J. Sturrock, "Reflections on Commercial Mediation in Scotland" (2007) 73 *Arbitration* 77.

L.E. Susskind, J.B. Stulberg, B.S. Mayer and J. Lande (Panel Discussion) "Core Values of Dispute Resolution: Is Neutrality Necessary?" (2012) 95 *Marquette L. R.* 805.

N. Susskind and L. Susskind, "Connecting Theory and Practice" (2008) *Negotiation J.* 201.

D. Tannen, *You Just Don't Understand: Women and Men in Conversation* (New York: Ballantine, 1990).

J.R. Tarpley, "ADR, Jurisprudence, and Myth" (2001–02) 17 *Ohio St. J. Disp. Resol.* 113.

I. Tavory and S. Timmermans, "Two Cases of Ethnography: Grounded Theory and the Extended Case Method" (2009) 10 *Ethnography* 243.

A. Taylor, "Concepts of Neutrality in Family Mediation: Contexts, Ethics, Influence, and Transformative Process" (1997) 14 *Mediation Q.* 215.

C. Tsay and M.H. Bazerman, "A Decision-making Perspective to Negotiation: A Review of the Past and a Look to the Future" (2009) *Negotiation J.* 467.

V.W. Turner, *Schism and Continuity in an African Society: A Study of Ndembu Village Life* (Oxford: Berg, 1996 edition).

W. Twining, "The Idea of Juristic Method: A Tribute to Karl Llewellyn" (1992–94) 48 *U. Miami L. Rev.* 119.

W. Twining, "Alternative to What? Theories of Litigation, Procedure and Dispute Settlement in Anglo-American Jurisprudence: Some Neglected Classics" (1993) 56 *Mod. L. Rev.* 380.

T. Tyler, "Procedure or Result: What Do Disputants Want From Legal Authorities?" in K.J. Mackie, ed., *A Handbook of Dispute Resolution: ADR In Action* (London: Sweet and Maxwell, 1991) 19.

K.L. Valley *et al.*, "Agents as Information Brokers: The Effects of Information Disclosure on Negotiated Outcomes" (1992) 51 *Organizational Behavior & Human Decision Processes* 220.

C.B. Vigouroux, "Trans-scription as a Social Activity" (2007) 8 *Ethnography* 61.

K. Visweswaran, *Fictions of Feminist Ethnography* (Minnesota: University of Minnesota Press, 1994).

K. von Benda-Beckmann and F. Pirie, eds, *Order and Disorder: Anthropological Perspectives* (New York: Berghahn Books, 2007).

L. Wacquant, "Scrutinizing the Street: Poverty, Morality, and the Pitfalls of Urban Ethnography" (2002) 107 *Am. J. of Sociology* 1468.

E.A. Waldman, "Identifying the Role of Social Norms in Mediation: A Multiple Model Approach" (1996–97) 48 *Hastings L. J.* 703.

J.A. Wall Jr and S. Chan-Serafin, "Do Mediators Walk Their Talk in Civil Cases?" (2010) 28 *Conflict Resol. Q.* 3.

J.A. Wall Jr and S. Chan-Serafin, "Processes in Civil Case Mediations" (2009) 26 *Conflict Resol. Q.* 261.

J.A. Wall and T.C. Dunne, "Mediation Research: A Current Review" (2012) *Negotiation J.* 217.

J.A. Wall, T.C. Dunne and S. Chan-Serafin, "The Effects of Neutral, Evaluative, and Pressing Mediator Strategies" (2011) 29 *Conflict Resol. Q.* 127.

J.A. Wall, J.B. Stark and R.L. Standifer, "Mediation: A Current Review and Theory Development" (2001) 45 *J. Conflict Resol.* 370.

M. Watkins, "Third-party Dilemmas: Are the Neutrals Working for Themselves?" (2002) 20 *Alternatives to High Cost Litig.* 119.

M. Watkins, *Breakthrough Business Negotiation: A Toolbox for Managers* (San Francisco: Jossey-Bass, 2002).

Webopedia: Online Dictionary for Computer and Internet Technology Definitions, http://www.webopedia.com/TERM/b/back_end_system.html (accessed 10 July 2012).

Webopedia: Online Dictionary for Computer and Internet Technology Definitions, http://www.webopedia.com/TERM/b/back_office.html (accessed 10 July 2012).

D.T. Weckstein, "In Praise of Party Empowerment – and of Mediator Activism" (1997) 33 *Willamette L. Rev.* 501.

E.A. Weitzman and P.F. Weitzman, "Problem Solving and Decision Making in Conflict Resolution" in M. Deutsch and P. T. Coleman, eds, *The Handbook of Conflict Resolution: Theory and Practice* (San Francisco: Jossey-Bass, 2000) 185.

N.A. Welsh, "Stepping Back Through the Looking Glass: Real Conversations with Real Disputants About Institutionalized Mediation and Its Value" (2004) 19 *Ohio St. J. Disp. Resol.* 573.

N.A. Welsh, "Disputants' Decision Control in Court-connected Mediation: A Hollow Promise without Procedural Justice" (2002) *J. Disp. Resol.* 179.

N.A. Welsh, "The Thinning Vision of Self-determination in Court-connected Mediation: The Inevitable Price of Institutionalization?" (2001) 6 *Harv. Negot. L. Rev.* 1.

G.D. Westermark, "Law, Anthropology and Mediation: 'Old Talk Dies Slowly': Land Mediation in Agarabi" (1983) 3 *Windsor Y.B. Access Just.* 186.

C.B. Wiggins and L.R. Lowry, *Negotiation and Settlement Advocacy: A Book of Readings* (St Paul, MN: West, 1997).

G.R. Williams, *Legal Negotiation and Settlement* (St Paul, MN: West, 1983).

P. Willis and M. Trondman, "Manifesto for Ethnography" (2000) 1 *Ethnography* 5.

T. Willis, "Creative Solutions When Only Money is at Stake" in C. Newmark and A. Monaghan, eds, *Butterworths Mediators on Mediation* (Haywards Heath: Tottel, 2005) 124.

W.J. Wilson and A. Chaddha, "The Role of Theory in Ethnographic Research" (2009) 10 *Ethnography* 549.

J. Winslade, "Mediation with a Focus on Discursive Positioning" (2006) 23 *Conflict Resol. Q.* 501.

J. Winslade and G. Monk, *Narrative Mediation: A New Approach to Conflict Resolution* (San Francisco: Jossey-Bass, 2000).

R.L. Wissler, "Court-connected Mediation in General Civil Cases: What We Know From Empirical Research" (2001–02) 17 *Ohio St. J. Disp. Resol.* 641.

R.L. Wissler and R.W. Rack Jr, "Assessing Mediator Performance: The Usefulness of Participant Questionnaires" (2004) *J. Disp. Resol.* 229.

P.Y. Wolfe, "How a Mediator Enhances the Negotiation Process" (2005) 46 *N. H. B. J.* 38.

J. Wood, "Mediation Styles: Subjective Description of Mediators" (2004) 21 *Conflict Resol. Q.* 437.

Lord Woolf, *Access to Justice Final Report*, Department for Constitutional Affairs, July 1996.

Lord Woolf, *Access to Justice Interim Report*, Department for Constitutional Affairs, June 1995.

M. Young and E. Schlie, "The Rhythm of the Deal: Negotiation as a Dance" (2011) *Negotiation J.* 191.

P.M. Young, "Teaching the Ethical Values Governing Mediator Impartiality Using Short Lectures, Buzz Group Discussions, Video Clips, a Defining Features Matrix, Games, and an Exercise Based on Grievances Filed Against Florida Mediators" (2011) 11 *Pepp. Disp. Resol. L. J.* 309.

R. Zamir, "The Disempowering Relationship Between Mediator Neutrality and Judicial Impartiality: Toward a New Mediation Ethic" (2011) 11 *Pepp. Disp. Resol. L. J.* 467.

W. Zartman, "Processes and Stages" in A.K. Schneider and C. Honeyman, eds, *The Negotiator's Fieldbook: The Desk Reference for the Experienced Negotiator* (Washington, DC: American Bar Association, Section of Dispute Resolution, 2006) 95.

Index

acceptance 52, 100, 186
active negotiator 66
adjudication 5, 7, 8
adviser *see* party adviser
advocacy 67, 209
agenda, composition of 79, 81, 88–9
agreement 4, 50, 78; execution of 80; joint decision-making for final 102–5; ritual affirmation 80, 81; *see also* compromise; settlement
'aha' moments 28, 44
Alfini, J.J. 54, 56
allegorical account, ethnography as an 21
alternative dispute resolution (ADR) 6, 46–7
ambivalence, in mediator identities 196–7
analytical constructs 28
analytical discourse 26
animosities 80
antagonism 80
anthropologists 17, 23
anthropology: cultural 26; legal 32; method 12, 24, 26; usefulness of 32
approximation to reality 19
arbitrator 63
Argonauts of the Western Pacific 16, 22
argumentation 77, 93
articulation of position 84–9, 106
Arusha 13, 78
assisted negotiation 15, 63–8
assumptions 29, 30
Astor, H. 54
attitudes 16

authority 5, 13, 55, 141, 204
autonomy 50, 51
awareness: of others 4; *see also* self awareness

Balinese cockfight 19–20
bargaining: phase 70; position, strengthening 91; power 75, 88, 92; proposals 56, 97, 98–102, 106; range 75, 77, 88, 93, 96, 100; strategy 56; *see also* final bargaining; pure bargaining
bashing 56
behaviour (mediator) 58–63
belonging 52
benign intervener 147
bi-directional plane, of phases 106
bias 31, 212
biased mediator 54
bilateral negotiation 5, 7
binary negotiation 13
blank canvas approach 119
blended paradigm 15
bluffs 76, 102
Bohannan, P. 30
Boskey, J.B. 50
Bowling, D. 63, 67, 150
breaches of norms 12–13, 23
British mediation agency study 33–44: fieldwork site 34–9; mediations 42–4; mediators 39–41; parties 41; training manual 68–9
broad-evaluative strategy 60
broad-facilitative strategy 60
Burns, S.L. 66
Bush, R.A. Baruch 50, 56, 62, 64

Carnevale, P.J.D. 58, 59, 87
case method 23
caucusing 58, 59
certainty 81
chairman 63
change 4, 15, 16, 56, 63, 94, 97
Chase, O.G. 7
Cheyenne 12, 32
The Cheyenne Way 23
choices 5
Christian religious groups 52
citizen participation 51
Civil Procedure Rules (CPR) 7: 44.3(5) 6
claimant, mediator as 166, 184, 185
Clammer, J. 29–30
Clarke, Lord 6
classic approach, to ethnography 28
Clifford, J. 20, 21, 28
codes of conduct 54
codes of standards 214
coercion 13, 75
cognitive barriers 94, 105
cognitive elements 73–4, 87, 91, 98
collaborative negotiation 7, 55
Comaroff, J. 17
Comaroff, J.L. 14, 15, 17, 24–5, 32
commercial mediations 35, 71, 130
commitment 76, 87, 94, 105
common ground 58
communication 50, 68: frankness in 139; importance to mediator 119, 129–30; mediation and improved 4; objectives 55; as a tool for persuasion 3; *see also* conversation; dialogue
communication-facilitation behaviour 59
community, mediation as 52
community empowerment 51
compassion 51
compensation strategy 58
competitive strategy 74, 75, 87, 88, 91, 102, 104, 105
composition of agenda and definition of issues 79, 81, 88–9
compromise 4, 80, 94, 98, 143
concessions 76, 80, 94, 101
conciliation 12
concluding phase 70

confidence 148
confidentiality 3, 49, 119, 130
confirmation, ritual 81
conflict: of interest 140; relationship between order and 12; state of 3–4
conflict specialists 67
Conley, J.M. 8, 17, 22, 32
consensual decision-making 53, 55
consensual negotiation 7, 65
consternation 75
content intervention 59
contextual intervention 59
contract zone 75–6, 100, 102
control *see* mediator control; party control
controversy, in ethnography 211
convergence: rules and processes 14, 15, 24; structures and processes 15, 23–4
conversation, protracted 7
cooperation 104
cooperative strategy 74, 75, 98, 100
coordination 80, 81, 102
corporate liquidation - shareholder conduct (case study) 98–102
cost sanctions 6
Crapanzano, V. 20, 27–8
Crime and Custom in Savage Society 12, 32
cultural anthropology 26
cultural interpretation 19, 20
cultural perspective 212
culture, and dispute resolution 52
customs 14, 23, 52
cyclical processual model, information exchange 78–9, 97

data, ethnographic 10, 18, 47, 58, 78, 82, 83, 109, 112, 120, 130, 209
data analysis 22–7, 212
data collection 22, 25, 26; *see also* fieldwork
De Bono, E. 64, 150
dealmakers, mediators as 143, 200
deception 75
decision-making: consensual 53, 55; crisis, precipitating 77; mediation as a social process of 50; in negotiation 73; strategic 74; *see also* joint decision-making
decisions, strategic 81

deductions 22
deductive interpretation 28
defensiveness 92
depersonalization 208, 209
description(s) 27, 29, 30
desired outcome(s) 79, 93, 108
developmental model 79, 88
devil's advocate 67, 186, 203
diachronic micro-sociology 24
diagnosis 78
dialogue 21, 46, 130, 140, 211
differences, narrowing 80, 101
directive approach 57, 59
discursive realities 57
dispute: issues *see* issues; *see also* conflict
dispute resolution: mediation as 4–9; through an ethnographic lens 11–16
Disputes and Negotiation 78
Douglas, A. 76, 77, 79, 88, 89, 96, 101
Druckman, D. 96
dualism, Tswana society 24
Dunne, T.C. 62
dyadic negotiation 66, 150

elicitive approach 57
elicitor 61
emergence and crisis 77–8
empathy 30, 59, 60, 131
empirical research, need for 45–6
employment dispute – the disabled worker (case study) 102–5
empowerment 4, 50, 51, 56, 148
England and Wales, judicial system 6
Enslin, E. 211
enunciator 63
equidistance: between parties 53, 55, 204, 205; *see also* impartiality; neutrality
equity seeking 91
escalation of commitment 87, 94, 105
establishing the bargaining range 77
establishing maximal limits to issues in dispute 79–80, 89, 92, 93–4
ethics 214
ethnographic data 10, 18, 47, 58, 78, 82, 83, 109, 112, 120, 130, 209
ethnography: application to mediation 27–31; data analysis 22–7; dispute resolution in 11–16; elements of 16–22; implications 209–10; limitations to 210–12; mediation study *see* British mediation agency study
evaluative approach 56, 146
evaluator 60, 147
Evans-Pritchard, E.E. 12, 27, 29
Exon, S.N. 54, 67
expectations 79, 100
experience, translation of 20–1
expert consultancy 201
exploration phase 70

facilitation 4, 5, 50
facilitative approach 56–7, 146
facilitator 50, 60, 118–19, 140, 143, 147, 199, 202, 207
fairness 4, 51, 52
female mediators 213
fieldsite 25, 34–9
fieldwork 17, 18
final agreement, joint decision making for 102–5
final bargaining 80, 81, 101
final stage, of negotiation 76
the fishing logo (case study): mediator identities 186–200; native voice 132–42
five-stage mediation process 60
flexible process, mediation as 130
Folberg, J. 50
Folger, J.P. 50, 56, 62
formulation 78
Fortune, R.F. 23
frames 55
framework (mediation) 70
frankness 139
free will 50
freedom of expression 139
functionalist approach 22, 23
future, focusing on 60

Garcia, A.C. 54
Geertz, C. 18, 19–20, 21, 22, 25, 26, 28, 34, 109, 214
gender 212, 213
general theory 25–6, 27
generalization(s) 18, 23, 27, 212
Genn, H. 50

go-betweens 67
goal, of mediation 144
Goldberg, S.B. 54
good mediators 68
good practice 46
good theory 46
Gulliver, P.H. 12–14, 19, 24, 32, 63, 64, 65–6, 68, 69, 78, 79, 80, 81–2, 88, 89, 92, 93, 106, 150

Hammersley, M. 18, 26, 30
Harper, C. 54
hashing it out 56
Hoebel, E.A. 8, 12, 23, 25, 26, 32
Hoffman, D. 63, 67, 150
Honeyman, C. 54
humour 59
hybrid model, of negotiation 78, 106–7

identification: of issues 81; strategic goals 74
identities (mediator) *see* quintet of identities
ideological banners 80
ignorance 80
impartiality 53, 59, 67, 140, 204, 213
inaction strategy 58
inductive generalization 23
influence, mediators 69
informality 144
information, as basis for intervention 60
information exchange: cyclical network of 78–9; functional ritualistic 75; importance of 3; mediator role 66, 70, 147; phase 89–92, 106; shift in position 97
initial stage, of negotiation 75
insight framework 57
instruction 59
integrative mediator 63
integrative strategy 58
interaction *see* mediator interactions; social interaction
intermediate stage, of negotiation 75–6
interpretation 19–20, 21, 22, 26, 28, 211
interpretive approach 28
interpretive exercises 110–11
interpretive schemes 55–6

interpretive sociology 30–1
intervention, models of 52–8
interventionist 183, 201
interview guideline, for participants, post-mediation 217
interview protocol, for mediators, post-mediation 215–16
ironic form of neutrality 204–5
issues: definition of 79, 81, 88–9; establishing maximal limits to 79–80, 89, 92, 93–4

Japanese culture 52
joint action 76
joint decision-making 55, 73, 102–5, 106
joint problem-solving 105
joint sessions 71
Jones, T.S. 59
judge 118, 119, 140, 143, 205
judgements 96
judicial system 5, 6, 7, 33
justice 4, 51, 52, 78, 209, 212–13

kinship 14, 24
Kolb, D.M. 50, 51, 55, 56, 204
Kressel, K. 50, 51, 55, 56, 57, 58, 59
kula 22
Kydd, A. 54

labels 8, 203, 208
'laissez-faire' approach 146
law: of the Cheyenne 23, 32; mediation and 6, 8, 12, 209, 213; *see also* natural law; role of law; rule of law
lawyers 8, 33
leader 63
learning, cyclical network 78–9, 97
legal anthropology 32
legal norms, use of 60
legal positivists 48
legal representatives 214
legal terminology 8
legalization of ADR 7
legitimacy 7, 54
limits to issues, establishing 79–80, 89, 92, 93–4
listening 111
literary report 27

240 *Index*

litigation 6, 49
Llewellyn, K.N. 8, 12, 23, 25, 26, 32

Mackie, K. 63
macro-level analysis, dispute resolution 15
Malinowski, B. 12, 14, 16, 17, 18, 19, 21–2, 23, 25, 26, 27, 28, 30, 32, 109
management services contract – unpaid invoices (case study) 94–9
manipulation: by mediator 120, 121, 131, 147; by parties 102, 139
Mansell, W. 8, 29
mantle of neutrality 205
Marcus, G.E. 28, 32
Matz, D.E. 50
Mayer, B. 54, 67
meaning: ascription of 19–20, 27; construction 18–19, 20
mediation: as an auxiliary to negotiation 144; as assisted negotiation 63–8; definitions 4–5, 6, 47–52; as a dispute resolution process 4–9; ethnography *see* ethnography; fugitive nature of 200, 201, 202; future research 212–14; institutionalization 6; and law 6, 8, 12, 209, 213; model 68–71; models of intervention 52–8; multidimensionality of 5; need for empirical research 45–6; as negotiation 3, 5, 7, 129, 141; perceptions of 207–8; power in 213–14; quintessence of 201; reconceptualization 210; reducing chasm between theory and practice 46–7; structure of 130; *see also* post-mediation
mediation quintet *see* quintet of identities
mediation team, British Organization 36
mediator control 40, 56, 58, 65, 66, 120, 130, 140, 144, 147, 214
mediator interactions 47, 54, 62, 71, *151*, 183, 207
mediator mythology 203
mediator style 120, 131, 141, 146, 147
mediator-centredness 140, 201

mediators 7, 8; awareness 214; behaviour 58–63; distinction between process and 120, 121, 142, 144–5, 208; ethnographic mediation study 39–41; identities *see* quintet of identities; influence 69; morphing of 200–1; personal involvement 67; post-mediation, interview protocol 215–16; professionalization 214; roles 63; vision 55–8; *see also* evaluator; facilitator
mekgwa le melao 14
Menkel-Meadow, C. 50, 79, 81
Merry, S.E. 46, 50, 56
Meteyard, B. 8
micro-sociology, diachronic 24
Milner, N. 46
mini-negotiations 105
miscommunication 130
Mnookin, R. 5
Moffitt, M.L. 47, 48
Moore, C.M. 51
moral growth 4, 51
morphing, of mediator 200–1
Mulcahy, L. 53–4, 66

narrative approach 57
narrow evaluative strategy 60
narrow facilitative strategy 60
narrowing the differences 80, 101
native voice 109–13: case studies; partnership gone awry 121–32; technology foul-up 113–21; the fishing logo 132–42
natural law 48
Ndembu 24
Ndendeuli 24, 78
needing to reality test 186
negotiated agreement 50
negotiated order 8, 16, 32, 52, 72–108
negotiation; assisted 15, 63–8; bilateral 5, 7; binary 13; collaborative 7, 55; decisions about progression 81; depersonalization of 209; mediation as 3, 5, 7, 129, 141; need for an understanding of 72–3; phases 74, 81–105, 106, *107*; processual arc 105–7, *108*; strategy and patterns 74–81; structure of 73; study of 73; trilateral 5

negotiation dyad 66, 150
negotiation map 64
negotiation range 75, 76
negotiation scripts 87–8
negotiation skills 214
negotiation triad 66, 68, 150
Neighbours and Networks 12, 14, 24
neutral adviser 131
neutrality 52–5, 68, 69, 120, 131, 140, 204–5, 208, 213
New New Grid 60–1
non-alignment 53, 55
non-determinative nature, mediator authority 55
non-western society 14
norm-advocating model 57
norm-educating model 57
norm-generating model 57
norms: breach of 12–13, 23; in dispute resolution 13, 14; rules and 5, 6, 34, 209; using social and legal 60
Nuer 12, 27, 29
nuisance claim – the showering softballs (case study) 89–92

O'Barr, W.M. 8, 17, 22, 32
Oberman, S. 60
objective scientific reporting 27
observation 19, 20, 22, 28, 38
observed, effect of observer on 31
observed mediations 70, 71
offer and counter-offer 97
Old Grid 60, 61
opening phase 70
opinions 131
opposing party, mediator as 152, 164–5, 185, 197, 203, 207
order *see* social order
orientation (mediator) 57, 60
orientation and positioning 77, 89
overconfidence 87, 91

Palmer, M. 64, 81, 150, 201
Pareto-optimal solutions 50
parochialism 9, 27
participant information 211
participant-observer 33, 81
parties: ethnographic mediation study 41; interview guideline, post-mediation 217; manipulation by 102, 139; neutrality as equidistance between 53; perception of mediator 207–8
partnership gone awry (case study); mediator identities 167–86; native voice 121–32
party actions 76–7
party adviser 152, 164, 166, 183–4, 185, 197, 198, 199, 201, 207
party advocate 36, 67; *see also* advocacy; devil's advocate
party against a party *see* opposing party
party control 4, 51, 68, 148
party participation 4
party proper, mediator as 152, 165–6, 167, 185, 197, 198, 201, 207
passivity 63
perceptions 16, 207–8
personal injury negotiation – the falling crane (case study) 84–9
personal involvement 67
personal lens 26, 29
personal narrative 27
physical environment 3–4; ethnographic mediation study 35–6
Picard, C. 57
position(s): articulation of 84–9, 106; shift in 94–9, 106; testing of 76, 92–4, 106; *see also* orientation and positioning
post-mediation: interview 199–200; interview guideline for participants 217; interview protocol for mediators 215–16
posturing 87, 88, 102
power, in mediation 213–14
power-balancing 59
powerful stories 21
practitioners, gap between theorists and 46
pragmatic lens 55, 56
pre-negotiation activities 82
pre-planned strategy 146
precipitating the decision-making crisis 77
preconceptions 27, 29
prefaces, mediator use of 164–5, 198
prejudices 30

preliminaries to final bargaining 80, 101
preparation phase 70
prescriptive definition, of mediation 48
present, focusing on 60
pressing strategy 58
primary classification criterion 75
private dispute resolution 7
private meetings 66, 70, 130, 141
problem-solving 50, 55, 57, 58, 104, 105, 207
procedural behaviour 59
process(es): convergence of rules and 14, 15, 24; convergence of structures and 15, 23–4; distinction between mediator and 120, 121, 142, 144–5, 208; road-map of 130
process intervention 59
processual forms 15
processual framework, of negotiation 72–108
processual theorists 74, 82; *see also* Douglas; Gulliver; Palmer; Roberts; Stenelo; Stevens
professionalization, of mediators 214
promises 76
prompter 63
Pruitt, D.G. 56, 58, 60, 87
pure bargaining 101, 105
purpose (observer) 30

qualifiers, mediator use of 164–5
quintet of identities 149–52, 207: case studies; partnership gone awry 167–86; technology foul-up 153–67; the fishing logo 186–200; depersonalization and 208

rapport 141, 147
rational discourses 56
real-life data 82
real-time mediation 110
reality, reconstruction of observed 21
reality construction 20
reality testing 60, 186, 203
recognisable data 26
recognition 4, 51, 52, 56
reconciliation 51, 52

reconnoitring the range 77, 93
reconstruction of reality 21
recording 22, 27, 28
reflective practitioner 30
reflexive intervention 59
relationship improvement 56
relationship-building 147
resoluteness 79, 92
resolution *see* dispute resolution
respect 50
Riskin, L.L. 56, 57, 60, 61
ritual affirmation by the parties of the agreement 80, 81
ritual confirmation 81
ritualistic information exchange 75
road-map, of process 130
Roberts, M. 55, 65, 66, 150
Roberts, S. 7, 14, 15, 24–5, 26–7, 29, 32, 64, 81, 201
role of law 5, 8, 23, 32, 41, 213, 214
rule of law 7
rule-centred paradigm 14
rules: of confidentiality 130; and norms 5, 6, 34, 209; and outcome 8; and processes, convergence of 14, 15, 24; Tswana society 14; *see also* Civil Procedure Rules
Rules and Processes 24–5

satisfaction story 56
Schelling, T.C. 101
Schism and Continuity in an African Society 15, 23–4
scientific approach 19, 21–2, 27, 28
search for an arena 79
self: mediator as 151–2, 164, 183, 185, 196, 197, 199, 208; strength of 51
self-assessment 147
self-awareness 52, 131, 183, 202
self-determination 4, 51, 207
self-empowerment 50
self-help 12, 13
self-interest(s) 31, 60, 88, 98, 209
self-worth 51
services contract – website malfunction (case study) 92–4
settlement 6, 7, 13, 50, 68, 70, 101
Shaw, M.L. 54
shift in position 94–8, 106

shifting identities 185, 196, 199, 204, 213, 214
shuttle mediation 66, 129–30
Silbey, S.S. 50, 56
silence (mediator) 208
social behaviour, breach of norms 12–13
social constructionist view 57
social contexts 24
Social Control in an African Society 12–13, 24
social drama(s) 12, 23, 34, 110–11
social interaction 4, 13, 14, 15, 16, 24, 73–4, 80, 81, 209
social life 15, 22
social norms, use of 60
social order 12, 13, 23, 209, 213
social process(es): conflict resolution 14; mediation as 8, 50
social relationships 13, 24
societal structures 15, 23–4; *see also* village structure
societies, dispute resolution in 12, 15
socio-emotional approach 56
Sorcerers of Dobu 23
sponsorship of settlements 7
standards, for cultural disputes 51
Stenelo, L.G. 74, 75, 76, 88
Stevens, C.M. 74, 75, 76, 88, 101
storytelling 60
strategic approach 74
strategic decisions 81
strategic distributive conduct 94
strategic game, mediation as 58
strategic goals 74, 75, 76
strategic movement 75
strategic moves 74
strategic planning 146
strategic style 57, 59
strategies, in negotiation 74–81
structure(s): convergence of processes and 15, 23–4; of mediation 130
Stulberg, J. 54
substantive goals 75
substantive intervention 59
substantive justice 213
substantive-directive behaviour 59
surprise 75
Susskind, L. 46

Susskind, N. 46
synchronic analysis, village structure 24

Tarpley, J.R. 68
task-oriented approach 56
task-oriented process, mediation as a 50
Taylor, A. 50
technology foul-up (case study): mediator identities 153–67; native voice 113–21
terminology, legal 8
testing of positions 76, 92–4, 106
textualization 20–1, 109, 111, 211
theoretical analysis 24–5
theoretical approach, to negotiation 73
theoretical creativity 29
theoretical knowledge 82
theorists, gap between practitioners and 46
theory, in ethnography 25–6
theory construction 23
theory formulation 26
theory generation 26, 29
theory of investigation 27, 34
therapeutic mediation 56
thick description 18, 27, 30, 32, 34, 109
third-party interveners 151, 201, 207, 208, 209, 213
third-party intervention 32, 52, 64, 65
Thomson, A. 8
threats 76, 79, 92, 102
three-fold model, of intervention 57
tradition, mediation-enriched 52
training manual, ethnographic mediation study 68–9
transcription 211
transformation story 56
transformative approach 62, 146
transformative lens 55, 56
translation of experience 20–1
transparency 22, 142
trashing 56
triadic negotiation 66, 68, 150
trilateral negotiation 5
Trobrianders 22
true fictions 28
trust 148
Tswana 14, 15, 24

Turner, V.W. 12, 15, 23–4, 110
turning points 96
Twining, W. 30–1
two-dimensional fight into a three-dimensional exploration 64
two-stage negotiation cycle 75

uncertainty 80
understanding 80
unilateral articulation of positions 84–9

values 29, 30, 57
village structure 12, 15, 24

vision, mediators' 55–8
voluntarism 50, 119

Waldman, E.A. 57
Wall, J.A. 62
western model, intervention 53
western terminology 8
Williams, G. 77, 78, 89
win-win solution 56
Winslade, J. 57
Wolfe, P.Y. 91

Zartman, W. 78

Taylor & Francis
eBooks
FOR LIBRARIES

ORDER YOUR FREE 30 DAY INSTITUTIONAL TRIAL TODAY!

Over 23,000 eBook titles in the Humanities, Social Sciences, STM and Law from some of the world's leading imprints.

Choose from a range of subject packages or create your own!

Benefits for you
- Free MARC records
- COUNTER-compliant usage statistics
- Flexible purchase and pricing options

Benefits for your user
- Off-site, anytime access via Athens or referring URL
- Print or copy pages or chapters
- Full content search
- Bookmark, highlight and annotate text
- Access to thousands of pages of quality research at the click of a button

For more information, pricing enquiries or to order a free trial, contact your local online sales team.

UK and Rest of World: **online.sales@tandf.co.uk**

US, Canada and Latin America:
e-reference@taylorandfrancis.com

www.ebooksubscriptions.com

A flexible and dynamic resource for teaching, learning and research.